A CONTINENTAL DISTINCTION
IN THE COMMON LAW

A CONTINENTAL DISTINCTION IN THE COMMON LAW

A Historical and Comparative Perspective on English Public Law

J. W. F. ALLISON

CLARENDON PRESS · OXFORD
1996

Oxford University Press, Walton Street, Oxford OX2 6DP

Oxford New York
Athens Auckland Bangkok Bombay
Calcutta Cape Town Dar es Salaam Delhi
Florence Hong Kong Istanbul Karachi
Kuala Lumpur Madras Madrid Melbourne
Mexico City Nairobi Paris Singapore
Taipei Tokyo Toronto
and associated companies in
Berlin Ibadan

Oxford is a trade mark of Oxford University Press

Published in the United States
by Oxford University Press Inc., New York

British Library Cataloguing in Publication Data
Data available

Library of Congress Cataloging in Publication Data
Allison, J. W. F.
A continental distinction in the common law: a historical and
comparative perspective on English public law / J.W.F. Allison.
p. cm.
Includes bibliographical references.
1. Administrative law—Great Britain. 2. Administrative law—France.
3. Common law. 4. Civil law. I. Title.
KJC5571.A93 1995 342.42—dc20 [344.202] 95–37005
ISBN 0–19–825877–1

1 3 5 7 9 10 8 6 4 2

Typeset by Hope Services, (Abingdon) Ltd.
Printed in Great Britain
on acid-free paper by
Bookcraft Ltd., Midsomer Norton, Avon

Preface

In completing this book, I benefitted greatly from the constructive, critical, and encouraging comments of others. I would like to thank Trevor Allan, John Bell, Peter Cane, Roger Cotterrell, Carol Harlow, Jeffrey Jowell, Martin Loughlin, Bob Summers, Colin Turpin, Sir William Wade, and Lord Woolf for their advice. I am particularly grateful to Professor Peter Stein for his continual support and for supervising the doctoral research upon which this book is based. I am indebted to two Cambridge colleges: Gonville and Caius College, for funding my initial research with a Tapp Studentship; and Queens' College, for a Research Fellowship that facilitated its development into a book. I am also grateful to Quentin Stafford-Fraser for his assistance with my computer, to Mary Munson for searching out the intrusive commas of an early draft, and to Richard Hart and John Whelan at OUP for their efficiency and friendliness. Finally, I would like to thank my family and friends for all their support.

J. W. F. ALLISON

Queens' College, Cambridge
August 1994

Contents

Table of Cases

1
Introduction

The origins of the Continental distinction between public and private law are ancient. Justinian's *Digest* opens with Ulpian's description of the distinction between a law pertaining to the Roman state and a law pertaining to the interests of individuals.[1] Ulpian's description served as the source for the development of the distinction in civil-law countries, a development that culminated in a separate system of courts for resolving public-law disputes in nineteenth-century France. In contrast, until this century, the distinction was little known in England. Despite the geographical proximity of England to civil-law countries and their similar social and economic development, the distinction remained a main point of difference.

In the course of this century, however, the distinction between public and private law developed or began to develop in English law in various ways. First, from about the turn of the century, administrative tribunals were created outside the structure of the ordinary courts and entrusted with the resolution of administrative disputes. Secondly, English judges and doctrinal writers have gradually developed distinct substantive principles of public law. Thirdly, the procedural reforms of the late 1970s and early 1980s have resulted in a distinct procedure—the application for judicial review (AJR)—for public-law disputes. And, fourthly, since 1981, the Crown Office List has been compiled to ensure that a particular set of judges, familiar with public-law cases, hears AJRs.

The emergence of the distinction in England has been the subject of ongoing debate. The proliferating administrative tribunals were denounced by one Chief Justice and investigated by two Committees of Inquiry.[2] The distinction in substantive law has been described as an excuse for administrative immunities and a guise for executive-minded decisions.[3] And the principle of procedural exclusivity

---

[1] D. 1. 1. 1. 2. See I. 1. 1. 4.

[2] Lord Hewart of Bury, *The New Despotism* (London, 1929); Donoughmore Committee, *Report of the Committee on Ministers' Powers* (1932), Cmnd. 4060; Franks Committee, *Report of the Committee on Administrative Tribunals and Enquiries* (1957), Cmnd. 218.

[3] See, e.g., C. Harlow, ' "Public" and "Private" Law: Definition Without Distinction' (1980) 43 *MLR* 241–65.

introduced in *O'Reilly* v. *Mackman*[4] has been much criticized as the cause of 'waste of time and money on litigation merely about procedure'.[5]

Contributors to the debate have raised and contested a variety of issues. Certain critical legal theorists, for example, have suggested that the distinction serves the ideological function of hiding the hand of the state: 'These authors argue that the distinction serves or seeks to maintain the belief that social and economic life—business, education, community, family—are outside government and law, simultaneously denying the role of political processes in constituting and maintaining them, and legitimating these arrangements by implying that they have arisen from decisions and choices freely made by individuals'.[6] Others have shown how the distinction is used rhetorically to achieve particular results in particular contexts. They describe the distinction's indeterminacy as an invitation to rhetorical abuse.[7] The debate about the distinction, however, has not been one-sided. While Cane, for example, has argued that 'there are sound reasons for drawing' a distinction between public and private law,[8] Samuel has stressed that the problem lies with the use of the distinction rather than with the distinction itself.[9]

Debate about the development of an English distinction has been extensive but not exhaustive. Usually, it has involved either sweeping allegations about the distinction or specific arguments about particular differences between public and private law. Since Hamson's important

---

[4] [1982] 3 All ER 1124 (HL).

[5] H. W. R. Wade, 'Procedure and Prerogative in Public Law' (1985) 101 *LQR* 180–99 at 189.

[6] N. Rose, 'Beyond the Public/Private Division: Law, Power and the Family' (1987) 14 *J of Law & Soc.* 61–76 at 63. See, e.g., K. O'Donovan, *Sexual Divisions in Law* (London, 1985).

[7] See, e.g., H. Collins, 'The Public/Private Distinction in British Labour Law', Critical Legal Conference (University of Kent, Sept. 1986), 12–14; *id., Justice in Dismissal: The Law of Termination of Employment* (Oxford, 1992), 187–92, especially at 191. Cf. K. E. Klare, 'The Public–Private Distinction in Labor Law' (1982) 130 *Univ. Penn. L Rev.* 1358–1422, especially at 1361; C. D. Stone, 'Corporate Vices and Corporate Virtues: Do Public/Private Distinctions Matter?' (1982) 130 *Univ. Penn. LRev.* 1441–1509.

[8] P. Cane, *An Introduction to Administrative Law* (Oxford, 1986), 4.

[9] G. Samuel, 'Public Law and Private Law: A Private Lawyer's Response' (1983) 46 *MLR* 558–83. See also H. Woolf, 'Public Law–Private Law: Why the Divide? A Personal View' [1986] *PL* 220–38; N. E. Simmonds, *The Decline of Juridical Reason: Doctrine and Theory in the Legal Order* (Manchester, 1984), ch. 9; T. R. S. Allan, *Law, Liberty, and Justice: The Legal Foundations of British Constitutionalism* (Oxford, 1993), 125–30.

work,[10] wide-ranging historical and comparative studies with which to help substantiate sweeping allegations and make sense of specific arguments have seldom been attempted.[11]

In this book, I hope to help fill the persisting gap in legal literature. My general aim is to explain and assess the emergence of a prominent English distinction by comparing the development of the French distinction. I will consider both the distinction's suitability to the English legal and political tradition and its justifiability in modern English law. In particular, I will assess its compatibility with prevailing attitudes to the state, approaches to law, understandings of the separation of powers, and established judicial procedures.

A wide-ranging analysis is ambitious but nonetheless necessary. In Chapter 2, I will argue that the distinction is a legal transplant to English law, which, because of the accompanying hazards, should have been assessed and must now be re-assessed by reference to its historical and political context. I will suggest that the distinction's transplantation to English law was ill-considered and therefore advocate that it be reconsidered. The wide-ranging analysis required to reconsider the distinction as a transplant necessitates methodological caution. I will consequently defend a historical-comparative jurisprudence that uses a Weberian method. In Chapter 3, I will describe a model of a working distinction between public and private law, which I will apply in subsequent chapters.

In this book, I will be focusing on public law in the sense of administrative law—the law relating to administrative authorities, powers, or functions. My analysis is relevant to constitutional law, but only in so far as administrative law can be regarded as applied constitutional law. I am excluding discussion of constitutional law as such and its relationship with private law. I am only concerned with the justifiability of an English distinction between private and administrative law.

---

[10] C. J. Hamson, *Executive Discretion and Judicial Control: An Aspect of the French Conseil d'Etat* (London, 1954).

[11] But see S. Flogaïtis, *Administrative law et droit administratif* (Paris, 1986); S. I. Benn and G. F. Gaus (eds.), *Public and Private in Social Life* (London, 1983).

2
A Method for Transplants

The English Distinction as a Transplant

The alien origins of the English distinction between public and private law have not always been clearly recognized. The judges who introduced the procedural distinction by their interpretation of Order 53 of the Rules of the Supreme Court[1] suggested that the distinction was an indigenous outgrowth rather than a transplant. In *O'Reilly* v. *Mackman*, Lord Denning in the Court of Appeal described the prerogative remedies as public-law precursors to the application for judicial review (AJR): 'For centuries there were special remedies available in public law. They were the prerogative writs of certiorari, mandamus and prohibition'.[2] In the House of Lords, Lord Diplock described, not the substantive distinction itself, but, 'the appreciation of the distinction in substantive law between what is private law and what is public law', as 'a latecomer to the English legal system'.[3] And Lord Woolf recently alleged that '[i]n drawing the distinction the House of Lords was doing no more than recognizing that our legal system has a feature derived from the ancient prerogative writs which is common to most if not all other advanced legal systems'.[4]

These pronouncements, however, are characteristically judicial claims to continuity, which belie the extent of the transformation. Before the judicial interpretation of Order 53, the prerogative remedies were not exclusive procedures in administrative disputes. The ordinary remedies were widely used where the prerogative remedies proved inadequate, and the declaration in particular played an important role in the development of English administrative law.[5] Just as criminal prosecutions in England can be either public or private, civil proceedings in administrative disputes could involve either the ordinary or the prerogative remedies.[6]

The prerogative remedies were not granted by a separate set of

---

[1] SI 1977 No. 1955. [2] [1982] 3 All ER 680 (CA) at 692H.
[3] [1983] 3 All ER 1124 (HL) at 1128B.
[4] H. Woolf, *Protection of the Public—A New Challenge* (London, 1990), 25–6.
[5] H. W. R. Wade and C. F. Forsyth, *Administrative Law* (7th edn., Oxford, 1994), 579 ff., 670–2.
[6] J. A. Jolowicz, 'Civil Proceedings in the Public Interest' [1982] *Cambrian LR* 32–52 at 39.

judges with a special knowledge of administrative law. They 'were awarded pre-eminently out of the Court of the King's Bench',[7] but alongside numerous other remedies. The King's Bench did have a Crown side and a Plea side but the same judges served on both sides. The prerogative remedies were anyway not confined to the Crown side. Certiorari was available on the Crown side; mandamus, on the Plea side;[8] and prohibition issued out of the King's Bench, Common Pleas, and Chancery.[9] The distinction between prerogative and ordinary remedies was not accompanied by an institutional distinction between public- and private-law judges.

A substantive distinction, a distinction within substantive law, is similarly alien to the English legal tradition. While the doctrine of *ultra vires* was central to the development of both company law and judicial review,[10] the history of public-law liability is intertwined with that of private-law liability. One has reason to argue either that public-law liability in England was established by extending private-law liability, or that private-law liability was established by extending public-law liability. On the one hand, section 2(1) of the Crown Proceedings Act 1947 introduced the liability of the Crown in tort by providing that 'the Crown shall be subject to all the liabilities in tort to which, *if it were a private person of full age and capacity*, it would be subject' (emphasis added). On the other hand, the English law of tort and contract developed earlier from the writ of trespass in which the plaintiff originally had to allege that wrongs had been committed *vi et armis* and *contra pacem regis*.[11]

The insignificance of the distinction in the English legal tradition[12] is reflected in legal doctrine. References to it are few and far between. Its first appearance in an English legal text would hardly be worthy of mention were it not portentous of its eventual adoption. In the

---

[7] S. A. de Smith, 'The prerogative writs: historical origins', App.1 to *Judicial Review of Administrative Action* (J. M. Evans (ed.)) (4th edn., London, 1980), 584–95 at 587.

[8] J. H. Baker, *An Introduction to English Legal History* (3rd edn., London, 1990), 59.

[9] De Smith, n. 7 above, 591.

[10] L. C. B. Gower *et al.*, *Principles of Modern Company Law* (4th edn., London, 1979), 51–2, 162–5; Wade and Forsyth, n. 5 above, 41 ff.

[11] Baker, n. 8 above, 71–5, 374–6.

[12] Cf. the distinction and teaching of public law in Scotland: see, e.g., J. Millar, *Historical View of English Government* (London, 1803), iv, essay 7, pp. 266–310, reproduced in W. C. Lehmann, *John Millar of Glasgow 1735–1801: His Life and Thought and His Contributions to Sociological Analysis* (Cambridge, 1960), 340–57, especially at 347; Lehmann, op. cit., 22; M. Loughlin, 'John Millar', Stevenson Lecture in Citizenship (University of Glasgow, 1990), 6, 14–16; *id.*, *Public Law and Political Theory* (Oxford, 1992), 6 ff.

thirteenth century, Bracton mangled or simply misunderstood Azo's discussion of the distinction.[13] Azo had argued that it could not arise from the classification of persons or things because they were infinite in number and so would give rise to an infinite number of different kinds of law. Azo had described the outcome of such a classification as absurd: 'hac enim ratione "infinitae" essent species iuris, quia infiniti sunt homines et infinitae sunt res, nam et sic diceretur ius aliud equinum, aliud asininum, aliud vineae, aliud agri, aliud Petri aliud Iohannis.'[14] Bracton either did not follow this *reductio ad absurdum* or misquoted Azo through an oversight.[15] In Bracton's discussion, the absurdity appears as sound doctrine: '[i]n finitae vero sunt iuris species, quia infiniti sunt homines et infinitae sunt res, nam et sic diceretur ius aliud equinum, aliud asininum, aliud vineae aliud agri, aliud Petri aliud Johannis. Est autem ius publicum quod ad statum rei Romanae pertinet, et consistit in sacris, in sacerdotibus et in magistratibus.'[16] Thorne tried to make sense of this passage by reading into it the following substantial changes: '[(r)ights are infinite], because men are infinite and things are infinite, but the kinds of law are [not] infinite, for we would then speak of equine and of asinine law, of the law of vineyards and that of fields, the law of Peter and that of John'.[17] Bracton's discussion, not surprisingly, had little influence.

The next known references are in the early seventeenth century when Lord Chancellor Bacon presupposed the distinction: 'I consider . . . that it is a true and received division of law into *jus publicum* and *privatum*, the one being the sinews of property, and the other of government.'[18] In another passage he stressed the supereminence of public law: 'Jus Privatum sub tutela Juris Publici latet. Lex enim cavet civibus magistratus legibus. Magistratuum autem auctoritas pendet et

[13] In F. W. Maitland (ed.), *Select Passages from the Works of Bracton and Azo* (8 Selden Society, 1895), 27–33.

[14] *Ibid.* 28, 30. See generally G. Chevrier, 'Les critères de la distinction du droit privé et du droit public dans la pensée savante médiévale' in *Etudes d'histoire du droit canonique dédiées à Gabriel le Bras* (Paris, 1965), ii, 841–59 at 847–51.

[15] Maitland (ed.), n. 13 above, 27, 29.

[16] *Ibid.* 27: 'the kinds of laws are indeed infinite because men and things are infinite in number. For we might thus speak of equine and asinine law, of the law of vineyards and that of fields, of the law of Peter and that of John. There is public law, which relates to the *statum* of the Roman *res publica* and deals with religion, priests, and public officers.'

[17] '[Infinita sunt iura], quia infiniti sunt . . . res; infinitae vero [non] sunt iuris species, nam et sic diceretur': *Bracton on the Laws and Customs of England* (S. E. Thorne (tr.)) (Cambridge, Mass., 1968), ii, 25.

[18] F. Bacon, *Works* (J. Spedding, R. L. Ellis, and D. D. Heath (eds.)), vii (London, 1859), 731.

majestate imperii, et fabrica politiae, et legibus fundamentalibus.'[19]
Bacon's analysis did not survive the Civil War. The victorious
Parliamentarians secured the overthrow of the prerogative courts and
the distinction came to be regarded[20] as a way of setting the King
above the law.

In his *De portibus maris*, Sir Matthew Hale distinguished between the
'*jus privatum* in the port'—the 'interest of propriety or franchise'—and
the '*jus publicum* in the port—'the common interest that all persons have
to resort to or from publick ports'.[21] He also stressed that where a
wharf is public, that is, where it is licensed by the Queen or is the only
wharf in the port, 'duties must be reasonable and moderate' because
the wharf is 'affected with a public interest' and ceases to be '*juris pri-
vati* only'.[22] Hale's distinction, however, was limited to a specific area
of law. In his systematic and comprehensive work, *An Analysis of the Civil
Part of the Law*, Sir Matthew Hale did not distinguish between public
and private law.[23] What we would classify as public law, he dealt with
under the 'rights of persons' and, more particularly, 'the political rights
of persons' (section 2), such as 'rights as relate to the King's person'
(section 3), 'rights concerning the Prerogatives of the King' (section 4),
'rights concerning the King's Rights of Dominium, or Power of
Empire' (section 5), etc. Within his category of the 'rights of persons',
Hale adopted not a dichotomy but a tripartite classification. He distinguished 'political relations' (between Magistrate and people) (section
2), 'oeconomical relations' (between husband and wife, parent and
child, Master and servant) (section 14), and 'civil relations' (between
ancestor and heir, lord and tenant, guardian and pupil, and Lord and
villein) (section 17).

Blackstone did distinguish between 'public relations' (between governors and governed) and 'private relations' (between master and servant, husband and wife, parent and child, and guardian and ward), but
still discussed public relations in his Book 1 entitled *Of the Rights of
Persons* and, so, did not recognize the independence of public law from

[19] *Ibid.*, i (1857), 804: 'Private Law depends on the Protection of Public Law. For the
law protects citizens, and magistrates protect the laws. But the authority of the magistrates depends on the power of the sovereign, the structure of the constitution, and the
fundamental laws.'

[20] T. Weir, 'Public and Private Law' *IECL*, ii, ch. 2, secs. 115–34 at sec. 115.

[21] In F. Hargrave (ed.), *Tracts* (Dublin, 1787), 45 ff., especially at 72.

[22] *Ibid.* 77–8. See also *Bolt* v. *Stennett* (1800) 8 TR 607, 101 ER 1572; *Allnutt* v. *Inglis*
(1810) 12 East 527, 104 ER 206. See generally P. P. Craig, 'Constitutions, Property and
Regulation' [1991] *PL* 538–554.

[23] 4th edn., London, 1779.

the law of persons.[24] Blackstone's other public/private distinction, his distinction between *Private Wrongs* and *Public Wrongs*, the titles to his third and fourth volumes, distinguishes torts and crimes rather than private and public law in the sense these terms are used in this book.

Austin explicitly rejected the traces of the public/private distinction in Blackstone, and, like Hale and Blackstone, preferred to classify public law as a mere branch of the law of persons.[25] He also explicitly rejected the Roman distinction.[26] Austin dealt with public law in a narrow and broad sense, exclusive and inclusive of criminal law. Austin defined public law in its narrow sense as 'that portion of law which is concerned with political *conditions*: that is to say, with the powers rights duties capacities and incapacities, which are peculiar to political superiors, supreme and subordinate'.[27] He inserted public law in this sense in the law of persons: '[t]here can be no more reason for opposing public law to the rest of the legal system, than for opposing any department of the Law of Persons to the bulk of the *corpus juris*.'[28] As for public law inclusive of criminal law, Austin rejected Blackstone's distinction between public and private wrongs for the reason that 'civil injuries affect the public interest as much as crimes'.[29] He preferred a distinction on the basis of whether the state is obliged to prosecute, a distinction he recognized as 'quite arbitrary'.[30]

The old English doctrinal authorities generally ignored, rejected, or rendered insignificant the distinction between public and private law. Only a few writers of books on general jurisprudence, such as Markby and Holland, provide feeble support for an English distinction.[31]

Markby made the bald assertion that '[t]he best-known and most widely accepted of these divisions of law is that which separates law into public and private' but stressed that the distinction is merely 'convenient' rather than 'scientific' or 'exact'.[32] He was therefore unconcerned to explain the distinction and rejected the only explanation he

[24] W. Blackstone, *Commentaries on the Laws of England* (Facsimile of 1st end of 1765–9, Chicago, 1979).

[25] J. Austin, *Lectures on Jurisprudence* or *The Philosophy of Positive Law*, (5th edn., London, 1885), 404–5, 744–59.

[26] *Ibid.* 404.   [27] *Ibid.* 744.   [28] *Ibid.* 750.   [29] *Ibid.* 751.
[30] *Ibid.* 752.

[31] W. Markby, *Elements of Law Considered with Reference to Principles of General Jurisprudence* (6th edn., Oxford, 1905); T. E. Holland, *The Elements of Jurisprudence* (13th edn., Oxford, 1924); F. Pollock, *A First Book of Jurisprudence* (6th edn., London, 1929); J. W. Salmond, *Jurisprudence* or *The Theory of Law* (London, 1902).

[32] Markby, n. 31 above, secs. 292–4.

did mention. He stressed that both the public interest and the interests of individuals were invariably involved in all kinds of law.[33]

Holland described the distinction as 'radical', 'natural', and of 'capital importance', but also justified it as only a matter of convenience.[34] Furthermore, he cited mainly the 'irrecusable' Roman and Continental authority for the distinction and recognized the weight of English authority against him.[35] He alleged a heresy by Blackstone and Austin but found a 'detailed disproof of heresy' unnecessary.[36] His one reason for adopting the distinction was the inadequacy of an alternative—the distinction between absolute and relative rights.[37] His other reason, his main reason for the distinction, was the peculiar position of the state as both party and judge in public-law cases:

> By adopting this subdivision of municipal law, its whole field falls at once into two natural sections. On the one hand is the law which regulates rights where one of the persons concerned is 'public'; where the State is, directly or indirectly, one of the parties. Here the very power which defines and protects the right is itself a party interested in or affected by the right. . . . Opposed to this is the law which regulates rights where both of the persons concerned are 'private' persons.[38]

But, because Holland seems to have presupposed an adjudicative triad[39] as a requirement for his law properly so called, his main reason for the distinction undermined the very basis of a legal distinction between public and private by precluding a categorization of public law as law at all. Holland therefore recognized that private law is 'in many respects the only typically perfect law'.[40]

For centuries, the maxim 'the king can do no wrong'[41] similarly undermined a distinction between legal liability in public and in private law. Public-law liability is precluded altogether, rather than distinguished from private-law liability: '[t]he now much-weakened doctrine that the King can do no wrong put him, and for a time his officers, outside the reach of much of the law, not into a special category of law.'[42]

---

[33] *Ibid.*, sec. 295.　　　　[34] Holland, n. 31 above, 127–9.
[35] *Ibid.* 130–1, 366–8.　　　[36] *Ibid.* 378.　　　[37] *Ibid.* 131–3.
[38] *Ibid.* 128–9.

[39] See generally M. Shapiro, *Courts: A Comparative and Political Analysis* (Chicago, 1981), 1–64.

[40] Holland, n. 31 above, 134.

[41] See generally C. Harlow, *Compensation and Government Torts* (London, 1982), 17–28.

[42] A. E. Tay and E. Kamenka, 'Public Law—Private Law' in S. I. Benn and G. F. Gaus (eds.), *Public and Private in Social Life* (London, 1983), 67–92 at 71.

Like Markby and Holland, Pollock recognized a distinction between public and private law but stressed that '[i]t is not possible to make any clear-cut division of the subject-matter of legal rules'.[43] Accordingly, he drew the distinction by reference to the degree to which the public interest is involved.[44] Pollock, however, did not even describe public and private law as poles to a continuum. He stressed the possibility of overlap both where the public interest is minimal and where it is extensive. In contrast to the modern English judges who introduced the principle of exclusivity in *O'Reilly*,[45] Pollock concluded: '[i]t will be seen, therefore, that the topics of public and private law are by no means mutually exclusive. On the contrary their application overlaps with regard to a large proportion of the whole mass of acts and events capable of having legal consequences.'[46]

Without citing any modern or English authority, Salmond asserted that '[b]y general consent this Roman distinction between *jus privatum* and *jus publicum* is accepted as the most fundamental division of the *corpus juris*.'[47] He expressed, however, a traditional English scepticism towards distinctions:

English law possesses no received and authentic scheme of orderly arrangement. Exponents of this system have commonly shown themselves too little careful of appropriate division and classification, and too tolerant of chaos. Yet we must guard ourselves against the opposite extreme. . . . It has been said by a philosopher concerning human institutions in general, and therefore concerning the law and its arrangement, that they exist for the uses of mankind, and not in order that the angels in heaven may delight themselves with the view of their perfections. In the classification of legal principles the requirements of practical convenience prevail over those of abstract theory.[48]

The authors of the books on jurisprudence generally gave little or no English authority for the distinction, did not justify it convincingly and were cautious in attributing to it any significance. Their attempts to distinguish between public and private law were no more than a superficial drawing on the concepts of Continental jurisprudence so as to facilitate teaching in the new law schools[49] and so as to conform to the axiomatic positivism typical of the time. Furthermore, their books

---

[43] Pollock, n. 31 above, 84–5.   [44] *Ibid.* 95–9.

[45] See above, nn. 2 and 3.   [46] Pollock, n. 31 above, 99.

[47] Salmond, n. 31 above, sec. 155.   [48] *Ibid.*, sec. 153.

[49] P. Stein, 'Continental influences on English legal thought, 1600–1900' in P. Stein, *The Character and Influence of the Roman Civil Law: Historical Essays* (London, 1988), 209–29 at 224–8.

on jurisprudence had limited influence. Maitland described their importance in the English legal tradition:

Writers on general jurisprudence are largely concerned with the classification of legal rules. This is a very important task, and to their efforts we owe a great deal—it is most desirable that law should be clearly stated according to some rational and logical scheme. But do not get into the way of thinking of law as consisting of a number of independent compartments, one of which is labelled constitutional, another administrative, another criminal, another property, so that you can learn the contents of one compartment, and know nothing as to what is in the others. No, law is a body, a living body, every member of which is connected with and depends upon every other member. There is no science which deals with the foot, or the hand, or the heart. Science deals with the body as a whole, and with every part of it as related to the whole.[50]

The influence of the writers on general jurisprudence was anyway negligible in comparison with the influence of Dicey's principled rejection of the French jurisdictional distinction. He regarded the second meaning he attributed to the rule of law as exclusive of an English *droit administratif*:

It [the rule of law] means, again, equality before the law, or the equal subjection of all classes to the ordinary law of the land administered by the ordinary law courts; the 'rule of law' in this sense excludes the idea of any exemption of officials or others from the duty of obedience to the law which governs other citizens or from the jurisdiction of the ordinary courts; there can be with us nothing really corresponding to the 'administrative law' (*droit administratif*) or the 'administrative tribunals' (*tribunaux administratifs*) of France.[51]

Despite the deficiencies of his analysis, Dicey expressed a tradition and exercised an enormous influence on successive generations.[52] Such was his influence that Robson described how in 1929, more than forty years after Dicey's *Law of the Constitution* was first published, the

[50] F. W. Maitland, *The Constitutional History of England: A Course of Lectures* (Cambridge, 1908), 539.
[51] A. V. Dicey, *An Introduction to the Study of the Law of the Constitution* (10th edn., London, 1959), 202–3.
[52] W. A. Robson, 'The Report of the Committee on Ministers' Powers' [1932] *Pol. Quat.* 346–64; W. I. Jennings, 'In praise of Dicey 1885–1935' (1935) 13 *Pub. Admin.* 123–34; *Grosvenor Hotel, London (No. 2), Re* [1965] Ch. 1210 at 1261EF; *Ministry of Housing and Local Government* v. *Sharp* [1970] 2 QB 223 at 266; R. W. Blackburn, 'Dicey and the Teaching of Public Law' [1985] *PL* 679–94; N. Johnson and P. McAuslan, 'Dicey and his Influence on Public Law' [1985] *PL* 717–23; H. W. Arthurs, 'Rethinking Administrative Law: A Slightly Dicey Business' (1979) 17 *Osgoode Hall LJ* 1–45; *id.*, '*Without the Law*': *Administrative Justice and Legal Pluralism in Nineteenth-Century England* (Toronto, 1985), especially at 5.

Donoughmore Committee 'started life with the dead hand of Dicey lying frozen on its neck'.[53] Robson was opposing the traditional English doctrinal rejection of a distinction between public and private law and, with others, was initiating a movement for its recognition in England, a movement inspired by the French model of administrative law[54] and culminating in *O'Reilly* v. *Mackman*[55] and the Crown Office List.

Possibly because of the influence of Dicey's negative description of French administrative law,[56] advocates of the distinction preferred to stress that it had already developed in England, rather than advocate its explicit transplantation.[57] But if, as I have argued, the distinction was alien to the English tradition, it must have been transplanted. That the distinction was in fact transplanted has occasionally been recognized by English judges. In *The Closing Chapter*, Lord Denning admitted that '[i]n the last few years we have thrown over Dicey and gone back to Justinian'.[58] And, in *Davy* v. *Spelthorne Borough Council*, Lord Wilberforce stressed the distinction's importation to emphasize his words of warning:

The expressions 'private law' and 'public law' have recently been imported into the law of England from countries which, unlike our own, have separate systems concerning public law and private law. No doubt they are convenient expressions for descriptive purposes. In this country they must be used with caution, for, typically, English law fastens not on principles but on remedies.[59]

Legal Transplantation

Originally Montesquieu drew attention to the hazards of legal transplantation:

Law in general is human reason insofar as it governs all the peoples of the earth; and the political and civil laws of each nation should be only the particular cases to which human reason is applied. Laws should be so appropriate to the people for whom they are made that it is very unlikely that the laws of one nation can suit another.[60]

---

[53] Robson, n. 52 above, 351.

[54] See, e.g., A. Denning, *Freedom under the Law* (London, 1949), 77–81.

[55] Above, nn. 2 and 3.   [56] Dicey, n. 51 above, ch. 12.

[57] See, e.g., Robson, n. 52 above.   [58] (London, 1983), 119.

[59] [1983] 3 All ER 278 (CA) at 285H; paraphrased by Sir John Donaldson in *R.* v. *East Berkshire Health Authority, ex p. Walsh* [1985] QB 152 at 162B.

[60] Montesquieu, *The Spirit of the Laws* (A. M. Cohler, B. C. Miller, and H. S. Stone (trs. and eds.)) (Cambridge, 1989), bk. 1, ch. 3, 8.

Montesquieu suggested that successful transplantation was 'un très grand hasard'[61] because laws should conform to the variety of factors that together constitute 'the spirit of the laws'—'the nature and the principle of the government', 'the climate, be it freezing, torrid or temperate', 'the properties of the terrain, its location and extent', 'the way of life of the peoples, be they plowmen, hunters or herdsmen' etc.[62] Montesquieu's insight has remained relevant and was the subject of a debate between Kahn-Freund[63] and Watson.[64]

The Debate between Khan-Freund and Watson

In an article on comparative law as a tool of law reform, Kahn-Freund updated Montesquieu's analysis and spelt out its implications. Whereas Montesquieu had stressed the importance of environmental obstacles to transplantation, Kahn-Freund argues that, because of a process of 'political differentiation' and 'economic, social, cultural assimilation', the political—the proximity of relationship between transplant and power structure—has become more important than the environmental.[65] Kahn-Freund stresses that transplantation is more difficult the closer the transplant is to the foreign power structure. He accordingly describes a continuum with the easy replacement of a mechanism like a carburettor at one end, and the difficult transplantation of an organ like a kidney at the other. What we would consider public-law rules he considers as the least transplantable:

All rules which organise constitutional, legislative, administrative or judicial institutions and procedures, are designed to allocate power, rule making, decision making, above all, policy making power. These are the rules which are closest to the 'organic' end of our continuum, they are the ones most resistant to transplantation.[66]

Kahn-Freund explains that, at the organic end of the spectrum, powerful institutions, deeply ingrained ideologies, and beneficiaries from

[61] Baron Montesquieu, *De l'esprit des loix* (J. Brèthe de la Gressaye (ed.)), i (Paris, 1950), bk. 1, ch. 3, 26.
[62] *The Spirit of the Laws*, n. 60 above, 8–9.
[63] O. Kahn-Freund, 'On Uses and Misuses of Comparative Law' (1974) 37 *MLR* 1–27. See also B. Kaplan, 'Civil Procedure—Reflections on the Comparison of Systems' (1960) 9 *Buffalo LRev.* 409–32. Cf. generally M. Loughlin, 'The importance of elsewhere: a review of *Public Law and Democracy in the United Kingdom and the United States of America* by P. P. Craig' (1993) 4 *PLR* 44–57.
[64] A. Watson, 'Legal Transplants and Law Reform' (1976) 92 *LQR* 79–84. See also A. Watson, *Legal Transplants: An Approach to Comparative Law* (Edinburgh, 1974).
[65] Kahn-Freund, n. 63 above, 8.   [66] *Ibid.* 17.

the existing allocation of power are more likely to frustrate transplantation. He therefore concludes that the use of the comparative method as a tool of law reform requires 'a knowledge not only of the foreign law, but also of its social, and above all its political context'.[67]

Kahn-Freund's analysis highlights the importance of considering context when contemplating transplantation. To determine whether a legal transplant is likely to suit its new context, its old context must at least be compared. And, once transplantation has taken place, contextual differences might explain accompanying problems.

Watson takes issue with Kahn-Freund. He denies the hazards of transplantation and their implications. He questions Montesquieu's warnings and challenges Kahn-Freund's argument by producing counter-examples. With particular reference to the reception of Roman law he stresses the 'amount of successful borrowing'[68] which he attributes, in part, to the judicial need for authority.[69] Generally, he depicts transplantation as a source of ideas and an opportunity for reforming the transplant.[70] He argues that political, social, and economic differences are not obstacles to transplantation and therefore that 'the recipient system does not require any real knowledge of the social, economic, geographical and political context of the origin and growth of the original rule'.[71]

Watson's theoretical argument, however, is flawed and his empirical evidence is unconvincing. By recognizing that transplantation is less likely where a rule is 'inimical' to the domestic context of the receiving system,[72] Watson exposes in effect the inadequacy of his own argument. One can only know whether a transfer is inimical by first comparing the foreign with the domestic context, by identifying features of the foreign context that are different from the domestic context. One can only reject the transplantation of English abortion or divorce laws to Ireland, for example, by knowing the religious/institutional differences.[73] That the differences are obvious does not make

---

[67] Kahn-Freund, n. 63 above, 27.

[68] Watson, 'Legal Transplants and Law Reform' n. 64 above, 80. See also *id.*, *Legal Transplants*, n. 64 above, 7, 22, 95.

[69] Watson, *Legal Transplants*, n. 64 above, 88–94, 99.

[70] *Ibid.* 79. See *ibid.* 97, 99.

[71] Watson, 'Legal Transplants and Law Reform', n. 64 above, 81. See also *id.*, *Legal Transplants*, n. 64 above, 9, 99.

[72] Watson, 'Legal Transplants and Law Reform', n. 64 above, 81.

[73] Kahn-Freund, n. 63 above, 15–16.

them any less important or the knowledge of the foreign context, which Watson presupposes, any less important.[74]

Furthermore, Watson's empirical evidence provides questionable support for his normative conclusions. Watson shows borrowing but not successful borrowing, the recurrence, but not the desirability, of transplantation. In *Legal Transplants*, Watson conceives of comparative law as descriptive rather than normative. His comparative law is 'a study of the relationship of one legal system and its rules with another' and is also about the 'nature of law, and especially about the nature of legal development'.[75] Consequently, Watson is concerned with the existence of rules rather than with their effect or interpretation in their new context.[76] Without a study of effect or interpretation, however, one cannot draw inferences concerning the success of transplantation. Watson nevertheless claims a normative significance for his work:

But the subject also has practical utility. It can enable those actively concerned with law reform to understand their historical rôle and their task better. They should see more clearly whether and how far it is reasonable to borrow from other systems, and whether it is possible to accept foreign solutions with modifications or without modifications.[77]

How the law reformer can be enlightened about what is reasonable or possible by a study that ignores the effect or interpretation of legal rules is unclear. In short, Watson expressly adopts a descriptive comparative law and does not explain how he can use it to reach normative conclusions concerning successful transplantation. A teleological organicism, a manifestation of a problem endemic to the subject of transplantation, may be behind the confusion. Watson concludes as follows:

First, *transplantation* of individual rules or a large part of a legal system *is extremely common*. This is true both of early times—witness the ancient Near East—and the present day. Secondly, transplantation *is, in fact, the most fertile source* of development. Most changes in most systems are the result of borrowing.[78]

In the transplanted acorn is the exotic oak tree. The organic metaphors implicit in discussion of transplantation must be treated with caution.

How exactly Watson's empirical evidence can support any general conclusions about transplantation, let alone successful transplantation,

---

[74] See Watson, 'Legal Transplants and Law Reform', n. 64 above, 82.
[75] Watson, *Legal Transplants*, n. 64 above, 6–7.   [76] *Ibid.* 20, 96, n. 3.
[77] *Ibid.* 9, 16.   [78] *Ibid.* 95 (emphasis added). For another metaphor, see *ibid.* 100.

is also questionable. Watson denies that his examples are, and doubts that they can be, typical.[79] He recognizes that they are 'arbitrary, in so far as they depend on the author's knowledge and background'.[80] The persuasiveness of his examples can therefore be undermined with counter-examples. I will argue that two far-reaching past interactions between English and French law—a transplantation and the rejection of a transplantation—confirm the need to consider both the present and proposed contexts of a transplant.

Montesquieu's Adoption of the English Separation of Powers

In his famous chapter entitled 'On the Constitution of England', Montesquieu advocated that executive, legislative, and judicial powers be kept separate for the sake of liberty.[81] He described all three powers but focused on the executive and legislative powers and on the need not to entrust them to the same institutions.[82] He envisaged legislative rather than judicial control over the executive. Montesquieu did mention the judicial power but described it as 'in some fashion, null' and the judges as 'only the mouth that pronounces the words of the law, inanimate beings who can moderate neither its force nor its rigor'.[83] Montesquieu's attitude to judicial power contrasted with earlier English attitudes to judicial lawmaking.[84] In short, Montesquieu underestimated the input of the courts and, except where he recognized checks and balances between executive and legislative powers,[85] overestimated the extent of separation.

Although recognizing some validity to Montesquieu's analysis of the English constitution, Holdsworth shows comprehensively how the separation between King, Parliament, and the courts was not complete or clear-cut in early eighteenth-century England.[86] Holdsworth draws attention to the Crown's legislative role, the legislative and judicial functions of the House of Lords, the occasional judicial function of the House of Commons, the nature of the Lord Chancellor as judge, minister, and Member of the House of Lords, the enormous influence exercised by the Cabinet over Parliament, and judicial use of the prerogative writs to control subordinate jurisdictions and the machin-

[79] Watson, *Legal Transplants*, n. 64 above, 19.   [80] *Ibid.*
[81] Montesquieu, n. 60 above, bk. 11, ch. 6, 156.
[82] M. J. C. Vile, *Constitutionalism and the Separation of Powers* (Oxford, 1967), 90–3.
[83] Montesquieu, n. 60 above, 160, 163; Vile, n. 82 above, 88–90.
[84] Vile, n. 82 above, 89. See also below,152 f.
[85] See Vile, n. 82 above, 93–6.
[86] W. S. Holdsworth, *A History of English Law*, x (London, 1938), 713–24.

ery of local government.[87] Holdsworth attributes Montesquieu's mis-understanding to neglect of context, especially historical context. Holdsworth criticizes the superficiality[88] of Montesquieu's study, his analytical method, and his failure to approach the English constitution historically. He argues that Montesquieu had consequently failed to notice that, because the separate English institutions pre-dated the division of functions and had developed along their own lines, the separation between them was not likely to be clear-cut and logical.[89]

Indeed, Montesquieu seems to have been more engaged in abstract political analysis[90] than in a detailed description of the English constitution in context. Montesquieu made few references to the actual English constitution, let alone to its history. His political analysis in Chapter Six, Book Eleven is dotted with occasional references, not only to England, but also to places such as Rome, Sparta, Carthage, Holland, and Venice. Furthermore, Montesquieu disclaimed any attempt to describe the English constitution in operation: '[i]t is not for me to examine whether at present the English enjoy this liberty or not. It suffices for me to say that it is established by their laws, and I seek no further.'[91] Montesquieu, however, was not simply engaged in abstract political discussion. He was laying claim to a knowledge of the English constitution and was advocating the further transplantation of an idea. His Chapter Six is entitled 'On the Constitution of England' and concludes with a reference to the origins of the English political system: '[i]f one wants to read the admirable work by Tacitus, *On the Mores of the Germans*, one will see that the English have taken their idea of political government from the Germans. This fine system was found in the forests.'[92] Shackleton's conclusion seems correct:

In the case of others among his ideas, there may be discussion about whether his mental process was a priori or empirical. Here there is no doubt. It is from his experience of the English Constitution and of political controversy in England that he empirically formed his theory of the separation of powers. . . . He did not understand the developing cabinet system. He did not understand the role of a minister. . . . He did not understand that there might be some good, even a small, relative, or dubious good, to be gained from ministerial exercise of influence; he saw it simply as corruption. . . . The separation of powers, during Montesquieu's stay in England, was no more than a partisan

[87] *Ibid.* 720.
[88] See also F. W. Maitland, 'The Shallows and Silences of Real Life' in *Collected Papers* (H. A. L. Fisher (ed.)) (Cambridge, 1911), i, 467–79 at 478.
[89] Holdsworth, n. 86 above, 717, 721.
[90] Vile, n. 82 above, 84–5.
[91] Montesquieu, n. 60 above, 166.
[92] *Ibid.* 165–6.

cry. It was he who dignified and rationalized the concept, linked it to a theory of liberty, and handed it to posterity.[93]

The consequences of Montesquieu's misunderstanding were serious. Watson mentions Montesquieu in his conclusion that borrowing can be influential without a knowledge of context and despite complete misunderstanding.[94] Montesquieu's theory of strictly separate powers was undoubtedly influential. It was reinforced by the pre-Revolutionary French experience of the power and pretensions of the *parlements*[95] and was radicalized by the 1790 Law of the Revolutionary Assembly which forbade the ordinary courts from interfering with the executive.[96] Montesquieu's theory of separate powers made a lasting contribution to liberal political theory, but the value of his immediate influence in France is questionable. About one hundred years were to pass before the French *Conseil d'Etat* could adjudicate administrative disputes as a judicialized body within the administration.[97] And about 190 years were to pass before a certain power of judicial review of legislation was assumed by the French *Conseil Constitutionnel*.[98] The slowness of these developments was, in part, due to Montesquieu's theory of strictly separate powers, therefore to his misunderstanding of the rough English separation, the result of his neglect of context, especially historical context.

Dicey's Rejection of Droit Administratif

In the absence of sufficient consideration of context, the refusal to transplant can also be hazardous. In his *Law of the Constitution*, Dicey rejected *droit administratif* as incompatible with the English tradition.[99] In Lecture Five of the first edition[100] and chapter 4 of the third and later editions, Dicey depicted *droit administratif* as incompatible with equality before the law. He concluded:

---

[93] R. Shackleton, *Montesquieu: A Critical Biography* (Oxford, 1961), 300–1.
[94] Watson, *Legal Transplants* n. 64 above, 99.
[95] J. P. Dawson, *The Oracles of the Law* (Ann Arbor, 1968), 350–71.
[96] Law of 16–24 August 1790, title 2, art. 13.   [97] Below, pp. 142–6.
[98] See M. Cappelletti, 'Repudiating Montesquieu? The Expansion and Legitimacy of "Constitutional Justice" ' in M. Cappelletti, *The Judicial Process in Comparative Perspective* (Oxford, 1989), 182–211; B. Nicholas, 'Fundamental Rights and Judicial Review in France' [1978] *PL* 82–101, 155–77; J. Bell, *French Constitutional Law* (Oxford, 1992).
[99] 10th edn., n. 51 above.
[100] A. V. Dicey, *Lectures Introductory to the Study of the Law of the Constitution* (London, 1885).

[T]he notion which lies at the bottom of the 'administrative law' known to foreign countries, that affairs or disputes in which the government or its servants are concerned are beyond the sphere of the civil courts and must be dealt with by special and more or less official bodies (*tribunaux administratifs*) is utterly unknown to the law of England, and indeed is fundamentally inconsistent with our traditions and customs.[101]

In his section on French administrative law in his original Lecture Five,[102] which was to expand into chapter 12 of his third and later editions, Dicey elaborated on the incompatibility. The normative importance of his rule of law and phrases like 'foreign' (page 181), 'totally different' (page 182), 'radically opposed' (page 191), 'absolutely inconsistent' (page 193), 'despotic' (page 194), 'utterly unknown' (page 216), and 'fundamentally inconsistent' (page 216), in his Lecture Five and repeated in chapter 12 of his third and later editions, betray at least his original antagonism to French administrative law.[103]

Dicey's antagonism was partly the product of a neglect of political and historical context. Dicey failed to appreciate the nature of the French separation of powers. He referred to their 'so-called "separation of powers" ' as a 'dogma' based on a 'double misconception'—Montesquieu's misunderstanding of the English constitution and the French revolutionaries' misunderstanding or misapplication of Montesquieu's doctrine.[104] Dicey did stress Montesquieu's 'extraordinary influence' in France but regarded further investigation as unnecessary.[105]

Apart from neglecting the French political context, Dicey neglected and misunderstood French history and, in particular, overemphasized the scope and nature of Napoleon's legacy.[106] Dicey condemned the *Conseil d'Etat* for its origins in the *ancien régime* and for its revival by the despot Napoleon. Dicey linked French administrative law to the Napoleonic legacy of the mid-nineteenth century and admitted to neglecting the recent French law. In the preface to the French edition of *Law of the Constitution*, he argued that 'for a comparison with English law, French administrative law, as it was in the middle of the nineteenth century, is as convenient as the more developed administrative law of to day'.[107] Dicey relied heavily on Tocqueville's comments on

---

[101] *Ibid.* 215–16.   [102] *Ibid.* 180–208.   [103] *Ibid.*
[104] N. 51 above, 337–8.   [105] *Ibid.*
[106] *Ibid.* 335–6. See S. Flogaïtis, *Administrative Law et droit administratif* (Paris, 1986), 35, 44–5, 56–7.
[107] Quoted by R. Errera, 'Dicey and French Administrative Law: A Missed Encounter?' [1985] *PL* 695–707 at 704.

French administrative law, although he recognized that Tocqueville 'knew little or nothing of the actual working of *droit administratif* in his own day' and had distorted French history by exaggerating the continuity of France before and after the Revolution.[108] Dicey did not perceive the extent to which French liberals like Tocqueville in effect contributed to the development of French administrative law.[109]

Not only, however, did Dicey misunderstand and neglect the French historical and political context, he was also insufficiently critical of his own basic presuppositions. Dicey did respond to the criticism of the translators of the French edition of *Law of the Constitution*,[110] but did not revise his basic thesis. Despite his recognition of 'official law' (the law determining the position of servants of the civil service), 'governmental law' (the law determining the functions of civil servants), the emergence of English administrative tribunals, the advances of French administrative law, and the unreliability of the authorities on which he relied, Dicey adhered to his original thesis concerning the incompatibility of *droit administratif* and the English rule of law.[111]

In the Harvard Law Review of 1905/6, Parker criticized Dicey's presentation of French law in chapter 12 as 'calculated to give an erroneous impression' and expressed surprise at Dicey's failure to re-write the chapter despite his 'virtual retraction' in notes x and xi of the appendix to the sixth edition.[112] Parker's call for the re-writing of chapter 12 was only partly answered. In his seventh edition, Dicey merely incorporated into chapter 12[113] his argument in notes x and xi of the sixth edition but did not alter the basic thesis of the chapter. In fact, Dicey explicitly wished to retain it: 'I have, lastly, wished to show that the modern administrative law of France, though, as amended since 1870 partly by legislation and still more by case-law, it approaches to a regular though peculiar system of law, is opposed in its fundamental principles to ideas which lie at the basis of English constitutional government'.[114]

In 1915 Dicey modified his position still further. He wrote an article entitled 'The Development of Administrative Law in England',[115]

---

[108] N. 51 above, 355–8, 392–3, especially at 392.   [109] See below, 55–6.

[110] A. V. Dicey, '*Droit administratif* in Modern French law' (1901) 18 *LQR* 302–18; incorporated as nn. x and xi in the app. to *Law of the Constitution* (6th edn.) p. xi.

[111] *Ibid.*

[112] E. M. Parker, 'State and official liability' (1905/6) 19 *Harv. LRev.* 335–49 at 347–9.

[113] See 364–89.   [114] *Law of the Constitution* (7th edn.), pp. ix and x.

[115] (1915) 31 *LQR* 148–53; incorporated as an appendix to *Law of the Constitution*, n. 51 above, 493–9.

and, in his introduction to the eighth edition of *Law of the Constitution*, the last which was published while he was still alive, Dicey recognized the 'approximation toward one another of what may be called the official law of England and the *droit administratif* of France'.[116] He began to think the unthinkable:

It is at least conceivable that modern England would be benefited by the extension of official law. Nor is it quite certain that the ordinary law courts are in all cases the best body for adjudicating upon the offences or the errors of civil servants. It may require consideration whether some body of men who combined official experience with legal knowledge and who were entirely independent of the Government of the day, might not enforce official law with more effect than any Division of the High Court.[117]

Dicey still, however, refused to revise his basic thesis in chapter 12. His refusal is a perplexing issue with methodological implications. It was not simply due to old age[118] or a reluctance to spoil his original text. Dicey did prefer to add the introduction to his eighth edition rather than revise the text of his seventh edition,[119] but to the very last Dicey regarded a real administrative law, a *droit administratif*, as alien to English law. As in his revisionary articles,[120] Dicey was imprisoned by an original presupposition: '[s]till it would be a grave mistake if the recognition of the growth of official law in England and the gradual judicialization of the Council as an administrative tribunal led any Englishman to suppose that there exists in England as yet any true administrative tribunals or any real administrative law.'[121] And, to the extent Dicey had become self-critical, his self-criticism was rendered ineffective by his attitude to his original work: 'The constant amendment of a book published in successive editions during thirty years is apt to take from it any such literary merits as it may originally have possessed. Recurring alterations destroy the *original tone and spirit of any treatise* which has the least claim to belong to the literature of England.'[122] As the editor of the ninth and tenth editions, E. C. S. Wade perpetuated this attitude in merely changing the introduction and not the main text: '[t]he influence of Dicey lies in the principles stated in the body of the book rather than in matters of contemporary controversy, such as figured in his Introduction in 1914. In this way it

---

[116] *Law of the Constitution* (8th edn.), p. xlii.   [117] *Ibid.*, p. xlviii.
[118] *Contra* F. H. Lawson, 'Dicey revisited' [1959] *Political Studies* 109, 207, at 109.
[119] See n. 116 above, p. xvii.   [120] See above, nn. 110 and 115.
[121] N. 116 above, p. xliv.   [122] *Ibid.* p. xvii (emphasis added).

is possible to preserve the text of a book which is a classic'.[123] Dicey's work had acquired a life of its own to its author and to others and had consequently become partly immune to change.

Lawson describes how Dicey's book became a 'phantom to replace the reality in the memory of those who had finished their university course' and stresses the need to read the book with reference to the changing conditions which existed when Dicey wrote.[124] The book, however, or at least Dicey's original thesis concerning French administrative law had become a phantom in which even Dicey to a certain extent believed. Ford depicts his slow adaptation of the book as a gradual facing of reality by a prophet who had created a myth for political ends and out of disillusion with British politics.[125] Be that as it may. Whether *Law of the Constitution* was created as a myth or became a myth, a methodology should be adopted which would prevent a thesis such as its thesis concerning French administrative law from being mistaken for reality.

The extent of our difficulty is apparent from Errera's comments on Dicey:

Dicey was a man of passion and of passions. . . . His definition of the concept of the Rule of law belongs to the realm of intellectual passions. Dicey's wide legal culture, his precise knowledge of French administrative law, his impeccable reading and use of the best French sources, his very honesty which led him to recognize, edition after edition, the progress of his 'anti-model,' all these qualities which it is only fair to state could not ultimately prevent him from remaining a prisoner of his own definition of the Rule of Law and overlooking, for that very reason, the true historical, legal and political meaning of the evolution of an institution he knew better than any other Englishman of his time.[126]

Dicey might have had a peculiar passionate wilfulness[127] but it was a wilfulness to which many of his readers succumbed. A national chauvinism was at work: 'Dicey's critical analysis of French administrative law was thus written only for the purposes of demonstration, the outcome of which was no doubt, in the author's and in his readers' minds,

---

[123] N. 51 above, pp. ix and x.   [124] Lawson, n. 118 above, 109, 221.

[125] T. H. Ford, 'Dicey as a political journalist' [1970] *Political Studies* 220–35, especially at 234–5.

[126] Errera, n. 107 above, 706.

[127] See generally F. Mount, *The British Constitution Now: Recovery or Decline?* (London, 1993), 47 ff.

the superiority of the English system, or, more precisely, of Dicey's analysis of it.'[128]

A different methodology might have bridled the passionate wilfulness which Errera describes. As things were, Dicey's political presuppositions denied by his analytical approach to constitutional law could operate unchecked. And his explicit rejection of the old historical approach in order to focus on the existing constitutional law[129] perhaps caused him to regard the English rule of law and French administrative law essentially as static and not fully to take account of their historical evolution or changing political[130] context. The irony would be that Dicey neglected history to focus on the present, which he could therefore see less clearly.

Dicey's influence was immense.[131] His neglect of political and historical context and his insufficiently self-critical approach to his basic presuppositions caused him to resist the transplantation of a *droit administratif* and, so, retard the development of an English administrative law at a time when its emergence would have been less inappropriate.[132] He might be excused as a doctrinal explorer[133] or pioneer rationalizing constitutional law without the help of authority,[134]but no similar excuse is available today.

Judicial Transplantation of the Distinction

The development of a significant English distinction between public and private law followed upon much academic discussion. In response to Dicey's analysis, academics frequently discussed *droit administratif* and the *Conseil d'Etat* in detail.[135] They diverged in their attitude to the general suitability of the French system. A few like Robson and Jennings

---

[128] Errera, n. 107 above, 699. See also Flogaïtis, n. 106 above, 34–5, 47–8; Jennings, n. 52 above, 127, 132–3.

[129] See *Law of the Constitution* (1st edn.), pp. v–vii; Loughlin, *Public Law and Political Theory*, n. 12 above, 13–17.

[130] See P. P. Craig, 'Dicey: Unitary, Self-correcting Democracy and Public Law' (1990) 106 *LQR* 105–43.

[131] See the references in n. 52 above. [132] See below, 82 ff.

[133] Flogaïtis, n. 106 above, 34, 36.

[134] Lawson, n. 118 above, 113–14, 121; Jennings, n. 52 above, 133.

[135] W. A. Robson, *Justice and Administrative Law: A Study of the British Constitution* (3rd edn., London, 1951), 28–34; F. J. Port, *Administrative Law* (London, 1929), ch. 7; W. I. Jennings, *The Law and the Constitution* (5th edn., London, 1959), 229–38; C. J. Hamson, *Executive Discretion and Judicial Control: An Aspect of the French Conseil d'Etat* (London, 1954); B. Schwartz, *French Administrative Law and the Common-Law World* (New York, 1954).

were enthusiastic; others like Schwartz and Hamson were cautious.[136] Despite his admiration for the French system, Hamson commented:

By way of caution, I desire to repeat what again I have said elsewhere: that I do not suggest that the answer to our difficulties is to seek to set up in England a body modelled upon the Conseil d'Etat. Human affairs, and comparative legal studies, do not unfortunately possess that degree of simplicity. The Conseil d'Etat is itself the creature of a peculiar history, it is conditioned by its own environment, it is the special response to the special set of circumstances existing in France. It cannot as such be transported across the Channel, it will not as such fit into our circumstances and our traditions and prejudices.[137]

About the possibility of an English *Conseil d'Etat*, a supreme administrative court within the executive, he asked: 'Would it be possible to promote or provoke a similar fit of conscience in the English executive? In such a matter the only effective gamekeeper is likely to be the really converted poacher. And would it be possible to secure the confidence of the public in the reality of the conversion?'[138]

The Committees of Inquiry listened to words of caution. Influenced by Dicey, the Donoughmore Committee declared the 'inexpediency of establishing a system of administrative law'.[139] The Committee rejected Robson's proposals for a system of administrative courts and administrative law as 'inconsistent with the sovereignty of Parliament and the supremacy of the law'.[140] Later, for similar reasons, the Franks Committee rejected proposals for a General Appeal Tribunal and Administrative Division of the High Court.[141]

The Law Commission in the 1970s was first bold, then cautious. In its 1971 Green Paper, it advocated that the AJR be exclusive for public-law issues,[142] but, in its 1976 Report, as a result of criticism, it retracted and recommended that the AJR not be exclusive.[143] The

---

[136] See also, e.g., J. D. B. Mitchell, 'The Causes and Effects of the Absence of a System of Public Law in the United Kingdom' [1965] *PL* 95–118, especially at 95. See generally M. Loughlin, 'Sitting on a Fence at Carter Bar: In Praise of J. D. B. Mitchell' (1991) 36 *Juridical Review* 135–53.

[137] Hamson, n. 135 above, 21.   [138] *Ibid.* 214.

[139] Donoughmore Committee, *Report of the Committee on Ministers' Powers* (1932), Cmnd. 4060, 110.

[140] *Ibid.*

[141] Franks Committee, *Report of the Committee on Administrative Tribunals and Enquiries* (1957), Cmnd. 218, 28 ff. See also Committee of the Justice–All Souls Review of Administrative Law in the United Kingdom, *Administrative Justice: Some Necessary Reforms* (Oxford, 1988), 168–70.

[142] *Remedies in Administrative Law* (working paper 40, 1971), paras. 76–82, 154(2).

[143] *Remedies in Administrative Law* (Law Com. 73, 1976), Cmnd. 6407, para. 34.

amendment to Order 53 of the Rules of the Supreme Court therefore provided for the use of the ordinary remedies under the umbrella of the AJR with permissive wording and did not determine that the AJR be an exclusive procedure in public law.[144]

Despite academic divergence, the caution of the Donoughmore and Franks Committees, and the retraction of the Law Commission, the English courts forged ahead.[145] In *O'Reilly* v. *Mackman*, Lord Denning in the Court of Appeal simply declared that '[i]n modern times we have come to recognize two separate fields of law, one of private law, the other of public law.'[146] The Court of Appeal proceeded to give the distinction procedural significance by relating it to an emergent principle of exclusivity.[147] To secure the protection afforded to authorities by the AJR procedure, the Court of Appeal determined that the AJR would be exclusive in public-law disputes. Lord Diplock in the House of Lords similarly assumed the distinction between public and private law and confirmed the decision of the Court on Appeal.[148] The Committee of the Justice–All Souls Review rightly criticized *O'Reilly* for having 'all the appearance of judicial legislation without the benefit of the consultation and debating process normally associated with legislation'.[149]

The Crown Office List was introduced by a few administrative changes[150] with even less consideration than the procedural distinction in *O'Reilly*. In January 1981, Order 53 was amended to provide for AJRs to be heard by a single judge of the Queen's Bench Division. The Lord Chief Justice then nominated judges known for their expertise in administrative law to hear the AJRs. Finally, in July 1981, the Lord Chief Justice issued Directions for London which established the Crown Office List to ensure that all administrative cases come before the nominated judges. Blom-Cooper comments: '[a] specialised administrative court—albeit one which lacks the distinctiveness and

[144] R. 1(2).

[145] But see dicta of Lord Wilberforce in *Davy* v. *Spelthorne BC*, n. 59 above, and of Parker LJ in *Bourgoin SA* v. *Ministry of Agriculture* [1986] QB 716 at 788C (but cf. *ibid.* 787F–G)

[146] See n. 2 above.

[147] See *Uppal* v. *Home Office*, *The Times*, 11 Nov. 1978; *Heywood* v. *Hull Prison Board of Visitors* [1980] 3 All ER 594.

[148] See n. 3 above.

[149] Committee of the Justice–All Souls Review of Administrative Law in the United Kingdom, n. 141 above, 150.

[150] L. Blom-Cooper, 'The New Face of Judicial Review: Administrative Changes in Order 53' [1982] *PL* 250–61.

constitutional status of a body like the French *Conseil d'Etat*—had been established, even if it has been achieved by administrative stealth rather than by the democratic process of legislation.'[151]

The English judiciary did not only develop a procedural and institutional distinction between public and private law. Since the 1970s, English judges, with little authority and without mentioning the traditional English rejection or academic discussion of the distinction, had also begun using the distinction to describe substantive law. In *Town Investments* v. *Department of the Environment*, Lord Diplock stressed that 'it is not private law but public law that governs the relationships between Her Majesty in her political capacity, the government departments among which the work of Her Majesty's government is distributed, the ministers of the Crown in charge of the various departments and civil servants of all grades who are employed in those departments'.[152] In *Gouriet* v. *Union of Post Office Workers*, Lord Diplock referred to the distinction in substantive law to demarcate the position of the courts and the Attorney-General in relator actions:

[T]he jurisdiction of a civil court to grant remedies in private law is confined to the grant of remedies to litigants whose rights in private law have been infringed or are threatened with infringement. To extend that jurisdiction to the grant of remedies for unlawful conduct which does not infringe any rights of the plaintiff in private law, is to move out of the field of private into that of public law with which analogies may be deceptive and where different principles apply.[153]

In *Anns* v. *Merton London Borough Council*, Lord Wilberforce simply assumed the distinction between public and private law in his discussion of a local authority's duty of care:

[T]he local authority is a public body, discharging functions under statute: its powers and duties are definable in terms of public not private law. The problem which this type of action creates, is to define the circumstances in which the law should impose, over and above, or perhaps alongside, these public law powers and duties, a duty in private law towards individuals such that they may sue for damages in a civil court.[154]

---

[151] Blom-Cooper, 'The New Face of Judicial Review', n. 150 above, 260.

[152] *Town Investments* v. *Department of Environment* [1978] AC 359 at 380F.

[153] *Gouriet* v. *Unioin of Post Office Workers* [1978] AC 435 at 500C–D. See also *ibid.* 494F–G, 518D–E.

[154] [1978] AC 728 at 754B.

Later, in *Bourgoin SA* v. *Ministry of Agriculture*, Parker LJ described the terms "public law rights" and "private law rights" as 'imprecise' and lacking in 'merit', but nevertheless used them to delimit the availability of damages for a breach by government of Article 30 of the EEC Treaty.[155] And, in the 'GCHQ' case, Lord Diplock used the terminology of public and private law and summarized the 'principles of public law'.[156] At no stage, however, did he discuss the distinction itself, the attitude of English academics or the distinction's compatibility with the English legal tradition.

English judges have introduced the distinction between public and private law without assessing the distinction itself or comparing its English and Continental historical and political contexts. Whatever the reason—whether a traditional judicial positivism, the practical irrelevance of academics, judicial denial of transplantation, or judicial acceptance that the distinction's reception was anyway inevitable via European Community law[157]—their work must be reconsidered. Montesquieu's adoption of the English separation of powers and Dicey's rejection of *droit administratif* illustrate the hazards and far-reaching implications of an ill-considered approach to transplantation. They are a reminder of the need for methodological caution and rigour when considering or reconsidering a legal transplant.

A Historical-Comparative Jurisprudence

The historical and comparative analysis which will be attempted in this book might seem misguided and old-fashioned. Until the first quarter of this century, theorists of legal evolution tackled general issues and reached general conclusions on the basis of historical and comparative studies.[158] Their theories have been widely discredited.[159] Therefore, to avoid their fate, a historical and comparative analysis at a high level of generality must confront the criticisms which discredited those theories.

[155] At 788C–D, 787F–G.

[156] *Council of the Civil Service Union* v. *Minister for Civil Service* [1985] AC 374 at 408E–11H.

[157] See *Marshall* v. *Southampton and South West Hampshire Area Health Authority (Teaching)* (C–152/84) [1986] ECR 723, [1986] QB 401; *Johnston* v. *Chief Constable of the Royal Ulster Constabulary* (C–222/84) [1986] ECR 1651, [1987] QB 129; *Foster* v. *British Gas plc* (C–188/89) [1990] ECR 1–3313, [1990] IRLR 353 (ECJ), [1991] IRLR 268 (HL); *Doughty* v. *Rolls-Royce plc* [1992] 1 CMLR 1045, [1992] IRLR 126.

[158] P. Stein, *Legal Evolution: The Story of an Idea* (Cambridge, 1980).

[159] *Ibid.* 99–127. See, e.g., Watson, *Legal Transplants*, n. 64 above, 12–15.

Maine's *Ancient Law* written at the heyday of historical jurisprudence is an exemplary theory of evolution.[160] Inspired by the nineteenth-century pretensions of science and challenged by those of natural-law theory, Maine abstracted scientific laws of legal evolution from a historical and comparative study mainly of the Roman, English, and German systems. A famous example is his generalization that ancient law was modified by three successive instruments of legal change: 'These instrumentalities seem to me to be three in number, Legal Fictions, Equity and Legislation. Their historical order is that in which I have placed them. . . . I know of no instance in which the order of their appearance has been changed or inverted.'[161]

By the end of the nineteenth century, however, his work was being discredited and historical jurisprudence endangered. Maine's laws of legal evolution were shown to have underestimated diversity and over-simplified development. Anthropologists questioned the features Maine attributed to his 'early law' and stressed that diversity precluded a universal evolutionary sequence.[162] Meanwhile, legal historians have shown that a few of Maine's generalizations do not even apply to the systems—Roman, English, and German—from which they were derived.[163] Baker, for example, concludes that Maine's thesis about the instruments of legal change 'in so far as it imposed an historical sequence . . . is difficult to square with the English experience'.[164]

Linguistic inabilities, the range of the subject matter, and the frequent absence of written law in remote legal systems induced an undue reliance on the accessible sources of the supposedly civilized legal systems and encouraged the cavalier use of fragmentary, literary, and anecdotal sources of other systems. Maine's bias in his selection of sources was characteristic of the chauvinism of theorists of social and legal evolution. To describe an abstract legal development by reference to more than one legal system is to distinguish the less developed from the more developed system. In an age of imperialism, distinctions were influenced by presuppositions of the progress and superiority of certain Western systems. The theorists of legal evolution revered the supposedly civilized legal systems of Rome, England, and Germany, and tended to dismiss remote systems as backward or unprogressive. Two world wars have exposed the chauvinism of their presuppositions and

---

[160] H. S. Maine, *Ancient Law: Its Connection with the Early History of Society and its Relation to Modern Ideas* (London, 1930); Stein, n. 158 above, 86–98.

[161] Maine, *ibid*. 31.   [162] Stein, n. 158 above, 101–6.

[163] *Ibid*. 106–10.   [164] Baker, n. 8 above, 224. See generally *ibid*. 223–52.

undermined the perception of progress and the faith in science that inspired the evolutionists.[165]

Today, theories of legal evolution are less appealing also because of the different conceptions of law[166] and legal change that now prevail. The school of historical jurisprudence was preoccupied[167] with private-law institutions like contract, property, and succession, and did not require[168] legislation by elected representatives for their progressive development. Now, democratic processes are usually seen as important to legal change. And law is not regarded simply as a collection of private-law institutions. It has, for example, been described as the 'literary presentation of social norms'[169] and famously likened to a chain novel.[170] The encroachment of public law upon private law is now widely recognized and, with it, the contextualized legal interpretation of the general and vague standards of public law.[171] Legal formalism has given way to a purposive approach to law for which context is all-important. To seek generalizations about legal institutions seems futile where their significance and interpretation is dependent on context.

But, despite the criticisms of legal evolutionists like Maine, and the decline of historical jurisprudence, and despite the presently unfavourable jurisprudential climate for the theories of legal evolution, many of the evolutionists' generalizations have become 'commonplaces of legal thought'.[172] Because they still influence the suppositions with which we approach remote legal systems, the theorists of legal evolution deserve reassessment and should not simply be discarded. To assess their contribution and the desirability of resuming historical and comparative studies at a high level of generality, we must realize the scope of the problems confronting the evolutionists and evaluate the adequacy of the answers and the alternatives.

The problems confronting the legal evolutionists were not peculiar to historical jurisprudence, but were part of a general and continuing

---

[165] See generally Stein, n. 158 above, 124; R. Cotterrell, *The Politics of Jurisprudence: A Critical Introduction to Legal Philosophy* (London, 1989), 50.

[166] Stein, n. 158 above, 125–6.

[167] But see J. Millar, *An Historical View of English Government, from the Settlement of Saxons in Britain to the Accession of the House of Stewart* (London, 1787); Loughlin, 'John Millar', n. 12 above, 4–13; Stein, n. 158 above, 46–50.

[168] See Cotterrell, n. 165 above,. 46–7.

[169] B. S. Jackson, *Essays in Jewish and Comparative Legal History* (Leiden, 1975), 11.

[170] R. A. Dworkin, 'Natural Law Revisited' (1982) 34 *Univ. of Florida LRev.* 165–88.

[171] R. M. Unger, *Law in Modern Society: Toward a Criticism of Social Theory* (New York, 1976), 192–237.

[172] Stein, n. 158 above, 98, 126.

predicament of social theory. Unger describes the social theorist as caught between conflicting demands—the demand for general truths and the demand for fidelity to concrete detail.[173] The description of a causal connection is a typical claim that, if x causes y, then wherever x occurs, y must or will probably follow. The theorist, however, when attempting to establish a causal connection, is confronted by the problem of either considering a multitude of causes and being unable to distinguish discrete causal judgements or wilfully distorting reality by tearing 'certain events out of the "seamless web" of history, in which everything seems to bear on everything else'.[174]

Another manifestation of this tension between the demand for general truths and the demand for fidelity to concrete detail is the inability of the theorist to devise a social theory that is both systematic and detailed.[175] The scientific laws and schemes of the nineteenth-century evolutionists, for example, stand in contrast to the detailed studies of the legal historians and anthropologists of this century. While the laws are discredited for their infidelity to concrete contexts, the detailed studies are often of uncertain relevance to our general understandings of social order and transformation. Generalization is still required for detailed studies to become relevant to the discussion of contemporary issues. Of necessity, generalizations such as Maine's have lived on despite the detailed studies which contradict them.[176] Unger concludes that:

> The recurring conflict between generality and accuracy is a constant preoccupation for 'social scientists' and historians alike. Its root is the tension between the concrete perception of particulars and the abstract knowledge of universals. . . . The conflict between historiography and systematic theory is really just an aspect of the larger issue of universality and particularity in knowledge, and it cannot be overcome as long as rational discourse continues to mean a kind of thinking that abstracts from the particularity of things.[177]

The theorists of legal evolution responded to the demand for generality and were accused of inaccuracy. Their response, however, should not simply be condemned when the problem they faced is a predicament for social theory in general. The alternative is a descent into detail of questionable relevance to our general concerns about social order and transformation. Furthermore, 'even the most focused histor-

---

[173] Unger, n. 171 above, 8–23.
[174] *Ibid.* 12.
[175] *Ibid.* 19–23.
[176] Stein, n. 158 above, 98, 126, 101–10.
[177] Unger, n. 171 above, 21–2.

ical statement must refer implicitly to general categories of thought and rely on general conceptions of social order and human action'.[178] The theorists of legal evolution were pierced by one horn of a dilemma; the writer of detailed historiography or social theory is unable completely to avoid either.

Possibly the dust kicked up by the critics of historical jurisprudence has sufficiently settled for a revival of a historical-comparative approach to general jurisprudential issues.[179] Indeed, a renewal of interest, comparable to developments in general social theory,[180] seems evident.[181] Much, however, depends on the adequacy of Weber's ideal type as the most advanced theoretical response to the problem of laws which do not do justice to the complexity and variety of contexts.[182]

Weber regarded analysis as necessarily involving abstraction from the unending complexity of reality.[183] He reduced laws or generalizations from the objectives of analysis to heuristic and expository devices for making explicit and unambiguous the selections and suppositions inevitably made by the theorist.[184] Weber called such devices ideal types and used them to make explicit the inevitably one-sided accentuation of a point of view on a particular situation without precluding the relevance of other points of view:

An ideal type is formed by the one-sided accentuation of one or more points of view and by the synthesis of a great many diffuse, discrete, more or less present and occasionally absent concrete individual phenomena, which are arranged according to those one-sidedly emphasized viewpoints into a unified analytical construct (*Gedankenbild*). In its conceptual purity, this mental construct (*Gedankenbild*) cannot be found empirically anywhere in reality. It is a utopia. Historical research faces the task of determining in each individual

---

[178] *Ibid.* 244.   [179] Jackson, n. 169 above, 8.

[180] See, e.g., Q. Skinner, 'Introduction: The Return of Grand Theory' in Q. Skinner (ed.), *The Return of Grand Theory in the Human Sciences* (Cambridge, 1985), 1–20; P. Birnbaum, *States and Collective Action: The European Experience* (Cambridge, 1988), especially at 4–8.

[181] See, e.g., Unger, n. 171 above; K. S. Newman, *Law and Economic Organization: A Comparative Study of Preindustrial Societies* (Cambridge, 1983); G. MacCormack, 'Historical Jurisprudence' (1985) 5 *Legal Studies* 251–60; P. Stein, 'The Tasks of Historical Jurisprudence' in P. Birks and N. McCormick (eds.), *The Legal Mind: Essays for Tony Honore* (Oxford, 1986), 293–305; R. C. Van Caenegem, *Judges, Legislators and Professors: Chapters in European Legal History* (Cambridge, 1987); *id.*, 'Max Weber: Historian and Sociologist' in *id.*, *Legal History: A European Perspective* (London, 1991), 201–22.

[182] M. Weber, *The Methodology of the Social Sciences* (Glencoe, Illinois, 1949). See A. Giddens, *Capitalism and Modern Social Theory: An Analysis of the Writings of Marx, Durkeim and Max Weber* (Cambridge, 1971), 133–44.

[183] Weber, n. 182 above, 81–2.   [184] *Ibid.* 76–80.

case, the extent to which this ideal-construct approximates to or diverges from reality.[185]

The knowledge furthered through the use of an ideal type is, then, not the grasp of generalizations or laws abstracted from the particularity of things, but a sense of the deviation of a particular situation from a general supposition.

The danger of the theorist's being imprisoned by the chosen type or model is reduced by the requirement that detailed research establish the extent to which the type diverges from reality. The Weberian method requires the theorist to become conscious of the prison. Further research and academic reaction can make the theorist aware of the need to abandon the chosen model or type. The consequent multiplication of models as the irrelevant or misleading are abandoned is not unduly problematic because the models are the means, not the objectives, of analysis. The enduring and underlying problem, however, is the determination of the appropriate level of generality for the type.[186]

Nevertheless, equipped with Weber's ideal type, the defender of a historical–comparative jurisprudence can answer pressing problems and even convert a few former methodological weaknesses into strengths. First, the discredited, but enduring, generalizations can become ideal types and, as such, devices for exposing their own deficiencies. Secondly, the Weberian method confronts the difficulty of inaccessible sources and the higher probability of error. Because the ideal type invites and even requires corrective research, error through linguistic inability or ignorance of context is an opportunity for correction and a reason for collaborative work.

Thirdly, any chauvinistic presuppositions we might have regarding less developed legal systems or the progress of our own become the explicit subjects of scrutiny. The type does not impose our own presuppositions but provides and calls for their exposure. Where we have no choice but to analyse Barotse jurisprudence in our own terms,[187] with the Weberian method, we can at least put them on trial. And we can avoid a moralistic ranking of legal systems by constructing an ideal

---

[185] Weber, n. 182 above, 90.   [186] Unger, n. 171 above, 22.

[187] See generally M. Gluckman, 'Concepts in the Comparative Study of Tribal Law' in L. Nader (ed.), *Law in Culture and Society* (Chicago, 1969), 349–73; P. Bohannan, 'Ethnography and Comparison in Legal Anthropology', *ibid.* 401–18.

type which focuses on functional and technical improvement as distinct from moral progress.[188]

Finally, we can construct ideal types to focus on law, not merely as an evolving collection of private-law institutions, but as the presentation and interpretation of rules, principles, or procedures in different contexts, whether by courts, citizens, or elected representatives. Jackson suggests that the 'literary presentation [of social norms] . . . would seem to provide the most promising area of law in which the search for universals may be conducted'.[189] However we may regard the prospect of such a treasure at the end of the rainbow, an analysis of the distinction between public and private law is an appropriate starting-point for considering the adaptability of a historical–comparative jurisprudence to a more contemporary conception of law.

Such a jurisprudence equipped with Weber's ideal type is suited to the reconsideration of the judicial transplantation of the distinction between public and private law. One has reason to hope that it demands both the sense of historical and political context and a self-critical attitude to one's basic presuppositions to avoid the far-reaching misunderstandings of Montesquieu and Dicey. My method, therefore, will be to present in the following chapter, and elaborate in subsequent chapters, a model or ideal type of a working distinction between public and private law in a legal and political setting where it is satisfactory.

---

[188] MacCormack, n. 181 above, 252–3.   [189] Jackson, n. 169 above, 11.

3
A Model Distinction in a Model Setting

The society in which the distinction is satisfactory is characterized by its theory of the state, its approach to law, and its judicial institutions and procedures.

The state administration, in the sense of the range of agents or activities organized to achieve the prevailing goals of a territorial community, is conceived as an important feature of reality in this society. A well-developed theory of the state prevails and influences legal doctrine, a theory that emphasizes the distinctness of the state administration—whether called the executive, the government, or the public power—and ascribes to it qualities that provide a justification for regulation and control with specially designed legal rules, institutions, and procedures.

Perhaps the state administration is regarded as distinct because it is centralized. At the centre, whether identified with a monarchy or with a democratic mechanism providing for the equal participation of all citizens, the state administration can be distinguished from other powerful institutions. Just as a centre can be identified because it is only one point on a line or in a circle, a centralized state administration is distinct and therefore identifiable. Or perhaps the state administration is regarded as distinct because of its unique powers and duties—whether arising from a monopoly of the use of force or some special role, such as that of night-watchman, moral exemplar, or provider of basic communal services. Whatever the reason, the state administration is not only conceived as somehow separate from, and thus amenable to, the application of legal rules, institutions, and procedures. It is also regarded as consistently identifiable through the elaboration of institutional or functional distinguishing criteria. In theory, disputes involving the state administration can therefore be identified and special legal rules, institutions, and procedures can therefore be applied.

In this society, special legal consequences are justified in administrative disputes by the qualities attributed to the state administration. While members of this society recognize its necessity, they are fearful that its peculiar powers will be abused or irresponsibly exercised. They recognize that the concentration of power in the state administration creates an enormous inequality between its power and the power of the individual. They therefore depend upon special judicial institutions and procedures and a distinct body of rules called public law to secure a responsible administration and to redress the imbalance of power. Whereas the formal equality of individuals is assumed in private law, substantive inequality of power is the main concern of public law. When dealing with administrative disputes, the courts are required to uphold the rights and freedoms of the individual threatened by administrative power. A distinction between public and private law expresses and entrenches the distinct character of the law required to regulate the relationship between the individual and the state administration.

The society in which the distinction is satisfactory is characterized not only by the theory of the state administration that prevails but also by a particular conception of law. The prevailing approach to law may be described as categorical. In other words, law is approached with a sense of system and of the whole of law. By system, I mean the ordering of law into exclusive categories and subcategories by way of division and subdivision according to clear criteria. By a sense of the whole of law, I mean a conception of law as a complete body of rules, which can be divided into main categories which together are exhaustive of all rules. Because jurists in this society separate law into individually exclusive and collectively exhaustive main categories, they can be sure that any particular case will neither fall beyond or be shared between categories. Because they are confident that a case will fall into either one or other of the categories, they can attribute significance to the categorization and so to the distinction that separates the categories. They can apply a separate set of rules, institutions, or procedures to particular cases. In short, jurists in this society approach law as a separable substantive body of rules. They are inclined to separate law into individually exclusive and collectively exhaustive main categories. They draw distinctions to reflect the reality of the society as conceived by its members and can ensure that such distinctions make a difference— whether to judicial institutions, procedures, or substantive law.

In this society, the distinction between public and private law makes an institutional difference. As a result of their understanding of the separation of powers, members of this society entrust the task of controlling the state administration and developing public law to courts that are known for both their independence and their expertise. Because of the independence of these courts from the administration, members of this society have faith in their impartial adjudication of administrative disputes despite the enormous power of the state administration. And, because of the expertise of these courts—an insight into the complexity of administrative needs, threats to administrative efficiency, and the adequacy of non-judicial controls over the administration—administrators have faith in their decisions and obey them accordingly. These courts can therefore intervene authoritatively and extensively to guide the administration. The distinct body of public law they develop therefore serves to control and facilitate, but not to stifle and obstruct, a responsible and effective administration.

In this society, the distinction between public and private law also makes a procedural difference, which can be illustrated with a few examples. An application for leave of the court might be required to serve as a procedural sieve and so protect the administration from being harassed by litigants without genuine complaints. Procedural time-limits might prevent the administration from being unduly disrupted long after the cause of complaint. Interlocutory procedures might be curtailed to minimize the disruption to the administration. But, most importantly, the courts conceive of the adjudication of administrative disputes as a kind of collaborative expert investigation. They generally follow inquisitorial or investigative procedures to resolve such disputes. They are able to reach a satisfactory decision by investigating the complex repercussions of judicial intervention and by consulting not merely the parties—the complainant and the administrative authority—but also those other persons or groups that are interested in the usually polycentric[1] disputes involving the administration. They can develop a body of public law without being blinded by the dust kicked up by the parties.

The Model's Main Features

Certain features of the model setting are more important to the distinction's success than others. Inquisitorial procedures, for example, are less dispensable than a particular procedural sieve where that sieve's function can be fulfilled by some other device. Therefore, to clarify the main features of my model of the working distinction between public and private law, I will suggest when the distinction would fail to work satisfactorily. I will argue that the absence of any of the following four features would seriously reduce the workability of the distinction: first,

---

[1] L. L. Fuller, 'The Forms and Limits of Adjudication' (1978) 92 *Harv. LRev.* 353-409.

a prevailing and well-developed theory of the state, which appreciates the distinctness of the state administration and ascribes to it qualities which can be used to justify special legal consequences; secondly, a categorical approach to law; thirdly, a separation of powers between judiciary and administration which ensures that the courts entrusted with administrative disputes have both independence and expertise; and fourthly, inquisitorial judicial procedures.

First, various theories of the state would negate the distinction. In a people's democracy, for example, where the state is equated with the people, a distinct branch of public law to defend the people against the state would be ideologically unnecessary and absurd. The problem for the distinction, however, is not restricted to the increasingly remote people's democracy. A theory of the welfare state might also affect the distinction between public and private law by not clearly specifying the functions that are to be assumed by the administration and the institutions that are to fulfil those functions. The state administration consequently assumes many new functions, but then off-loads existing functions on other institutions to limit the expanding bureaucracy. While administrative authorities fulfil formerly private functions, formerly private bodies begin to fulfil public functions. Amidst the fluctuations, the meanings of public and private become increasingly unclear, and distinguishing criteria, whether institutional or functional, become obviously unattainable. The state administration is no longer regarded as consistently identifiable, and the special legal rules, institutions, or procedures of public law can no longer be applied with any confidence to a special category of cases.

Meanwhile, the very inclination to continue conceiving of the state might be the target of other theories. The state might, for example, be described as a relic surviving the secularization of god's transcendence over the world[2] or as a misleading organicist concept projecting our vision of our brain in command of our body. In either case, the state ceases to be a self-evident governmental apparatus of which the administration can be a part.

However one might assess such theories, their concurrence would suggest a collapse of consensus about the state. The notion of public law regulating the state administration would be ambiguous. Criteria for distinguishing public law from private law would not be agreed upon. Doctrinal suggestions would be unpersuasive. Courts would be

---

[2] See generally R. M. Unger, *Knowledge and Politics* (New York, 1975), 157–64.

left to their own devices. In the absence of rough consensus about the state administration, and thus about the scope of public law, the distinction would be reduced to a rhetorical tool used for diverse purposes in diverse contexts. Vacuous rhetoric, legal uncertainty, and wasted litigation would be the result.

Secondly, the distinction would not work where law is not approached categorically either for want of system or for want of a sense of the whole of law. On the one hand, if a distinction is drawn where system is lacking, it would not give rise to exclusive categories. In the absence of clear criteria with which to put cases in one or another category, borderline cases would pose insurmountable problems. Because cases might partly belong to both categories divided by the distinction, it cannot be applied to give a sure result. On the other hand, if a distinction is drawn without a conception of the whole that is being divided, it would not give rise to categories that together are exhaustive. Because cases might arise that fall into an indeterminate residue and so into neither of the categories separated by the distinction, it cannot be applied with confidence. Its indeterminacy—whether because of a lack of system or a sense of the whole of law—makes it difficult to apply, its benefits uncertain, and its application therefore unattractive. It would therefore not readily be given institutional, procedural, or substantive legal significance. And any use of the distinction would be hedged with exceptions which would be left open just in case.

Thirdly, the distinction would be peculiarly problematic in the absence of a satisfactory separation of powers between the judiciary and the state administration. On the one hand, where the courts entrusted with public law are not independent, whether because they are conveniently loaded with administrative and judicial tasks or whether because they are staffed by judges sharing interest and outlook with administrators, executive-minded decisions would make public law an unacceptable realm of immunity. One branch of the state would be seen exonerating another branch of the state. On the other hand, where the courts are so independent as to lack insight into administrative needs, they would be unable to intervene confidently in the administrative process. Their occasional interventions would be arbitrary, suspect to administrators, and evaded where possible. The substantive public law that they develop would therefore be unacceptable and ineffective. Where the courts, because of an inevitable contradiction, cannot be expected to have both insight into administrative needs and independence from the administration, then at least the absence of a rough but satisfactory compromise would undermine the distinction. Whether because of their lack of judicial independence or expertise, widespread dissatisfaction with public law would call into question the underlying distinction between public and private law.

Fourthly, the distinction would be unsatisfactory where the courts entrusted with public law do not follow inquisitorial procedures. When procedures are adversarial rather than inquisitorial, courts are judicially informed only by the representations of two parties to the administrative dispute—usually the administration and the complainant— and are unable properly to investigate the complex repercussions of judicial intervention. Improperly informed, the courts are unable to intervene confidently. And, informed as if the administrative dispute only involves two parties, they struggle to develop acceptable principles sufficiently different to those designed for the bipolar disputes of private law.

Other Points of View

The main features of the model of the working distinction are the outcome of particular points of view on the English and French legal traditions, on their respective conceptions of the state administration, approaches to law, interpretations of the separation of powers, and judicial procedures for resolving administrative disputes. They are the outcome of an explicitly 'one-sided accentuation'[3] of these viewpoints and do not preclude the relevance of other points of view.

Analysis of the distinction from various other viewpoints might prove useful. The following are exemplary analyses that would be distinguishable from the analysis in this book. First, a normative political analysis might seek to assess the distinction by reference to a theorist's own normative political theory of the state or separation of powers. This book is not normative in that way. It elaborates on a model that does accentuate norms, such as those relating to control of the administration and the desirability of judges with both administrative expertise and judicial independence, but it accentuates those norms to explain the development of the distinction. This book does not advocate a general normative theory of the state or separation of powers. It does, however, espouse a norm of systemic rationality, a certain

---

[3] M. Weber, *The Methodology of the Social Sciences* (Glencoe, Illinois, 1949), 90.

congruence between the features of a legal system and the way in which that system undertakes certain tasks. It elaborates on the particular theoretical, institutional, and procedural setting that is required in order to control and facilitate administration with a separate body of public law.

Secondly, an analysis might assess the distinction between public and private law in relation to the problems experienced in a particular kind of dispute before a particular court or tribunal. In contrast, this book provides an overview by drawing on disputes about matters ranging from government contracts and torts to expropriation and employment in the civil service. It discusses the role of administrative tribunals but focuses on the work of the French *Conseil d'Etat* and the English superior courts because of their leading role in developing public law in France and England respectively.

Thirdly, an analysis might explain public law principally by reference to judicial attitudes to the adequacy of non-judicial controls over the administration. This book takes account of such attitudes, but only as an aspect of the expertise of judges in the model setting. An expert judge intervenes in an administrative dispute with regard to the adequacy of non-judicial controls.

Fourthly, an analysis might focus on judicial attitudes to involvement in the merits of administrative decision-making. It might compare the English judicial reluctance to negate the distinction between appeal and review with the reluctance of the French administrative courts to interfere with *l'opportunité*. This book deals briefly with the vague English distinction between appeal and review but doubts its independent significance and presents it as an outcome of the English separation of powers.

Fifthly, an analysis of the distinction between public and private law in some other context, perhaps the Dutch or the German, might accentuate features other than those in the model setting. For example, an analysis of the Australian departure from the English system of judicial review might accentuate the Law Commission's role[4] in a federal state and attitudes to received institutions in a post-colonial context. The scope of this book, however, is limited to the analysis of legal traditions in England and France, traditions that are influential, contrasting, and comparable because they have developed in geographical proximity and have been accompanied by similar social and economic development.

---

[4] Cf. P. Cane, 'The Law Commission on Judicial Review' (1993) 56 *MLR* 887–96.

The story of the elephant and the three blind men illustrates the relevance of multiple viewpoints. One man touched the trunk; one, the ears; and, one, the tail. They were surprised when they compared notes. They were unsure and could not agree but they continued to talk and listen because they knew that their experience was limited. Each of their one-sided and tentative descriptions is comparable to the features accentuated in a model. Even if a model were describing an organic or functioning whole, it could not do so comprehensively.

In subsequent chapters, I will elaborate on the model setting for a working distinction between public and private law. I will use its four main features to explain the relative success of the distinction in changing contexts. I will focus on the required conception of the state administration in Chapters 4 and 5, the required approach to law in Chapter 6, the required institutional separation of powers in Chapters 7 and 8, and the required judicial procedures in Chapters 9 and 10. Finally, in Chapter 11, I will draw conclusions and consider their implications for the reform of English law.

4
French Approximations

The model described in the last chapter refers to the peculiar conception of the state administration that must prevail for the distinction between public and private law to be satisfactory. It identifies three general features of that conception: first, a well-developed theory of the state; secondly, a conception of a distinct state administration; and, thirdly, the attribution of qualities to the state administration that can be used to justify special legal rules, institutions, or procedures. In the next two chapters, I will suggest that, whereas the French distinction developed because such a conception became prevalent, an English distinction was undeveloped and the transplanted distinction is not working because such a conception did not and does not prevail in English legal doctrine. With particular reference to pluralist theories of the state, I will show that the prevalence of such a conception is required for the use of a distinct set of rules, institutions, or procedures in resolving administrative disputes, that is, for a workable substantive, institutional, or procedural distinction between public and private law.

The Feudal Setting

The Roman distinction reappeared with the renaissance of Roman law in a setting to which it was unsuited.[1] At least in form, the feudal relationship was voluntary and reciprocal. The liegeman would agree to serve while the liege-lord would agree to provide and protect.[2] The feudal relationship was between persons and did not give rise to an administration that was powerful and centralized or indeed to any administration for the community as such. Those who served the King in the royal domain or a lord in the large seigneuries sought to feudalize their offices and performed relatively limited functions like the waging of war, the administration of justice, the raising of taxes, and the coining of money.[3] From the beginning of the thirteenth century, the King's officials acted with increasing independence in their day-to-

---

[1] See G. Chevrier, 'Remarques sur l'introduction et les vicissitudes de la distinction du «jus privatum» et du «jus publicum» dans les œuvres des anciens juristes Français' [1952] *Archives de philosophie du droit* 5–77 at 22–5.

[2] M. Bloch, *Feudal Society* (London, 1961), 219–30. But cf. *ibid.* 244–7.

[3] J. Brissaud, *A History of French Public Law* (London, 1915), secs. 204–9.

day decisions but 'power remained rooted in household government and consecrated authority': '[t]he household was still the centre of power, the place where the head of the family had his seat and, with the advice of his council, administered his lordship.'[4] Furthermore, feudal relationships overlapped. The liegeman might owe an allegiance to various authorities[5] and was therefore subject not to a body of public law but to various kinds of law or custom, such as royal law, canon law, and manorial law, associated with those authorities.[6]

In the absence of a conception of a state administration distinct from the various feudal authorities, the medieval Romanists could not go beyond theoretical discussion of the Roman distinction between public and private law. They did not apply the distinction to the feudal setting, failed to settle on a distinguishing criterion, and discussed Roman private-law texts regardless of their original contexts.[7] The medieval Romanists might well have used Roman-law concepts to begin to develop both a theory of public law conducive to state centralization and some conception of the state in the vague sense of the King's realm and the welfare of his realm.[8] Nevertheless, for want[9] of a conception of the state administration, the medieval Romanists were unable to attribute institutional, substantive, or procedural significance to the distinction. For similar reasons, from the thirteenth to the fifteenth centuries, writers on French customary law did not use the Roman distinction;[10] and, courts did not demarcate their jurisdiction by reference to it.[11]

---

[4] G. Duby, *France in the Middle Ages 987–1460* (J. Vale (tr.)) (Oxford, 1991), especially at 298.

[5] See, e.g., Bloch n. 2 above, 211–18, 241–54, 345–55, 382–3.

[6] A. E. Tay and E. Kamenka, 'Public Law—Private Law' in S. I. Benn and G. F. Gaus (eds.), *Public and Private in Social Life* (London, 1983), 67–92 at 69–70.

[7] See below, 112–13.

[8] See G. Post, *Studies in Medieval Legal Thought: Public Law and the State, 1100–1322* (Princeton, 1964), especially at 3–24. Cf. Q. Skinner, 'The State' in T. Ball, J. Farr, and R. Hanson (eds.), *Political Innovation and Conceptual Change* (Cambridge, 1989), 90–131, especially at 102–4; M. Gilmore, *Argument from Roman Law in Political Thought, 1200–1600* (Cambridge, Mass., 1941), 15–44.

[9] See also below, 113–14.

[10] Chevrier, n. 1 above, 36–9.

[11] C. Szladits, 'The Distinction between Public Law and Private Law' in *IECL*, vol. 2, ch. 2, secs. 25–57 at sec. 27.

The Beginnings of a Distinct State Administration

Administrative Centralization

Institutional changes accompanied conceptual development. Towards the end of the fifteenth century, after the plagues and the Hundred Years War, a centralized administration identified with the person of the monarch began to prevail over the multiplicity of feudal authorities. Its dependence upon the King was furthered by a basic change in administrative organization. The fief was gradually replaced by the office, and the office by the commission, as the principal administrative function. Revocable and granted to persons of relatively low social status, the commission became a supple instrument in the hands of the King.[12] It was used in special circumstances and in day-to-day administration. Commissioners especially empowered by the King, whether in judicial, financial, or police affairs, would enjoy precedence over the King's other administrators according to the scope of their commissions.[13] In day-to-day administration, the few dispatch clerks, formerly attached to the person of the King and entrusted with the power of signing papers in financial matters, became prominent, and, by about 1560, were called *Secrétaires d'Etat*. They were consulted about the drafting of the King's orders; they saw to their execution; and, by the end of the sixteenth century, they dispatched the orders themselves. Their loyalty to the King was secured by their commissions' revocability and intransmissibility at least until the reign of Louis XV.[14]

Generally during the sixteenth and seventeenth centuries, whether because of economic crisis, technological advances, demands of war, or refinements to the raising of revenue, the *Secrétaires* were entrusted with more extensive tasks.[15] Of necessity they delegated work to their clerks so that, while the clerks became masters of bureaux, they became heads of departments of state concerned with matters ranging from the army, the church, and foreign policy to the colonies, fisheries, and fine arts. The *Secrétaires* became surrounded by an administration, extensive and increasingly centralized, although still lacking in functional specialization.[16]

[12] Brissaud, n. 3 above, sec. 370. See generally E. Le Roy Ladurie, *The Royal French State 1460-1610* (Oxford, 1994), 22–4.

[13] H. A. Lloyd, *The State, France, and the Sixteenth Century* (London, 1983), 80–3.

[14] Brissaud, n. 3 above, sec. 375; Lloyd, n. 13 above, 57–8.

[15] See generally Lloyd, n. 13 above, 48–83, especially at 61–7; T. Aston (ed.), *Crisis in Europe 1560–1660* (London, 1965); Le Roy Ladurie, n. 12 above.

[16] Brissaud, n. 3 above, sec. 375. See Lloyd, n. 13 above, 58, 60.

In the provinces, the *intendants* came to exercise wide-ranging powers relating *inter alia* to taxation, the military, agriculture, public works,
relief of the poor, and the administration of justice. They were answer-
able to the *Secrétaires*, did not come from the nobility, and held revocable commissions. Therefore with 'everything to fear and everything
to hope from the royal authority', they were generally active and obe-
dient agents of the central administration.[17]

Before the Revolution, however, administration centralization was
limited. The royal administration did not achieve a monopoly of
administrative power. Rather, it continued to co-exist with numerous
other authorities,[18] and, through the sale of judicial offices, even
enhanced the power and independence of the *Parlements*.[19] Indeed, the
Parlements illustrate a continuing confusion between public and private.
They were public because of the origin and nature of their functions;
private, because of the ownership of offices and consequent independence from the central administration.

The State

The administrative centralization that was achieved in the royal
domain brought the monarch's right to exercise authority to the forefront of debate, and so prompted[20] an important conceptual development. Influenced by ideas developed in the Italian cities, writers ceased
to use the concept of the state only to refer to the standing of the King,
his kingdom, or the prevailing system of government. Authors of books
written as advice to the Prince began to conceptualize the state as a
distinct apparatus of government albeit in the hands of the Prince.
Furthermore, whereas Republican writers detached the state from the
Prince, their opponents distinguished it from the sovereignty of the
people. The outcome was a concept of a distinct state—isolated from
the general conditions of the kingdom, no longer identified with the
prevailing system of government, not necessarily linked to the
monarch, and distinguished from a sovereign people.[21]

This concept of a distinct state began to crystallize for the first time
in late sixteenth-century France where 'the material preconditions for

[17] Brissaud, n. 3 above, secs. 383–8, especially at 411.
[18] See, e.g., Le Roy Ladurie, n. 12 above, especially at 7–16.
[19] J. P. Dawson, *The Oracles of the Law* (Ann Arbor, 1968), 350–71, 373; Lloyd, n. 13
above, 72–3, 162–3.
[20] Lloyd, n. 13 above, 54–5, 81–2, 148–9.
[21] Skinner, n. 8 above; *id.*, *The Foundations of Modern Political Thought: The Age of
Reformation*, (Cambridge, 1978), ii, 349–58.

such a development were all present: a relatively unified central authority, an increasing apparatus of bureaucratic control, and a clearly defined set of national boundaries'.[22] Bodin not only used the concept of the state in the traditional way to refer to the standing of the King or his kingdom. He also used it in phrases like *en matiere d'estat* and *l'estat en soy* to refer to an apparatus of government distinct from its citizens, its rulers, and any specific form of government:[23] '[a]nd albeit that the government of a Commonweale may be more or lesse popular, aristocratique, or royall . . ., yet so it is that the state in it selfe [*l'estat en soy*] receiveth no comparison of more or lesse. For the soveraigntie is alwaies indivisible and incommunicable in one alone.'[24] As a result partly of administrative centralization and partly of the accompanying conceptual developments, the state had become identifiable as a distinct apparatus.

Montesquieu's Executive and Intermediate Powers

While the state was being conceptualized as a distinct apparatus of government, the parts of that apparatus remained theoretically obscure. During the sixteenth century, judicial and executive or administrative powers were confused. In other words, 'authority comprehended both *gubernatio* and *jurisdictio*'.[25] Accordingly, Bodin merely listed the powers of sovereignty to cover *inter alia* the making of laws, the waging of war, the appointment of magistrates, the hearing of appeals, the coining of money, and the imposition of taxes.[26]

Only in the eighteenth century did the conception of an executive power separate from the judicial power begin to develop.[27] Montesquieu's analysis in *The Spirit of the Laws* was a pivotal attempt to conceptualize the executive power.[28] It illustrates both the earlier

[22] Skinner, *Foundations of Modern Political Thought*, n. 21 above, 354.

[23] 'Et combien que le gouvernement d'une Republique soit plus ou moins populaire, ou aristocratique, ou Royale, si est ce que *l'estat in soy* ne reçoit comparaison de plus ny de moins: car toujours la souveraineté indivisible & incomunicable est à un seul': J. Bodin, *Les Six Livres de la république* (Paris, 1583), bk. 2, ch. 7, 338, 339 (emphasis added); Skinner, 'The State', n. 8 above, 120; *id.*, *Foundations of Modern Political Thought*, n. 21 above, 355–6, 358. See Lloyd, n. 13 above, 155–62.

[24] From the 1606 Knolles translation of *De la république*, reprinted in *The Six Bookes of a Commonweale* (K. D. McRae (ed.) (Cambridge, Mass., 1962), 250.

[25] Lloyd, n. 13 above, 52–4, especially at 52.

[26] Bodin, n. 23 above, bk. 1. ch. 10.

[27] M. J. C. Vile, *Constitutionalism and the Separation of Powers* (Oxford, 1967), 28–9.

[28] Montesquieu, *The Spirit of the Laws* (A. M. Cohler, B. C. Miller, and H. S. Stone (trs. and eds.)) (Cambridge, 1989), bk. 11, ch. 6; Vile, n. 27 above, 86–8. See R. Shackleton, *Montesquieu: A Critical Biography* (Oxford, 1961), 286–7, 298–301.

confusion and the later clarification. In his short chapter advocating separate powers for the sake of liberty, Montesquieu conceptualized the executive power in no fewer than three ways. First, he opened the chapter by defining the three powers as 'legislative power, executive power over the things depending on the right of nations, and executive power over the things depending on civil right'.[29] Like his predecessors, he confused the governmental and the judicial under the notion of executive power. Secondly, Montesquieu then immediately redefined the executive power to refer solely to the conduct of foreign affairs as distinct from the punishing of criminals and the resolution of disputes. According to his redefinition, he omitted any account of executive acts other than those relating to the conduct of foreign affairs. Thirdly, in the rest of his analysis, he disregarded both his definition and redefinition to distinguish the three powers 'of making the laws, . . . of executing public resolutions, and . . . of judging the crimes or the disputes of individuals'.[30] Here he did conceptualize the executive power to refer to the conduct of both internal and external affairs. Therefore, despite overall confusion, Montesquieu did produce the conceptualization of the executive power that would prevail and be identified with the state administration as distinct from legal institutions and procedures.

Montesquieu not only described separate executive, judicial, and legislative powers as the safeguard of liberty. He also emphasized an ill-defined category of intermediate powers, which included the *Parlements*, the church, and the nobility, as a guard against despotism in a monarchy: '[t]he checks upon the royal power operate as a result of the existence of the various orders of society through which that power must be channelled'.[31] In Book Six, Chapter Five, of *The Spirit of the Laws*, Montesquieu stated: '[i]n despotic states the prince himself can judge. He cannot judge in monarchies: the constitution would be destroyed and the intermediate dependent powers reduced to nothing.'[32] In the original manuscript of Book Two, Chapter Four, he wrote: '[l]es pouvoirs intermédiaires constituent la nature du gouvernement monarchique, c'est-à-dire de celui où un seul gouverne par

[29] Montesquieu, n. 28 above, 156.
[30] *Ibid.* 157.
[31] Vile, n. 27 above, 80–2, especially at 82; F. Ford, *Robe and Sword: The Regrouping of the French Aristocracy after Louis XIV* (New York, 1965), 222–45, especially at 239; C. J. Friedrich, *The Philosophy of Law in Historical Perspective* (Chicago, 1958), 106.
[32] N. 28 above, 78.

des lois fondamentales.'[33] Because he was 'anxious not to appear to be raising up other powers against the King',[34] he made changes so that the published text is translated as follows:

Intermediate, subordinate, and dependent powers constitute the nature of monarchical government, that is, of the government in which one alone governs by fundamental laws. I have said intermediate, subordinate, and dependent powers; indeed, in a monarchy, the prince is the source of all political and civil power.[35]

Even in the published manuscript, Montesquieu still described the intermediate powers as essential, albeit subordinate, to monarchical as opposed to despotic government. Because he recognized and could rely upon intermediate powers, his perception of administrative centralization and the state administration's potential dangerousness was not as acute as the perception of others[36] would become after the Revolution.

The Pre-Revolutionary Distinction

As the royal administration became increasingly centralized and as the state began to be conceived as a distinct apparatus of government, the distinction between public and private law became more prominent. Although writers on French law failed to abide by the distinction, around 1600, a few, such as Charondas le Caron and Guy Coquille, began to emphasize it.[37] In the seventeenth and eighteenth centuries, they were followed by others, such as Le Bret, Fleury, and Pothier. Specialists began to write books, and, in the second half of the eighteenth century, taught the first courses on public law.[38] And a few special courts, such as the *Cour des Aides* and *Chambres des Comptes*, developed an administrative jurisdiction.[39] By the end of *l'Ancien Régime*, a range of rules relating to the administration had been elaborated.[40]

Before the Revolution, however, a coherent and systematic body of public law was not developed and its autonomy was not formally declared.[41] The distinction was not yet rigorously drawn or applied. It

---

[33] Quoted by Shackleton, n. 28 above, 279: '[i]ntermediate powers constitute the nature of monarchical government, that is, of the government in which one alone governs by fundamental laws.'

[34] Shackleton *ibid.*   [35] Montesquieu, n. 28 above, 17.

[36] See, e.g., below, 52 ff.

[37] Chevrier, n. 1 above, 39–50; Szladits, n. 11 above, sec. 27.

[38] Chevrier, n. 1 above, 50–65.

[39] Szladits, n. 11 above, sec. 28; Brissaud, n. 3 above, sec. 468. See generally J.-L. Mestre, *Introduction historique au droit administratif Français* (Paris, 1985).

[40] Mestre, n. 39 above.   [41] *Ibid.*, secs. 4 and 5.

did not prevent overlap between public and private law,[42] the
Parlements from meddling with administrative matters, and the *Conseil
du Roi* from hearing *évocations* from the ordinary courts.[43] The origins
of French administrative law were pre-Revolutionary, but only after
the Revolution did the distinction become formally instated and institutionally significant.

The distinction's continuing informality and institutional
insignificance were partly[44] due to the continuing absence of the
required conception of the state administration. The effect of this
absence is suggested by Mestre despite his emphasis on the pre-
Revolutionary origins of French administrative law. By reference to the
'administration', Mestre explains the lack of autonomy of the administrative rules elaborated in *l'Ancien Régime*:

[L]es juristes de l'Ancien Régime ne reconnaissaient pas de façon formelle
l'autonomie du droit administratif. Ils ignoraient cette expression qui ne s'est
répandue qu'au XIXe siècle. Ils n'ont même donné que tardivement au mot
'administration' son sens général actuel.[45]

Before the Revolution, executive and judicial powers were still confused. Until Montesquieu's theory of separate powers began to prevail,[46] the state administration was not clearly distinguished from, and
thus, in theory, clearly amenable to, judicial power. Furthermore,
while Montesquieu had reason to claim that '[i]ntermediate . . . powers constitute the nature of monarchical government',[47] the state
administration remained generally indistinct. Montesquieu could rely
upon various intermediate powers to check the royal administration. In
short, the perception of administrative centralization and the threat
that it poses were insufficiently acute for a separate body of public law
to be applied and justified as such.

[42] Chevrier, n. 1 above, 71–7.
[43] Brissaud, n. 3 above, sec. 367; Szladits, n. 11 above, sec. 28.
[44] See also below,117–18, 138 ff.
[45] Mestre, n. 39 above, sec. 4, p. 12: '[t]he jurists of the *Ancien Régime* did not formally
acknowledge the autonomy of administrative law. They knew nothing of that expression,
which did not become well-known until the nineteenth century. It was even only very
belatedly that they gave the word "administration" its current general meaning.'
[46] See below, 141 f.   [47] See n. 35 above.

Liberal Apprehension of Administrative Centralization

Rousseau's View of Government

In *The Social Contract*, Rousseau conceived of government as an administrative entity, 'a new body within the state, distinct from both people and sovereign', ' a body charged with the execution of the laws and the maintenance of freedom, both civil and political'.[48] He entrusted to government what he called the executive power, the power of acting in accordance with the instructions of the general will.

Rousseau developed the conception of the state administration in two important respects. First, although, like his predecessors and many of his contemporaries, he failed to distinguish the executive and judicial powers,[49] he did otherwise conceive of government as centrally important and distinct—the agent or instrument of the general will. He suggested its peculiar importance and centrality in relation to the rest of the state by comparing the executive power to the brain commanding the limbs of the body: '[t]he principle of political life dwells in the sovereign authority. The legislative power is the heart of the state, the executive power is the brain, which sets all the parts in motion'.[50]

Secondly, Rousseau anticipated subsequent developments by attributing to government qualities that would later be used to justify special legal consequences. Although he conceptualized the general will as infallible,[51] he regarded government as a threat to liberty. He argued that the participation of people in the general will decreases in proportion to the enlargement of the state. He concluded as follows:

Whence it follows that the more the state is enlarged, the more freedom is diminished. . . . The smaller the ratio between the particular wills and the general will, that is, between the people's morals and the law, the more will repressive force have to be employed. Hence, for the government to be good, its strength must be increased to the extent that the people is more numerous. In proportion as the enlargement of the state means offering the holders of public authority more temptations and more opportunities to abuse their power, it follows that the more power the government needs to control the people, the more power the sovereign needs, in its turn, to control the government.[52]

[48] J.-J. Rousseau, *The Social Contract* (M. Cranston (tr.)) (Harmondsworth, 1968), bk. 3, ch. 1, 105, 102.
[49] Vile, n. 27 above, 179.
[50] Rousseau, n. 48 above, bk. 3, ch. 11, 135. See *ibid.*, bk. 3, ch. 1.
[51] *Ibid.*, bk. 2, ch. 3. See also *ibid.*, bk. 2, ch. 4; bk. 4, ch. 1.
[52] *Ibid.*, bk. 3, ch. 1, 104.

Rousseau, however, did not elaborate on control of the government by the sovereign people. He only suggested the desirability of small states and mentioned the drastic consequences of abuse of government power—dissolution of the state, dismissal of government officers, and changing the form of the government.[53] Possibly because he still confused executive and judicial powers, he neglected control of government by law. In his Book Three, Chapter Ten, he expressed his resignation to an increasing abuse of government power. He described how government would not remain counterpoised with the sovereign people, but would inevitably degenerate:

> Just as the particular will acts unceasingly against the general will, so does the government continually exert itself against the sovereign. And the more this exertion increases, the more the constitution becomes corrupt, and, as in this case there is no distinct corporate will to resist the will of the prince and so to balance it, sooner or later it is inevitable that the prince will oppress the sovereign and break the social treaty. This is the inherent and inescapable defect which, from the birth of the political body, tends relentlessly to destroy it, just as old age and death destroy the body of a man.[54]

Rousseau viewed government as a threat to liberty but failed to restrict that threat with appropriate control.

Furthermore, the men of 1789 neglected Rousseau's perception of the potential abuse of government power as they adopted him as the 'only tutor of the Revolution in its youth'[55] and laid claim to his notion[56] of an infallible general will. Rousseau had stressed that the general will could not be represented and could only become apparent from an actual meeting of all citizens.[57] Most of the revolutionaries, however, accepted the legitimacy of representation by deputies.[58] They confused Rousseau's infallible general will with the ordinary legislature, and its implementation with ordinary acts of the administration. Therefore, as Rousseau's theory was popularized, while his conceptualization of the infallibility of the general will reinforced, by implication,

---

[53] *Ibid.*, bk. 3, chs. 1, 3, 4, 10, and 18. [54] *Ibid.* bk. 3, ch. 10, 131.
[55] Tocqueville quoted by F. Furet, *Interpreting the French Revolution* (E. Forster (tr.)) (Cambridge, 1981), 45.
[56] See generally Furet, *ibid.*, especially at 30–2; K. M. Baker, *Inventing the French Revolution: Essays on French Political Culture in the Eighteenth Century* (Cambridge, 1990), especially at 25–6.
[57] See below, 140–1.
[58] N. Hampson, 'The Heavenly City of the French Revolutionaries' in C. Lucas (ed.), *Rewriting the French Revolution* (Oxford, 1991), 46–68, especially at 49–50, 54; F. Furet, *Revolutionary France 1770–1880* (Oxford, 1992), 77; J. Hayward, *After the French Revolution: Six Critics of Democracy and Nationalism* (Hemel Hempstead, 1991), 11–14.

the idea of a centralized state administration, his perception of the potential abuse of government power had little effect. Neither Rousseau nor the men of 1789 used his perception to justify special legal consequences. Rousseau's own neglect of legal controls of government, the popularization of his theory of the state, and the general distrust of the courts in the wake of the *Parlements*, all contributed to the 1790 Law prohibiting judicial interference with the administration.[59] In the Revolution's immediate aftermath, the sense of the administration's potential dangerousness did not yet prevail so as to justify a public law distinct from private law.

Constant

Enlightened by what was done in the name of the general will after the Revolution, Constant was critical of Rousseau.[60] He alleged that Rousseau had provided a pretext for despotism by not limiting the sovereignty of the people, that is, the supremacy of the general will, and by not clarifying a workable relationship between that sovereignty and government. Constant argued as follows: '[w]hen you establish that the sovereignty of the people is unlimited, you create and toss at random into human society a degree of power which is too large in itself, and which is bound to constitute an evil, in whatever hands it is placed.'[61] He also suggested that Rousseau had been preoccupied with securing the old form of liberty—the freedom to participate in the exercise of authority—and had failed to appreciate the modern form of liberty— the freedom to further private interests and, particularly, the freedom to engage in commercial activity.[62] He argued that this modern freedom necessitated representative government:

[S]ince the liberty we need is different from that of the ancients, it needs a different organization from the one which would suit ancient liberty. In the latter, the more time and energy man dedicated to the exercise of his political rights, the freer he thought himself; on the other hand, in the kind of liberty of which we are capable, the more the exercise of political rights leaves us the time for our private interests, the more precious will liberty be to us. Hence, Sirs, the need for the representative system. The representative system

---

[59] Law of 16–24 August 1790.

[60] B. Constant, *Principles of Politics Applicable to All Representative Governments* and 'The Liberty of the Ancients Compared with That of the Moderns' in B. Constant, *Political Writings* (B. Fontana (ed. and tr.)) (Cambridge, 1988), 169–305, 307–28; S. Holmes, *Benjamin Constant and the Making of Modern Liberalism* (London, 1984), 79–103.

[61] Constant *Principles of Politics*, n. 60 above, 176.

[62] See generally Holmes, n. 60 above, 53–78.

is nothing but an organisation by means of which a nation charges a few individuals to do what it cannot or does not wish to do herself. Poor men look after their own business; rich men hire stewards. . . . The representative system is a proxy given to a certain number of men by the mass of the people who wish their interests to be defended and who nevertheless do not have the time to defend them themselves.[63]

Constant was reconciled to representative government, but, because he feared 'a degree of power which is too large in itself',[64] he was preoccupied with limiting governmental powers and guarding against governmental abuse and irresponsibility. He therefore stressed the importance of individual rights, 'active and constant surveillance' over representatives, a constitutional framework for government, and both ordinary and extraordinary legal institutions to control ministers and their subordinates.[65] In short, Constant justified legal controls by reference to the qualities he attributed to government—its peculiar power, and potential irresponsibility and abusiveness. His analysis exemplifies the theory required to justify public law.

The Doctrinaire Liberals

Whereas Constant did not specifically describe representative government as centralized, the Doctrinaire liberals and, later, Tocqueville focused on administrative centralization and its implications. Their approach, unlike that of the English liberals, was characterized by two preoccupations—one with history and continuity and one with the Revolution and its impact.[66] Administrative centralization was important to both.

First, the Doctrinaire liberals such as Guizot regarded administrative centralization as the outcome of an alliance between the Crown and bourgeoisie, originating in the early Middle Ages. They described how the Crown supported, and derived support from, the bourgeoisie against the feudal nobility. They emphasized the nature of the alliance

---

[63] Constant, 'The Liberty of the Ancients', n. 60 above, 325–6.

[64] Constant, *Principles of Politics*, n. 60 above, 176.

[65] Constant, 'The Liberty of the Ancients', n. 60 above, 326; *id.*, *Principles of Politics*, n. 60 above, chs. 9, 11, 15–18. See generally Vile, n. 27 above, 204–6.

[66] See S. Mellon, *Political Uses of History: A Study of Historians in the French Restoration* (Stanford, 1958), 5–57; *id.*, in F. Guizot, *Historical Essays and Lectures* (S. Mellon (ed.)) (Chicago, 1972), pp. xxi–xxxix; D. W. Johnson, *Guizot: Aspects of French History 1787–1874* (London, 1963), 323–7; L. Siedentop, 'Two Liberal Traditions' in A. Ryan (ed.), *The Idea of Freedom: Essays in Honour of Isaiah Berlin* (Oxford, 1979), 153–74; *id.*, *Tocqueville* (Oxford, 1994); Hayward, n. 58 above, 141–71; Furet, *Revolutionary France*, 291–4, 367–71.

by contrasting it with the English alliance between the nobility and bourgeoisie. They described how, in England, the nobility had limited the powers of the Crown by strengthening Parliament with representatives of the bourgeoisie. They compared the consequences of these contrasting English and French alliances: in England, a limited legislative centralization in Parliament; in France, an extensive administrative centralization in the executive.[67] Imbued with the historical analysis of the Doctrinaires,[68] Alexis de Tocqueville alleged continuity between the centralized administrative state of Napoleon and that of Louis XIV.[69]

Secondly, liberals in the Doctrinaire tradition regarded the French Revolution as a further impetus to centralization. Tocqueville in *De la Démocratie en Amérique* suggested that, because of the destruction of the intermediate powers that had formerly restricted the power of the royal administration, Napoleon could reinstate, refine, and further centralize it.[70] Furthermore, he stressed that the pre-eminence of equality and the relative neglect of liberty in the theory culminating in the Revolution left individuals equally subservient to an overarching state administration in democratic society.[71] By repeatedly personifying[72] the administration, Tocqueville expressed an overwhelming perception of administrative centralization as the outcome of the Revolution and pre-Revolutionary history.

Liberals such as Constant, Guizot, and Tocqueville were prominent in the administration, in Parliament, and in academia.[73] Constant

---

[67] See, e.g., F. Guizot, *Histoire générale de la civilisation en Europe* (Paris, 1828); Siedentop, 'Two Liberal Traditions', n. 66 above, 163–5; *id.*, *Tocqueville*, n. 66 above, 35–6, 115–16. Cf. A. de Tocqueville, *L'Ancien Régime* (G. Headlam (ed.)) (Oxford, 1904), bk. 2, chs. 9–12.

[68] See Furet, *Interpreting the French Revolution*, n. 55 above, 135–9; Siedentop, *Tocqueville*, n. 66 above, 20–40.

[69] De Tocqueville, *L'Ancien Régime*, n. 67 above, bk. 2, chs. 2–7; Siedentop, *Tocqueville*, n. 66 above, 113 ff., 140.

[70] A. de Tocqueville, *De la démocratie en Amérique* (Paris, 1850), Introduction, i, 11; ch. 17, 379–380; ii, pt. 4, chs. 3 and 4. Cf. De Tocqueville, *L'Ancien Régime*, n. 67 above, Foreword, 5; bk. 1, ch. 2, 17–19; bk. 2, chs. 2 and 5; bk. 2, ch. 11; Siedentop, 'Two Liberal Traditions', n. 66 above, 165–6.

[71] De Tocqueville, *De la démocratie en Amérique*, n. 70 above, i, ch. 5, 116–17; ch. 17, 381–3; ii, pt. 4, chs. 2–4. Cf. De Tocqueville, *L'Ancien Régime*, n. 67 above, bk. 2., chs. 8 and 11; bk. 3., chs. 3 and 8. See generally Siedentop, 'Two Liberal Traditions', n. 66 above, 163; *id.*, *Tocqueville*, n. 66 above, 49, 97–106; C. Lefort, *Democracy and Political Theory* (Cambridge, 1988), 183–209.

[72] See, e.g., De Tocqueville, *De la démocratie en Amérique*, n. 70 above, ii, pt. 4, ch. 3, 333–4; *id.*, *L'Ancien Régime*, n. 67 above, bk. 2, ch. 11., 116; bk. 3, ch. 7, 207.

[73] See, e.g., Furet, *Revolutionary France*, n. 58 above, 169–71, 211–12, 359–67, 428–9, 456; Siedentop, *Tocqueville*, n. 66 above, 14–15, 96.

served on the *Conseil d'Etat*, as did Guizot.[74] The Doctrinaire liberals were leading politicians and historians. As politicians, they used history in politics.[75] As historians, they spoke what had become the 'language of politics'[76] and educated generations of Frenchmen with a confident history which claimed to be enlightened[77] by the Revolution and its aftermath. Although their immediate political success varied,[78] their ultimate influence was pervasive. They influenced Tocqueville for one, who was also active in politics and was similarly influential. Tocqueville's *De la Démocratie en Amérique* was to become central[79] to the political education of the generation that produced the 1875 Constitution.

Distinguishing and Developing Public Law

In the second half of the nineteenth century and in the early twentieth century, reformist politicians, *Conseillers d'Etat*, and doctrinal writers, through the lasting influence of liberals like Constant, attributed to the state administration qualities of potential irresponsibility and abusiveness that rendered legal controls justifiable. At the same time, through the influence of liberals like Guizot and Tocqueville, they perceived a centralized and, therefore, distinct and identifiable administration that could be subject to a distinct body of law. To such reformers, it made sense to extend the judicial role of the *Conseil d'Etat*, to establish the *Tribunal des Conflits*,[80] to declare the autonomy of public law,[81] to work with the notion of *la puissance publique*, and eventually to settle on *service public* as the general criterion for determining the *Conseil d'Etat*'s

[74] See B. Fontana, 'Introduction' in Constant, *Political Writings*, n. 60 above, 12–13; Johnson, n. 66 above, 31–2.

[75] Mellon, *Political Uses of History*, n. 66 above; Furet, *Revolutionary France*, n. 58 above, 306–8. Cf. Johnson, n. 66 above, 320–76.

[76] Mellon, *Political Uses of History*, n. 66 above, 1.

[77] F. Guizot, *Histoire des origines du gouvernement représentatif en Europe*, (Paris, 1851), i, lecture 1, 13–15.; S. Mellon in Guizot, *Historical Essays*, n. 66 above, pp. xxxi–xxxii; Johnson, n. 66 above, 324–6.

[78] See Mellon, *Political Uses of History*, n. 66 above, Mellon in Guizot, *Historical Essays*, n. 66 above, pp. xvii–xxi; Johnson, n. 66 above, 432–42; Furet, *Revolutionary France*, n. 58 above, 377 ff., 513; A. Ryan in his 'Introduction' to a translation of De Tocqueville, *De la démocratie en Amérique*, n. 70 above, *Democracy in America* (P. Bradley (ed.)) (London, 1994) pp. xiv–xvii; Siedentop, *Tocqueville* n. 66 above, 13–17.

[79] J. Barthélémy in *Traité de droit constitutionnel*, quoted by J. P. Mayor in his 'Introduction' to a translation of De Tocqueville, *De la démocratie en Amérique*, n. 70 above, *Democracy in America* (J. P. Mayer and M. Lerner (eds.)) (London, 1968), i, p. xxi; Hayward, n. 58 above, 170. See generally Siedentop, *Tocqueville*, n. 66 above, 17, 138, 141–4.

[80] Law of 24 May 1872.   [81] *Blanco*, TC, 8 Feb. 1873.

jurisdiction.[82] In theory, public law could be distinguished from private law; and, significance could be attributed to the distinction. Public law could serve as a corrective to a potentially irresponsible and abusive administration.[83]

Tocqueville did not himself especially advocate law as the answer to the problems posed by the administration. The Doctrinaires had shown that, because of the revolutionary annihilation of the intermediate powers that Montesquieu presupposed, Montesquieu's theory advocating a separate judicial power could not by itself secure liberty.[84] Furthermore, Tocqueville opposed an answer that required the further centralization of power in the *Conseil d'Etat*. He criticized the *Conseil d'Etat*, not only for violating judicial independence, but also for perpetuating the centralization of power in the *Conseil du Roi*.[85] In theory, Tocqueville and other liberals prescribed decentralization rather than the legal controls of the *Conseil d'Etat*.[86] Tocqueville's own prescription, however, was incongruous outside his idealized[87] picture of American democracy. In practice, he voted for reforming rather than abolishing the *Conseil d'Etat*.[88] And, in effect, his focus on the centralized French administration helped clarify the conception of a distinct state administration required for the *Conseil d'Etat* to develop a distinct body of public law.

Furthermore, the limited regional decentralization that was achieved in the mid- to late-nineteenth century probably promoted public law in another way. As local authorities were made more powerful, central

---

[82] See J. Rivero, 'Hauriou et l'avènement de la notion de service public' in *L'Evolution du droit public: études offertes à Achille Mestre* (Paris, 1956), 461–71; See generally A. De Laubadère, *Traité de droit administratif* (J.-C. Venezia and Y. Gaudemet (eds.)) (11th edn., Paris, 1990), secs. 35–8; L. N. Brown and J. S. Bell, *French Administrative Law* (4th edn., Oxford, 1993), 124–8; H. S. Jones, *The French State in Question: Public Law and Political Argument in the Third Republic* (Cambridge, 1993), ch. 4.; L. Duguit, *Law in the Modern State* (F. and H. Laski (tr.)) (New York, 1970), 153–8.

[83] Cf. generally M. Waline, *Droit administratif* (9th edn., Paris, 1963), secs. 21–2; P. Weil, 'The Strength and Weakness of French Administrative Law' [1965] *CLJ* 242–59 at 244; J. Brèthe de la Gressaye in O. Kahn-Freund, C. Lévy and B. Rudden (eds.), *A Source-book on French Law* (3rd edn., Oxford, 1991), 148–50.

[84] Siedentop, 'Two Liberal Traditions', n. 66 above, 166–7; *id.*, *Tocqueville*, n. 66 above, 37–8, 139–40.

[85] De Tocqueville, *L'Ancien Régime*, n. 67 above, bk. 2, ch. 4; *id. De la démocratie en Amérique*, n. 70 above, i, ch. 6, 126; ii, pt. 4, ch. 5, 347–8.

[86] Cf. Constant, *Principles of Politics*, n. 60 above, ch. 12. See generally Siedentop, 'Two Liberal Traditions', n. 66 above, 167–72; *id.*, *Tocqueville*, n. 66 above, 36–68.

[87] See generally A. Ryan in De Tocqueville, *Democracy in America*, n. 78 above, pp. xxi–xxiii.

[88] C. E. Freedeman, *The Conseil d'Etat in Modern France* (New York, 1961), 14.

government extended its legal controls.[89] In 1864, it facilitated access to the *Conseil d'Etat* by substantially reducing the costs of a *recours* and by abolishing compulsory legal representation.[90] Meanwhile, the *Conseil d'Etat* itself began to extend *le recours pour excès de pouvoir* to cover *détournement de pouvoir*. Its first decisions finding abuse of power concerned the acts of local authorities—a mayor's prohibition in *Vernhes*[91] and a prefect's refusal of a permit in *Lesbats*.[92] Later, Parliament dispensed with a filing fee in the case of a successful *recours* and so further reduced costs of successful litigation before the *Conseil d'Etat*.[93] By developing the *Conseil d'Etat*'s judicial role, the central government sought to discipline and unify the whole administration including local authorities.[94]

In *Terrier*, the *Conseil d'Etat* used the criterion of *service public* to extend its jurisdiction to cover the activities of a *département*. The *Commissaire du Gouvernement* declared: '[t]out ce qui concerne l'organisation et le fonctionnement des services publics . . . généraux ou locaux . . . constitue une *opération administrative*, qui est, *par sa nature*, du domaine de la juridiction administrative'.[95] In *Feutry*,[96] the *Tribunal des Conflits* followed the lead of the *Conseil d'Etat*, and, in *De Fonscolombe*,[97] found that the *Conseil d'Etat* similarly had jurisdiction over the activities of *communes*. The *Commissaire* in *Feutry* declared categorically:

Il semble *a priori* qu'on ne puisse même pas concevoir la possibilité d'une différence entre la situation des départements ou des communes et celle de l'Etat. *La puissance publique est une*, le caractère de ses actes ou de ses opérations ne change pas suivant l'importance territoriale de l'administration qui agit. Les actes accomplis par les représentants ou les agents de l'administration ont la même nature, quelle que soit l'étendue de la circonscription où exercent ces agents.[98]

---

[89] J.-M. Auby, 'The Abuse of Power in French Administrative Law' (1970) 18 *AJCL* 549–64 at 549–53.

[90] Decree of 2 Nov. 1864. [91] CE, 19 May 1858.

[92] CE, 25 Feb. 1864. [93] Law of 17 Apr. 1906, art. 4.

[94] See generally M. Shapiro, *Courts: A Comparative and Political Analysis* (Chicago, 1981), 49–50, 55, 153–4.

[95] CE, 6 Feb. 1903: '[e]verything connected with the organization and functioning of public services . . . general or local . . . constitutes an *administrative task*, which is, *by its nature*, within the jurisdiction of the administrative courts'.

[96] TC, 29 Feb. 1908. [97] TC, 11 Apr. 1908.

[98] Emphasis added: '[i]t seems *a priori* that one cannot even conceive of the possibility of a difference between the position of *départements* and *communes* and that of the State itself. *The Public power is one*—the nature of its acts or its tasks does not change according to the territorial importance of the administration that performs them. Acts done by representatives or agents of the administration are of the same kind, whatever the extent of the territorial competence exercised by such agents.'

Despite moves to decentralization in the nineteenth century, partly
through the role played by the *Conseil d'Etat*, local authorities remained
subordinate to central government[99] and the French administration
remained centralized. The administration could be, and still was, conceived as a distinct entity—*la puissance publique*—that could be subject
to the jurisdiction of a distinct court and the application of a distinct
body of law.

In England, Dicey popularized Tocqueville's theoretical criticism of
the *Conseil d'Etat*[100] but failed to realize the extent to which
Tocqueville's analysis and that of other French liberals of the nineteenth century had contributed to the theoretical framework for a
significant distinction between public and private law.

The Blurring of the State Administration

Tocqueville's Prescription

Although Tocqueville's analysis contributed, in effect, to the theoretical framework for the distinction, it also foreshadowed the difficulties
that extensive decentralization would pose for that framework.
Tocqueville prescribed decentralization for the sake of a conception of
freedom developed from that of the Doctrinaires—a conception of free
moeurs involving participation rather than merely freedom from physical interference:

By free *moeurs* they meant a sense of personal capacity, which promoted both
self-reliance and the habit of free association, and thus moulded all social relations. Free *moeurs* created an active citizenry attached to local freedom and
joined together in numerous voluntary associations—the only real safeguard against
excessive centralisation, which, in turn, destroys free *moeurs*.[101]

Tocqueville stressed the importance of participation in associations that
were not necessarily political, associations ranging from the industrial
and commercial to the religious and moral.[102]

---

[99] F. Ridley and J. Blondel, *Public Administration in France* (London, 1969), 85–8.

[100] A. V. Dicey, *An Introduction to the Study of the Law of the Constitution* (10th edn.,
London, 1959), 355–8.

[101] Siedentop, 'Two Liberal Traditions', n. 66 above, 168–72, especially at 170; I
have italicized the phrase. See also Siedentop, *Tocqueville*, n. 66 above, 51–5, 66–8, 90–2.
See, e.g., Guizot, *Histoire générale de la civilisation en Europe*, n. 67 above, lecture 1, 18 ff.;
lecture 2, 33–5; De Tocqueville, *De la démocratie en Amérique*, n. 70 above, i, ch. 5, 98; ch.
14, 292–7; ii, pt. 4, ch. 6.

[102] De Tocqueville, *De la démocratie en Amérique*, n. 70 above, ii, pt. 2, ch. 5.

In a decentralized system, however, the state administration becomes difficult to distinguish from other associations. Tocqueville accordingly described its complete disappearance from his idealized view of American democracy:

Nothing is more striking to a European traveler in the United States than the absence of what we term the government, or the administration. Written laws exist in America, and one sees the daily execution of them; but although everything moves regularly, the mover can nowhere be discovered. The hand that directs the social machine is invisible. . . . The administrative power in the United States presents nothing either centralized or hierarchical in its constitution; this accounts for its passing unperceived. The power exists, but its representative is nowhere to be seen.[103]

In a thoroughly decentralized democracy, the administration is difficult to distinguish and the distinction between public and private is difficult to apply.

Durkheim, Duguit, and the Proliferation of Hybrid Institutions

Unlike Tocqueville, Durkheim[104] did not project his prescriptions upon distant American democracy. Rather, he expressed them as normal manifestations of the development of industrial society in nineteenth-century France. He was a liberal Republican who had inherited a liberal apprehension of administrative centralization but sought to come to terms with the social needs of industrial society and the influence of socialist ideas. Because Durkheim regarded the state and, accordingly, its administration as answers to those needs and as enduring problems, his attitude to their distinctness was ambivalent.

On the one hand, in response to sceptical socialist attitudes to the state, Durkheim stressed the state's distinctness and necessity. He regarded it as a central, representative, and deliberative body of officials, and the administration, as its subordinate, the executor of its decisions.[105] He argued that the development of the state was a necessary concomitant of the transition from 'mechanical' to 'organic

---

[103] A. de. Tocqueville, *Democracy in America*, n. 78 above, i, ch. 5, 70, 71.

[104] See generally E. Durkheim, *The Division of Labour in Society*, (G. Simpson (tr.)) (New York, 1964); *id.*, *Le Suicide: étude de sociologie* (Paris, 1930), 434–42; *id.*, 'L'Etat' (1958) 148 *Revue Philos.* 433–7; *id.*, *Politics and the State* (A. Giddens (ed.), W. D. Halls (tr.)) (Stanford, 1986); A. Giddens, *Durkheim* (Glascow, 1978), 9–20, 49–62; *id.*, *Profiles and Critiques in Social Theory* (London, 1982), 117–32.

[105] Durkheim, *Politics and the State*, n. 104 above, 37–40, 57; *id.*, 'L'Etat', n. 104 above, 433–5.

solidarity' and of the complex division of labour in industrial society.[106] He described the democratic state as a responsible institution with an extended role both moral and economic: the moral role of securing individual rights and so the self-realization of the individual; and, the economic role of preventing exploitation and securing equal opportunity in the workplace.[107]

On the other hand, by recognizing the state's extended role, Durkheim aggravated the liberal apprehension of administrative centralization. He therefore envisaged a decentralized system in which individuals play a prominent social role through intermediate powers like the family and especially through various national occupational associations.[108] He advocated that these associations regulate industrial relations, prevent exploitation of the weak by the strong, complement and counterbalance the power of the state, and even serve as electoral colleges in place of regional institutions. These associations, however, are not clearly distinguished from the state and especially from its administration. Secondary groups like the occupational associations are central to Durkheim's very definition of the state. His secondary groups come together in political society to constitute the state as the supreme authority:

[T]hey . . . form the primary condition for any higher organization. Far from being in opposition to the social group endowed with sovereign powers and called more specifically the State, the State presupposes their existence: it exists only where they exist. No secondary groups, no political authority—at least, no authority that this term can apply to without being inappropriate.[109]

Durkheim's occupational associations regulate, as does the state, and so, presumably, have in some degree the qualities of deliberativeness and representativeness with which Durkheim attempted to distinguish the state. Repeatedly, Durkheim tried to clarify the state's distinctness by resorting to the organic metaphor of the state as the brain operating through its intermediary organs.[110] To the extent that he nonetheless failed, he left the administration without a distinct category of

---

[106] Durkheim, *Division of Labour*, n. 104 above.

[107] Durkheim, *Politics and the State*, n. 104 above, 41–5, 51–9, 79–83; *id.*, 'L'Etat', n. 104 above, 435–7; Giddens, 'Introduction' in Durkheim, *Politics and the State*, n. 104 above, 30–1.

[108] Durkheim, *Le Suicide*, n. 104 above, 434–42; *id.*, *Division of Labour*, n. 104 above, 1–31 (pref. to 2nd Fr. edn.); Giddens, *Durkheim*, n. 104 above, 60–2.

[109] Durkheim, *Politics and the State*, n. 104 above, 34–7, especially at 35.

[110] See, e.g., Durkheim, *Politics and the State*, n. 104 above, 41; Giddens, 'Introduction' in Durkheim, *Politics and the State*, n. 104 above, 9.

decisions to implement and therefore similarly indistinct or blurred. Furthermore, Durkheim stressed that occupational associations are public, not private, associations,[111] and seems to have distinguished them from administrative agencies only with the vague notion of the directness of their subordination to the state. Whereas the administrative agencies are directly subordinate to the state,[112] his occupational associations are subject to its action and general influence.[113] By stressing the role of occupational associations, Durkheim negated the centrality and, so, the distinctness of the state and its administration.

Although Durkheim was disdainful of practical politics, his sociology was generally representative and influential. In the late nineteenth and early twentieth centuries, his sociology converged with the official ideology of Republicanism. He was a prominent professor who provided Republicanism with a sociological basis.[114] In particular, he influenced Duguit[115] and, through him, the development of French public law.

Duguit explicitly rejected the German political tradition dominated by Kant and Hegel and enshrining the sovereign powers of the state. He preferred the French tradition, exemplified in Constant's analysis, long preoccupied with limiting the state's powers and recently enlightened by the sociological interpretation of Durkheim and others.[116] Like Durkheim, Duguit was both sensitive to social needs and concerned to limit the powers of the state. He required that the state further social solidarity, in other words, facilitate social interdependence, and respect civil liberties to enable individuals and other associations to do likewise.[117] Accordingly, his inclinations, like Durkheim's, were twofold: the inclination to rely on the state as a distinct entity to meet social needs; and, the inclination to limit the state's powers by extolling decentralization and so negating the state's distinctness.

---

[111] Durkheim, *Division of Labour*, n. 104 above, 6, 22; *id.*, *Le Suicide*, n. 104 above, 436.

[112] Durkheim, *Politics and the State*, n. 104 above, 41; *id.*, *L'Etat*, n. 104 above, 434.

[113] Durkheim, *Le Suicide*, n. 104 above, 437–9; *id.*, *Division of Labour*, n. 104 above, 24.

[114] Giddens, *Durkheim*, n. 104 above, 19; *id.*, 'Introduction' in Durkheim, *Politics and the State*, n. 104 above, at 15, 27.

[115] L. Duguit, 'The Law and the State: French and German Doctrines' (1917/18) 31 *Harv. LRev.* 1–185 at 177–85, especially at 178. See generally H. J. Laski, 'A Note on M. Duguit' (1917/18) 31 *Harv. LRev.* 186–92.

[116] Duguit, 'Law and the State', n. 115 above. See generally Duguit, *Law in the Modern State*, n. 82 above; W. J. Brown 'The Jurisprudence of M. Duguit' (1916) 32 *LQR* 168–83; Laski, 'Note on Duguit', n. 115 above; H. J. Laski, 'M. Duguit's Conception of the State' in W. I. Jennings *et al.*, *Modern Theories of Law* (London, 1933), 52–67; Jones, n. 82 above, 159–79.

[117] Laski in Jennings *et al.*, n. 116 above, 54.

First, Duguit conceptualized a state without rights but with the capacity to bear duties.[118] He conferred upon the state the special responsibility of furthering social solidarity by providing a widening range of public services in response to growing social needs. Duguit described a state that must provide, and an administration that must operate, services, such as education, charity, and transport, in addition to the traditional police, justice, and defence.[119] Duguit's state would be responsible for 'the development of the individual well-being, physical, intellectual and moral, and the material prosperity of the nation'.[120] Duguit denied that state officials had remained the 'masters of men' but nevertheless identified them as the 'managers of the nation's business'.[121] By substituting state responsibility for state rights, Duguit was reacting[122] against the theorists of a sovereign state but sharing their conception of its distinctness.[123]

Secondly, Duguit extolled an increasingly decentralized system with public services not only provided by central government but also by regional representatives, industrialized departments, 'autonomous group[s] of officials', 'technical experts' within a department and 'private citizen[s] acting under government control'.[124] In the social system described by Duguit, central government, officials in decentralized institutions, as well as other associations and individuals are all concerned with social solidarity. Their acts in its furtherance are similar in substance and similarly subject to the rule of law.[125]

Duguit refused to distinguish the state by conferring upon it sovereignty or corporate identity. He regarded such notions as mythical, fictional, or unscientific: at worst, perpetuating extensive state powers; at best, useless in protecting individuals from their exercise.[126] Duguit rather tried to establish the distinctness of the state by accepting the notion of public service in place of the notion of sovereignty: 'The state is no longer a sovereign power issuing its commands. It is a group of individuals who must use the force they possess to supply the public need. The idea of public service lies at the very basis of the theory of

---

[118] See Brown, n. 116 above, 181–3; Laski in Jennings *et al.*, n. 116 above, 55–6.

[119] Duguit, *Law in the Modern State*, n. 82 above, pp. xlii–xliii, 30–67, 150–1.

[120] *Ibid.* 30.   [121] *Ibid.* 51.

[122] See generally, 'Law and the State', n. 115 above.

[123] See Laski in Duguit, *Law in the Modern State*, n. 82 above, pp. xxix–xxx.

[124] *Ibid.* 52–4, 20–2; Laski, 'Law and the State', n. 115 above, 190–1. See generally Laski in Duguit, *Law in the Modern State*, n. 82 above, pp. xi–xv, xxiii–xxiv.

[125] Laski in Jennings *et al.*, n. 116 above, 53–5.

[126] See, e.g., Duguit, *Law in the Modern State*, n. 82 above, p. xli; *id.*, 'Law and the State', n. 115 above, 8; Laski, 'Note on Duguit', n. 115 above, 189.

the modern state.'[127] Duguit failed, however, to define public service with any precision and without begging numerous questions:

[The elements of public service] consist essentially in the existence of a legal obligation of the rulers in a given country, that is to say of *those in fact who possess power*, to ensure without interruption the fulfilment of certain tasks. . . . A public service . . . may be defined as follows: Any activity that has to be governmentally regulated and controlled because it is indispensable to the realization and development of social solidarity is a public service so long as it is of such a nature that it cannot be assured save by governmental intervention.[128]

Duguit replaced the conceptualization of a sovereign state with an indirect reference to the powerful in society, entrusted with an increasing and indeterminate range of tasks.

Durkheim and Duguit were both[129] ambivalent towards the distinctness of the state but differed in their emphasis. Durkheim emphasized the state's distinctness; Duguit, its indistinctness. Durkheim emphasized evolutionary change; Duguit described a dramatic development—'The Eclipse of Sovereignty'.[130] And, whereas Durkheim pioneered the discipline of sociology, Duguit familiarized public lawyers with a new conception of the state[131] and provided public law with a new framework. During the Third Republic, French law faculties became peculiarly receptive to other disciplines and particularly to sociological approaches.[132] In France, Duguit influenced a generation of jurists and produced an effect which has been compared to that of *The Spirit of the Laws*.[133]

By stressing, on the one hand, state responsibility and, on the other, the role of intermediate bodies and the decentralization of public services, Durkheim and especially Duguit marked the emergence, and anticipated the proliferation, of hybrid institutions, in the sense of corporations, organizations, and enterprises variously named and variously related to and independent from an interventionist central government. From early in the Third Republic and especially in the

---

[127] Duguit, *Law in the Modern State*, n. 82 above, p. xliv.
[128] *Ibid.* 39, 48 (emphasis added).
[129] Cf. generally Jones, n. 82 above, 105–11, 124–41, 154–79.
[130] *Law in the Modern State*, n. 82 above, 1.
[131] See, e.g., the debates about public service syndicalism in Jones, n. 82 above, especially chs. 6 and 7.
[132] See *ibid.* 32–48.
[133] Laski, 'Note on Duguit', n. 115 above, 188; *id.* in Jennings *et al.*, n. 116 above, 52.

Fourth and Fifth Republics, central government increasingly operated through, and together with, other institutions to meet social needs. The resulting variety of hybrid institutions came to include the following:

(a) the *établissements publics administratifs*, specialized agencies established by government to fulfil special functions but with financial autonomy and separate legal personality, e.g. various universities, schools, and hospitals;

(b) the *établissements publics à caractère industriel et commercial* and free from the restrictions of public accounting, e.g. *Electricité de France* and *Gaz de France*;

(c) the *entreprises d'économie mixte*, companies with shares partly owned by private persons and partly by the state, e.g. *Air France* and *Société Nationale des Chemins de Fer Français*;

(d) the *entreprises publiques* with nationalized assets but required to continue functioning in the same way as commercial companies, e.g. the nationalized banks;

(e) the *établissements d'utilité publique*, institutions recognized to be private but declared to be acting in the public interest and therefore supervised by government, e.g. the local savings banks;

(f) the *ordres professionnels*, with their supervisory functions subject to the jurisdiction of the administrative courts;

(g) trade unions, influencing the determination of wages and working conditions while sanctioned and regulated by law; and,

(h) private enterprises subject to administrative regulation concerning, for example, public health and safety.[134]

These hybrid institutions were the ambiguous outcome of an ambivalence towards the state exemplified in the analyses of Durkheim and Duguit. While decentralized and institutionally autonomous in varying degrees, these institutions were also manifestations of the supremacy of a responsible and centralized state. Their institutional and functional hybridity rendered the state and its administration less

---

[134] R. Drago, 'Public Enterprises in France' in W. Friedmann and J. F. Garner (eds.), *Government Enterprise: A Comparative Study* (London, 1970), 107–22; *id.*, 'The Public Corporation in France' in W. Friedmann (ed.), *The Public Corporation: A Comparative Symposium* (London, 1954), 108–37; J. Rivero, *Droit administratif* (13th edn., Paris, 1990), secs. 484–637; De Laubadère, n. 82 above, secs. 395–419; Szladits, n. 11 above, secs. 53–5; Ridley and Blondel, n. 99 above, 233–55, 299–307. See generally V. Wright, *The Government and Politics of France* (2nd edn., London, 1983), 100–2, 219–54, 293–303; A. Shonfield, *Modern Capitalism: The Changing Balance of Public and Private Power* (London, 1965), 71–87.

distinct and the application of the terms public and private more problematic.

Durkheim's and Duguit's ambivalence towards the distinctness of the state and its administration was reflected in an ambivalent attitude to the distinction between public and private law. While Durkheim recognized the practical usefulness of the distinction and stressed that administrative law was developing together with the state in advanced societies, he nevertheless also explicitly rejected the distinction between public and private law:

The most accepted [of the distinctions used by the jurisconsults] is that which divides law into public and private; the first is for the regulation of the relations of the individual to the State, the second, of individuals among themselves. But when we try to get closer to these terms, the line of demarcation which appeared so neat at the beginning fades away. All law is private in the sense that it is always about individuals who are present and acting; but so, too, all law is public, in the sense that it is a social function and that all individuals are, whatever their varying titles, functionaries of society. Marital functions, paternal, etc., are neither delimited nor organized in a manner different from ministerial and legislative functions . . . What, moreover, is the State? Where does it begin and where does it end? We know how controversial the question is; it is not scientific to make a fundamental classification repose on a notion so obscure and so badly analyzed.[135]

Duguit was similarly ambivalent. On the one hand, to the extent that he recognized the peculiar responsibility of government, he justified the development of public law and, so, the distinction between public and private law. Laski described the one implication of Duguit's analysis as follows:

It [the rule of law] is imposed upon public persons, even more than upon private, because their situation makes incumbent upon them a greater sense of their responsibility for its realisation. These public persons are, in their totality, what we call government; for, to M. Duguit, a state is simply a society divided into government and subjects. It would, then, be clearly absurd if the more important position of government, relative to the general social end, did not involve greater responsibility for that end.[136]

Duguit identified public law with the sanctioning of a twofold responsibility of government: '[a]ny system of public law can be vital only so

---

[135] Durkheim, *Division of Labour*, n. 104 above, 68, 126–7, 219 ff., especially at 68.
[136] Laski in Duguit, *Law in the Modern State*, n. 82 above, pp. xvii–xviii. See also Laski in Jennings *et al.*, n. 116 above, 54; Jones, n. 82 above, 178.

far as it is based on a given sanction to the following rules: First, the holders of power cannot do certain things; second, there are certain things they must do.'[137] Because Duguit both recognized the necessity of the state and had inherited the liberal concern to limit its powers, he envisaged a public law that both facilitates and controls the operation of public services. He celebrated in the 'new and fruitful jurisprudence' of the *Conseil d'Etat*[138] and himself contributed to the elaboration of its principles of legality and liability.[139]

On the other hand, to the extent that Duguit denied a distinct state as 'nothing more formidable than a particular grouping of men seeking to achieve and intensify social solidarity',[140] he blurred the public law/private law distinction. Laski asserted that, in Duguit's theory, 'there is no distinction between the nature of public and of private law, since each is subject to the criterion of social solidarity'.[141] Indeed, Duguit did repeatedly stress the similarities between public and private law. He suggested that both are similarly affected by the dislocation of earlier political theory and based both upon the idea of social function—that of the state and that of the individual.[142] He was concerned that principles be imposed equally on the state and on individuals. For example, in a discussion of abuse of power, he described how the central idea of purpose equally affects public and private law.[143] And, in a discussion of contractual liability, he equated the state with the private citizen: '[a] contract is a legal act with the same character both in public and in private law; or rather *no distinction exists between public and private law* and the state is bound by its contracts exactly as a private citizen is bound.'[144] Because Duguit lacked an unequivocal conception of a distinct state administration, he denied or negated the distinction.

The Search for Distinguishing Criteria

In the absence of theoretical clarification of a distinct state administration amidst the proliferating hybrid institutions, the *Conseil d'Etat* and the *Tribunal des Conflits* struggled to develop institutional and functional

---

[137] Duguit, *Law in the Modern State*, n. 82 above, 26–9, especially at 26.
[138] *Ibid.* 31.   [139] *Ibid.* 54–67, 164–242.
[140] Laski in Jennings *et al.*, n. 116 above, 54.
[141] *Ibid.* 56. See Jones, n. 82 above, 165–6.
[142] Duguit, *Law in the Modern State*, n. 82 above, pp. xxxvi, 49, 243–5. See L. Duguit, 'Changes of Principle in the Feld of Liberty, Contract, Liability, and Property' in *The Progress of Continental Law in the Nineteenth Century* (London, 1918), 65–146.
[143] Duguit, *Law in the Modern State*, n. 82 above, 186–7.
[144] *Ibid.* 148–9 (emphasis added).

criteria with which to apply the distinction consistently. The *Tribunal* used the notion of *service public* in *Blanco* but did not define it then or, later, when it was established.[145] Doctrinal writers provided only vague definitions. Rolland, for example, defined *service public* as the 'entreprise ou . . . institution d'intérêt général qui, sous la haute direction des gouvernants, est destinées à donner satisfaction à des besoins collectifs du public'.[146] Meanwhile, the *Conseil d'Etat* and *Tribunal des Conflits* extended *service public ad hoc* and without clear justification to cover activities of a range of hybrid institutions such as professional associations, sporting bodies, and what were traditionally private social welfare agencies.[147] Furthermore, when confronted with the proliferation of the *établissements publics à caractère industriel et commercial* after the First World War, the *Tribunal* established an exception to the criterion of *service public*. It recognized the jurisdiction of the civil courts where an authority provided a *service public* by adopting the forms of private law.[148] For example, in the *'Bac d'Eloka'* case, the *Tribunal des Conflits* held that a civil court was competent to hear a claim for damages arising from a ferry-boat service where the authority operated it as a private business.[149] The *Tribunal*, however, was not consistent. In the *Effimief* case, for example, the *Tribunal* held that an administrative court had jurisdiction where the authority employed private firms to develop slum areas.[150]

Because of such inconsistency, especially evident in the field of *contrats administratifs*, and because of a variety of other exceptions and exceptions to exceptions,[151] a number of doctrinal writers questioned the usefulness of the general criterion of *service public* and despaired of establishing a satisfactory substitute. Waline, for example, called *service*

---

[145] *Blanco*, TC, 8 Feb. 1873; Rivero, 'L'Avènement de la notion de service public', n. 82 above; De Laubadère, *Droit administratif*, n. 82 above, secs. 35–8; Szladits, n. 11 above, sec. 39, 25.

[146] L. Rolland, *Précis de droit administratif* (9th edn., Paris, 1947), sec. 2: 'the undertaking or . . . general-interest institution which, under the overall direction of those who govern, is intended to satisfy the collective needs of the public'. See Waline, n. 83 above, sec. 1124.

[147] See, e.g., *Caisse Primaire 'Aide et Protection'*, CE, 13 May 1938; *Bouguen*, CE, 2 Apr. 1943; *Peschaud* v. *Groupement du Football Professionnel*, TC, 7 July 1980.

[148] Brown and Bell, n. 82 above, 128–30, 136 ff.

[149] *Société Communale de l'Ouest Africain*, TC, 22 Jan. 1921.

[150] TC, 28 Mar. 1955.

[151] See, e.g., *Competition Law*, CC decision no. 86–224–DC, 23 Jan. 1987; Brown and Bell, n. 82 above, 130–44; J. Hill, 'Public Law and Private Law: More (French) Food for Thought' [1985] *PL* 14–21; Szladits, n. 11 above, sec. 39, 24–5; J. D. B. Mitchell, *The Contracts of Public Authorities: A Comparative Survey* (London, 1954), 167–182.

public a 'pseudo critère' and 'purement verbal', while Chenot argued that judicial use of the criterion was existential.[152] In 1964, Weil described the overall confusion accompanying the search for distinguishing criteria: 'la recherche se perd dans les subtilités des exceptions aux principes, des dérogations aux exceptions, des présomptions susceptibles d'être renversées, et la réflexion tourne rapidement au vertige'.[153] Such confusion has been lasting.[154]

Sympathetic and less sympathetic foreign observers regarded the lasting confusion as the cost of the French distinction.[155] Indeed, the confusion was not simply academic. It aggravated the litigant's burden of choosing the appropriate forum and was costly in judicial resources. The *Tribunal des Conflits* might have dealt with few cases over the years,[156] but it has been staffed by the *Conseil d'Etat*'s and the *Cour de Cassation*'s highest judicial officers. Usually they have been required to decide, not major issues of substance, but mere matters of jurisdiction. Hamson implied that the cost of the distinction was raised by 'a fantastic spirit of legal refinement or by the mere obstinacy and caste-sense of the French fonctionnaire'.[157] But a less nationalistic part explanation, which avoids the 'pons asinorum of "national character" ',[158] stresses the proliferation of institutions regarded as hybrid:

Des transformations accélérées à partir de la période de l'entre deux-guerres ont imposé des orientations nouvelles à notre droit administratif et conduit à repenser les problèmes des idées-clefs et des critères d'application de ce droit. Les deux phénomènes majeurs à cet égard ont été, d'une part la multiplication des services publics à caractère économique, d'autre part l'association des personnes privées à la réalisation des services publics. . . . La conséquence de ces diverses transformations de la vie administrative, en ce qui concerne la théorie du service public, a été . . . que la démarcation, autrefois aisément repérable, entre le secteur des services publics et celui des activités privées, est *devenue beau-*

---

[152] De Laubadère, n. 82 above, secs. 40–1; Waline, n. 83 above, secs. 109 ff., especially at 72, 75. See also *ibid.*, secs. 1109 ff.; B. Chenot, 'La notion de service public dans la jurisprudence économique du Conseil l'Etat' (1950) 4 *EDCE* 77–83; *id.*, 'L'existentialisme et le droit ' (1953) 3 *Revue Française de science politique* 57–68.

[153] P. Weil, *Le Droit administratif* (Paris, 1964), 68: 'the search loses itself in the subtleties of exceptions to principles, derogations from exceptions, presumptions that can be rebutted, and thought rapidly turns to dizziness'.

[154] See De Laubadère, n. 82 above, secs. 42–5.

[155] See, e.g., C. J. Hamson, *Executive Discretion and Judicial Control: An Aspect of the French Conseil l'Etat* (London, 1954), 84–8; Hill, n. 151 above, 20–1; Brown and Bell, n. 82 above, 280–1.

[156] See Brown and Bell, *ibid.*   [157] N. 155 above, 87.

[158] B. Kaplan, 'Civil Procedure—Reflections on the Comparison of Systems' (1960) 9 *Buffalo LRev.* 409–32 at 421.

coup moins claire. Il est devenu difficile de déterminer, dans les applications con-crètes, si telle ou telle institution est gestionnaire d'un service public. La notion de service public n'est *plus apparue comme une notion 'opérationnelle'*.[159]

The prevalence of a political theory comparable to Duguit's made the state administration less distinct, administrative disputes difficult to identify, and satisfactory distinguishing criteria difficult to attain. The distinction between public and private law was becoming increasingly difficult to draw.

Continuing Acceptance

Despite the difficulties in distinguishing public and private and despite academic criticism of attempts to develop distinguishing criteria, academic lawyers were generally resigned to the distinction. While Waline, for example, accepted the impossibility of unifying public and private law and the possibility only of cross-fertilization,[160] Brèthe de la Gressaye accepted that, as a result of extending the distinguishing criteria to cover hybrid institutions, 'le Droit administratif n'a pas une unité parfaite'.[161] Radical positions[162] had little practical influence.

To most French lawyers, the distinction remained 'indisputable . . . natural, just and necessary':[163]

For a Frenchman, the most basic distinction is that between public and private law. The line between public and private law may sometimes be unclear. The very principle of the distinction, from the point of view of logic or rationality, may be disputed. But the distinction, based on a tradition as ancient as the

---

[159] De Laubadère, n. 82 above, secs. 38–9, 37, 38: '[c]hanges which have accelerated since the period between the two World Wars have imposed new directions on our administrative law, and have led to a rethinking of the problems involving key ideas and the criteria for applying the law. The two major phenomena in this regard have been, on the one hand, the multiplication of public services that are economic in character and, on the other, the involvement of private persons in the carrying out of public ser-vices. . . . The consequence of these various changes in administrative life, as far as the theory of public service is concerned, has been . . . that the demarcation line, once eas-ily identified, between the sector of the public services and that of private activities has *become less well-defined.* It has become difficult to decide, in practical applications, whether this or that institution is supplying a public service. The notion of public service is *no longer seen as an "operational" notion.*' See also *ibid.*, sec. 44.

[160] Waline, n. 83 above, sec. 28.   [161] N. 83 above, 147.

[162] See, e.g., Jones, n. 82 above, 124–41, 208.

[163] R. David, 'Public Law and Private Law: Romanist Countries' in *IECL*, ii, ch. 2, sec. 18, 10. See also J. H. Merryman, 'The Public Law-Private Law Distinction in European and American Law' (1968) 17 *J Publ. L* 3–19 at 3–4; *id.*, *The Civil Law Tradition* (2nd edn., Stanford, 1985), 91.

Roman Empire, remains the basic division in French law. French lawyers are either private law specialists or public law specialists. It matters little that both sometimes claim the same contested area and sometimes deal with the same questions.[164]

The 'excessive technicality' of the rules governing the distinction between public and private law, rather than the distinction itself, remained the main subject of criticism.[165] In the 1980s, a French author observed:

Il reste que les notions de droit public et de droit privé restent très vivaces dans le monde du droit, tout particulièrement dans les Facultés où elles dominent à la fois programmes et diplômes. La distinction entre le droit public et le droit privé s'y trouve renforcée par celle entre 'publicistes' et 'privatistes'.[166]

The jurisdictional distinction's constitutional status and a degree of flexibility in the allocation of cases between the ordinary and administrative courts have now been recognized by the *Conseil Constitutionnel.*[167]

Despite the reservations that were expressed,[168] acceptance of the distinction remained widespread for at least[169] two reasons. First, French *publicistes* and *privatistes* were inclined to accept a distinction with a long-established institutional, substantive, and procedural significance to which they were oriented by education and career. Secondly, they did not become merely dismissive of the notion of a distinct state administration but inherited an ambivalence like Duguit's. That ambivalence did not turn to rejection. French lawyers continued to be influenced, although not exclusively, by an old theoretical tradition emphasizing the state administration's centrality and potential irresponsibility.[170] They still attributed qualities to the state administration

[164] R. David, *French Law: Its Structure, Sources, and Methodology* (M. Kindred (tr.)) (Baton Rouge, 1972), 98.

[165] See, e.g., P. Weil, 'The Strength and Weakness of French Administrative Law', n. 83 above, 252.

[166] J.-L. Sourioux, *Introduction au droit* (Paris, 1987), 114: '[i]t remains the case that the concepts of public law and private law are still very much alive in the world of law, most particularly in the university faculties, where they dominate both curricula and diplomas. The distinction between public law and private law has there been reinforced by that between "publicists" and "privatists".'

[167] *Competition Law*, CC decision no. 86–224–DC, 23 Jan. 1987; *Entry and Residence of Foreigners*, CC decision no. 89–261–DC, 28 July 1989.

[168] See, e.g., C. Eisenmann, 'Droit public, droit privé' (1952) 68 *RDP* 903–79.

[169] See also below, 119 ff., 149 ff., 176 f.

[170] See Wright, n. 134 above, 97–110; Shonfield, n. 134 above, 71–87; K. H. F. Dyson, *The State Tradition in Western Europe: A Study of an Idea and Institution* (Oxford, 1980), 282; Jones, n. 82 above.

that made the distinction seem applicable and justifiable. In short, entrenched within the French legal and political tradition, the distinction did not succumb to the difficulties posed by a less distinct modern state administration.

5
A Trojan Horse of the English Legal Tradition

Neglect of the State Administration

In contrast to the French distinction between public and private law, the English distinction has developed too recently to be entrenched. It has not had a long-standing institutional, procedural, and substantive significance.[1] And it has been developed by academic and practising lawyers unaccustomed to theorizing about the state and its administration. A traditional neglect of the state administration is related to two features of the English context—the lateness and limited extent of administrative centralization and the theoretical insularity of the English legal profession.

First, while the economic troubles of seventeenth-century Europe were contributing to administrative centralization in France,[2] they were fuelling conflicts resulting in the destruction of the royal bureaucracy in England.[3] The emerging revolutionary settlement between Parliament and the English Crown precluded the establishment of a powerful centralized administration. It did not express a theory of popular sovereignty conducive to administrative centralization and comparable to the Rousseauist theory of the general will.[4] Rather, by enshrining the sovereignty of Parliament and the supremacy of the common-law courts, it confirmed legislative and judicial centralization[5] which do have a long history in England. Later, Dicey described as a fundamental feature of the English Constitution 'the omnipotence or undisputed supremacy throughout the whole country of the central government', but by that supremacy he meant the sovereignty of Parliament that had replaced the supremacy of the Crown.[6]

---

[1] See above, 4–12.   [2] See above, 44–5

[3] C. Hill, *Reformation to Industrial Revolution: A Social and Economic History of Britain 1530–1780* (London, 1967), especially at 3–5, 74–6.

[4] See K. H. F. Dyson, *The State Tradition in Western Europe: A Study of an Idea and Institution* (Oxford, 1980), 40–1.

[5] See generally R. C. Van Caenegem, *The Birth of the English Common Law* (2nd edn., Cambridge, 1988); id., *Judges, Legislators and Professors: Chapters in European Legal History* (Cambridge, 1987), 93–6.

[6] A. V. Dicey, *An Introduction to the Study of the Law of the Constitution* (10th edn., London, 1959), 183.

Whereas the beginnings of administrative centralization in France were pre-Revolutionary,[7] only through the course of the nineteenth century did central government in England similarly begin to extend its administrative controls by replacing boards and commissions with ministries and by providing for government inspectors in legislation on factories, public health, and relief for the poor. About the turn of the century, when countervailing calls for decentralization were being heard in France, the English administrative system was still in the process[8] of becoming more centralized. The administrative centralization that did occur remained limited by the role of local authorities, which continued to provide numerous services albeit subject to the limited supervision of central government.[9]

English administrative centralization, later and more limited than that in France, did not command the same attention. It did not bring the state to the forefront of academic debate. In the seventeenth century, Hobbes had been preoccupied with 'that great Leviathan called a common-wealth, or state'[10] but 'left an abiding impact' in France, not England.[11] In the eighteenth and nineteenth centuries, his concept of the state did not become the theoretical cornerstone of the English political system. The administrative role of central government did increase in the nineteenth century but was neglected by the prescriptive *laissez-faire* theory of the time.[12] And the English concepts of the state and the Crown were left theoretically unelaborated by a philosophical tradition which was to become predominantly linguistic and analytic and by an historiography and a political science which were inclined to be empirical and mistrustful of abstractions.[13]

---

[7] See above, 44 ff.

[8] M. Hill, *The State, Administration and the Individual* (London, 1976), 17–52; C. Harlow and R. Rawlings, *Law and Administration* (London, 1984), 6–10. See generally R. Barker, *Political Ideas in Modern Britain* (London, 1978), 7–49, 126–8; P. P. Craig, *Administrative Law* (2nd. edn., London, 1989), 34–52, 59–61.

[9] S. Flogaïtis, *Administrative Law et droit administratif* (Paris, 1986), 59–65.

[10] T. Hobbes, *Leviathan* (R. Tuck (ed.)) (Cambridge, 1991), 9. See Q. Skinner, 'The State' in T. Ball, J. Farr, and R. L. Hanson (eds.), *Political Innovation and Conceptual Change* (Cambridge, 1989), 90–131 at 121.

[11] Q. Skinner, 'Thomas Hobbes and his Disciples in France and England' (1966) 8 *Comparative Studies in Soc. & Hist.* 153–67, especially at 154.

[12] A. J. Taylor, *Laissez-faire and State Intervention in Nineteenth-Century Britain* (London, 1972), 18–26, 39–49, 53–4; Hill, n. 8 above, 25–9. See generally the debate amongst historians: Taylor, *op. cit.*; Craig, n. 8 above, 43–6.

[13] Dyson, n. 4 above, 196–201; A. Vincent, *Theories of the State* (Oxford, 1987), 1–2. See generally Dyson, 36–44, 186–96.

74 *A Continental Distinction in the Common Law*

Secondly, the English legal profession, traditionally independent[14] and historically linked to the Inns of Court, has been generally insulated from political theory,[15] from the influence of conceptions of the state like those of Constant, Tocqueville, and Durkheim. Brown's argument against Duguit's sociological analysis illustrates the insulation:

> [T]he whole system of M. Duguit, while professing to be based on facts, so confuses the various social sciences that a science of law, as distinct from a science of politics, ethics, or sociology, is an impossibility. . . . By all means let us get away from legal fiction and construct our legal theory on a basis of facts; but the facts must be such as a court of law takes cognizance of. . . . The way to distinguish between legal fiction and legal theory is to be found, not so much by concentrating our vision upon the world of fact external to the courts, as by regarding the world of fact as it is reflected in the rules and principles which the courts recognize, apply, and enforce.[16]

Unlike the *Conseillers d'Etat*, English academic and practising lawyers have long been preoccupied with remedies, the practice of law, and the law as posited.

Dicey's analytical method provides a further example of insularity. Even though Dicey was both a civil servant and political critic in his early career, he eschewed explicit political theory when, as a law professor, he wrote his legal analysis. In *Law of the Constitution*, Dicey's political prescriptions, although not derived from case law,[17] take the form of analytical descriptions of the fundamental legal rules and principles of the English Constitution.[18] Well into the twentieth century, the positivist separation of description and prescription, fact and value, generally insulated law from political theory with a normative emphasis on the state.[19]

The Crown and its Officers

Whereas, in France, the concept of the state was developed to describe the governmental apparatus, in England, academic and practising

[14] See below, 152 ff.　　[15] Dyson, n. 4 above, 41–3.
[16] W. J. Brown, 'The Jurisprudence of M. Duguit' (1916) 32 *LQR* 168–83 at 183.
[17] W. I. Jennings, 'In Praise of Dicey 1885–1935' (1935) 13 *Pub. Admin.* 123–34 at 129–31; P. P. Craig, 'Dicey: Unitary, Self-correcting Democracy and Public Law' (1990) 106 *LQR* 105–43 at 105, 142–3.
[18] Jennings, n. 17 above, 127–8, 132; R. W. Blackburn, 'Dicey and the Teaching of Public Law' [1985] *PL* 679–94 at 683–4. Cf. T. H. Ford, 'Dicey as a Political Journalist' [1970] *Pol. Stud.* 220–35.
[19] See M. Loughlin, 'The Importance of Elsewhere: A Review of *Public Law and Democracy in the United Kingdom and the United States of America* by P. P. Craig' (1993) 4 *PLR* 44–57.

lawyers used various other concepts to deal with government. In particular, they used two concepts that exemplify the traditional neglect of the state administration. Apart from the vague concept of the public interest,[20] they used an abstract concept of the Crown and the familiar concept of the person or individual—the individual official or officer, the public or political person.

The origins of the abstract concept of the Crown are medieval.[21] In the thirteenth century, jurists began to refer to the Crown as a symbol of the King's office. They developed the notion of an invisible and immaterial Crown distinct from the visible and material Crown of the King. This Crown connoted the King and his Kingdom but was something more than the Kingdom's territory or the King's physical body. The King, in his coronation oath, would promise not to alienate the rights and possessions of the Crown. Towards the end of the thirteenth century, through interpretation of the maxim *quod omnes tangit*,[22] the King would be bound by the oath to do nothing that affected the Crown without first consulting his counsel of prelates and magnates. The Crown thus involved not only the King, but what was vaguely called the whole body politic through its highest representatives.[23]

In a number of ways the medieval concept of the Crown differed from the concept of the state that began to crystallize in late sixteenth-century France.[24] First, the concept connoted both the King and the whole body politic. It did not describe an abstract government apparatus, an apparatus distinguishable from the King and his subjects. Secondly, the concept of the Crown had 'innumerable aspects'.[25] Apart from the material Crown, the concept could refer to the King alone, the King as head of the body politic, the body politic itself, the inalienable rights of that body or those jointly responsible for it. Thirdly, the Crown was a symbol with a mystical quality evoking reverence rather than requiring reasoned elaboration. Kantorowicz suggests that the 'indefiniteness itself of the symbol may have been its

---

[20] See A. E. Tay and E. Kamenka, 'Public Law—Private Law' in S. I. Benn and G. F. Gaus (eds.), *Public and Private in Social Life* (London, 1983), 67–92 at 79. See, e.g., P. Finn, 'Public Function—Private Action: A Common Law Dilemma' in Benn and Gaus (eds.), 93–111.

[21] See F. Pollock and F. W. Maitland, *The History of English Law before the Time of Edward I* (2nd edn., Cambridge, 1898), i, 511–26, especially at 524–6.

[22] See below, 113.

[23] E. H. Kantorowicz, *The King's Two Bodies: A Study in Medieval Political Theology* (Princeton, 1957), 336 ff.

[24] See above, 45–6   [25] Kantorowicz, n. 23 above, 381.

greatest value, and haziness the true strength of the symbolic abstraction'.[26] The Crown was certainly a hazy fiction with which to symbol-
ize dynastic continuity and the perpetuity of the body politic.[27]

The concept of the Crown did not become clearer with the passing
of time. In the Tudor period, the Crown was, for the first time, conceived as a corporation sole, a corporation of one, not unlike a parson
in church property law.[28] That enduring[29] conception amounted to
metaphysical or, rather, 'metaphysiological',[30] even metapsychological,
fiction: 'the personality of the corporate body is concentrated in and
absorbed by the personality of its monarchical head'.[31] With time, the
fiction became greater as the exercise of the monarch's powers became
further removed from the person and diadem of the monarch. The
concept of Crown was rendered increasingly problematic by the gradual transfer of the monarch's powers to new authorities that did not
seem to deserve the same privileges and immunities.[32]

Around 1900, Maitland famously exposed the absurdities of viewing
the Crown as corporation sole.[33] He also stressed that it was being used
in a variety of related senses to refer not only to the royal corporation
sole, but also to the King and the Commonwealth. He quoted Lord
Penzance—'We all know that the Crown is an abstraction'—and
added 'I do not feel quite sure of knowing even this'.[34] In one of his
lectures he observed:

There is one term against which I wish to warn you, and that term is 'the
crown'. You will certainly read that the crown does this and the crown does
that. As a matter of fact we know that the crown does nothing but lie in the
Tower of London to be gazed at by sight-seers. No, the crown is a convenient
cover for ignorance: it saves us from asking difficult questions, questions which
can only be answered by study of the statute book.[35]

---

[26] Kantorowicz, n. 23 above, 340.   [27] *Ibid.* 381–3.

[28] F. W. Maitland, 'The Crown as Corporation' (1901) 17 *LQR* 131–46. See generally F. W. Maitland, 'The Corporation Sole' (1900) 16 *LQR* 335–54.

[29] See, later, e.g., W. Blackstone, *Commentaries on the Laws of England* (facsimile of 1st
edn. of 1765–9, Chicago, 1979), i, bk. 1, ch. 18, 457–8; H. W. R. Wade and C. F.
Forsyth, *Administrative Law* (7th edn., Oxford, 1994), 819–20.

[30] Maitland, 'The Crown', n. 28 above, 134.   [31] *Ibid.* 133.

[32] E. C. S. Wade and A. W. Bradley, *Constitutional and Administrative Law* (10th edn.,
London, 1985), 692–3. See H. J. Laski, 'The Responsibility of the State in England'
(1919) 32 *Harv. LRev.* 447–72.

[33] 'The Crown as Corporation', n. 28 above. See also F. Pollock, *A First Book of
Jurisprudence for Students of the Common Law* (6th edn., London, 1929), 121.

[34] 'The Crown' as Corporation', n. 28 above, 139.

[35] F. W. Maitland, *The Constitutional History of England: A Course of Lectures* (Cambridge,
1908), 418.

To the conception of the Crown as corporation sole, Maitland pre-ferred the conception of a 'corporation aggregate of many', like other corporations, but 'complex and highly organized', headed by the monarch and called the Commonwealth.[36]

In the early twentieth century, the English concept of the Crown, still unclear and confused, whether understood as corporation sole or corporation aggregate, did not approximate to a developed concept of the state administration. On the contrary, it provoked Laski's com-ment:

In England, that vast abstraction we call the state has, at least in theory, no shadow even of existence; government, in the strictness of law, is a complex system of royal acts based, for the most part, upon the advice and consent of the Houses of Parliament. We technically state our theory of politics in terms of an entity which has dignified influence without executive power.[37]

Similarly, Barker referred to the Crown to show that the state barely existed in England: '[o]ur State is on its executive side a bundle of officials, individually responsible for their acts, and only united by a mysterious Crown which is responsible for nothing and serves chiefly as a bracket to unite an indefinite series of $1+1+1$.'[38]

Barker's description of a bundle of officials bracketed by the Crown refers to a traditional preoccupation with official persons to the exclu-sion of a concept of the state. Hale, Blackstone, and Austin dealt with what we might call public-law issues under the law of persons.[39] Austin did, in an early article that referred mainly to French developments, advocate governmental centralization, a relationship of subordination between a sovereign power and numerous functionaries with delegated authority.[40] But, in his discussion of the distinction between public and private law,[41] Austin did not use the concept of the state to refer to the English apparatus of government that was becoming more centralized. Rather, he suggested a 'rule of men'[42] by emphasizing the role of

[36] 'The Crown as Corporation', n. 28 above, 140.

[37] H. J. Laski, 'The Responsibility of the State in England' (1919) 32 *Harv. LRev.* 447–72 at 447.

[38] E. Barker, 'The Discredited State: Thoughts on Politics before the War' [1915] *Pol. Quat.* 101–21 at 101.

[39] See above, 7 ff.

[40] J. Austin, 'Centralization' (1847) 85 *Edinburgh Rev.* 221–58. See R. Cotterrell, *The Politics of Jurisprudence: A Critical Introduction to Legal Philosophy* (London, 1989), 77–9.

[41] J. Austin, *Lectures on Jurisprudence or The Philosophy of Positive Law* (5th edn., London, 1885), 744–60.

[42] See Cotterrell, n. 40 above, 74.

'public or political persons' and of 'political superiors, supreme and subordinate'.[43]

Austin recognized 'the difficulty of drawing the line of demarcation, by which the conditions of private persons are severed from the conditions of political subordinates'.[44] His classification of public law under the law of persons also provoked Paton's criticism: '[t]o consider the powers of the State in connection with the status of married women, infants, and lunatics seems to suggest a lack of proportion.'[45] Through the emphasis on persons, the state administration remained obscure. Even Holland, who did refer to the state and was sympathetic to the distinction between public and private law, was affected, although differently, by the preoccupation with persons, the subjects of private law. He defined 'public law' and 'administrative law' by reference to the state but did not define the state more specifically than as 'a great juristic person' with rights and duties resembling those of individuals.[46] For Holland, the state was itself a person, a juristic person.

To some extent, Dicey did take account of the apparatus of central government. His concepts of parliamentary sovereignty and the rule of law, which enshrined the roles of Parliament and of the ordinary courts, recognized legislative and judicial centralization.[47] Dicey was also politically motivated by his opposition to the increasing intervention of central government in the nineteenth and early twentieth centuries.[48] He nevertheless stressed the individual role of officials and, in each of the three meanings he attributed to the rule of law, negated a distinct state administration. First, he described 'the exercise by persons in authority of wide, arbitrary, or discretionary powers of constraint' as contrary to the rule of law and, so, precluded discretion as the distinguishing feature of government.[49] Secondly, he equated individuals and officials by requiring that 'every man' be 'subject to the

---

[43] Austin, *Lectures on Jurisprudence*, n. 41 above, 749, 744.   [44] *Ibid.* 747.

[45] G. Paton, *A Textbook of Jurisprudence* (4th edn., Oxford, 1972), 328, n. 2.

[46] T. E. Holland, *The Elements of Jurisprudence* (13th edn., Oxford, 1924), 127–8, 374–5, 387–8, especially at 387. See also Pollock, n. 33 above, 95–6, 121; F. W. Maitland, 'Introduction' in O. Gierke, *Political Theories of the Middle Ages* (Cambridge, 1900), especially at pp. xi, xxxvii.

[47] Dicey, *Law of the Constitution*, n. 6 above. Cf. generally, H. W. Arthurs, *'Without the Law': Administrative Justice and Legal Pluralism in Nineteenth-Century England* (Toronto, 1985); P. P. Craig, 'Dicey: Unitary, Self-correcting Democracy and Public Law' (1990) 106 *LQR* 105–43, especially at 128 ff.

[48] T. H. Ford, 'Dicey as a Political Journalist' [1970] *Pol. Stud.* 220–35; W. I. Jennings, n. 17 above. See generally A. V. Dicey, *Lectures on the Relation between Law and Public Opinion in England During the Nineteenth Century* (2nd. edn., London, 1962), xxxii–liii, 211 ff.

[49] Dicey, *Law of the Constitution*, n. 6 above, 188.

ordinary law of the realm'.[50] Instead of conceptualizing the state administration as a subject of law, he referred to it only indirectly in defining 'officials' to include 'all persons employed in the service of the state'.[51] Thirdly, he omitted any reference to the state administration where he asserted that 'the general principles of the constitution . . . are with us the result of judicial decisions determining the rights of *private persons* in particular cases brought before the courts'.[52]

In short, when a conception of the state would have been used in France, English academic and practising lawyers used various vague conceptions, such as the Crown, officials, political superiors, officers of the Crown, and public or political persons. These conceptions not only did not approximate to a conception of the state administration. They also continued to obscure the extent to which the apparatus of government had become centralized.

The traditional confusion about the state and its administration has persisted.[53] It is illustrated in numerous cases this century. In *Chandler* v. *Director of Public Prosecutions*,[54] the House of Lords struggled to define 'safety and interests of the State' in section 1 of the Official Secrets Act 1911. Lord Reid recognized the difficulty and uncertainty:

'State' is not an easy word. It does not mean the Government or the Executive. . . . [W]e have seen only too clearly in some other countries what can happen if you personify and almost deify the State. Perhaps the country or the realm are as good synonyms as one can find and I would be prepared to accept the organised community as coming as near to a definition as one can get.[55]

In *Attorney-General* v. *Jonathan Cape Ltd*, regardless of the propriety of applying the notion of confidence to government officials rather than private persons with commercial and domestic secrets, Lord Widgery extended the doctrine of breach of confidence to give courts the power to restrain, when in the public interest, the publication of Cabinet minutes.[56] Only a lack of any conception of the state can explain the passage in *Malone* v. *Metropolitan Police Commissioner* where the court applied the principle that everything is lawful unless expressly

---

[50] *Ibid.* 193.   [51] *Ibid.* 195.
[52] *Ibid.* (emphasis added). See Harlow and Rawlings, n. 8 above, 14–17.
[53] Cf. T. R. S. Allan, *Law, Liberty, and Justice: The Legal Foundations of British Constitutionalism* (Oxford, 1993), 157–62.
[54] [1964] AC 763.
[55] *Ibid.* 790. Cf. *ibid.* 807–8, 813. See *R.* v. *Ponting* [1985] Crim. LR 318.
[56] [1976] QB 752. Cf. Allan, n. 53 above, 160–1.

prohibited equally and explicitly to smoking by individuals and tele-phone tapping on the warrant of the Home Secretary.[57] Even more recently, in *Air Canada* v. *Secretary of State for Trade*,[58] Lord Fraser was confronted with a dispute between, on the one hand, a group of air-lines, and, on the other, a government department and the British Airports Authority. He nevertheless saw only individuals when he stated generally that '[i]n an adversarial system such as exists in the United Kingdom, a party is free to withhold information that would help his case if he wishes—perhaps for reasons of *delicacy or personal pri-vacy*'.[59] Often, English courts still equate the state administration (or the powerful institution) with individuals and, accordingly, do not regard its potential abusiveness and irresponsibility as a peculiar threat.

Negation of the Distinction

In the absence of any traditional legal conception of the state, let alone a developed theory, the old English legal authorities[60] rejected the dis-tinction between public and private law or rendered it insignificant. Hale and Blackstone negated the distinction by classifying what we might call public law under the law of persons. Austin adopted a sim-ilar classification and explicitly rejected the Roman distinction. Others such as Holland defended the distinction as a mere matter of conve-nience. And Dicey expressed a tradition where he defined the rule of law to exclude a distinction with institutional or substantive legal significance. Without a clear conception of the state administration, Dicey, like Austin,[61] had no clear reason to distinguish the legal con-sequences of administrative disputes from those of private disputes.[62]

Furthermore, to the extent that English courts and academic lawyers have been motivated by a vague Diceyan appreciation of the threat posed by the administration, they have been handicapped in develop-ing a satisfactory body of public law that would entrench the distinc-tion between public and private law. In 1919, Laski commented: '[t]he

---

[57] [1979] Ch. 344 at 366E–367A. Cf. generally B. V. Harris, 'The "Third Source" of Authority for Government Action' (1992) 109 *LQR* 626–51.

[58] [1983] 2 AC 394.

[59] *Ibid.* 434D (emphasis added). See J. A. Jolowicz, 'Adversarial and Inquisitorial Approaches to Civil Litigation' in E. G. Baldwin (ed.), *The Cambridge Lectures* (Toronto, 1983), 237–43 at 239–41; T. R. S. Allan, 'Abuse of Power and Public Interest Immunity: Justice, Rights and Truth' (1985) 101 *LQR* 200–16 at 209–10, 216.

[60] See above, 7–11.　　　　　　　　　　　　[61] Cf. Cotterrell, n. 40 above, 83.

[62] See P. Cane, 'Public Law and Private Law: A Study of the Analysis and Use of a Legal Concept' in J. Eekelaar and J. Bell (eds.), *Oxford Essays in Jurisprudence* (Oxford, 1987), 57–78 at 61.

state cannot be sued, because there is no state to sue. There is still no more than a Crown, which hides its imperfections beneath the cloak of an assumed infallibility. The Crown is irresponsible save where, of grace, it relaxes so stringent an attitude.'[63] Equipped only with a confused conception of the Crown, English courts and academic lawyers have struggled to come to terms with Crown immunities, to develop principles of public law systematically in response to perceived needs, and, in short, to write a black-letter public law beneath the dim glow of red-light theory.[64] Their traditional theoretical handicap is manifest in the *Malone* case where Sir Robert Megarry declared that 'telephone tapping is a subject which cries out for legislation'[65] and so abrogated judicial responsibility.

Opening the Gates to the Trojan Horse

In spite of the traditional neglect, English academic and practising lawyers have, in this century, less frequently neglected the state and its administration. Slowly, they responded to the limited centralization that had occurred through the course of the nineteenth century. Around 1900, a few academics began to draw attention to governmental expansion and the conception of the state. Maitland observed:

We are becoming a much governed nation, governed by all manner of councils and boards and officers, central and local, high and low, exercising the powers which have been committed to them by modern statutes. . . . The governmental powers, the subordinate legislative powers of the great officers, the Secretaries of State, the Treasury, the Board of Trade, the Local Government Board, and again of the Justices in Quarter Sessions, the Municipal Corporations, the Guardians of the Poor, School Boards, Boards of Health and so forth; these have become of the greatest importance, and to leave them out of the picture is to make the picture a partial one-sided obsolete sketch.[66]

Salmond also emphasized the extension of government and analysed the state with care: '[b]ut the modern state does many things, and different things at different times and places. It is a common carrier of

---

[63] Laski, n. 37 above, 450.

[64] J. D. B. Mitchell, 'The Causes and Effects of the Absence of a System of Public Law in the United Kingdom' [1965] *PL* 95–118, especially at 113–15. See generally Harlow and Rawlings, n. 8 above, ch. 1.

[65] At 380G.

[66] Maitland, *Constitutional History of England*, n. 35 above, 501, 506.

letters and parcels, it builds ships, it owns and manages railways, it conducts savings-banks, it teaches children, and feeds the poor.'[67]

The increasing concern with the state administration was stimulated
by Continental contacts of varying intensity. Maitland, for example,
was influenced by German jurisprudence, and later writers, such as
Robson, Jennings, and Mitchell, were influenced by Continental theory or by English theorists like Laski at LSE, who initially derived ideas
about the state from Duguit.[68] Laski presented Duguit as a source of
'enlightenment and inspiration' and alleged that France 'holds open
the gate through which the sister nations pass'.[69] He summarized
Duguit's contribution with approval:

He [Duguit] saw that the government of a State is simply a body of men issuing orders, and that these, in themselves, have no colour of any kind. Orders
of government do not embody the will of the nation, for the simple reason that
the nation, as such, has no will. The State, so to say, is a parallelogram of
forces in which now one element, now another, prevails.[70]

The state administration that began to receive attention, however, was
particularly alien and problematic. The uncertain starting-point for
Laski's subsequent vacillations[71] was not the traditional French conception of the state, but the recent conception of Duguit, ambivalent
towards the distinctness of the state and its administration.[72]

English legal academics began to consider a conception of the state
that was changing as its capacities were enhanced by advances in technology and communications and as social problems were aggravated
by industrialization and urbanization. Changes affecting the distinctness of the state administration were evident in three general areas—
liberal theory, institutional forms, and governmental processes.

First, liberal theory shifted between poles that may be described by
reference to conceptions of either individual freedom or the role of the
state. It shifted from what Berlin famously called a negative freedom,

[67] J. W. Salmond, *Jurisprudence* or *The Theory of Law* (London, 1902), 184–216, especially at 184–5.

[68] See, e.g., H. J. Laski, 'A Note on M. Duguit' (1917/18) 31 *Harv. LRev.* 186–92; *id.*,
'Duguit's Conception of the State' in W. I. Jennings *et al.*, *Modern Theories of Law* (London,
1933), 52–67, especially at 65–6; Harlow and Rawlings, n. 8 above, 35–9.

[69] Laski in Duguit, *Law in the Modern State* (F. and H. Laski (trs.)) (New York, 1970),
pp. xxxiv, xxxvi.

[70] Laski in Jennings *et al.*, n. 68 above, 65.

[71] See H. A. Deane, *The Political Ideas of Harold J. Laski* (New York, 1955); R. Barker,
n. 8 above, 97–8, 129–31, 165–71.

[72] See above, 61–3.

requiring a certain freedom from governmental interference, towards a positive freedom, allowing or requiring government to facilitate individual development and fulfilment by providing services and enabling meaningful political participation.[73] Lawyers and legal writers began to be influenced not simply by a 'passive individualism' but also by a 'developmental individualism'.[74] Changes in the conception of the state roughly corresponded to changes in the conception of individual freedom. Hill describes the change from the state as 'controller' to the state as 'provider'.[75] The night-watchman state with relatively discrete law-and-order functions was replaced by the welfare state with an indeterminate range of functions relating *inter alia* to health, housing, and social security.

Consequently, in his *Jurisprudence*, Salmond struggled to identify 'the modern state'.[76] Salmond still regarded the state's old night-watchman functions—'*war* and the *administration of justice*'—as 'primary and essential' but recognized an open-ended category of secondary functions:

The secondary functions of the state may be divided into two classes. The first consists of those which serve to secure the efficient fulfilment of the primary functions, and the chief of these are two in number, namely legislation and taxation. . . . *The remaining class of secondary functions comprises all other forms of activity which are for any reason deemed especially fit to be undertaken by the state.* . . . Considerations such as these have, especially in modern times, induced the state to assume a great number of secondary and unessential functions, which in a peaceful and law-abiding community *tend even to overshadow and conceal from view those primary functions in which the essential nature of the state is to be found.*[77]

By implication, Salmond recognized that the secondary functions assumed by the state had rendered it less distinct.

Secondly, in response to overriding social goals, hybrid institutional forms increased in importance in England,[78] as they did in France.

---

[73] See I. Berlin, 'Two Concepts of Liberty' in A. Quinton (ed.), *Political Philosophy* (London, 1967), 141–52.

[74] See Cane, n. 62 above, 57–61.

[75] M. Hill, n. 8 above, 29–44, especially at 44; Craig, *Administrative Law*, n. 8 above, 51–3.

[76] Salmond, n. 67 above, 184.   [77] *Ibid.* 185, 190–1 (emphasis added).

[78] W. Friedmann, 'The Public Corporation in Great Britain' in W. Friedmann (ed.), *The Public Corporation: A Comparative Symposium* (London, 1954), 162–89; W. Friedmann and J. F. Garner (eds.), *Government Enterprise: A Comparative Study* (London, 1970); A. Barker (ed.), *Quangos in Britain: Government and the Networks of Public Policy-Making* (London, 1982); I. Harden and N. Lewis, *The Noble Lie: The British Constitution and the Rule of Law* (London, 1986), 56–62, 153–87; N. Lewis, 'Regulating Non-government Bodies: Privatisation, Accountability, and the Public–Private Divide' in J. Jowell and D. Oliver (eds.), *The*

84   *A Continental Distinction in the Common Law*

Public corporations, resulting from the nationalization of industries, such as the Port of London Authority (1908) and the Central Electricity Board (1926), proliferated, as did QUANGOs (quasi-autonomous non-governmental organizations),[79] such as the Independent Television Authority (1954) and National Economic Development Council (1962). Especially after the Second World War, the number of public corporations increased as a result of various nationalizing statutes, such as the Coal Industry Nationalisation Act 1946, the Gas Act 1948, and the Iron and Steel Act 1949. In 1965, Mitchell recognized the problem posed by hybrid institutions for the conceptualization of the state administration: '[t]he "administration" does not exist. Instead the law contemplates two things: "the crown"—which is very broadly the central government, and other public authorities—largely local authorities with *public corporations existing in an uncanny half-world*.'[80] The relationship of these public corporations to central government has remained uncertain. Supposedly autonomous in day-to-day administration but subject to ministerial determination of overall policy, they have been caught between commercial and central-governmental pressures, between the demands of private enterprise and those of an ill-defined public interest.[81]

The hybridity of another category of institutions and the concomitant conceptual problems are evident in the contradictory, changing, and qualified references to government in the terminology[82] used to describe them. 'QUANGOs' has been used to refer to organizations which are 'non-governmental' but only 'quasi-autonomous'. The more recent 'NDPBs' (non-departmental public bodies) avoids any reference to government but is still only a negative conceptualization. And the term 'fringe organizations' is further subdivided by Craig into 'quasi-governmental organisations' and 'quasi non-governmental organisation[s]'.[83] Because of the difficulties in classifying QUANGOs and public corporations, Cane has recognized the inadequacy and indeter-

Changing Constitution (2nd edn., Oxford, 1989), 219–45; P. Birkinshaw, I. Harden, and N. Lewis, *Government by Moonlight: The Hybrid Parts of the State* (London, 1990).

[79] See, e.g., A. Shonfield, *Modern Capitalism: The Changing Balance of Public and Private Power* (London, 1965), 151–75.

[80] Mitchell, n. 64 above, 113 (emphasis added).

[81] Craig, *Administrative Law*, n. 8 above, 85–6.

[82] See generally A. Barker, 'Governmental Bodies and the Networks of Mutual Accountability' in A. Barker (ed.), n. 78 above, 3–33 at 3–5; *id.*, App., *ibid.* 219–31; C. Hood, 'Governmental Bodies and Government Growth', *ibid.* 44–68 at 51–7.

[83] Craig, *Administrative Law*, n. 8 above, 72–3.

minacy of institutional and functional criteria and concluded that 'no sharp distinction can be drawn between public and private'.[84]

The cases defying classification are not restricted to public corporations and QUANGOs. Apart from trade unions, mixed enterprises, pressure groups,[85] and professional associations, huge industrial corporations have developed through the course of this century: '(I)mportant changes have taken place since the late nineteenth century in the structure of British industry. The revolution in technology has encouraged the emergence of very large, highly capitalized firms; and the internal growth of industrial firms, together with mergers and acquisitions, has resulted in a substantial degree of concentration in many sectors of industry.'[86] Huge industrial corporations have approximated to administrative agencies in various respects. They have acquired a bureaucratic control over their own employees. Their employment and pricing decisions may have a widespread effect on the national economy and the public at large. Their standardized contracts, facilitated by disparities in bargaining power, may have a dimension of generality and a detrimental effect (e.g. by limiting liability) comparable to that of executive regulations. The managers of corporations, like administrators, are supposed to act on behalf of others, and the corporation itself may even, to a certain extent, develop a 'corporate conscience', a consciousness 'of its public functions, its social responsibilities, and of the force of public opinion'.[87] In the light of the role of big corporations and other groups, Friedman struggled to distinguish the state and stressed 'the blurring of the traditional distinctions between public authority and private power'.[88]

Thirdly, central governmental processes adapted to the increasing importance of corporations and to the enhanced potential of greater governmental wealth. From about the 1930s onwards and especially in the 1960s and 1970s, central government used its bargaining and contractual powers to achieve extraneous policy objectives, for example, to enforce a pay policy in the fight against inflation and a 'Buy British'

---

[84] P. Cane, *An Introduction to Administrative Law* (Oxford, 1986), 6–8, especially at 8.

[85] T. C. Daintith, 'The Mixed Enterprise in the United Kingdom' in Friedmann and Garner (eds.), n. 78 above, 53–78. See 'Pressure Politics' *The Economist*, 30 May 1992, 36.

[86] C. Turpin, *Government Contracts* (Harmondsworth, 1972), 261. See generally J. K. Galbraith, *The New Industrial State* (London, 1972).

[87] W. Friedmann, *Law in a Changing Society* (2nd edn., London, 1972), 329–30.

[88] *Ibid.* 119–60, 312–72, especially at 366. See also H. Collins, *Justice in Dismissal: The Law of Termination of Employment* (Oxford, 1992), especially at 271–2.

policy in the exploitation of North-Sea Oil.[89] Daintith identifies a general shift from governmental use of *imperium*, the power to pass prohibitive and authorizing statutes, to the use of its *dominium* or wealth to secure its policy objectives.[90] Interpenetration of public and private was the result:

Most important is the way in which discussion of government contracting concentrates our minds on the whole division between public and private bodies. Private institutions become involved in making decisions which have public impact. The government both plays an increasing role as manufacturer in its own right and becomes more reliant upon a private enterprise to carry out its policies.[91]

Because of the increasing use of contractual powers, in Turpin's first edition of *Government Contracts* (1972), he described the 'New Partnership', 'a much closer relationship of mutual dependence' involving continuing consultation and co-operation in planning and research between central government and big industry to secure the most efficient and productive use of resources.[92] Although Turpin denied a blurring of public and private sectors comparable to that in the USA, his concept of partnership with its implicit notion of partners equal in important respects, together with his description of the public functions devolved to corporations and their public importance,[93] suggest the increasing indistinctness of the state administration.

In trying to clarify the state administration's distinctness despite its extended functions, the proliferation of hybrid institutions, and governmental use of its contractual and bargaining powers, academics and practising lawyers have not been assisted by theories of corporatism. Those theories have not only generally failed to clarify the specificity of the state in various countries[94] but have also explicitly denied its distinctness and recognized its amorphousness.[95] Under the influence of

---

[89] Turpin, n. 86 above, 244–65; T. C. Daintith, 'The Executive Power Today: Bargaining and Economic Control' in Jowell and Oliver (eds.), n. 78 above, 193–218. Cf. generally J. Jowell, 'The Limits of Law in Urban Planning' [1977] *CLP* 63–83 at 70–4.

[90] Daintith in Jowell and Oliver (eds.), n. 78 above. See generally P. P. Craig, *Public Law and Democracy in the United Kingdom and the United States of America* (Oxford, 1990), 187 ff.

[91] Craig, *Administrative Law*, n. 8 above, 94.

[92] Turpin, n. 86 above, 260–5, especially at 260, 261. Cf. C. Turpin, *Government Procurement and Contracts* (2nd edn., Harlow, 1989), 257–67.

[93] Turpin, *Government Contracts*, n. 86 above, 263–5.

[94] P. Birnbaum, *States and Collective Action: The European Experience* (Cambridge, 1988), 107–16.

[95] See, e.g., Birkinshaw, Harden, and Lewis, n. 78 above, especially at 7–12, 224–7.

welfare-corporatist theories, Unger declared: '[t]he spearhead of corporatism is the effacement both in organization and in consciousness of the boundary between state and society, and therefore between the public and the private realm. As the state reaches into society, society itself generates institutions that rival the state in their power and take on many attributes formerly associated with public bodies.'[96]

The state has often been referred to as a Trojan horse brought into the midst of unsuspecting English society during the reign of *laissez-faire* economic theory in the nineteenth century.[97] The metaphor, however, is a particularly apt indication of legal recognition of the state through the course of this century. When the state began to attract the attention of academic and practising lawyers, it was especially alien. Not only was it unfamiliar to lawyers unaccustomed to theorizing about the state, but it was no longer distinct. Emerging from the Trojan horse into the midst of the unsuspecting English legal community was a mixed battalion of civil servants and corporate managers.

Implications for an English Distinction

The emerging theory of the state and its administration affected the justification of public law and the application of the distinction between public and private law. Its effect on the distinction's workability was twofold. First, in stressing the desirability of extended administration, the emerging theory downplayed administrative qualities of potential irresponsibility and abusiveness or at least did not elevate them to justify legal controls. Jennings, for example, advocated that administrative law facilitate rather than control administrative action: '[t]he task of the lawyer as such is not to declare that modern interventionism is pernicious, but, seeing that all modern States have adopted the policy, to advise as to the technical devices which are necessary to make the policy efficient and to provide justice for individuals.'[98] In his *Parliamentary Government in England* Laski expressed a distrust in legal controls. He emphasized parliamentary controls and citizen participation through advisory committees rather than law as answers to administrative

[96] R. M. Unger, *Law in Modern Society: Toward a Criticism of Social Theory* (New York, 1976), 192–3, 200–3, especially at 200–1. See also R. M. Unger, *Knowledge and Politics* (New York, 1975), 174–6; A. Asaro, 'The Public/Private Distinction in American Liberal Thought: Unger's Critique and Synthesis' (1983) 28 *Am. J Juris* 118–48.

[97] See, e.g., M. Hill, n. 8 above, 25–9, especially at 26; Harlow and Rawlings, n. 8 above, 8.

[98] W. I. Jennings, 'Courts and Administrative Law—The Experience of English Housing Legislation' (1936) 49 *Harv. LRev.* 426–54 at 430.

problems.[99] Because of such changes in emphasis, theorists of corporatism have described a shift away from legalism at least as traditionally understood.[100] The overall impact of this shift was to leave
administrative disputes beyond law rather than subject them to a separate body of law.

Furthermore, practising and academic lawyers who did continue to
stress the need for legal controls contributed to create overall confusion
and uncertainty about the appropriate response to administrative disputes. Contradictory commands to the administration—'[s]top, go,
amber'—accompanied contradictory red- and green-light theories of
judicial review.[101] If the emerging theory of the state administration
did not preclude a distinction between public *law* and private *law*, it
did not justify its application by establishing a clear justification for special legal consequences in administrative disputes.

Secondly, the emerging theory of the state did not clarify the distinctness of the state administration and so enable administrative disputes, and accordingly, their legal consequences to be distinguished.
Already in the first decade of this century, Salmond was struggling to
distinguish public from private law because of the extended functions
of the state:

In many of its actions and relations the state stands on the same level as its
subjects, and submits itself to the ordinary principles of private law. It owns
land and chattels, makes contracts, employs agents, and servants, and enters
into various forms of commercial undertaking; and in respect of all these matters it differs little in its juridical position from its subjects. Public law, therefore, is not the *whole* of the law that is applicable to the state and to its relations
with its subjects, but only those parts of it which are different from the private
law concerning the subjects of the state and their relations to each other.[102]

In this passage, Salmond offers no applicable criterion to distinguish
public from private law. He merely defines public law as an indefinite
residue—the law applicable to the state that differs from private law.

Later writers such as Jennings, Friedmann, and Mitchell experi-

---

[99] See, e.g., H. J. Laski, *Parliamentary Government in England: A Commentary* (London,
1938), 147–50, 211–12, 344–50, 360–87. Cf. Laski, 'The Responsibility of the State in
England', n. 37 above; W. B. Gwyn, 'The Labour Party and the Threat of Bureaucracy'
[1971] *Pol. Stud.* 383–402, especially at 389.

[100] See, e.g., Unger, *Law in Modern Society*, n. 96 above, 192–200; Jowell, n. 89 above,
77–8; Harlow and Rawlings, n. 8 above, 50–1.

[101] Harlow and Rawlings, n. 8 above, 1–59, especially at 47. Cf. generally the categories recently developed by M. Loughlin, *Public Law and Political Theory* (Oxford, 1992).

[102] Salmond, n. 67 above, 484–5. See also Paton, n. 45 above, 328–9.

enced similar difficulties and were similarly imprecise. Jennings defined administrative law as follows:

Administrative law is the law relating to the Administration. It determines the organisation, powers, and duties of administrative authorities. Where the political organisation of the country is highly developed, as it is in England, administrative law is a large and important branch of the law. It includes the law relating to the civil service, local government law, the law relating to nationalised industries, and the legal powers which these authorities exercise. Or, looking at the subject from the functional instead of the institutional point of view, we may say that it includes the law relating to public health, the law of highways, the law of social insurance, the law of education, and the law relating to the provision of gas, water, and electricity. These are examples only, for a list of the powers of the administrative authorities would occupy a long catalogue.[103]

Here, Jennings defines administrative law by reference to administrative authorities or powers, but does not define either administrative authorities or powers, and merely illustrates both with examples. Friedmann supported an institutional distinction between public and private law but stressed that 'the borderlines . . . between public and private law . . . are shifting'[104] and acknowledged that the Continental distinction hindered the legal assimilation of public corporations with their blend of public- and private-law elements.[105] Mitchell supported both an institutional and a substantive legal distinction, but recognized problems. He stressed the difficulty of distinguishing administrative from private contracts[106] and described the 'uncanny half-world' of public corporations as partly responsible for obstructing the development of a system of public law.[107]

Enlightened by the French experience of struggling to establish criteria with which to distinguish consistently between public- and private-law disputes, a number of English academics expressed reservations about the distinction or about attributing to it institutional consequences.[108] Carol Harlow was mindful of the French experience

---

[103] W. I. Jennings *The Law and the Constitution* (5th edn., London, 1959), 217.

[104] Friedmann, *Law in a Changing Society*, n. 87 above, 432–37, especially at 431.

[105] In Friedmann and Garner (eds.), n. 78 above, 322–5.

[106] J. D. B. Mitchell, *The Contracts of Public Authorities: A Comparative Survey* (London, 1954), 224–6.

[107] J. D. B. Mitchell, 'Causes and Effects of the Absence of a System of Public Law', n. 64 above, 113–15, especially at 113. See generally M. Loughlin, 'Sitting on a Fence at Carter Bar: In Praise of J. D. B. Mitchell' (1991) 36 *Juridical Review* 135–53.

[108] See, e.g., C. J. Hamson, *Executive Discretion and Judicial Control: An Aspect of the French Conseil d'Etat* (London, 1954), 87–8; J. F. Garner, 'Public Law and Private Law' [1978] *PL* 230–8.

when she responded to Mitchell's and Friedman's advocacy of a distinction between public and private law.[109] She rejected an institutional distinction as the occasion for 'sterile jurisdictional litigation'.[110] She explained the insufficiency of organic distinguishing criteria and the 'vagueness and imprecision' of functional criteria by reference to the modern state:

> The structure of the modern state is such that public and private industry, autonomous statutory bodies, regional boards and central government departments all jostle for place. They carry on identical functions which are allocated in a haphazard fashion. Some, like the Post Office, are transmogrified from departments of state to autonomous bodies overnight, yet carry out the same task and retain the same privileges. No activity is typically governmental in character nor wholly without parallels in private law. Even the most characteristic function may be delegated—as when the law and order function is exercised by private armies levied by Securicor, a private service employed on occasion by government agencies.[111]

Harlow quoted with approval theorists who describe the distinction as increasingly inappropriate or merely rhetorical in the modern state.[112] She concluded by warning against adopting 'an outmoded distinction at the very moment when our continental neighbours are questioning its validity and usefulness'.[113]

Judicial Attempts to Apply the Procedural Distinction

Order 53 and *O'Reilly* v. *Mackman*, which introduced a procedural distinction[114] regardless of warnings such as Harlow's, did not clearly indicate the circumstances in which the AJR would be required or available. Order 53 ruled that the court have regard to the uncertain ambit[115] of the prerogative remedies and 'all the circumstances of the case'.[116] Lord Diplock in *O'Reilly* did not elaborate on a distinguishing

---

[109] C. Harlow, ' "Public" and "Private" Law: Definition without Distinction' (1980) 43 *MLR* 241–65.

[110] *Ibid.* 250.   [111] *Ibid.* 556, 257.

[112] *Ibid.* 257–8. See D. Kennedy, 'The Stages of the Decline of the Public/Private Distinction' (1982) 130 *Univ. Penn. LRev.* 1349–57; Tay and Kamenka, n. 20 above. Cf. Unger, *Law in Modern Society*, n. 96 above, 200–3; M. J. Horwitz, 'The History of the Public/Private Distinction' (1982) 130 *Univ. Penn. LRev.* 1423–8.

[113] Harlow, n. 109 above, 265.

[114] See above, 25; *O'Reilly* v. *Mackman* [1982] 3 All ER 680 (CA), 1124 (HL).

[115] Craig, *Administrative Law*, n. 8 above, 385–7, 419–20. See, e.g., *R.* v. *Electricity Commissioners, ex p. London Electricity Joint Committee Co (1920) Ltd* [1924] 1 KB 171; *R.* v. *Criminal Injuries Compensation Board, ex p. Lain* [1967] 2 QB 864 at 882AB.

[116] RSC, O. 53, r.1(2).

criterion. He simply laid down the general rule that it would 'be contrary to public policy, and as such an abuse of the process of the court,
to permit a person seeking to establish that a decision of a public
authority infringed rights to which he was entitled to protection under
public law to proceed by way of an ordinary action'.[117] He did not
clarify the meaning either of 'public authority' or of 'rights protected
by public law'.[118]

Unassisted by clear guidelines for determining the availability or
necessity of an AJR, the English courts have resorted to two general
approaches both of which are proving problematic.

Their first approach is formalistic. The courts focus upon the source
of the authority's power or upon the source or apparent nature of the
individual litigant's right. In other words, they consider whether the
source of power is statutory or contractual or whether the individual
litigant seeks to uphold a contractual or other private-law right.[119] In
cases involving national sporting associations,[120] the courts have been
preoccupied with source of power. In the leading case of *Law* v. *National
Greyhound Racing Club Ltd*, the Court of Appeal held that the contractual source of the Club's powers would have precluded a challenge by
way of AJR.[121] In subsequent cases, the District Court suggested dissatisfaction but followed the binding authority of *Law's case*.[122] Then,
in *R.* v. *Jockey Club, ex p. Aga Khan*, the majority of the Court of Appeal
confirmed that the Jockey Club was not amenable to judicial review
where 'the powers which the Jockey Club exercises over those who . . .
agree to be bound by the Rules of Racing derive from the agreement
of the parties'.[123]

---

[117] N. 114 above, at 1134E.

[118] *Ibid.* 1134E,D. See also *ibid.* 1126H–7A, 1130BC, 1129J.

[119] See, e.g., *R.* v. *BBC, ex p. Lavelle* [1983] 1 WLR 23; *Davy* v. *Spelthorne BC* [1983] 3
All ER 278; *Roy* v. *Kensington and Chelsea and Westminster Family Practitioner Committee* [1992]
2 WLR 239; *R.* v. *Lloyd's of London, ex p. Briggs and Others* (1993) 5 *Admin. LR* 698. On *Roy*,
see P. Cane, 'Private Rights and Public Procedure' [1992] *PL* 193–200; S. Fredman and
G. Morris 'A Snake or a Ladder? *O'Reilly* v. *Mackman* Reconsidered' (1992) 108 *LQR*
353–7.

[120] See generally M. J. Beloff, 'Pitch, Pool, Rink, . . . Court? Judicial Review in the
Sporting World' [1989] *PL* 95–110; D. Pannick, 'Who is Subject to Judicial Review in
Respect of What?' [1992] *PL* 1–7.

[121] [1983] 1 WLR 1302.

[122] *R.* v. *Jockey Club ex p. Massingberd-Mundy* [1993] 2 All ER 207, especially at 219EF,
222A–3B; *R.* v. *Jockey Club, ex p. RAM Racecourses* [1993] 2 All ER 225, especially at 244D,
245F, 248EF. Cf. *R.* v. *Football Association, ex p. Football League* [1993] 2 All ER 833, especially at 849B–C.

[123] [1993] 1 WLR 909 at 924C. See also *ibid.* 929G-30D. Cf. *ibid.* 932FG. See generally N. Bamforth, 'The Scope of Judicial Review: Still Uncertain' [1993] *PL* 239–48.

The desirability of a formalistic preoccupation with source of power is questionable. The source of an authority's power may bear little relation to its extent or public importance.[124] In *Aga Khan*, all the judges recognized the immense or monopolistic powers of the Jockey Club.[125] Sir Thomas Bingham MR and Farquharson LJ also recognized that 'if the applicant wished to race his horses in this country he had no choice but to submit to the club's jurisdiction'.[126] The Master of the Rolls nevertheless[127] concluded that the relevant powers of the Jockey Club 'derive from the agreement of the parties and give rise to private rights on which effective action for a declaration, an injunction and damages can be based without resort to judicial review'.[128] His conclusion on the effectiveness of a private-law action, however, is undermined by his recognition of the applicant's limited choice. Because the applicant could only race by contracting with the Jockey Club, his contractual private-law action was not complemented by the controls of a market, the constraints imposed on the Jockey Club by the possibility that its members or potential members would contract with another club. The criterion of the majority of the court in *Aga Khan*—a contractual source of power—does not indicate those cases in which judicial review is rendered superfluous by an adequate alternative.

The formalistic preoccupation with private-law right is also problematic. The conception of a private-law right cannot be treated as self-evident. In *Cocks* v. *Thanet District Council*, the House of Lords determined that a council's decision whether a person is homeless so as to be entitled to housing as a homeless person must be challenged by an AJR because the decision only affects 'a necessary condition precedent to the statutory private law right' and not a private-law right itself.[129] The House's distinction which it has reiterated[130] is artificial and difficult to comprehend. Wade commented: '[t]he difficulty in this case is to understand how a single statutory duty (to provide housing in certain circumstances) can be dichotomized into both public and

---

[124] See, e.g., *Law*, n. 121 above, 1311G; *Massingberd-Mundy*, n. 122 above, 222F; *RAM Racecourses*, n. 122 above, 243GH; *Football League*, n. 122 above, 848H, 850C.

[125] N. 123 above, 918I–9A, 923G, 928B, 930H–1A.

[126] *Ibid.* 928H. See also 924B and 930D.

[127] Cf. *R.* v. *Panel on Take-overs and Mergers, ex p. Datafin Plc* [1987] QB 815 at 846A.

[128] N. 123 above, 924C–D.

[129] [1983] 2 AC 286 at 294EF. See also *Ettridge* v. *Morrell* (1986) 85 LGR 100 at 106–7; *Cato* v. *MAFF* [1989] 3 CMLR 513, para. 36.

[130] *Roy*, n. 119 above, 263H–264D.

private law'.[131] In *Wandsworth London Borough Council* v. *Winder*, the House of Lords distinguished *Cocks* v. *Thanet District Council* by reference to Winder's 'pre-existing private law right' and determined that Winder could challenge a council resolution raising rent by way of a defence in ordinary proceedings.[132] Lord Woolf criticizes the decision: '[i]t could be said that Winder had no private law right. All that he had was the same right, as had other members of the public in the locality, to challenge the resolution of the local authority to increase the rents.'[133] Lord Woolf further criticizes the decision for negating the procedural protections for public authorities. Indeed, the House's conception of private-law right does not indicate disputes in which the procedural protections of an AJR are unnecessary. The House of Lords recognized the importance of procedural protections to Wandsworth LBC but held that 'the arguments for protecting public authorities' were outweighed by 'the arguments for preserving the ordinary rights of private citizens to defend themselves against unfounded claims'.[134] Through its formalistic preoccupation with private-law right, the House negated what Lord Diplock identified[135] as the central purpose of the process of judicial review.

An ill-defined criterion is open to manipulation. In *Roy*, the House of Lords accepted that an NHS doctor had 'either a contractual or statutory private law right to his remuneration' although his terms of service were statutory.[136] Lord Lowry ruled that private-law rights were in issue 'almost inevitab[ly]' as a result of the 'contractual echoes in the relationship' between a general practitioner and his family practitioner committee.[137] His Lordship does not seem to require that the contractual echoes be loud. After a passing reference to the 'contractual overtones' of the expression 'terms of service' in the statutory scheme, he recognized that 'the discretion which the scheme confers

---

[131] H. W. R. Wade, *Administrative Law* (6th edn., Oxford, 1988), 682. See also Wade and Forsyth, n. 29 above, 686–7; *An Bord Bainne Co-operative Ltd. (Irish Dairy Board)* v. *Milk Marketing Board* [1984] 2 CMLR 584, paras. 13 and 15; *Mohram Ali* v. *Tower Hamlets LBC* [1992] 3 WLR 208, especially at 214F–G.

[132] [1985] AC 461, especially at 508F, 510D–F.

[133] H. Woolf, 'Public Law–Private Law: Why the Divide? A Personal View' [1986] *PL* 220–38 at 233–5, especially at 234. Cf. J. Beatson, ' "Public" and "Private" in English Administrative Law' (1987) 103 *LQR* 34–65 at 59–61; Allan, *Law, Liberty, and Justice*, n. 53 above, 127–30.

[134] N. 132 above, 508H–9D.   [135] *O'Reilly* v. *Mackman*, n. 114 above.

[136] N. 119 above, at 265B. See also *Ettridge* v. *Morrell*, n. 129 above, 106.

[137] N. 119 above, 261B. See Cane, 'Private Rights and Public Procedure', n. 119 above, 197.

on the committee is not typically characteristic of a contractual relationship'.[138] In the light of *Roy*, the Law Commission has rightly suggested that the 'present trend is towards limiting insistence on use of Order 53 to claims raising issues solely of public law'.[139] Some or other private-law element, however small, seems sufficient to circumvent an AJR and its procedural protections for public authorities. The criterion of private-law right is close to vanishing. In the absence of a clear alternative, 'uncertainty and the potential for continuing litigation' continues.[140]

The second general approach of the courts is to determine the availability of judicial review by surveying various aspects of a case and deciding whether a public duty, governmental interest, or sufficient public element is involved. In *Datafin*, for example, the Court of Appeal rejected any single test of jurisdiction and considered various circumstances suggesting the 'giant's strength' of the Panel on Take-overs and Mergers.[141] The Court of Appeal held that the Panel is susceptible to judicial review because, although its powers do not have a statutory or prerogative origin, it is performing a 'public duty' or 'exercising public law functions'.[142]

This second approach, however, is problematic because it does not clarify the crucial aspects which distinguish one case from another. References to public duty, public-law functions, governmental interest, or sufficient public element or issue either beg the question or are conclusory.[143] The position of Walsh, a senior nurse employed by a Health Authority on contractual terms incorporating the agreement negotiated by the Whitley Council,[144] becomes difficult to distinguish from the

---

[138] N. 119 above, 261C.

[139] *Administrative Law: Judicial Review and Statutory Appeals* (consultation paper 126, 1993), para. 3.23. Cf. Law Commission, *Administrative Law: Judicial Review and Statutory Appeals* (Law Com. 226, 1994), HC 669, para. 3.15. See also, e.g., *Lonrho plc* v. *Tebbit* [1992] 4 All ER 280.

[140] Law Commission, *Administrative Law* (consultation paper), n. 139 above, para. 3.23.

[141] N. 127 above, at 845F.

[142] 838F, 847C–D, 848G–H, 852C–D. See also *R.* v. *Advertising Standards Authority, ex p. the Insurance Service plc* (1990) 2 *Admin. LR* 77; *R.* v. *Code of Practice Committee of the British Pharmaceutical Industry, ex p. Professional Counselling Aids Ltd* (1991) 3 *Admin. LR* 697. See generally C. Forsyth, 'The Scope of Judicial Review: "Public Duty" not "Source of Power" ' [1987] *PL* 356–67.

[143] See Craig, *Administrative Law*, n. 8 above, 420–1.

[144] See *R.* v. *East Berkshire Health Authority, ex p. Walsh* [1985] QB 152. Cf. *R.* v. *Civil Service Appeal Board, ex p. Bruce* [1988] 3 All ER 686; *R.* v. *Derbyshire CC, ex p. Noble* [1990] IRLR 332. See generally B. A. Walsh, 'Judicial Review of Dismissal from Employment: Coherence or Confusion?' [1989] *PL* 131–55.

position of Benwell, a prison officer disciplined under a statutory code.[145] And the position of Benwell becomes difficult to distinguish from the position of Nangle, a civil servant in the Lord Chancellor's Department and subject to its internal disciplinary proceedings of an 'informal' and 'domestic nature'.[146] Accordingly, the decisions that the AJR be unavailable to Walsh and Nangle but available to Benwell become difficult to defend.

In cases involving self-regulatory bodies, the courts have tried to facilitate their survey of circumstances with a hypothetical test. They have tried to determine the governmental interest by asking whether Parliament would have created a regulatory body if the self-regulatory body did not exist. In *Aga Khan*, this test was unhelpful, the attempts to apply it, tentative and contradictory. Whereas Sir Thomas Bingham MR accepted that a regulatory body would be established if the Jockey Club did not exist, Farquharson LJ and Hoffmann LJ found no evidence of that likelihood.[147] Furthermore, because the courts have not related the test to a clear and justified criterion, the question remains: '[w]hy should the jurisdiction of the court depend on a hypothesis as to what Parliament would do but for the existence of the body in question?'[148] Whether the courts have applied a distinguishing criterion or surveyed the circumstances with the help of their hypothetical test, their decisions on the procedural distinction have remained unconvincing.

Dissatisfaction and Debate

Judicial attempts to apply the procedural distinction have provoked extensive criticism. Academics such as Wade, Cane, and Craig have drawn attention to the wasted litigation, arbitrary distinctions, and inadequacy of distinguishing criteria.[149] Even Lord Woolf, who

---

[145] See *R.* v. *Home Secretary, ex p. Benwell* [1985] QB 554. On *Benwell*, see Y. Cripps, 'Dismissal, Jurisdiction and Judicial Review' (1985) 44 *CLJ* 177–80. Cf. *McClaren* v. *Home Office* [1990] ICR 824; *R.* v. *Home Secretary ex p. Attard* (1990) 2 *Admin. LR* 641. See generally S. Fredman and G. Morris, 'Public or Private? State Employees and Judicial Review' (1991) 107 *LQR* 298–316, especially at 305–8.

[146] See *R.* v. *Lord Chancellor's Department, ex p. Nangle* [1991] IRLR 343 at 348; S. Fredman and G. Morris, 'Judicial Review and Civil Servants: Contracts of Employment Declared to Exist' [1991] *PL* 485–90.

[147] N. 123 above, 923G, 930B, 932B. Cf. *R.* v. *Chief Rabbi, ex p. Wachmann* [1992] 1 WLR 1036 at 1041I–2A; *Football League*, n. 122 above, 848J.

[148] Pannick, n. 120 above, 5–6.

[149] H. W. R. Wade, 'Procedure and Prerogative in Public Law' (1985) 101 *LQR* 180–99; *id.* and Forsyth, n. 29 above, 680–95; P. Cane, 'Standing, Legality and the Limits of Public Law' [1981] *PL* 322–39; *id.*, 'Public Law and Private Law Again: *Davy*

defends *O'Reilly* and the distinction between public and private law, accepts the damning analogy of the progress of the courts to a game of snake and ladders.[150] Academics have generally criticized the procedural dichotomy and advocated the full or partial assimilation of public-law procedure to private-law procedure. Wade and Forsyth, for example, blame the dichotomy for 'a great deal of fruitless litigation' and continuing uncertainty 'as to the boundary between public and private law, since these terms have no clear or settled meaning'.[151] They recommend the replacement of the dichotomy of procedures with a single procedure—the ordinary procedure of private law—possibly modified only on the application of the relevant authority.[152]

The courts seem to be responding to the extensive criticism. Wade and Forsyth argue that the varying reasons given by the House of Lords for allowing Mrs Gillick to bring ordinary proceedings against a government department suggest that the House is 'disinclined to press the logic of *O'Reilly* to its limit'.[153] In *Roy*, the House was similarly disinclined. Lord Lowry concluded that 'unless the procedure adopted by the moving party is ill suited to dispose of the question at issue, . . . a court having jurisdiction ought to let a case be heard rather than entertain a debate concerning the form of the proceedings'.[154] And, in a recent article, Lord Woolf praised the 'judicial ingenuity' displayed by the Court of Appeal in *Foster* and stressed 'the responsibility of the courts to chip away at the grey area (whether a case is a public-law case) by successive decisions'.[155] The prevailing judicial pragmatism seems to be motivated by a faith in procedural ingenuity and incre-

---

v. *Spelthorne Borough Council* [1983] 3 WLR 742 (HL)' [1984] *PL* 16–22; *id.*, *An Introduction to Administrative Law* (2nd edn., Oxford, 1992), 88–104; Craig, *Administrative Law*, n. 8 above, 410–26. See also Fredman and Morris, 'Public or Private?', n. 145 above; Collins, n. 88 above, 128–32, 140.

[150] Woolf, n. 133 above, 227–8.

[151] Wade and Forsyth, n. 29 above, 682. See also *Doyle* v. *Northumbria Probation Committee* [1991] 1 WLR 1340 at 1347H–8B.

[152] Wade and Forsyth, n. 29 above, 684–6.

[153] *Ibid.* 687–8; *Gillick* v. *West Norfolk and Wisbech AHA* [1986] AC 112 at 163E–F, 177F–8G. See J. A. Jolowicz, 'Justiciable Questions are Justiciable after All' (1986) 45 *CLJ* 1–3.

[154] *Roy*, n. 119 above, 266B. See also *ibid.* 258H, 265A; Lord Bridge's judgment at 241F–H.

[155] H. Woolf, 'Judicial Review: A Possible Programme for Reform' [1992] *PL* 221–37 at 232; *Chief Adjudication Officer* v. *Foster* [1992] 1 QB 31 at 49E–50E, 56E, 60G (CA), [1993] 1 All ER 705.

mental clarification. Such defensive pragmatism is facilitated[156] and indeed required by the flexibility of the statutory criteria, the open-ended exceptions recognized in *O'Reilly*, Lord Diplock's ambivalent appreciation that the AJR both removed procedural disadvantages and incorporated procedural protections, and the general uncertainty about the approach to applying the distinction.

The adequacy of judicial pragmatism, however, depends upon the scope of the problem facing the courts. Jolowicz attributes 'the complications and difficulties to which the procedural dichotomy gives rise' to its incongruity in contemporary society:

> It [the technique of the procedural dichotomy] . . ., by implication, holds that decisions which are not 'administrative', that is, which are not decisions of public authorities, have little or nothing in common with administrative decisions, however important and however wide-spread their consequences may be. That might have been satisfactory in the past, on the hypothesis that society consists of the state, on the one hand, and of individuals on the other, with all power centred in the state. That this simplistic view bears little relation to contemporary society, however, needs no demonstration.[157]

Indeed, the disputes provoking litigation and posing difficult classificatory problems for the courts have generally related either to the state's extended functions,[158] such as the provision of housing and health services, or to the hybrid institutions[159] of modern society, such as the BBC, national sporting associations, and the Panel of Takeovers and Mergers.

---

[156] See *O'Reilly*, n. 114 above, 696F, 1134F–G; A. Denning, *The Closing Chapter* (London, 1983), 122–5. Cf. generally D. Feldman, 'Public Law Values in the House of Lords' (1990) 106 *LQR* 246–76 at 271–6.

[157] J. A. Jolowicz, 'Civil and Administrative Procedure: National Report for England and Wales' in J. P. Gardner (ed.), *United Kingdom Law in the 1990s: Comparative and Common Law Studies for the XIIIth International Congress of Comparative Law* (London, 1990), 160–75 at 165–6. See also J. A. Jolowicz, 'Civil Proceedings in the Public Interest' [1982] *Cambrian LR* 32–52 at 45–6.

[158] See, e.g., *Cocks*, n. 129 above; *Winder*, n. 132 above; *An Bord Bainne Co-operative Ltd (Irish Dairy Board)*, n. 131 above; *Walsh*, n. 144 above; *R. v. National Coal Board, ex p. National Union of Mineworkers* [1986] ICR 791; *Cato*, n. 129 above; *Roy*, n. 119 above; *Lonrho plc*, n. 139 above; *R. v. British Coal Corporation, ex p. Vardy* [1993] ICR 720.

[159] See, e.g., *R. v. BBC, ex p. Lavelle*, n. 119 above; *Law v. National Greyhound Racing Club Ltd*, n. 121 above; *R. v. Jockey Club, ex p. Aga Khan*, n. 123 above; *R. v. Panel on Takeovers and Mergers, ex p. Datafin Plc*, n. 127 above. See also *R. v. Advertising Standards Authority, ex p. Insurance Service plc*, n. 142 above; *R. v. Code of Practice Committee of the British Pharmaceutical Industry, ex p. Professional Counselling Aids Ltd*, n. 142 above; *R. v. Lloyd's of London, ex p. Briggs and Others*, n. 119 above.

In *Aga Khan*, Hoffmann LJ referred to public and private power in the mixed economy of contemporary society:

All this leaves is the fact that the Jockey Club has power. But the mere fact of power, even over a substantial area of economic activity, is not enough. In a mixed economy, power may be private as well as public. Private power may affect the public interest and the livelihoods of many individuals. But that does not subject it to the rules of public law.[160]

But how to distinguish public from private power is the crucial difficulty. Precisely because what Hoffmann LJ calls 'private power may affect the public interest and the livelihoods of many individuals',[161] it is not clearly private. In *Doyle*, Henry J rightly recognized 'that the circumstances in which there may be . . . a mixture of private and public law claims are infinitely various and can arise in very disparate situations'.[162] The concepts of public and private lack a reality that is clearly conceived and to which they can refer. Because the state administration has been rendered indistinct by its extended functions and hybrid institutions, administrative disputes cannot be clearly identified and their legal consequences determined. Disentangling public and private pragmatically in every case or by developing satisfactory distinguishing criteria seems to have become a task too great for Hercules.

But the English debate about the distinction, provoked by *O'Reilly*, is not one-sided. Despite his criticism of the procedural dichotomy, Cane suggests that 'there are sound reasons for drawing' a distinction between public and private law.[163] He rejects the 'descriptive attack' on the distinction, the argument, such as Harlow's, that the distinction has become incongruous in contemporary society:

The descriptive attack is, however, flawed in a fundamental way. The terms 'public' and 'private' are, in a very important sense, not descriptive terms. To say of some body or activity that it is 'public' or 'private' is not to say that it possesses some 'brute' characteristics but rather that, according to some norm or set of norms, the terms 'public' or 'private' is appropriately applied to that body.[164]

---

[160] N. 123 above, 932I.   [161] *Ibid.*   [162] N. 151 above, 1348A.

[163] Cane, *Introduction to Administrative Law*, n. 84 above, 4.

[164] Cane, 'Public Law and Private Law', n. 62 above, 64–6, especially at 65. For analyses of the distinction with an exemplary normative emphasis, see C. A. Reich, 'The New Property' (1964) 73 *Yale LJ* 733–87; N. E. Simmonds, *The Decline of Juridical Reason: Doctrine and Theory in the Legal Order* (Manchester, 1984), ch. 9.

The terms public and private, however, while not simply referring to 'some "brute" characteristics' are nevertheless still descriptive in a very important sense. Benn and Gaus, cited by Cane as the authority for his argument that the terms public and private are normative, stress that they are also descriptive:

[I]t does not follow from a concept's being normative in the sense specified that it cannot also function descriptively. On the contrary: precisely because 'private' relates to social norms, to describe an object as private implies that it satisfies some, at least, of a bounded set of conditions specified in the norms, without which the normative implications would not hold.[165]

Precisely because the norms[166] specifying the consequences of administrative disputes no longer clearly identify the state administration, the term public law is not fulfilling its descriptive function satisfactorily and the distinction between public and private law is not working.

Cane recognizes the difficulty of distinguishing public and private institutions or functions but suggests that public and private law be distinguished by reference to the relevant reasons for drawing a distinction in particular cases—whether they relate to the extent of government power, access to government information, the separation of powers, or procedural protections for public authorities.[167] Where the underlying reasons, however, refer to concepts like government, governmental functions, or public authorities, the question of distinguishing public from private is begged. And, where they do not, the reasons themselves are determinate and the distinction is merely conclusory. Cane is not defending a determinate distinction between public and private law but illustrating its indeterminacy.

Cane recognizes that what he calls 'developmental individualism' (and 'Diceyan integrationism'), in contrast to 'passive individualism', blurs the distinction between public and private spheres, but he nevertheless denies the importance of his abstract analysis:

I have suggested that different attitudes to the public-private distinction can be related, at a very abstract level, to different accounts of the role of the

[165] S. I. Benn and G. F. Gaus, 'The Public and the Private: Concepts and Action' in Benn and Gaus (eds.), n. 20 above, 3–27 at 12.

[166] Except, possibly, for religious freedom with its relatively established distinction between Church and State: see *Wachmann*, n. 147 above, 1041I–2A, 1042I–3B; *R. v. Imam of Bury Park, ex p. Sulaiman Ali* [1992] COD 132.

[167] Cane, *Introduction to Administrative Law*, n. 149 above, 12–19, 237–40; *id.*, 'Public Law and Private Law', n. 62 above, 64–5, 71–8. See also the Opinion of Van Gerven A.G. in *Foster* v. *British Gas plc* (Case C–188/89) [1990] ECR I–3313 at 3334 (para. 11) and 3339–40 (para. 21).

individual in political life and hence to different accounts of the nature of democracy and the state. But at a more concrete level, attitudes to the distinction are more complex than the abstract analysis can capture.[168]

If abstract and concrete levels of analysis, however, are related, if the indistinctness of the state administration is characteristic of 'developmental individualism' and if political theory shifted away from 'passive individualism', then the distinction must have become increasingly indeterminate as the state administration became increasingly indistinct.

Like Cane, Samuel seeks to defend the distinction.[169] He regards it as a jurisprudential device with which to confer rights upon individuals like Malone[170] in the absence of suitable private-law devices. By advocating the application of substantive public law to corporations,[171] however, his analysis illustrates the difficulty of applying the distinction when the state administration has become less peculiarly powerful. The indistinctness of the state administration renders administrative disputes and, so, their legal consequences—whether procedural, institutional, or substantive—difficult to distinguish.[172] The substantive distinction, like the institutional distinction, falls with the procedural dichotomy.

Legal academics, such as Robson, who advocated or explained the development of English administrative law by reference to the emergence of the modern state, generally ignored the increasing indistinctness of its administration.[173] As legal academics became aware of the state administration, they did not and could not clearly distinguish it. The recent adoption, nonetheless, of a procedural distinction was not a triumph for political theory but a further exposure of judicial ignorance.[174]

[168] Cane, 'Public Law and Private Law', n. 62 above, 57–64, especially at 78.

[169] G. Samuel, 'Public and Private Law: A Private Lawyer's Response' (1983) 46 *MLR* 558–83. Cf. generally Allan, *Law, Liberty, and Justice*, n. 53 above, 125–30.

[170] *Malone*, n. 57 above.

[171] N. 169 above, 574–6. See also H. Woolf, *Protection of the Public—A New Challenge* (London, 1990), 31; D. Pannick, 'What is a Public Authority for the Purposes of Judicial Review?' in J. L. Jowell and D. Oliver (eds.), *New Directions in Judicial Review* (London, 1988), 23–36 at 30–2. Cf. H. W. R. Wade, 'Beyond the Law: A British Innovation in Judicial Review' (1991) 43 *Admin. LRev.* 559–70.

[172] See C. Harlow, *Compensation and Government Torts* (London, 1982), 30–1.

[173] W. A. Robson, *Justice and Administrative Law: A Study of the British Constitution* (3rd edn., London, 1951), 33. See also Shonfield, n. 79 above, 411 ff.; Flogaïtis, n. 9 above, 59–94. Cf. Harden and Lewis, n. 78 above, 188–218; Birkinshaw, Harden, and Lewis, n. 78 above, 274–6.

[174] See generally T. R. S. Allan, 'Pragmatism and Theory in Public Law' (1988) 104 *LQR* 422–47; P. McAuslan, 'Administrative Justice—A Necessary Report?' [1988] *PL* 402–12.

The Distinction's Prospects

The Implications of Privatization

The present task of academic and practising lawyers is doubly difficult. In applying the distinction between public and private law, they must not only overcome a traditional judicial ignorance, but also take account of the developments of the last fifteen years. In particular, they must come to terms with privatization, which has affected the three general manifestations of the increasingly indistinct state described above[175]—the state's extension, hybrid institutional forms, and governmental contracting with industry.

First, statutes, such as the British Aerospace Act 1980 and the Telecommunications Act 1984, have sought to reduce the role of the state, but the state's former role, together with its continuing role chiefly through regulation,[176] contributes to a vague sense that a public function is still being performed by the privatized industry. A commentator in *The Economist* observed: '[m]any of the once-nationalised companies do retain much of the feel of state behemoths'.[177] The contraction of the state administration, like its earlier extension, obscures its distinctness.

Secondly, after initially attempting to reduce the number of hybrid institutions, central government has increased expenditure on them, hived off more governmental functions to quasi-governmental agencies (e.g. the Housing Action Trusts), and created new agencies (e.g. OFTEL and OFGAS) to regulate the privatized industries.[178] Pronouncing the 'death of corporatism', central government abolished the National Economic Development Council,[179] but still relies on numerous other hybrid institutions.

Thirdly, although central government has preferred regulation as the formal corrective to privatization, it has nevertheless continued, in fact, to bargain with the privatized industries[180] and has increasingly

---

[175] At 82 ff.

[176] See generally C. Graham and T. Prosser, *Privatizing Public Enterprises: Constitutions, the State, and Regulation in Comparative Perspective* (Oxford, 1991); C. D. Foster, *Privatization, Public Ownership and the Regulation of Natural Monopoly* (Oxford, 1992).

[177] 27 July 1991, 16.

[178] Lewis in Jowell and Oliver (eds.), n. 78 above, 223–4; R. Baldwin and C. McCrudden, *Regulation and Public Law* (London, 1987), 28–30; Birkinshaw, Harden, and Lewis, n. 78 above.

[179] 16 June 1992.

[180] Lewis in Jowell and Oliver (eds.), n. 78 above, 242–3; Graham and Prosser, n. 176 above, 164 ff.

advocated the 'contracting-out' of service functions.[181] In the second edition of his book on government contracts, Turpin describes how the new emphasis on *'value for money, competition* and *arm's length bargaining'* did not end the close relationship between government and industry:

> Despite the radical changes which have taken place in the aims and procedures of government contracting since 1979, there still exists a 'procurement community' of purchasing departments and their major suppliers, and in some important sectors of government procurement this is a restricted community whose members are locked together in a relationship of interdependence and shared interests. Features of this relationship are a continuous exchange of information, migration of personnel, hard bargaining and search for common ground. The Government concerns itself with the health of supplying industries, with their capacity to deliver what is wanted and to innovate so as to meet future governmental requirements. Industry looks to government for a flow of orders, seeks to resist foreign intrusion, and keeps up the pressure on government for improved levels of profit and more favourable contractual conditions.[182]

The state administration remains at least as indistinct within the procurement community as it was within the earlier partnership. It is unlikely to be rendered more distinct by the development of Majorism. In a speech to the CBI,[183] Prime Minister John Major advocated yet another 'new partnership' between government and industry, again,[184] by implication, a relationship between partners, who are equal in important respects.

In short, privatization has not resulted in a clearly-defined minimal state administration. Lewis rightly concludes his analysis of the effect of privatization as follows: 'there is no clear divide between the public and the private spheres. . . . We should not, in particular, be confused by the labels ordinarily attached to functions as being distinctly private or public.'[185]

The blurring of the public/private divide has continued to blur the distinction between public and private law. Lord Woolf describes the implications of privatization:

> The interests of the public are as capable of being adversely affected by the decisions of large corporations and large associations, be they of employers or

---

[181] See generally I. Harden, *The Contracting State* (Buckingham, 1992).
[182] Turpin, *Government Procurement and Contracts*, n. 92 above, 257–67, especially at 263, 259.
[183] 18 May 1993.   [184] See above, 86.
[185] Lewis in Jowell and Oliver (eds.), n. 78 above, 244–5.

employees, and should they not be subject to challenge on *Wednesbury* grounds if their decision relates to activities which can damage the public interest? . . . Powerful bodies, whether they are public bodies or not, because of their economic muscle may be in a position to take decisions which at the present time are not subject to scrutiny and which could be unfair or adversely affect the public interest.[186]

In a later discussion of *O'Reilly* v. *Mackman*, Lord Woolf stresses that '[i]n the days of privatisation and the creation of non-statutory regulatory bodies it is very important that the courts should not be prevented by a strict definition of what is the boundary of public law from extending supervision of the courts to bodies which otherwise would exercise uncontrolled power'.[187] Sir Gordon Borrie, Director General of Fair Trading, goes further than Lord Woolf:

[S]urely the citizen is concerned that *all* power, public or private, should be conformable with liberty, fair dealing and good administration. . . . As power shifts from the public sector to the private sector, it seems to me desirable that instruments of control and accountability forged to ensure that the public sector behaves itself are considered for appropriate adaptation to the private sector. That is why some convergence between judicial supervision over powerful public bodies and such supervision over powerful private bodies is desirable.[188]

Sir Gordon Borrie praises the extension of judicial review and explicitly calls for 'some convergence' between public and private law,[189] a convergence that had raised the spectre of 'judicial review *ad infinitum*'.[190]

Disagreement about the State

Academic and practising lawyers intent on applying the distinction would look in vain to party politics and political theory for clarification of the state and its administration. Party-political disagreement and uncertainty about the proper role of the state have accompanied privatization. Despite election defeats, the Labour Party has continued to dispute privatization, especially as regards the exploitation of energy resources.[191] The Labour Party's opposition to the government's

[186] Woolf, 'Public Law–Private Law', n. 133 above, 224, 225.
[187] Woolf, *Protection of the Public*, n. 171 above, 26.
[188] G. Borrie, 'The Regulation of Public and Private Power' [1989] *PL* 552–67 at 559, 564. See also D. Oliver, 'Is the *Ultra Vires* Rule the Basis of Judicial Review?' [1987] *PL* 543–69, especially at 565–9.
[189] *Ibid.* 564.   [190] Wade, 'Beyond the Law', n. 171 above, 570.
[191] Cf. Conservative Party, *The Best Future for Britain: The Conservative Manifesto 1992* (London, 1992), 10–11; Labour Party, *Labour's Election Manifesto: It's Time to Get Britain Working Again* (London, 1992), 13.

health reforms has placed the very meaning of privatization in issue. Furthermore, neither the Labour Party nor the Conservative Party has been consistent in its attitude to privatization. For example, before the 1992 General Election, the Labour Party committed itself to allowing British Rail to raise funds in the City through the introduction of leasing schemes.[192] At the same time, the Conservative Party presented the privatized corporations—British Telecom and British Gas—under the rubric of 'Public Services' and the 'Citizen's Charter'.[193]

In academia, the conception of the state and, accordingly, the conception of its administration are no clearer than in party politics. Various political theorists have suggested the demise of the notion of the state,[194] stressed its complexity and contestability,[195] challenged the traditional conception of a private sphere or of the family as private,[196] described increasing disagreement about the state,[197] and even regarded such disagreement as a source of stability.[198] In England, neither party politics nor political theory is, at present, likely to produce the theory of a distinct state administration required for a working distinction between public and private law.

The Judicial Refusal to Reconceive the Crown

The traditional concept of the Crown has long required judicial clarification. In this century, the English courts have attributed to it

---

[192] Labour Party Conference, 1 and 2 Oct. 1991. See Labour Party, n. 191 above, 13.

[193] Conservative Party, n. 191 above, 13–14. See Government White Paper, *The Citizen's Charter: Raising the Standard* (1991), Cmnd. 1599, 28 ff.

[194] Dyson, n. 4 above, 282–7.

[195] See, e.g., Vincent, n. 13 above, 3–4, 42–3, 223–5.

[196] See, e.g., C. Pateman, 'Feminist Critiques of the Public/Private Dichotomy' in Benn and Gaus (eds.), n. 20 above, 281–303; M. D. A. Freeman (ed.), *State, Law, and the Family: Critical Perspectives* (London, 1984); M. D. A. Freeman, 'Towards a Critical Theory of Family Law' (1985) 38 *CLP* 153–85; K. O'Donovan, *Sexual Divisions in Law* (London, 1985); C. A. MacKinnon, 'Feminism, Marxism, Method, and the State: Toward Feminist Jurisprudence' (1983) 8 *Signs* 635–58 at 656–7; F. E. Olsen, 'The Family and the Market: A Study of Ideology and Legal Reform' (1983) 96 *Harv. LRev.* 1497–1578 at 1509–13. Cf. N. Rose, 'Beyond the Public/Private Division: Law, Power and the Family' (1987) 14 *J of Law & Soc.* 61–76.

[197] See, e.g., R. Barker, n. 8 above, 177 ff.

[198] See, e.g., D. Held, 'Power and Legitimacy in Contemporary Britain' in G. McLennan, D. Held, and S. Hall (eds.), *State and Society in Contemporary Britain: A Critical Introduction* (Cambridge, 1984), 299–369; id., *Political Theory and the Modern State: Essays on State, Power and Democracy* (Cambridge, 1989), 79–157. See generally, e.g., J. B. Thompson, *Studies in the Theory of Ideology* (Cambridge, 1984), 61–4, 192–3; R. Cotterrell, *The Sociology of Law: An Introduction* (2nd edn., London, 1992), 291–8.

different meanings in different contexts.[199] That the courts might themselves clarify their concept of the Crown and develop it into a concept of government or the state administration was remotely possible after the decision of the House of Lords in *Town Investments* and before their recent decision in *M* v. *Home Office.*

In *Town Investments*, Lord Diplock distinguished public from private law by reference to a concept of government. He explained that public law 'governs the relationships between Her Majesty acting in her political capacity, the government departments among which the work of Her Majesty's government is distributed, the Ministers of the Crown in charge of the various departments and civil servants of all grades who are employed in those departments'.[200] Lord Diplock suggested that the concept of government replace that of the Crown. He criticized the concept of the Crown as anachronistic:

[T]he vocabulary used by lawyers in the field of public law . . . remains more apt to the constitutional realities of the Tudor or even the Norman monarchy than to the constitutional realities of the 20th century. To use as a metaphor the symbol of royalty, 'the Crown', was no doubt a convenient way of denoting and distinguishing the monarch when doing acts of government in his political capacity from the monarch when doing private acts in his personal capacity, at a period when legislative and executive powers were exercised by him in accordance with his own will. But to continue nowadays to speak of 'the Crown' as doing legislative or executive acts of government, which, in reality as distinct from legal fiction, are decided on and done by human beings other than the Queen herself, involves risk of confusion. . . . Where, as in the instant case, we are concerned with the legal nature of the exercise of executive powers of government, I believe that some of the more Athanasian-like features of the debate in your Lordships' House could have been eliminated if instead of speaking of 'the Crown' we were to speak of 'the Government'.[201]

Lord Diplock understood 'the government' to 'embrace both collectively and individually all of the ministers of the Crown and parliamentary secretaries under whose direction the administrative work of Government is carried on'.[202] His concept of government identifies the Crown with its officers. He stressed that '[e]xecutive acts of government that are done by any of them are acts done by "the Crown" in the fictional sense in which that expression is now used in English

---

[199] See, e.g., *Merricks* v. *Heathcote-Amory and the Minister of Agriculture, Fisheries and Food* [1955] Ch. 567; *Town Investments* v. *Department of the Environment* [1978] AC 359; *M* v. *Home Office* [1993] 3 WLR 433; P. Cane, *Introduction to Administrative Law*, n. 149 above, 64–5, 235–40.

[200] N. 199 above, 380F. [201] *Ibid.* 380G–1B. [202] *Ibid.* 381B–C.

public law'.[203] His Lordship therefore held that the Crown was the tenant where a lease was granted to a Minister.

But Lord Diplock's identification of the Crown with its officers under the rubric of government did not take account of the Crown's traditional immunity from legal process. If the Crown were to be identified with its officers, its immunity should extend to them. Such an extension would preclude review proceedings against officers of the Crown and their personal liability for wrongful acts in the course of their duties, both of which are fundamental to the English rule of law.[204] Wade has therefore long criticized the identification of the Crown with its officers in *Town Investments* as contrary to constitutional principle.[205] He rejects Lord Diplock's concept of government in so far as it involves such an identification:

Of course it is convenient to speak of 'the Government' as carrying out the services of the Crown, but that does not mean that 'the Government' has any meaning in law, or that we ought to say goodbye to the vital distinction between the Crown and its servants upon which so much constitutional law is based.[206]

In spite of Maitland's scorn,[207] Wade and Forsyth still prefer the old concept of the Crown as corporation sole,[208] a corporation of one rather than a government of many.

Wade's traditional view of the Crown, rather than the innovation of Lord Diplock, has prevailed. In *M* v. *Home Office*, the House of Lords restricted *Town Investments* to its facts[209] and confirmed the traditional distinction between the Crown and its servants emphasized by Wade. Lord Woolf observed that, '[a]lthough in reality the distinction between the Crown and an officer of the Crown is of no practical significance in judicial review proceedings, in the theory which clouds this subject the distinction is of the greatest importance'.[210] The House interpreted section 21 of the Crown Proceedings Act 1947 only to bar an injunction against an officer of the Crown in the rare situation[211] where the relevant statutory power is conferred upon the Crown itself

---

[203] N. 199 above 381C.   [204] See Dicey, n. 6 above, ch. 4.
[205] Wade, n. 131 above, 52, n. 2.
[206] H. W. R. Wade, 'The Crown—Old Platitudes and New Heresies' (1992) 142 *NLJ* 1275–6, 1315–17 at 1275–6.
[207] See above, 76.
[208] Wade, n. 206 above, 1317; Wade and Forsyth, n. 29 above, 819–20.
[209] N. 199 above, 456C–D.   [210] 448G.
[211] But see M. Gould, '*M* v. *Home Office*: Government and the Judges' [1993] *PL* 568–78 at 577.

as opposed to one of its officers. The House's curtailment of the Crown's immunity was achieved by confirming the distinction between the Crown and its officers, a distinction precluding the concept of government which unites them.

Before the decision of the House of Lords in *M* v. *Home Office*, with a reference to Francis Bacon's metaphor, Lester had claimed that 'British judges remain lions firmly beneath the throne of the Crown in Parliament'.[212] He had suggested that 'our judicial lions will have to move from their relatively sheltered position beneath the throne'.[213] In *M* v. *Home Office*, they did leave that sheltered position by refusing to countenance an extension of the Crown's immunity from injunction to officers of the Crown. They are nevertheless peculiarly traditional. They have remained instinctively preoccupied with individual people—whether or not they be officers of the Crown—but they are still the Queen's lions with an irrational reverence for her Crown. They have given effect to Dicey's rule of law, according to which all individuals, including officers of the Crown, are subject to the ordinary law of the ordinary courts. To that rule of law, however, they still add a mystical notion of a Crown that can do no wrong.[214] *M* v. *Home Office* might be the most important constitutional case for more than 200 years[215] but it also exemplifies traditional judicial attitudes to the Crown and its officers, attitudes that continue to cloud the prospects of a working distinction between public and private law.

The Irony of the English Distinction

In France, the distinction between public and private law acquired significance as the political conception of a centralized and, therefore, distinct state administration began to prevail and be regarded as a threat. By the time that conception was being questioned, the French distinction was already entrenched.

In England, the distinction was traditionally negated because academic and practising lawyers were insulated from any developed theory of the state and its administration. Ironically, as they began to take account of the state, and as they transplanted[216] the distinction

---

[212] A. Lester, 'English Judges as Law Makers' [1993] *PL* 269–90 at 270.
[213] *Ibid.* 289.   [214] *M* v. *Home Office*, n. 199 above, 451E, 453H.
[215] Wade, 'The Crown', n. 206 above, 1275; M. Beloff QC in *The Times*, 28 July 1993, 20.
[216] See above, 4 ff., 23 ff.

between public and private law, the state administration was becoming increasingly indistinct and administrative disputes difficult to identify. The distinction was becoming incongruous. Since then, its prospects have not been improved by privatization and are still clouded by traditional attitudes to the Crown. The recent confused attempts to apply the distinction, to attribute special procedural consequences to administrative disputes, illustrate the absence of appropriate theory and the ironical consequences of ill-considered transplantation.

For a working distinction to be established, whether procedural, substantive, or institutional, a peculiar theory of the state is required—a theory prevalent in nineteenth-century France and difficult to attain in twentieth-century England.

6

A Categorical Approach to Law

In the last chapter, I concluded that the English distinction is proving unsatisfactory in the absence of the peculiar conception of the state administration described in Chapter 3. In the rest of this book, I will argue that, even if the conception of the state administration is irrelevant or unproblematic, an English distinction is not working for want of the other features of the legal and political context described in my model. To persuade the reader who is unconvinced by my earlier analysis, whether because of a distrust in abstract argument,[1] a faith in judicial pragmatism,[2] or a rejection of pluralist theories of the state, I will make a heuristic assumption. To focus attention on other features of my model, I will assume that the state administration is distinct and that administrative disputes are accordingly identifiable.

In this chapter, I will focus on the effect of prevailing conceptions of law in the French and English traditions. I will suggest that, in England, the distinction has traditionally been unimportant and is now proving unsatisfactory for want of the peculiar, categorical, approach to law[3] once evident in France.

Historic Precursors

The Distinction in Roman Law

The role of the distinction in Roman law illustrates the effect of a prevailing conception of law. The Roman lawyers were familiar with some sort of notion of the state expressed with words and phrases like *civitas*, *res publica*, and *senatus populusque Romanus*.[4] Their distinction between public and private law, standing at the forefront of both Justinian's *Institutes* and *Digest*,[5] was nevertheless not attributed the significance of the later Continental distinction. In the famous passages of the *Corpus Iuris Civilis*, it is presented as a didactic distinction: '[h]uius studii duae

---

[1] See, e.g., P. Cane, 'Public Law and Private Law: A Study of the Analysis and Use of a Legal Concept' in J. Eekelaar and J. Bell (eds.), *Oxford Essays in Jurisprudence* (Oxford, 1987), 57–78 at 78.

[2] See, e.g., H. Woolf, 'Judicial Review: A Possible Programme for Reform' [1992] *PL* 221–37 at 231–2.

[3] See above, 35, 38.

[4] See J. M. Kelly, *A Short History of Western Legal Theory* (Oxford, 1992), 63–6.

[5] D. 1. 1. 1. 2; I. 1. 1. 4.

sunt positiones, publicum et privatum. publicum ius est quod ad statum rei Romanae spectat, privatum quod ad singulorum utilitatem.'[6]
Moreover, because no text links public law, for example, to the immunity of magistrates or to the exemption of the state from the rules of
conveyancing, H. F. Jolowicz concludes that the distinction was not of
any technical significance to Roman lawyers.[7]

The technical insignificance of the Roman distinction is related to
two features of the Roman conception of law. First, the casuistic and
pragmatic Roman jurists did not approach law systematically. They
were not minded to clarify their conceptual distinction, varied their use
of the concepts *ius publicum* and *ius privatum* from case to case, and did
not try to develop distinguishing criteria with which to use the distinction effectively.[8]

Secondly, the Roman jurists did not conceive of law as a whole. The
casuistic Classical jurists were concerned with specific cases and
focused on the private-law problems of inheritance, ownership, and
obligations. Whether because magistrates were generally controlled
through the senate and criminal prosecutions[9] or because the jurists
were preoccupied with a law of nature and regarded the time-bound
and particular as unworthy of scholarly treatment,[10] problems like
those relating to the public ownership of land or public-law limitations
on land ownership were neglected.[11] The Roman jurists even seem to
have avoided public law. With reference to the example of Q. Scaevola
who had refused to give legal opinions on issues of public law, Cicero
stressed that such opinions should be sought from practitioners—imperial administrators—rather than jurists.[12] Later imperial legislation did
not change the overall emphasis on private law. Imperial legislation
was generally clarificatory of private law rather than a source of public law.[13] Nevertheless, private law was not the whole of Roman law.
The public law governing magistrates, for example,[14] or, as identified

---

[6] D. 1. 1. 1. 2; I. 1. 1. 4: '[t]his study has two aspects, public and private. Public law
is that which concerns the Roman state, private that which concerns the well-being of
individuals'.

[7] H. F. Jolowicz, *Roman Foundations of Modern Law* (Oxford, 1957), 50–2.

[8] *Ibid.*

[9] P. G. Stein in discussion.

[10] F. Schulz, *Principles of Roman Law* (Oxford, 1936), ch. 3, especially at 34–5. Cf. E.
Levy, 'Natural Law In Roman Thought' (1949) 15 *Studia et Documenta Historiae et Iuris*
1–23, especially at 6, 9–10.

[11] Schulz, n. 10 above, 26–31.   [12] Cicero, *Pro Balbo*, 19. 45.

[13] G. Gualandi, *Legislazione imperiale e giurisprudenza* (Milan, 1963), ii.

[14] D. 1. 1. 1. 2.

with *ius sacrum*,[15] was occasionally recognized but generally neglected. Justinian's *Corpus Iuris Civilis* initiated a conception of law as a whole but, despite his 'non exemplis sed legibus judicandum est', was a collection of juristic texts, inheriting their focus on private law, rather than a comprehensive code.[16]

Because the Roman lawyers did not conceive of law as a whole, they were unable to separate law into public and private categories. Their inability can be explained by contrasting the ancient notions of *divisio* (*diairesis*) and *partitio* (*merismos*).[17] While material is 'divided' into *genera*, a whole is 'separated' into *partes*, the sum of which comprises the whole. In other words, one can classify by bringing together similar institutions into *genera*, or by separating a whole into its component *partes*. A *partitio* is more significant than a *divisio* because it can be relied upon to have an effect. While data may fall in an indeterminate residue on neither side of a *divisio*, data must fall in the exhaustive categories separated by a *partitio*. The methodological distinction between *divisio* and *partitio* is related to a philosophical distinction between inductive and deductive, or casuistic and theoretical, reasoning. Whereas similar institutions are identified empirically and distinguished from others by *divisio*, a whole is separated theoretically (or mathematically) into its component *partes* by *partitio*.

The pragmatic and casuistic Roman jurists struggled to move from *divisio* to *partitio*.[18] Possibly because, as a Sabinian, he was influenced by the Stoics, and probably because his *Institutes* was designed as a textbook, Gaius preferred *partitio* to *divisio*.[19] Gaius, however, only achieved his *partitio* of private law into persons, actions, and things, by placing obligations illogically under things.[20] And the compilers of Justinian's *Institutes* simply adopted his system of classification, although they included titles on criminal law and the office of the judge.[21] Where they declare that all law concerns persons, things, or actions,[22] they neglect the place of public law, which they therefore leave as an indeterminate residue rather than as a residual category. The Roman jurists lacked the sense of the whole of law required for a distinction to

---

[15] *Ibid.* See generally M. Crawford, 'Aut sacrum aut poublicom' in P. Birks (ed.), *New Perspectives in the Roman Law of Property: Essays for Barry Nicholas* (Oxford, 1989), 93–8.
[16] See J. P. Dawson, *The Oracles of the Law* (Ann Arbor, 1968), 93–8.
[17] P. G. Stein, 'The Development of the Institutional System' in P. G. Stein and A. D. E. Lewis, *Studies in Justinian's Institutes: In Memory of Thomas* (London, 1983), 151–63.
[18] *Ibid.*   [19] *Ibid.* 156.   [20] *Ibid.* 154–8.   [21] *Ibid.* 159.
[22] I. 2. 12.

separate public and private *partes* of that whole and, so, to become significant as a *partitio*.

In short, an essential element of my model of the working distinction between public and private law was missing. The Roman distinction was technically insignificant because of the lack of a categorical—systematic and all-embracing—approach to law.

The Distinction in the Middle Ages

A categorical approach to law did not develop with the renaissance of Roman law in the twelfth century. Justinian's ideal of a 'complete code of laws without contradiction or imperfection'[23] was unfulfilled in the *Corpus Iuris Civilis* which was received. And the *Corpus Iuris Canonici*, like the *Corpus Iuris Civilis*, was merely a compilation of texts—conciliary canons, Gratian's papal decretals, and subsequent official collections—rather than a systematic and comprehensive code. Accordingly, the medieval Romanists generally envisaged the distinction between public and private law as a *divisio* rather than a *partitio*, without always using the term *divisio* or clearly distinguishing a separation of *partes*.[24] The Glossators usually wrote of two *species* of a genre.[25] Only Bartolus and Paul de Castro describe *partes* of law and envisaged a separation between categories exhaustive of the whole of law—a 'divisio bimembris, distinctio bimembris videlicet quod *omne jus* aut est publicum aut privatum'.[26] Later Commentators did not follow Bartolus and Paul de Castro. Baldus typically combined the various descriptions of public and private law to write of *duas partes* and *species*.[27]

The medieval Romanists did not approach the distinction systematically. The early Romanists rejected the distinguishing criterion of object—*respublica/ res privata*—put forward by Placentinus but were generally not disposed to develop their own criteria.[28] The Commentators

[23] Dawson, n. 16 above, 122.

[24] G. Chevrier, 'Remarques sur l'introduction et les vicissitudes de la distinction du *«jus privatum»* et du *«jus publicum»* dans les œuvres des anciens juristes Français' [1952] *Archives de philosophie du droit* 5–77 at 32–3.

[25] *Ibid.*

[26] Paul de Castro quoted by Chevrier, n. 24 above, 32 (emphasis added): a 'dividing of two limbs, a distinction separating two limbs cledarly because *all law* is either public or private'. See also G. Chevrier, 'Les critères de la distinction du droit privé et du droit public dans la pensée savante médiévale' in *Etudes d'histoire du droit canonique dédiées à Gabriel Le Bras* (Paris, 1965), ii, 841–59 at 854–5.

[27] Chevrier, 'Remarques sur l'introduction de la distinction', n. 24 above, 33, nn. 2 and 3.

[28] *Ibid.*, 26–31; *id.*, 'Critères de la distinction', n. 26 above, 846–9. See, e.g., Azo, Ch. 1 above, p. 6.

who followed them discussed criteria at length but did not settle on a criterion, and the purposive criterion they usually stated engendered scepticism of the 'possibilité de couper le droit en deux parties, en raison de la connexité de ses fins privées et publiques.'[29] Baldus, for example, wrote: '[i]llud est publicum quod continet publicum bonum principaliter et per prius. Illud vero est privatum, quod continet privatum bonum principaliter et per prius'.[30] His distinction, however, hinges loosely on the vague notions of main purpose and public good.

The medieval Romanists did discuss the distinction by reference to theoretical legal problems. They also had a vague and limited sense of its scientific and methodological value.[31] They were insufficiently systematic, however, to apply the distinction with any consistency. They remained unconscious of the intermingling of public and private in the feudal setting.[32] And they applied Roman private-law texts regardless of context. The maxim *necessitas non habet legem*, which explained why a thief might lawfully be killed in the night,[33] was used from the twelfth century onwards to justify the rulers' overriding right to take whatever action was necessary to maintain the *status regni*.[34] Similarly, 'quod omnes tangit ab omnibus comprobetur', which had applied to a context where several tutors were jointly administering a ward's estate,[35] was freely used by medieval jurists as a principle of procedural consent or participation outside the private-law context.[36] Whereas in other instances the medieval Romanists might have succeeded in applying texts from the *Corpus Iuris Civilis* in a radically different setting,[37] in the case of Justinian's distinction between public and private law, they failed. Through their work the distinction became known but, partly for want of a conception of the state administration[38] and partly for

[29] Chevrier, 'Critères de la distinction', n. 26 above, 849–52, especially at 849: 'possibility of dividing law into two parts, by reason of the connection between its private and public ends'. See also Chevrier, 'Remarques sur l'introduction de la distinction', n. 24 above, 32–5.

[30] Quoted by Chevrier, 'Remarques sur l'introduction de la distinction', n. 24 above, 33, n. 5: '[t]hat which is public concerns the public good first and foremost. That which is private concerns private interests first and foremost.'

[31] See Chevrier, 'Critères de la distinction', n. 26 above, 856–8.

[32] Jolowicz, n. 7 above, 52.   [33] D. 9. 2. 4: 'necessity knows no law'.

[34] G. Post, *Studies in Medieval Legal Thought: Public Law and the State, 1100–1322* (Princeton, 1964), 20–2.

[35] C. 5. 59. 5. 2: 'that which affects all must be approved by all'.

[36] Post, n. 34 above, 168–80.

[37] See M. Gilmore, *Argument from Roman Law in Political Thought, 1200–1600* (Cambridge, Mass., 1941).

[38] See above, 42–3

want of a systematic and comprehensive approach to law, it could not yet become significant.

The Development of a Categorical Approach in France

The French Customs

In the centuries before the Revolution, the resilience of the French customs retarded the development of a systematic approach to law. Partly because of the codification of the customs in the sixteenth century,[39] a range of diverse rules and differences between the *pays de coutumes* and the *pays de droit écrit* were preserved. Furthermore, the separate judicial powers of the thirteen *Parlements* and the uneven reception of Roman law added to the legal confusion and fragmentation. Dawson describes French law in the 200 years before the Revolution as 'more a kaleido-scope, presenting different views to different observers, than it was a structure with a firm foundation that called for the talents of an archi-tect'.[40] As a myriad of reflections, French law could not be partitioned into two grand parts.

Before the fifteenth century, customary-law works seldom mentioned the concepts of public and private law.[41] And, even in the sixteenth century, despite administrative centralization and the development of the concept of the state, authors, such as Guy Coquille in his *Institution au droit des Français*, slipped from public to private law in the same work and were unable to abide by any rigid partitioning of the law.[42] Constructive attempts at categorization were initially frustrated by the confused and fragmented sources of law.[43]

Systematization and Early Codes

The required categorical approach to law emerged from the confusion through development along two lines. First, from the late sixteenth cen-tury, French humanists, such as Baron, Le Douaren, Connan, Doneau, Cujas, and Hotman, began to show a concern for system.[44] They

[39] Dawson, *Oracles*, n. 16 above, 347–8. See generally J. P. Dawson, 'The Codification of the French customs' (1940) 38 *Michigan LRev.* 765–800.

[40] Dawson, *Oracles*, n. 16 above, 348 and 409, n. 22 (where Dawson recognizes his indebtedness to C. J. Friedrich for the metaphor of the kaleidoscope).

[41] Chevrier, 'Remarques sur l'introduction de la distinction', n. 24 above, 37–9.

[42] *Ibid.* 43, 50.   [43] *Ibid.* 48–9.

[44] D. R. Kelley, '*Vera Philosophia*: The Philosophical Significance of Renaissance Jurisprudence' (1976) 14 *Journal of the History of Philosophy* 267–79. See, e.g., P. Stein, 'Donellus and the Origins of the Modern Civil Law' in J. A. Ankum *et al.* (eds.), *Mélanges Felix Wubbe* (Fribourg, Switzerland, 1993), 439–52.

questioned and undermined the authority of the *Corpus Iuris Civilis* and, mainly to facilitate teaching, began a process of re-arrangement. Reminded of the Ciceronian ideal of recasting *ius civile in artem*, and influenced by a model of mathematics, they adopted a method of explaining by moving through a system of concepts from the more general to the more particular by division and subdivision. Although the humanists attacked orthodoxy and accordingly had little immediate influence on French law,[45] by the end of the sixteenth century, they did have some influence on legal form. In the case of the distinction between public and private law, it was the humanist Charondas le Caron who retrieved the Roman distinction and made it the basis for his *Pandectes du droit Français*.[46] He described a *partitio*: 'hoc studium . . . in duabus thesibus totum est: aut enim in jure publico aut privato ponitur.'[47] Charondas le Caron, however, did not apply his distinction rigorously. Instead of trying to separate feudal law into public and private *partes*, he simply annexed it to private law by incorporating it in his discussion of things.[48] His lead was nevertheless followed by Fleury who based his *Institution au droit Français* on the distinction.[49]

Secondly, law began to be conceived as a whole, as a body of law for the whole of France, requiring systematic exposition and enactment. A national French private law was, for example, the subject of the systematic works of Charondas le Caron and Fleury, which adopted the distinction between public and private law. Furthermore, to become authoritative the emerging body of law was enacted in stages, and to be so enacted it was further systematized.

Watson attributes what Weber called the formal rationality of the civil-law systems to acceptance of the *Corpus Iuris Civilis* as authoritative.[50] He describes how such acceptance necessitated the teaching of the *Corpus Iuris Civilis* at universities, and its systematic exposition by teachers for students. His argument, however, cannot explain legal systematization in France when the universities were in decline[51] and where the reception of the *Corpus Iuris Civilis* was uneven because of the resilience of the French customs. At one point Watson does suggest that acceptance of any part of the *Corpus Iuris Civilis* would explain

---

[45] Dawson, *Oracles*, n. 16 above, 342.

[46] Chevrier, 'Remarques sur l'introduction de la distinction', n. 24 above, 45–8, 76.

[47] Quoted in Chevrier, *ibid.* 46, n. 4: '[t]he whole of this study has two subjects: it is concerned either with public or private law'.

[48] *Ibid.* 48.   [49] *Ibid.* 57, 76.

[50] A. Watson, *The Making of the Civil Law* (London, 1981), ch. 3.

[51] See Dawson, *Oracles*, n. 16 above, 339–41.

formal rationality,[52] but it is unclear how accepting the authority of mere fragments of the *Corpus Iuris Civilis* in the French customs could justify the learning of the whole of the *Corpus Iuris Civilis* by students at universities. Rather, the reception of the whole or a part of the *Corpus Iuris Civilis* stimulated systematization by initiating the conception of a body of law, requiring systematic exposition and enactment.

In France the conception of law as a whole did continue to evolve despite the resilience of the French customs and, so, can partly explain the French path to systematization. The codification of the French customs in the sixteenth century, on the one hand, preserved the diversity of the French customs but, on the other, laid the basis for the Napoleonic Code. Dawson comments:

> The codification of the French customs represents merely one stage in a continuous development. . . . At a later stage another and more sweeping reformulation was still to be necessary, in order to unify French law and adjust it to the needs of modern society. But the codification of the customs prepared the way for the great codification of the early nineteenth century, both by preserving the main elements of the customary systems and by supplying a more tractable material for the skilled legal technicians of the intervening centuries.[53]

In the seventeenth and eighteenth centuries, the Royal Ordinances, especially those of Louis XIV, such as the Code Louis on civil procedure in 1667, and the Code Marchand on commercial law in 1673,[54] popularized the idea of a comprehensive, systematic, and authoritative body of law applicable throughout France.

Montesquieu confirmed this idea with his notion of laws enacted by the legislature to conform to the conditions of a country.[55] He related these laws to different objects and therefore divided laws into different kinds.[56] In particular, he worked with a distinction between public and private law by dividing *droit politique* and *droit civil*: '[c]onsidered as living in a society that must be maintained, they [men] have laws concerning the relation between those who govern and those who are governed, and this is the *political right* (*droit politique*). Further, they have laws concerning the relation that all citizens have with one another,

---

[52] Watson, n. 50 above, 24. Cf. *ibid.* 32.

[53] Dawson, 'Codification of the French Customs', n. 39 above, 800.

[54] See generally W. Johnson, *Chapters in the History of French Law* (Montreal, 1957), ch. 17, 228 ff., reprinted in J.-G. Castel, *The Civil Law System of the Province of Quebec: Notes, Cases, and Materials* (Toronto, 1962), 35–55 at 46–52.

[55] Montesquieu, *The Spirit of the Laws* (A. M. Cohler, B. C. Miller, and H. S. Stone (eds. and trs.)) (Cambridge, 1989), bk. 1, ch. 3, 7–9.

[56] C. J. Friedrich, *The Philosophy of Law in Historical Perspective* (Chicago, 1958), 107–8.

and this is the *civic right (droit civil)*.'[57] His divisions, however, were not rigid and were to be drawn by the legislature[58] which until after the Revolution did not seek to embrace the whole of law.

The Pre-Revolutionary Division

The conception of French law as a whole was expanding but was not yet all-embracing. The Royal Ordinances dealt with specific areas, rather than the whole, of French law. In the seventeenth and eighteenth centuries, writers tried to extract a national French private law from the confusion of the customs but lacked that systematic sense of the whole of law necessary to elaborate a public-law, or to remain within a private-law, category. For example, they continued to discuss public-law aspects of feudal law under the private law of things. Similarly, professors who used Justinian's distinction to present their course in French law did not adhere to it.[59] Chevrier comments: '[c]'est pourquoi le plan de leur cours n'a plus qu'une portée limitée: loin d'être un canevas général pour l'exposé du *jus* dans son ensemble, il n'est qu'un moyen d'exposition du seul droit privé.'[60]

Before the Revolution, a clear doctrinal separation of the whole of law into categories of public and private law was absent. A range of rules relating to the administration was developed by special courts such as the *Cour des Aides* and the *Chambres des Comptes*, but its autonomy was not formally declared.[61] Furthermore, the distinction was not attributed institutional significance. The *Parlements* still meddled with administrative matters, and the *Conseil du Roi* unified judicial practice by deciding ordinary cases through *évocations* from the ordinary courts.[62] The distinction between public and private law had the limited significance of a *divisio* rather than the importance of a *partitio*.

---

[57] Montesquieu, n. 55 above, p. 7 (author's insertions). 'Droit' is translated as 'right' although usually closer to 'law' in English: *ibid.* n. n.

[58] Friedrich, n. 56 above, 107–8.

[59] Chevrier, 'Remarques sur l'introduction de la distinction', n. 24 above, 66–77, especially at 68–9.

[60] *Ibid.* 69: '[t]his is why their course outline has only a limited scope: far from being a general canvas for expounding law in its entirety, it is merely a means to the exposition of private law alone.'

[61] J.-L. Mestre, *Introduction historique au droit administratif Français* (Paris, 1985), especially at secs. 4–5; J. Brissaud, *A History of French Public Law* (London, 1915), s. 468; C. Szladits, 'The Distinction between Public Law and Private Law' in *IECL*, ii, ch. 2, secs. 25–57 at s. 28.

[62] Brissaud, n. 61 above, s. 367; M. Waline, *Droit administratif* (9th edn., Paris, 1963), sec. 32; Szladits, n. 61 above, sec. 28.

The Nineteenth-century Categorical Separation

The nineteenth-century institutional separation followed upon post-Revolutionary institutional and conceptual changes—the introduction of a radical separation of powers, the judicialization of the *Conseil d'Etat*, and the emergence of a conception of the state as a distinct and potentially abusive entity[63]—but was also made possible by the impetus to systematization given by the great French codes at the start of the nineteenth century. Codification of the law was a demand of the Revolution answered by Napoleon. Its impetus to systematization was multiple. First, the subject-areas of the great French codes had further to be classified in order to be researched and drafted concisely and comprehensively by a team of jurists. H. F. Jolowicz rightly stresses that '[c]lassification is particularly necessary when it is desired to enact a code or codes, for it is only by very careful analysis of the subject-matter that it is possible to express a body of law within a reasonable compass and without omission or overlapping.'[64] Secondly, logical arrangement was encouraged by the demand that the codes be complete, simple, and accessible.[65] Thirdly, once the codes were enacted, systematic exposition was necessary for them to be learned. Finally, the codified areas—civil law, commercial law, civil procedure, and criminal law and procedure—were hived off to develop as autonomous categories of law, while the uncodified areas in general, and public law in particular, were left exposed as an indeterminate residue. But the logic inspiring codification—a clear body of law for all Frenchmen—required that the indeterminate residue of public law at least be transformed into a residual category alongside private law and part of a greater body of law.

The Exegetical School which dominated French doctrine in the nineteenth century took the logic of codification to extremes[66] and made the indeterminacy of French public law more apparent. The School refused to acknowledge law beyond the codes, beyond the will of the legislature. The *Conseil d'Etat*, entrusted with the resolution of

---

[63] See above, 52–8, below, 138–46.

[64] H. F. Jolowicz, *Lectures on Jurisprudence* (J. A. Jolowicz (ed.)) (London, 1963), 319. See also O. W. Holmes, 'Codes, and the Arrangement of the Law' (1931) 44 *Harv. LRev.* 725–37, especially at 726.

[65] See A. Tunc, 'The Grand Outlines of the Code' in B. Schwartz (ed.), *The Code Napoleon and the Common-Law World* (New York, 1956), 19–45.

[66] F. Geny, *Méthode d'interprétation et sources en droit privé positif: essai critique* (Paris, 1919), pt. 1; J. Stone, *The Province and Function of Law* (London, 1947), 149–59; Dawson, *Oracles*, n. 16 above, 392–4.

administrative disputes, and the doctrinal writers in its shadow, gradually through the course of the nineteenth century answered the challenge by evolving and systematizing public law. The *Conseil d'Etat* adopted a style of judicial opinion if anything more laconic than that of the *Cour de Cassation*[67] to suggest that it is the law, if not the code, that speaks. Crucially in 1873 in *Blanco*, the *Tribunal des Conflits* authoritatively defined an autonomous category of public law by explicitly contrasting it with private law. In the familiar single sentence of judgment, it declared, first, that 'the liability which may fall upon the state for damage caused to individuals by the act of persons which it employs in the public service cannot be governed by the principles which are laid down in the Civil Code for relations between one individual and another', secondly, 'that this liability is neither general nor absolute', and, thirdly, 'that it has its own special rules which vary according to the needs of the service and the necessity to reconcile the rights of the state with private rights'.[68] After decades of judicial development, David could comment: '[a]lthough no codes exist for administrative law, the situation there is fundamentally the same, except that logical interpretation of statutes is guided not by rules of law formulated by the legislature, but by unwritten rules of law.'[69] Satisfactory criteria distinguishing the two categories were hard to find[70] but, unlike the criteria loosely asserted in earlier centuries, their importance was emphasized by the categorical approach to law that had developed.

Codification in nineteenth-century France centred on private not public law,[71] but the accompanying code-conception of law, the conception of law as an exhaustive and systematic body of rules, championed by the Exegetical School in its attitude to the codes, provoked a doctrinal separation between public and private law to which institutional and substantive significance could be given.

The Persistence of the French Categorical Approach

Since its heyday in the nineteenth century, the code-conception of law has been much criticized. In 1899, Geny published his influential

---

[67] Dawson, n. 16 above, 410–11, 416, 426.

[68] TC, 8 Feb. 1873. Translation by L. N. Brown and J. S. Bell, *French Administrative Law* (4th edn., Oxford, 1993), 174.

[69] R. David, *French Law: Its Structure, Sources, and Methodology* (M. Kindred (tr.)) (Baton Rouge, 1972), 159.

[70] See above, 66 ff.

[71] B. Schwartz, 'The Code and Public Law' in Schwartz (ed.), n. 65 above, 247–66.

critique of the Exegetical School.[72] He stressed that the codes could not provide answers to all legal problems and recognized that French law had been transformed through judicial interpretation of the codes. His call for 'la libre recherche scientifique' where the judge has the burden of choice became a movement's banner.[73] Nevertheless, Geny did not regard judicial decisions as an independent source of law. He still presupposed a conception of law as a whole by requiring that judicial decisions be incorporated as rules of custom in order to produce new law.[74] The code-conception of law persisted despite Geny's perception of its inadequacies.

In the course of this century, recognition of the role of case law, by which the general phrases of the code have been adapted to a changing society, has become commonplace.[75] The words of Portalis in his 'Discours Préliminaire' to the Code Napoleon which were ignored by the French Exegetical School have been repeatedly confirmed:

L'office de le loi est de fixer, par des grandes vues, les maximes générales du droit; d'établir des principes féconds en conséquences, et non de descendre dans le détail des questions qui peuvent naître sur chaque matière. *C'est au magistrat et au jurisconsulte, pénétres de l'esprit général des lois, à en diriger l'application.*[76]

Dawson therefore concludes that the French judges, rather than merely apply the provisions of the code, began again to whirl the kaleidoscope:

The doctrines to be found in French opinions thus consist of an enormous number of detached propositions, competing, conflicting and overlapping. There are many thousands, indeed hundreds of thousands if one takes account of significant variations in their language. . . . But so many subordinate propositions have been invented by the court and used in the past that the range of choice is enormously wide. As was true in France under the old regime with its multiplicity of sources of law, French judges seem to sit before a whirling

[72] Geny, n. 66 above, i, pt. 2; Stone, n. 66 above, 149–53.
[73] See Stone, n. 66 above; W. Friedmann, *Legal Theory* (3rd edn., London, 1967), 227–46.
[74] Geny, n. 66 above, i, secs. 109–11, ii, secs. 146–9.
[75] See, e.g., M. Ancel, 'Case Law in France' (1934) 16 *Jnl. of Comp. Leg. & Int. L* 1–17; F. H. Lawson, *Negligence in the Civil Law* (London, 1950), 231–82, especially 234–5; A. Sereni, 'The Code and Case Law' in Schwartz (ed.), n. 65 above, 55–79; Dawson, *Oracles*, n. 16 above, ch. 5; Watson, n. 50 above, 39 ff.; M. Shapiro, *Courts: A Comparative and Political Analysis* (Chicago, 1981), ch. 3.
[76] Quoted in Tunc, n. 65 above, 26: '[t]he function of the law is to lay down, in broad outline, general legal maxims; to establish principles capable of bearing much fruit, and not to descend into the detail of the questions that may arise in each case. *It is for the judge and the jurisconsult, imbued with the general spirit of the laws, to see to their application.*'

kaleidoscope, watching for the screen to flash the image that fits the particular case before them.[77]

Dawson's perspective, however, is external.[78] In France judicial decisions did not become authoritative in themselves. In accordance with Geny's argument, their authority still depended on their incorporation as custom through the consent of courts and jurists.[79] French judges still did not acknowledge their own lawmaking.[80] Through a conception of the legal rule as general and abstract,[81] and, through a teleological approach to the interpretation of statutes,[82] they were able to regard their decisions as mere applications of the rule, statute, or code. The conception of law as a body of rules which can be separated into parts could therefore persist. Indeed, it had to persist if the courts were to remain true to the Revolution and avoid becoming like the pre-Revolutionary *Parlements*.[83]

The impact of the development of French public law has been ambivalent. It has both challenged and confirmed the conception of law as a body of rules. On the one hand, French administrative law is recognized to have been made by judges and systematized by academics.[84] In the 1930s, Waline commented that '[i]t has been only sixty years that the theory of governmental liability has been being built up gradually by the repetition of judicial precedents, each of which adds elements to only one aspect of the problem.'[85] Furthermore, by developing *violation de la loi* as a ground of review since the Second World War, the *Conseil d'Etat* has introduced a notion of *loi* that does not entail codification, enactment, or even written formulation.[86] It has interpreted *loi* to include 'les principes généraux du droit' such as equality before the law, protection of the environment, and even social and economic rights. Since 1971, the *Conseil Constitutionnel* has been prepared to use similarly abstract standards which it has taken from the Republican tradition as a whole.[87]

---

[77] Dawson, n. 16 above, 409. [78] Cf. *ibid*. 414.

[79] *Ibid*. 429–30; David, n. 69 above, pp. xi–xii.

[80] David, n. 69 above, 56, 167. [81] *Ibid*. 78–83.

[82] *Ibid*. 185. [83] Dawson, n. 16 above, 362–73, 415.

[84] See generally J. Rivero, 'Jurisprudence et doctrine dans l'élaboration du droit administratif' (1955) 9 *EDCE* 27–36; B. Chenot, 'L'Existentialisme et le droit' (1953) 3 *Revue Française de science politique* 57–68.

[85] Quoted in S. Riesenfeld, 'The French System of Administrative Justice: A Model for American Law? Part II' (1938) 18 *Boston Univ. LRev.* 400–32 at 410.

[86] Brown and Bell, n. 68 above, 205–23.

[87] J. Bell, *French Constitutional Law* (Oxford, 1992), ch. 2; B. Nicholas, 'Fundamental Rights and Judicial Review in France' [1978] *PL* 82–101, 155–77.

On the other hand, despite these developments, French administrative law has continued to be evolved and conceived as a body of law to stand alongside the code and statutes of private law. A *Conseiller d'Etat*, for example, described the role of the judge in public law in contrast to his role in private law as follows:

> The role of the judge is thus very often not only to interpret the written texts, but to create an applicable law when none exists. It is therefore incumbent upon him to establish *a coherent body of judicial decisions, which will take the place of statute*.[88]

A coherent body of public law has been developed to take the place of a code. Its development confirms the pervasive categorical approach to law. Furthermore, the *Tribunal des Conflits* has evolved rules for separating public and private law which, although complex and often arbitrary,[89] are settled and the occasion of relatively few cases.[90] Despite the problems, the distinction and the underlying categorical approach to law are entrenched.[91]

The Contrasting Tradition in England

The Absence of a Categorical Approach to Law

The influence of Roman law in England was negligible in contrast to its influence on the Continent. The early reform of the common law and, in particular, the development of powerful central courts anticipated and made less necessary the reforms that were to occur through the Continental reception of Roman law.[92] The authority of the *Corpus Iuris Civilis* was consequently not pervasive and, so, could not initiate a conception of law as a body of rules requiring codification and systematic exposition.

At no stage did a code-conception of law become dominant. From the seventeenth to the nineteenth centuries, calls for codification were repeatedly made on the English side of the Channel but had little effect. In the seventeenth century, both Bacon and, later, the Puritan

---

[88] M. Letourneur, 'The Concept of Equity in French Public Law' in R. A. Newman (ed.), *Equity in the World's Legal Systems: A Comparative Study* (Brussels, 1973), 261–75 at 261 (emphasis added).

[89] See above, 66–9.   [90] Brown and Bell, n. 68 above, 280.

[91] J. H. Merryman, *The Civil Law Tradition* (2nd edn., Stanford, 1985), 91, 97–8.

[92] R. C. van Caenegem, *The Birth of the English Common Law* (2nd edn., Cambridge, 1988), ch. 4; *id.*, *Judges, Legislators and Professors: Chapters in European Legal History* (Cambridge, 1987), 114–24.

Revolutionaries advocated codification. As Attorney-General and then as Lord Chancellor, Bacon proposed the 'Compiling and Amendment of the Laws of England', but, amidst political controversy, his proposals came to nothing.[93] The Puritan Revolutionaries went further and advocated comprehensive codification to democratize the common law and curtail the monopoly of lawyers,[94] but their ambitions were similarly frustrated with the Restoration of the Monarchy. In the late eighteenth century, Bentham coined the very word codification and advocated it passionately so that the law could be known, but he lacked the political leverage to bring it about.[95] His followers in the nineteenth century were almost as unsuccessful. Sir James Stephen drafted a criminal code but could not get it enacted.[96] And the trend to codification at the end of the nineteenth century[97] resulted only in specific statutes—for example, the Sale of Goods Act 1893 and the Partnership Act 1890—on specific areas of law. Whether because of judicial opposition, the belief in the common law's evolution from time immemorial,[98] the faith of the propertied in judges rather than the legislature, or the associating of codification with the Puritans, the French Revolution, and Napoleon Bonaparte,[99] English law remained uncodified.

Without codification as an impetus to classification and without an authoritative body of law which had to be systematically expounded, a systematic approach to law was slow to develop. Those who did advocate codification confirm its links to legal system. Francis Bacon both advocated codification and tried to rationalize law as a science. He even distinguished between public and private law specifically for the purpose of 'A Preparation toward the Union of Laws', which, he argued, should affect only public law.[100] Similarly, Bentham advocated codification as part of his endeavour to establish a science of

---

[93] R. Pound, 'Codification in Anglo-American law' in Schwartz (ed.), n. 65 above, 267–97 at 267–8.

[94] Van Caenegem, *Judges, Legislators and Professors*, n. 92 above, 45–6.

[95] *Ibid.* 47.   [96] *Ibid.* 47–8.

[97] P. Stein, 'Continental Influences on English Legal Thought, 1600–1900' in P. G. Stein, *The Character and Influence of the Roman Civil Law: Historical Essays* (London, 1988), 209–29 at 228.

[98] M. Loughlin, *Public Law and Political Theory* (Oxford, 1992), 42–8. See generally G. J. Postema, *Bentham and the Common Law Tradition* (Oxford, 1986), especially at 4–13, 63–6.

[99] Van Caenegem, *Judges, Legislators and Professors*, n. 92 above, 48–50.

[100] *Works* (J. Spedding, R. L. Ellis and D. D. Heath (eds.)), vii (London, 1859), 731.

legislation.[101] To his followers in the nineteenth century he bequeathed his concern for both system and codification: '[f]rom Bentham Austin inherited a triple passion for legislation, classification and codification.'[102]

The nineteenth-century English attempts at classification, however, were as indecisive as the calls for codification. They did not mark the development of a categorical approach to law. Analytical legal positivists, such as Markby, Holland, and Salmond, in their books on general jurisprudence, described divisions of law, including that between public and private law, but stressed that they were only for convenience.[103] Mainly, they classified for academic purposes. Markby, for example, designed his *Elements of Law* for the emergent university courses in law, which, he wrote, must consider law 'as a science; or at least, if that is not yet possible . . . as a collection of principles capable of being systematically arranged, and resting, not on bare authority, but on sound logical deduction'.[104] Outside the realm of academia, and in the absence of an imperative of codification, the nineteenth-century classifications did not need to be rigorous and, so, could not have much substantive,[105] procedural, or institutional effect.

In contrast to the code-conception of French exegetical positivism, Austin's command-theory of law came to dominate English analytical positivism in the nineteenth century.[106] Whereas the exegetical code-conception provoked the development of a body of public law to stand alongside the *Code Civil*, Austin's command-theory had an opposite effect. It did not focus on law as a whole. By describing laws as commands, Austin emphasized, not a separable body of law, but the courts and the procedures by which those commands are sanctioned. Furthermore, he regarded the sovereign as the source of commands concerning both public authorities and private persons: '[i]t is somewhat difficult to describe the boundary by which the conditions of political subordinates are severed from the conditions of private persons. The rights and duties of political subordinates, and the rights and duties of

[101] Stein, 'Continental Influences', n. 97 above, 223. See generally Postema, n. 98 above, ch. 12.

[102] Stein, 'Continental Influences', *ibid.* 224–5.   [103] See above, 8–11.

[104] W. Markby, *Elements of Law Considered with Reference to Principles of General Jurisprudence* (6th edn., Oxford, 1905), pp. iii–iv, ix–xii, especially at p. x. See Stein, 'Continental Influences', n. 97 above, 224–6.

[105] See Stein, 'Continental Influences', *ibid.* 209, 226–8.

[106] J. Austin, *The Province of Jurisprudence Determined and the Uses of the Study of Jurisprudence* (H. L. A. Hart (ed.)) (London, 1954).

private persons, are creatures of a common author: namely the sovereign or state.'[107] Austin struggled to distinguish between public and private law and relegated the distinction to an imprecise and 'extremely vague' subdivision of the law of persons.[108]

The English Remedial Conception of Law: Ubi Remedium, Ibi Ius

Austin conceived of law in a typically English way by focusing on the remedy, by requiring that a sanction be annexed to a command for 'law properly so-called'.[109] Dicey was similarly preoccupied with remedies. His preoccupation contributed to his analysis that rejected a distinction between public and private law. Each of the three meanings he attributed to the rule of law not only negated a distinct state administration, but also enshrined the role of the ordinary courts and the remedies they provide. First, Dicey stressed that the rule of law requires that a breach of law be 'established in the ordinary legal manner before the ordinary courts of the land'.[110] Secondly, he equated equality before the law with 'the equal subjection of all classes to the ordinary law of the land administered by the ordinary law courts'.[111] Thirdly, Dicey regarded the action of the courts as the source of individual rights:

The 'rule of law', lastly, may be used as a formula for expressing the fact that with us the law of the constitution, the rules which in foreign countries naturally form part of a constitutional code, are not the source but the consequence of the rights of individuals, as defined and enforced by the courts; that, in short, the principles of private law have with us been by the action of the courts and Parliament so extended as to determine the position of the Crown and of its servants; thus the constitution is the result of the ordinary law of the land.[112]

Dicey did envisage some body of law with his notion of the 'ordinary law of the land' but only by neglecting courts and tribunals of local and special jurisdiction, following a range of special procedures, and often free from the effective control of the superior courts.[113]

---

[107] J. Austin, *Lectures on Jurisprudence or The Philosophy of Positive Law* (5th edn., London, 1885), i, p. 71.

[108] *Ibid.* ii, 748.

[109] Austin, *Province of Jurisprudence*, 133–4; *id.*, *Lectures on Jurisprudence*, i, 178.

[110] A. V. Dicey, *An Introduction to the Study of the Law of the Constitution* (10th edn., London, 1959), 188.

[111] *Ibid.* 202.   [112] *Ibid.* 203.

[113] See H. W. Arthurs, 'Rethinking Administrative Law: A Slightly Dicey Business' (1979) 17 *Osgoode Hall LJ* 1–45 at 11–14; *id.*, *'Without the Law': Administrative Justice and Legal Pluralism in Nineteenth-Century England* (Toronto, 1985).

Below the clouds of jurisprudence the English remedial conception of law was pervasive. For centuries practitioners were preoccupied with the forms of action. They had good reason, because choosing the wrong form of action would result in failure.[114] They had to know the legal requirements relating to each form of action, which therefore developed in each case to fill a 'procedural pigeon-hole'.[115] Through their efforts they contributed to the development of a law confusing substance and procedure. The role of conclusive presumptions, the development of promissory estoppel, and the rule of the Statute of Frauds that no action be brought on certain kinds of contract unless in writing, all illustrate the confusion.[116]

Maine concluded his discussion of classification in 'early law' with his famous words:

So great is the ascendency of the Law of Actions in the infancy of Courts of Justice, that substantive law has at first the look of being gradually secreted in the interstices of procedure; and the early lawyer can only see the law through the envelope of its technical forms. It would even seem that civilised societies experience reversions towards this condition of thought.[117]

Maine argued that the analytical positivists like Austin were recovering 'from its hiding-place the force that gives its sanction to law'.[118] In other words, the judicial remedies that had secured the 'law-abiding habit'[119] were being rediscovered. The remedies, however, were at no stage lost from the view of at least the practitioner. The forms of action were abolished but the causes of action in their wake remained of decisive importance. 'The forms of action we have buried, but they still rule us from their graves' were the equally famous words that Maitland added to Maine's description.[120] The preoccupation with remedies was not restricted to 'early law' and the occasional reversions of 'civilised societies' as Maine had suggested.[121]

Only an overwhelming remedial conception of law can explain *Malone* v. *Metropolitan Police Commissioner* where the court claimed it was powerless to declare telephone-tapping by the police unlawful because there was no recognized remedy.[122] Furthermore, the procedural

---

[114] F. W. Maitland, *The Forms of Action at Common Law: A Course of Lectures* (A. H. Chaytor and W. J. Whittaker (eds.)) (Cambridge, 1948), 1–11.

[115] *Ibid.* 4.   [116] Jolowicz, n. 64 above, 361–2.

[117] H. S. Maine, *Dissertations on Early Law and Custom* (London, 1891), 389.

[118] *Ibid.* 388–9.   [119] *Ibid.*

[120] Maitland, n. 114 above, 2.   [121] Maine, n. 117 above, 389.

[122] [1979] Ch. 344. See G. Samuel, 'Public and Private Law: A Private Lawyer's Response' (1983) 46 *MLR* 558–83 at 574–7.

requirements of the prerogative remedies continued to dominate judicial review, even after the procedural reforms of the late 1970s. They were fossilized because section 31(1)(2) of the Supreme Court Act 1981 (Order 53, rule 1 (2)) demarcated the scope of the AJR partly by reference to the scope of the prerogative remedies. If anything, the importance of the procedural requirements of the AJR was enhanced when, in *O'Reilly* v. *Mackman*, the House of Lords confirmed the principle of exclusivity.[123]

The English remedial conception of law has affected legal system. Whatever the reason for the remedial conception—whether it be the role of equity or the faith in an independent judiciary—English lawyers have been proudly pragmatic rather than theoretical[124] or systematic. They have been preoccupied with the question: what's to be done? Case by case, they have asked: can these facts lead to such-and-such a remedy? Their casuistic fact-orientation has had at least two consequences. First, English law has developed through 'the increasingly detailed consideration of facts'.[125] Secondly, English law has therefore had to be classified through the ordering of more and more relevant facts. For a classification to be determinate it has had to indicate the facts that would lead to a particular remedy. Accordingly, at an English conference on division and classification of the law, J. A. Jolowicz typically advocated 'fact based classification of law' for study purposes, and rejected conceptual classification through an examination of the 'law's internal logic or theoretical consistency'.[126]

A fact-based classification, however, cannot be attributed practical significance because of its unclearness and instability. Facts or classifications of facts are not self-evident. And the range of relevant facts has been increased by the courts casuistically, but without overall classification, to leave 'the uncharted vastness of the law'.[127] Pollock appreciated the unclearness of fact-based classification. He wrote: '[i]t is not possible to make any clear-cut division of the subject-matter of legal rules. The same facts are often the subject of two or more distinct

---

[123] [1982] 3 All ER 1124. See also *Uppal* v. *Home Office, The Times*, 11 Nov. 1978; *Heywood* v. *Hull Prison Board of Visitors* [1980] 3 All ER 594.

[124] P. S. Atiyah, *Pragmatism and Theory in English Law* (London, 1987), 18–26, 112–19.

[125] S. Milsom, 'Law and Fact in Legal Development' (1967) 17 *U of Toronto LJ* 1–19 at 1.

[126] J. A. Jolowicz, 'Fact Based Classification of Law' in J. A. Jolowicz (ed.), *The Division and Classification of the Law* (London, 1970), 1–9 at 3.

[127] M. Amos, 'Have we too Much Law?' [1931] *Jnl. of the Soc. of Pub. Teachers of L* 1–7 at 6.

rules, and give rise at the same time to distinct and different sets of duties and rights'.[128] Furthermore, any particular fact-based classification will become outmoded as the facts are seen to change. For example, Jolowicz's suggestion that the 'law relating to . . . relations between the State and the Individual' be a main heading for a fact-based classification of the law[129] has become increasingly problematic as the identity of the modern state has become increasingly unclear.[130]

With a positivist remedial conception of law, Austin negated and Dicey rejected the distinction between public and private law. Occasionally, English judges have recognized the implications of a remedial conception of law. A few years ago, Lord Wilberforce warned that '[i]n this country they [the expressions 'private law' and 'public law'] must be used with caution, for, typically, English law fastens not on principles but on remedies.'[131] Indeed, the traditional English concern with remedies has encouraged a casuistic fact-orientation which has undermined the importance of any system or classification. It has helped preclude a conception of law as a whole and has permitted only the secretion of principles and a limited systematization of procedures.

The Secretion of Legal Principles

Despite the traditional remedial conception of law, English courts have at times openly developed substantive legal principles. Their recent contribution has been most marked in the area of judicial review. The limited intervention of the courts in administrative disputes was mandated by the doctrine of *ultra vires*. With specific remedies, the courts could be required to intervene where the administration acted beyond the scope of its statutory powers. Nevertheless, at an early stage, they were prepared to develop principles of judicial review regardless of statute and their limited mandate. In the case of *Cooper* v. *Wandsworth Board of Works*, for example, where a local authority had exercised a statutory power to demolish a house, the court awarded the owner damages for trespass because the authority had not given the owner a hearing and so violated a rule 'of universal application, and founded upon the plainest principles of justice'.[132] The court introduced a

---

[128] F. Pollock, *A First Book of Jurisprudence* (6th edn., London, 1929), 84.

[129] Jolowicz, n. 126 above, 9.   [130] See above, Chs. 4 and 5.

[131] *Davy* v. *Spelthorne BC* [1983] 3 ALL ER 278 at 285H; paraphrased by Sir John Donaldson in *R.* v. *East Berkshire Health Authority, ex p. Walsh* [1985] QB 152 at 162B.

[132] (1863) 14 CBNS 180; excerpts reprinted in J. Beatson and M. H. Matthews, *Administrative Law: Cases and Materials* (2nd edn., Oxford, 1989), 304–6, especially at 305.

principle of natural justice by openly invoking 'the justice of the common law' to 'supply the omission of the legislature'[133] (which had not provided for a hearing). Subsequent courts were more restrained[134] but, after the Second World War and especially from the mid-1960s onwards, judges such as Lord Denning, Lord Reid, and Lord Radcliffe openly developed principles of reasonableness, fairness, and procedural justice to constrain the growing administration.[135] To the extent that they acknowledged their own innovations, they furthered a conception of law as a collection of principles rather than a mere range of remedies.[136]

Their contribution was reinforced by jurisprudential developments in response not only to the casuistic common-law tradition, but also to the challenge of American legal realism. In denying the limitations of formal legal logic, the legal realists conceived of law as a 'seamless web' rather than as a 'bundle of sticks' which could be separated into smaller bundles.[137] They described the judge spinning the seamless web as unconstrained by legal system.[138] In answer to the scepticism of the realists, later legal positivists have confirmed the constraints upon the judge. Hart describes how the judge, even when he must choose because of the 'open texture of law', should be concerned 'to deploy some acceptable general principle as a reasoned basis for decision'.[139]

[133] *Ibid.* 306.

[134] See H. W. R. Wade and C. F. Forsyth, *Administrative Law* (7th edn., Oxford, 1994), 502–10.

[135] A. Denning, *Freedom under the Law* (London, 1949), 99–126, especially at 125–6; *id.*, 'The Way of an Iconoclast' (1959/60) 5 *Jnl. of the Soc. of Pub. Teachers of L* 77–89, especially at 87–9; Lord Reid, 'The Judge as Law Maker' (1972/73) 12 *Jnl. of the Soc. of Pub. Teachers of L* 22–9; L. L. Jaffe, *English and American Judges as Lawmakers* (Oxford, 1969), especially at 78–84; S. Flogaïtis, *Administrative Law et droit administratif* (Paris, 1986), 105–9; J. Jowell, 'Courts and the Administration in Britain: Standards, Principles and Rights' (1988) 22 *Is. LR* 409–23. See, now, Lord Browne-Wilkinson, 'The Infiltration of a Bill of Rights' [1992] *PL* 397–410; J. Laws, 'Is the High Court the Guardian of Fundamental Constitutional Rights?' [1993] *PL* 59–79; A. Lester, 'English Judges as Law Makers' [1993] *PL* 269–90, especially at 278–86; Loughlin, n. 98 above, 206 ff.; D. Rose, 'Silent Revolution', *Observer*, 9 May 1993, 45–6; J. Clark, 'The Politics of Precedents', *The Times*, 28 July 1993, 12.

[136] C. J. Radcliffe, *The Law and its Compass* (London, 1961). See Jaffe, n. 135 above, 5–8. Cf. K. C. Davis, 'The Future of Judge-made Law in England: A Problem of Practical Jurisprudence' (1961) 61 *Columbia LRev.* 201–20; Atiyah, n. 124 above, 143–84.

[137] W. L. Twining, K. O'Donovan, and A. Paliwala, 'Ernie and the Centipede: Some Theoretical Aspects of Classification for the Purposes of Law Reform' in Jolowicz (ed.), n. 126 above, 10–29 at 13, 18.

[138] See, e.g., *ibid.* 18; J. H. Merryman, 'The Public Law–Private Law Distinction in European and American Law' (1968) 17 *J Publ. L* 3–19 at 9.

[139] H. L. A. Hart, *The Concept of Law* (Oxford, 1961), 121–50, especially at 200.

And, in hard cases, Dworkin's Hercules is bound to justify his decision by reference to principles underlying the legal and political institutions of his jurisdiction.[140]

The normal judge, however, in contrast to Dworkin's Hercules, has struggled to articulate and systematize principles of judicial review.[141] The difficult distinction between jurisdictional and non-jurisdictional error, the varying and vague meanings attributed to unreasonableness,[142] the unclearness of improper purpose,[143] and the relevance of the concept of legitimate expectation to both the procedure and substance of decision-making,[144] are the result of the struggle. The absence of clearly articulated principles is consequently still the cause of academic[145] and judicial dissatisfaction. Lord Scarman recognized the continuing lack of system in the 1990s:

Since 1948 [the year in which the *Wednesbury* case appeared in the Law Reports] there has, of course, been remarkable progress in the development of judicial review. But we have not achieved a coherent body of law. Today's administrative law is made up of bits and pieces. . . . It is still no more than an *ad hoc* bunch of restraints, controls, and procedures wrung from government and encapsulated in statutes and statutory instruments of limited operation.[146]

Articulation and systematization of principles are difficult for at least two reasons. First, the vagaries of statutory interpretation still required by the doctrine of *ultra vires* confuse the principles and, in particular, preclude clear categorization of public and private. For example, in *Anns* v. *Merton London Borough Council*, Lord Wilberforce distinguished between private- and public-law liability in tort. He stressed that 'the local authority is a public body, discharging functions under statute: its

[140] R. Dworkin, *Taking Rights Seriously* (London, 1978).

[141] See generally H. W. R. Wade, 'Crossroads in Administrative Law' [1968] *CLP* 75–93; Davis, n. 136 above.

[142] See, e.g., *Associated Provincial Picture Houses Ltd* v. *Wednesbury Corporation* [1948] 1 KB 223.

[143] See, e.g., *Wheeler* v. *Leicester CC* [1985] AC 1054; J. Jowell and A. Lester, 'Beyond *Wednesbury*: Substantive Principles of Administrative Law' [1987] *PL* 368–82 at 373–4.

[144] G. Ganz, 'Legitimate Expectation' in C. Harlow (ed.), *Public Law and Politics* (London, 1986), 145–62; C. Forsyth, 'The Provenance and Protection of Legitimate Expectations' [1988] *CLJ* 238–60.

[145] See, e.g., Jowell and Lester, n. 143 above; *eid.*, 'Proportionality: Neither Novel nor Dangerous' in J. L. Jowell and D. Oliver (eds.), *New Directions in Judicial Review* (London, 1988), 51–72; T. R. S. Allan, 'Pragmatism and Theory in English Administrative Law' (1988) 104 *LQR* 422–47; Lester, n. 135 above, especially at 280–6.

[146] 'The Development of Administrative Law: Obstacles and Opportunities' [1990] *PL* 490–5 at 491–2. See also Laws, n. 135 above.

powers and duties are definable in terms of public not private law.'[147] But he made the distinction between the principles of public- and private-law liability in tort depend upon twin uncertainties—statutory authorization for the administrative policy on the one hand, and the distinction between that policy and operations in its furtherance on the other. Secondly, a collection of principles is less amenable to categorization than a body of law. Generally applicable and often submerged, principles have a weight that cannot easily be confined to specific categories. For example, a principle of consistency was blocked where the Court of Appeal restricted the operation of estoppel in public-law cases,[148] but re-emerged through judicial development of the public-law doctrine of legitimate expectation.[149] '[D]epartments of law' are 'condemn[ed]' by the 'general spirit' of the interpretive method advocated by Dworkin.[150]

Because of the traditional casuistry of English law, David likened its overall appearance to that of an impressionist painting.[151] Because of the role of legal principles, however, its appearance is now rather that of a masterpiece made by a chain[152] of avant-garde artists from the principles secreted in the interstices of procedure.

The Systematization of Procedures

Although the emerging unruly principles, like the facts justifying a remedy, have not been able to be categorized, the procedures central to the English remedial conception of law have themselves been amenable to limited systematization in a traditional way. The traditional paths to legal system in English and Continental law have been divergent. While Continental law was generally being systematized through the reception and reworking of the *Corpus Iuris Civilis*, English law was being, or had been, partially systematized through the development of the science of pleading and a rational writ system at the Inns of Court.[153]

---

[147] [1978] AC 728 at 754B.

[148] *Western Fish Products Ltd* v. *Penwith DC* [1981] 2 All ER 204.

[149] *R.* v. *Home Secretary, ex p. Khan* [1984] 1 WLR 1337; *R.* v. *Home Secretary, ex p. Ruddock* [1987] 2 All ER 518. See Case Comment [1988] *Jnl. of Plan. & Environ. L* [1988] 705.

[150] R. Dworkin, *Law's Empire* (London, 1986), 250–4, especially at 251.

[151] David, n. 69 above, 77.

[152] See R. Dworkin, 'Law as Interpretation' (1982) 60 *Texas LRev.* 527–50, especially at 540–6.

[153] F. W. Maitland, *English Law and the Renaissance with Some Notes* (Cambridge, 1901);

The Order 53 reforms are the most recent example of the traditional attempt at systematizing procedures. The AJR was introduced to meet the need for a simple, inexpensive, and speedy procedure for judicial review.[154] In *O'Reilly* v. *Mackman*,[155] Lord Diplock justified its exclusivity in public-law cases as necessary to safeguard its procedural protections for public authorities—its time limit, standing requirement, and the need to obtain leave of court. The House of Lords would not tolerate the procedural anomaly of having legislative protections for public authorities that could be circumvented simply by a litigant's choosing another form of action.[156] Therefore, ironically, a public/private distinction was introduced through the remedial conception of law that traditionally precluded its development.

The divergent paths to legal system in English and Continental law, however, have different destinations. Because procedures remain the means to an end (albeit indefinite), their systematization in England has not been categorical. For centuries the requirements of the forms of action were subverted by the use of fiction.[157] Meanwhile, the prerogative writs defied systematization and survived the Judicature Acts abolishing the forms of action. As late as 1923, Jenks declared that '[t]here is no definition' of a prerogative writ and added '[t]hat is not how we do things'.[158] Furthermore, the prerogative remedies did not come to be regarded as exclusive procedures in public-law cases. Rather, the ordinary remedies of action for damages, injunction, and, especially, the declaration were widely used where the prerogative remedies proved inadequate. They played an important role in the development of judicial review.[159] The ordering of procedures has only ever resulted in limited systematization rather than legal categorization.

J. H. Baker, 'English Law and the Renaissance', Introduction *The Reports of Sir John Spelman*, ii (J. H. Baker (ed.)) (94 Selden Society, 1977), i, 23–51 at 23–8. Cf. generally Martin Loughlin's view of the anti-rationalist character of the common law: n. 98 above. Cf. R. Cotterrell, *The Politics of Jurisprudence: A Critical Introduction to Legal Philosophy* (London, 1989), 22–5.

[154] See Law Commission, *Remedies in Administrative Law* (Law Com. 73, 1976), Cmnd. 6407.

[155] N. 123 above.

[156] H. W. R. Wade, 'Procedure and Prerogative in Public Law' (1985) 101 *LQR* 180–99 at 185–6.

[157] See Maitland, *The Forms of Action*, n. 114 above, 7–11.

[158] E. Jenks, 'The Prerogative Writs in English Law' (1923) 32 *Yale LJ* 523–34 at 533.

[159] See, e.g., *Dyson* v. *Attorney-General* [1911] 1 KB 410; *Barnard* v. *National Dock Labour Board* [1953] 2 QB 18; *Anisminic Ltd* v. *Foreign Compensation Commission* [1969] 2 AC 147; Wade and Forsyth, n. 134 above, 579–600, 670–2.

The Order 53 reforms introducing the distinction between public- and private-law procedures illustrate the limits to procedural systematization in England. They are and have remained fundamentally confused in at least three respects. First, no clear criterion has been adopted for determining whether the AJR should be used.[160] Order 53 of the Rules of the Supreme Court[161] refers only to 'all the circumstances of the case' and to the varying ambit[162] of the prerogative remedies. In *O'Reilly*, the House of Lords introduced the principle of exclusivity but did not clarify the criterion.[163] More recently, in *R. v. Panel on Take-overs and Mergers, ex p. Datafin plc*, the judges of the Court of Appeal did at times suggest public duty as a criterion for determining the availability of the AJR,[164] but did not define it and stressed the relevance of multiple factors.[165] Like the Court of Appeal in *R. v. East Berkshire Health Authority, ex p. Walsh*, the judges chose to survey all the circumstances, including the *ad hoc* availability of alternative relief,[166] rather than apply any clear criterion. In *R. v. Football Association, ex p. Football League*, Rose J also stressed the increasing scarcity of the judicial resources of the Crown Office.[167] Judicial pragmatism has prevailed over legal system.[168]

Secondly, the reforms are confused by Lord Diplock's exceptions to the principle that the AJR be an exclusive procedure in public-law cases.[169] In *O'Reilly*, Lord Diplock mentioned two exceptions—where

---

[160] See above, 90 ff.　　　　　　　[161] R. 1(2); s. 31(2) of Supreme Court Act 1981.

[162] P. P. Craig, *Administrative Law* (2nd edn., London, 1989), 385–7, 419–20. See, e.g., *R. v. Electricity Commissioners, ex p. London Electricity Joint Committee Co. (1920) Ltd* [1924] 1 KB 171; *R. v. Criminal Injuries Compensation Board, ex p. Lain* [1967] 2 QB 864 at 882A–B.

[163] N. 123 above.

[164] [1987] QB 815 at 848G–H, 852C–D; C. Forsyth, 'The Scope of Judicial Review: "Public Duty" not "Source of Power" ' [1987] *PL* 356–67.

[165] N. 164 above, 838E–G, 847A–B, 848C–D and 852C–D.

[166] *Ibid.* 845F–G; *Walsh*, n. 131 above, especially at 170A and 173B–D; S. Fredman and G. Morris, 'Public or Private? State Employees and Judicial Review' (1991) 107 *LQR* 298–316 at 308–9. See generally C. Forsyth, 'The Boundaries of Judicial Review', Public Seminar (QMW College, Dec. 1991).

[167] [1993] 2 All ER 833 at 849C. See also *R. v. Code of Practice Committee of the British Pharmaceutical Industry, ex p. Professional Counselling Aids Ltd* (1991) 3 Admin. LR 697 at 718H–19A; *R. v. Jockey Club, ex p. Aga Khan* [1993] 1 WLR 909 at 922E, 923B–D, 924E; M. J. Beloff, 'Pitch, Pool, Rink, . . . Court? Judicial Review in the Sporting World' [1989] *PL* 95–110 at 110; D. Pannick, 'Who is Subject to Judicial Review in Respect of What?' [1992] *PL* 1–7 at 6–7; J. Laws, 'Procedural Exclusivity', Conference on the Law Commission's consultation paper 126 (University of Cambridge, May 1993).

[168] See D. Feldman, 'Public Law Values in the House of Lords' (1990) 106 *LQR* 246–76 at 271–5.

[169] *O'Reilly*, n. 123 above, 1134F–G; J. McBride, 'The Doctrine of Exclusivity and Judicial Review: *O'Reilly v. Mackman*' [1983] *CJQ* 268–81 at 279–80.

the administrative decision is challenged collaterally to a private-law action, and where the parties do not object to the use of private-law remedies. These exceptions, however, raise questions which undermine Lord Diplock's argument for exclusivity. Why should an authority forfeit the procedural protections of an AJR merely because a challenge is collateral? And why should the AJR generally be required if the parties may have good reason not to use it? Lord Diplock does not justify his exceptions and leaves them open-ended, 'to be decided on a case to case basis'.[170] Consequently, the further exceptions, such as that created in *Wandsworth London Borough Council* v. *Winder* (the challenge to an administrative decision raised as a defence to a private-law action),[171] and the 'liberal attitude towards the exceptions' adopted by the House of Lords[172] and recommended by Lord Woolf[173] further undermine Lord Diplock's reasoning by denying the authorities the procedural protections which the House in *O'Reilly* was concerned to uphold. Another of Woolf's recommendations—that the present overload on the Crown Office be spread among other Divisions and part-time judges—is a comparable denial of the institutional advantages of the Crown Office List.[174]

Thirdly, the judicial approach to distinguishing private- from public-law procedures is different from the judicial approach to distinguishing public- from private-law procedures. After *O'Reilly*, to determine the availability of private-law remedies, courts generally worked with a criterion of private-law rights.[175] But, apart from begging the question by not defining their criterion, they have not related it to Lord Diplock's reasoning for making the AJR an exclusive procedure in public-law cases. They have not adequately explained why an authority should forfeit an AJR's procedural protections merely because a private-law right is in issue. While they determine the avail-

---

[170] *O'Reilly*, n. 123 above, 1134F–G; J. McBride, 'The Doctrine of Exclusivity and Judicial Review: *O'Reilly* v. *Mackman*' [1983] *CJQ* 268–81 at 279–80.

[171] [1985] AC 461, especially at 509A–B, where Lord Fraser recognizes the need to protect Wandsworth LBC from prolonged uncertainty about the validity of its rent decisions; C. Forsyth, 'The Principle of *O'Reilly* v. *Mackman*: A Shield but not a Sword?' [1985] *PL* 355–61. See also, e.g., *An Bord Bainne Co-operative Ltd (Irish Dairy Board)* v. *Milk Marketing Board* [1984] 2 CMLR 584; *R.* v. *Oxford Crown Court and Another, ex p. Smith* (1990) 2 Admin. LR 389; M. J. Beloff, 'The Boundaries of Judicial Review' in J. Jowell and D. Oliver (eds), *New Directions in Judicial Review* (London, 1988), 5–21 at 12–14.

[172] *Roy* v. *Kensington and Chelsea and Westminster Family Practitioner Committee* [1992] 2 WLR 239 at 261H–2A, 264H–6B, especially at 265E.

[173] Woolf, 'Programme for Reform', n. 2 above, 231.

[174] *Ibid.* 225–6. Cf. *ibid.* 228–31.

[175] *Cocks* v. *Thanet DC* [1983] 2 AC 286; *Davy*, n. 131 above; *Roy*, n. 172 above.

ability of private-law procedures according to an independent notion of private-law right, they are required by Lord Diplock's reasoning to give the procedural protections priority when deciding on the availability of the AJR. In short, the judicial approaches to using the private-law remedies on the one hand, and the application for judicial review on the other hand, are asymmetrical.[176]

Because of the confusion, the Order 53 reforms have been much criticized for creating a procedural minefield for the litigant. While Jolowicz calls the Order 53 reforms 'a singularly unfortunate step back to the technicalities of a bygone age',[177] Wade stresses the consequent waste of time and money on procedural litigation.[178] In response to such criticism, the courts seem to be reducing the significance of the procedural distinction by relying on the exceptions recognized in *O'Reilly*. Without the required categorical approach to law, the English distinction between public- and private-law procedures is proving unsatisfactory and is becoming less significant.

In contrast to the categorical approach to law accompanying the French distinction in the nineteenth century, the English remedial conception of law has negated the importance of legal system. In England, only with difficulty have legal principles been articulated and systematized and only to a limited extent have procedures been ordered. For want of a categorical approach to law,[179] the recent attempt to introduce a procedural distinction between public and private law has been accompanied by confusion and obscured by open-ended exceptions. It does not signify the coming together of the civil and common-law traditions.[180] Rather, it confirms their traditional differences and illustrates the hazards of ill-considered transplantation.

---

[176] C. Forsyth, 'Beyond *O'Reilly* v. *Mackman*: The Foundations and Nature of Procedural Exclusivity' [1985] *CLJ* 415–34; Craig, n. 162 above, 413–18.

[177] J. A. Jolowicz, 'The Forms of Action Disinterred' [1983] *CLJ* 15–18 at 18. See also *Doyle* v. *Northumbria Probation Committee* [1991] 1 WLR 1340 at 1348B.

[178] Wade, n. 156 above, 189. See also McBride, n. 169 above.

[179] See also above, 95 ff., below, 230 ff.   [180] *Contra* Flogaïtis, n. 135 above.

7
The Separation of Powers

In the last chapter, I elaborated on one aspect of my model of the working distinction between public and private law, which I described in Chapter 3. I suggested that a categorical approach to law is required for the distinction to be given significance in general—whether substantive, institutional, or procedural. In this chapter, I will elaborate on the theory of institutional separation required for the distinction to be given institutional significance in particular. I will argue, first, that institutions dealing with administrative disputes must meet demands for expertise and independence; secondly, that the *Conseil d'Etat*, because of a unique political history, has broadly satisfied those demands; and, thirdly, that those demands have not been met by separate institutions in the English context because of the English approach to the separation of powers—its vagueness and its emphasis on judicial independence. I will conclude that the institutional distinction which has emerged in England as a result of the Crown Office List is therefore proving inadequate. In this chapter, I will again[1] presuppose a distinct state administration so as to focus attention on another aspect[2] of my model.

Institutional Expertise and Independence

Contradictory claims of subjectivity and objectivity upon social theory are described by Unger:

If we disregard the meanings an act has for its author and for the other members of the society to which he belongs, we run the risk of losing sight of what is peculiarly social in the conduct we are trying to understand. If, however, we insist on sticking close to the reflective understanding of the agent or his fellows, we are deprived of a standard by which to distinguish insight from illusion . . . Thus, subjective and objective meaning must somehow both be taken into account.[3]

The claims of subjectivity and objectivity are not restricted to social theory and the predicament created by Weber's call for interpretive

---

[1] See above, 109. [2] See above, 35–6, 38–9.
[3] R. M. Unger, *Law in Modern Society: Toward a Criticism of Social Theory* (New York, 1976), 15.

explanation. Whether the viewpoint of the observed or the observer is adopted matters partly because of the proximity accordingly required of the observer to the situation of the observed. The claims of subjectivity and objectivity can be broadly conceptualized to refer to that proximity. As such, they are almost common sense and are expressed in everyday figures of speech. While we are aware that 'distance lends enchantment to a view', we try to avoid 'not seeing the wood for the trees'. We realize that to know, we must have both insight and perspective. We must be involved in order to understand, and detached in order not to be deluded.

Particularly, a court which must intervene authoritatively in a dispute on the basis of its understanding of the facts feels the weight of the claims of subjectivity and objectivity. The court must understand the subject matter of the dispute and the position of the parties, but must not be blinded by the dust they kick up. It must have the expertise so as not to be obstructive and the independence so as not to be partisan. In short, if the court is to avoid depending on its access to the coercive powers of the state, it must derive authority for its decisions from its institutional assurances of subjectivity and objectivity—judicial expertise and independence.

When a court must resolve a dispute involving an administrative body or function, the demands both of expertise and independence are aggravated. The court must understand the nature of administrative needs despite the complexity of modern administration. It must appreciate the circumstances possibly relevant to the intensity of its involvement—the administrator's relative expertise, the effectiveness of non-judicial controls, and whatever interests are being threatened or promoted. It must also be able to determine administrative policy because, for example, in reviewing the relevance of considerations taken into account by administrators, it cannot distinguish between policy and the execution of policy. But, at the same time, because the court is inevitably drawn into policy determination and because of the involvement of an administrative body in the dispute, the court's independence is especially necessary. The court must negate that institutional link between itself and the administration as both part of the state for fear that the 'basic social logic' of the adjudicative triad—two disputants' appealing to a third—will collapse into the unacceptable situation of 'two against one'.[4] The position of the state as both party and

⁴ M. Shapiro, *Courts: A Comparative and Political Analysis* (Chicago, 1981), 1–2, 27.

judge in administrative disputes has been used to explain the distinctness of public law.[5] It also, however, demands that a theory of institutional separation somehow ensure that the court has the expertise and
independence to deal with administrative disputes.

The demands of expertise and independence are contradictory. The
court must be sufficiently associated with the administration to understand its activities, and sufficiently detached so as not to be partial.
Critical legal theorists have regarded contradictions, such as that
between objectivity and subjectivity, between the demand for independence and the demand for expertise, as a means to social transformation. They have faith in the escalation of argument around
contradictions into conflict about fundamentals.[6] Their faith, however,
is opposed by the realist or cynical understanding that contradictory theory is politically effective and conducive to stability precisely because it
can satisfy contradictory human sensibilities in a particular context. The
development of the French and English institutional distinctions between
public and private law in response to the demands of expertise and independence is therefore a test case for the stability of contradictions.

The Development of an Institutional Distinction in France

I will argue that the French distinction between public- and private-
law courts developed in two stages. In the first stage, the ordinary
courts were prohibited from resolving administrative disputes. In the
second stage, separate administrative courts were created to resolve
such disputes. The two stages were motivated by different theories, or
different aspects of the same theory, of the separation of powers: in the
first, by a radical assertion of the complete independence of the executive from the ordinary courts; and, in the second, by a demand for
the judicial independence of the emergent administrative courts.[7]

The Radical French Separation of Powers

In pre-Revolutionary France, the *Parlements* had wide-ranging powers.
Apart from fulfilling their normal judicial functions, they exercised

---

[5] See, e.g., T. E. Holland, *The Elements of Jurisprudence* (13th edn., Oxford, 1924),
128–9, 366.

[6] Cf., e.g., R. M. Unger, *False Necessity: Anti-Necessitarian Social Theory in the Service of
Radical Democracy*, Pt. 1 of *Politics, a Work in Constructive Social Theory* (Cambridge, 1987),
355–62.

[7] Cf. B. Schwartz, *French Administrative Law and the Common-Law World* (New York,
1954), 8.

administrative functions, issued regulatory decrees, and could veto royal legislation by refusing to register royal acts.[8] They wielded their enormous powers according to their interest. Because judicial offices came to be bought, sold, and inherited,[9] a 'huge and rapacious bureaucracy' exacted excessive returns from litigants.[10] And, because judicial offices accumulated in the hands of those families who could afford them, the *Parlements* came to be administered by a *noblesse de robe* intent on defending the privileges of the nobility and resisting the reforms that might have saved the monarchy.[11]

The *Parlements* came into conflict with an increasingly centralized administration. They competed with the *Intendants*,[12] the King's administrative officers, for judicial and political power. They resented the judicial powers conferred by the King upon the *Intendants* and protected by way of *évocations* to the *Conseil du Roi*.[13] In turn, they were resented for the extent and nature of their political involvement which the French kings could restrict only temporarily.[14] At the time of the Revolution, the resentment turned to wrath and, in its aftermath, to a lasting distrust and fear of *gouvernement des juges*.

As a noble who became a *Président à Mortier* of the *Parlement* of Bordeaux, Montesquieu was concerned with the judicial role of the administration rather than with the political role of the *Parlements*.[15] But, because of his political ambivalence to the monarchy, his general theory advocating that legislative, executive, and judicial powers be kept separate could have widespread appeal at the time of the Revolution.[16] In his famous chapter on the English constitution in *The Spirit of the Laws*, Montesquieu presented the confusing of powers as a

---

[8] J. Brissaud, *A History of French Public Law* (London, 1915), secs. 413, 416; J. P. Dawson, *The Oracles of the Law* (Ann Arbor, 1968), 305–14.

[9] E. Le Roy Ladurie, *The Royal French State 1460–1610* (Oxford, 1994), ch. 13; H. A. Lloyd, *The State, France, and the Sixteenth Century* (London, 1983), 72 ff.

[10] Dawson, n. 8 above, 355–6.

[11] F. Ford, *Robe and Sword: The Regrouping of the French Aristocracy after Louis XIV* (New York, 1965); Dawson, n. 8 above, 353–73.

[12] See generally Brissaud, n. 8 above, secs. 383–8; J.-L. Mestre, *Introduction historique au droit administratif Français* (Paris, 1985), secs. 124 ff.

[13] M. Waline, *Droit administratif* (9th edn., Paris, 1963), sec. 33.

[14] See, e.g., Brissaud, n. 8 above, secs. 418, 419; Dawson, n. 8 above, 368.

[15] Montesquieu, *The Spirit of the Laws* (A. M. Cohler, B. C. Miller, and H. S. Stone (eds. and trs.)) (Cambridge, 1989), bk. 2, ch. 4; bk. 12, ch. 22. See Ford, n. 11 above, 222–45, especially at 239; M. J. C. Vile, *Constitutionalism and the Separation of Powers* (Oxford, 1967), 80.

[16] Vile, *ibid.*, 78.

threat to liberty. He stressed the need not to entrust legislative, executive, and judicial powers to the same institutions:

> Nor is there liberty if the power of judging is not separate from legislative power and from executive power. If it were joined to legislative power, the power over the life and liberty of the citizens would be arbitrary, for the judge would be the legislator. If it were joined to executive power, the judge could have the force of an oppressor.[17]

Although Montesquieu derived his theory of separate powers from the English constitution, he envisaged a rigid rather than a rough separation of powers.[18] In his chapter on the English constitution, he also did not describe the three powers as equally important. Whereas he described the legislative power as 'the general will of the state' and the executive power as 'the execution of that general will', he regarded the judicial power, which he introduced into analytical discussion of a separation of powers, as 'in some fashion, null'.[19] Elsewhere, Montesquieu did recognize and defend the role of the *Parlements* amongst other intermediate groups in a normal monarchy,[20] but, in his chapter on the constitution of England (which he regarded as a disguised republic),[21] he expressed a preference for a system of checks and balances, depending on legislative rather than judicial control over the administration.[22]

Rousseau's theory of the general will accentuated the disparity of the three powers.[23] Rousseau conceptualized the general will as infallible,[24] but nevertheless recognized that the government which was to enact it would inevitably subvert it,[25] and that even the people could make wrong decisions. Chapter 3, Book 2, of *The Social Contract* opens with the following famous passage:

> It follows from what I have argued that the general will is always rightful and always tends to the public good; but it does not follow that the decisions of the

---

[17] Montesquieu, n. 15 above, bk. 11, ch. 6, 157. See generally Vile, n. 15 above, 90–3.

[18] See above, 16–18.

[19] Montesquieu, n. 15 above, 158, 160. See Vile, n. 15 above, 88–90; C. J. Friedrich, *Constitutional Government and Politics* (New York, 1937), 147–8.

[20] Ford, n. 11 above, 222–45, especially at 239; M. Cappelletti, 'Repudiating Montesquieu? The Expansion and Legitimacy of "Constitutional Justice"' in M. Cappelletti, *The Judicial Process in Comparative Perspective* (Oxford, 1989), ch. 5, 192–3, n. 28.

[21] See Montesquieu, n. 15 above, bk. 5, ch. 19; Vile, n. 15 above, 80–5.

[22] Montesquieu, n. 15 above, bk. 11, ch. 6.

[23] J.-J. Rousseau, *The Social Contract* (M. Cranston (tr.)) (Harmondsworth, 1968).

[24] *Ibid.* bk. 2, ch. 3. See also *ibid.* bk. 2, ch. 4; bk. 4, ch. 1.

[25] *Ibid.* bk. 3, ch. 10. See generally *ibid.* bk. 3, ch. 1.

people are always equally right. We always want what is advantageous but we do not always discern it. The people is never corrupted, but it is often misled; and only then does it seem to will what is bad.[26]

Rousseau's theory of the general will is confusing and contradictory. He left his general will suspended in mid-air by conceiving of it both as a transcendent abstraction of a sovereign people and as a real expression of willing individuals when they come together to legislate.[27] Therefore, as his theory was popularized, as it became the ideology of the Revolution, it was susceptible to a simplified identification of the infallible general will with the legislature, and the execution of the general will with the administration. The revolutionaries of 1789 attributed to the ordinary legislature and administration certain of the qualities that Rousseau had attributed to his sovereign people and government.[28] Rousseau derided the separation of powers in one chapter[29] and generally ignored the judicial power, but his theory of the general will, as popularized, enhanced the status of the legislature and executive at the expense of the judiciary.

The experience of the power and political involvement of the *Parlements*, Montesquieu's advocacy of separate powers, his recognition but immediate relegation of the judicial power, and the accentuation of the executive power derived from Rousseau all contributed, at the time of the Revolution, to a radical and repeated prohibition of interference by the courts with the executive. Article 16 of the Declaration of Human Rights of 26 August 1789 declared that a separation of powers was indispensable for constitutional government. On 3 November 1789, the Constituent Assembly placed the *Parlements* on indefinite vacation, and, on 22 December 1789, it attempted to prevent their recurrence and to ensure a separation of powers by passing a law proclaiming that the judicial power should not interfere with administrative authorities. Decisively, in 1790, it proclaimed the prohibition that was repeated in the Constitution of 1791 and, after the Jacobin period, in the Constitution of 1799:

Judicial functions are distinct and will always remain separate from administrative functions. It shall be a criminal offence for judges of the ordinary courts

---

[26] *Ibid.* 72.

[27] C. J. Friedrich, *The Philosophy of Law in Historical Perspective* (Chicago, 1958), 123–5. See N. Hampson, 'The Heavenly City of the French Revolutionaries' in C. Lucas (ed.), *Rewriting the French Revolution* (Oxford, 1991), 46–68 at 48–50.

[28] Vile, n. 15 above, 177–88. See above, 51.

[29] Rousseau, n. 23 above, bk. 2, ch. 2.

to interfere in any manner whatsoever with the operation of the administration, nor shall they call administrators to account before them in respect of the exercise of their official functions.[30]

As separated by Montesquieu and derived from Rousseau's theory of the general will, the executive and judicial functions were not of equal status. As understood and enacted by the revolutionaries, the separation of powers was radical but pointedly one-sided: 'the judges were . . . prevented from administering, but the administrators were not prevented from judging'.[31] Indeed, administrators soon were required to judge administrative disputes; and, when they were, their institutional position ensured that they would at least have the administrative expertise to do so effectively.

Judicial Independence and the Judicialization of the Conseil d'Etat

The prohibition of judicial interference with the administration left both the administration and individuals aggrieved by administrative action in an unacceptable situation. On the one hand, the central administration was without that source of information which complaints about administrative injustices would have provided and which could have been used to discipline subordinate administrators. On the other hand, the aggrieved individuals had no one to complain to other than the offending administrators or their immediate superiors.[32]

Napoleon began the process by which the situation was rectified. In his Constitution of 1799 he established the *Conseil d'Etat*, a post-Revolutionary analogue to the pre-Revolutionary *Conseil du Roi*.[33] It was intended generally to serve as the technical legal advisor to the government and particularly to draft laws and administrative regulations, and 'to resolve difficulties which might occur in the course of the administration'.[34] By way of a decree later that year, he explicitly gave it the power to advise him on the setting aside of improper administrative acts. But, because of its restricted appellate role, its mixed functions and the form of its decisions, appeal to the *Conseil d'Etat* did not amount to recourse to an independent judicial body. First, the individual aggrieved by an administrative act could only appeal after his

---

[30] Law of 16–24 Aug. 1790, ch. 2, art. 13 (translation by L. N. Brown and J. S. Bell, *French Administrative Law* (4th edn., Oxford, 1993)), 123; Constitution of 1791, art. 203; Constitution of 1799, art. 75.

[31] Waline quoted by Schwartz, n. 7 above, 7.

[32] Waline, n. 13 above, sec. 36.   [33] See below, 209–11.

[34] Constitution of 1799, art. 53 (translation by Brown and Bell, n. 30 above, 44).

complaint had been heard by the appropriate minister. Secondly, the *Conseil d'Etat* itself fulfilled both administrative and judicial functions according to procedures which were neither public nor governed by clear procedural rules. Thirdly, it could make decisions only in the form of administrative proposals to the Head of State and not in the form of judgements.[35]

In the first half of the nineteenth century, the *Conseil d'Etat* was much criticized by liberals influenced by English ideas. Whereas the revolutionaries had stressed the need for the courts not to interfere with administrative agencies, the liberals of the nineteenth century began to stress a notion of judicial independence and apply it to the judicial functions of the *Conseil d'Etat*.

While Benjamin Constant served as Napoleon's constitutional adviser on the *Conseil d'Etat*, he championed a notion of judicial independence as an aspect of his theory of constitutional monarchy involving co-operation but checks and balances between the executive, legislative, and judicial branches of government.[36] In his *Principles of Politics*, Constant advocated that judges be irremovable, well paid, few in number, protected against declamations, and subject to procedural safeguards.[37] Amidst repeated references to the English model, Constant argued that the responsibilities of subordinate officials for the execution of illegal orders should be determined by jurors because of their independence:

And, who, anyway, is going to be entrusted with this examination? Not, I believe, the same authority who issued the order which you wish to examine. You will have to find a way of pronouncing a judgement in each case, and the best method is precisely to confer the right to pronounce a judgement on those men who are the most impartial, the most identified with both private and public interest. These men are the jurors.[38]

Similarly, he argued that ministerial responsibility for abuse of power should be determined by a tribunal of peers who are 'initiated through their offices into most of the secrets of the administration' but are independent from the interests of both people and government.[39]

Whereas Constant championed the notion of judicial independence, others also applied it to the *Conseil d'Etat*. Tocqueville's application of

---

[35] Waline, n. 13 above, sec. 39.   [36] See generally Vile, n. 15 above, 201–6.

[37] B. Constant, *Principles of Politics Applicable to All Representative Governments* in B. Constant, *Political Writings* (B. Fontana (ed. and tr.)) (Cambridge, 1988), 169–305 at ch. 19.

[38] *Ibid.*, ch. 11, at 249.   [39] *Ibid.*, ch. 9, especially at 234–5.

the notion typified liberal criticism of that body. Tocqueville identified the problem of an administrative tribunal as pre-Revolutionary in origin, even praised the pre-Revolutionary *Parlements* for their courageous defence of their own independence from interference by the central administration,[40] and explicitly criticized the *Conseil d'Etat* because of its lack of independence. In *Democracy in America*, he described the incredulous response of people in England and America to his description of the *Conseil d'Etat*:

But when I told them that the council of state was not a judicial body in the common sense of the term, but an administrative council composed of men dependent on the crown, so that the king, after having ordered one of his servants, called a prefect, to commit an injustice, has the power of commanding another of his servants, called a councillor of state, to prevent the former from being punished. When I showed them that the citizen who has been injured by an order of the sovereign is obliged to ask the sovereign's permission to obtain redress, they refused to credit so flagrant an abuse and were tempted to accuse me of falsehood or ignorance.[41]

Elsewhere in the same work, Tocqueville commented on the one-sidedness of the French separation of powers:

A strange sophism has been uttered on this subject in France. When a suit arises between the government and a private person, it is not to be tried before an ordinary judge, in order, they say, not to mix the administrative and the judicial powers; as if it were not to confuse those powers and in the most dangerous and oppressive manner to invest the government with the office of judging and administering at the same time.[42]

Liberal critics of the *Conseil d'Etat*[43] were particularly prominent in the French legislature in the early and middle decades of the nineteenth century. They argued either that it should be suppressed as unconstitutional and its judicial business transferred to the ordinary courts, or that special administrative courts should be created. The *Conseil d'Etat* was not suppressed but, in response to liberal criticism like that of Tocqueville, was transformed by a series of reforms through the course of the nineteenth century.

---

[40] A. De Tocqueville, *L'Ancien régime* (G. Headlam (ed.)) (Oxford, 1904), bk. 2, chs. 4, 11.

[41] A. De Tocqueville, *Democracy in America* (P. Bradley (ed.)) (London, 1994), i, ch. 6, 104–5.

[42] *Ibid.* ii, bk. 4, ch. 5, 308–9, n. 4.

[43] See, e.g., H. S. Jones, *The French State in Question: Public Law and Political Argument in the Third Republic* (Cambridge, 1993), 50.

Within the *Conseil d'Etat*, a section was first created to deal with its judicial work, and then gradually judicialized to meet a demand for judicial independence.[44] In 1806, the *Commission du Contentieux* (called the *Section du Contentieux* after 1849) was created to stand alongside advisory sections of the *Conseil d'Etat*.[45] In 1831, first an ordinance provided for a public hearing at which the parties to an administrative dispute could be represented by counsel.[46] Then, a second ordinance established the office of *Commissaire du Gouvernement* and excluded members associated with the active administration from judicial deliberations.[47] The office of *Commissaire* was originally intended to limit the independence of the judicial section by representing the government's interest in the judicial proceedings of the *Conseil*. But, in effect, it furthered that independence by acquiring the role of representing the public interest free from hierarchical control. In 1849, an ordinance further detached the judicial section from the rest of the *Conseil d'Etat* by dispensing with the requirement that decisions of the judicial section be formally approved by the *Conseil d'Etat*'s General Assembly.[48]

The judicial independence of the *Conseil d'Etat* was symbolically enacted in 1872 when it was no longer required to make its decisions in the form of advice to the Head of State and was empowered to pronounce judgments in the name of the French people.[49] In 1879, when the Republicans gained full control of the Republic, the Vice-president of the *Conseil* was forced to resign and nine *Conseillers d'Etat* were dismissed, but, thereafter, the independence of the *Conseil* was accepted by the government.[50] Only after the fall of the Vichy government were *Conseillers* again purged, and, then, alongside ordinary judges. During the Third Republic, the independence of *Conseillers d'Etat* was further entrenched as seniority became the basis for advancement.[51] Crucially, recourse to a more independent judicial body was ensured in 1889, when the individual aggrieved by administrative action was no longer required first to complain to the appropriate minister, who would be

---

[44] Waline, n. 13 above, secs. 40 and 41; Brown and Bell, n. 30 above, 44–7; C. J. Hamson, *Executive Discretion and Judicial Control: An Aspect of the French Conseil d'Etat* (London, 1954), 74–83, 145–8.

[45] Decree of 11 June 1806, art. 24. [46] Ordinance of 2 Feb. 1831.

[47] Ordinance of 12 Mar. 1831. [48] Ordinance of 26 May 1849.

[49] Law of 24 May 1872, art. 9. See generally R. Drago, 'La loi du 24 Mai 1872' (1972) 25 *EDCE* 13–20; V. Wright, 'La réorganisation du Conseil d'Etat en 1872' (1972) 25 *EDCE* 21–61; C. E. Freedeman, *The Conseil d'Etat in Modern France* (New York, 1961), 16–34.

[50] Freedeman, *ibid.*, 34–6. [51] *Ibid.* 10–11, 58.

judge in his own cause, but was entitled by the *Cadot* decision to take his case directly to the *Conseil d'Etat*.[52]

As the *Conseil d'Etat* was judicialized, its liberal critics were silenced. Even Tocqueville, while a member of the Committee considering the reform of the *Conseil d'Etat* in 1845, voted against abolishing it.[53] And, in 1872, the Committee of the National Assembly, considering its reform, both advocated that it be given full powers of judgment and conclusively defended the separation of jurisdictions: first, because of the expertise required when judging cases involving the administration and, secondly, because the ordinary courts would otherwise interfere with the administration.[54] Duguit later described how the *Conseil d'Etat* had won confidence: '[t]he movement towards suppression has had considerable result. The Act of 1872 has not only made the Council of State a sovereign jurisdiction; but the learning and the impartiality of its members has made of it a power which inspires an unlimited confidence.'[55] Duguit praised the administrative courts because of their cognizance 'of the conditions under which it is necessary to operate the state' and because of their 'guarantees of independence and impartiality'.[56] By the early twentieth century, after more than a hundred years of difficult reform, the judicial independence of the *Conseil d'Etat statuant au contentieux* and the administrative expertise assured by its links to the administration had entrenched the institutional distinction between public- and private-law courts. The distinction's constitutional status and its connection with the French conception of the separation of powers have now been confirmed by the *Conseil Constitutionnel*.[57]

The Independence and Expertise of the *Conseil d'Etat*

Despite its judicialization, the judicial section of the *Conseil d'Etat* has retained its links with the administration.[58] It remains part of the *Conseil d'Etat* which recruits members mainly from *l'Ecole Nationale d'Administration* and partly from the active administration. Many members spend periods away to serve as administrators, while distinguished

---

[52] *Cadot*, CE, 13 Dec. 1889.   [53] Freedeman, n. 49 above, 14.
[54] *Ibid.* 19–21, 124–5.
[55] L. Duguit, *Law in the Modern State* (F. and H. Laski (trs.)) (New York, 1970), 137.
[56] *Ibid.* 159.
[57] *Competition Law*, CC decision 86–224–DC, 23 Jan. 1987; *Entry and Residence of Foreigners*, CC decision 89–261–DC of 28 July 1989.
[58] R. David, *French Law: Its Structure, Sources and Methodology* (M. Kindred (tr.)) (Baton Rouge, 1972), 34–6; Brown and Bell, n. 30 above, ch. 4.

administrators spend periods *en service extraordinaire* on the *Conseil d'Etat.*

Together with the judicial section, advisory sections make up the *Conseil d'Etat.*[59] While the judicial section judges the administration, the other sections serve as its confidential legal advisor on proposed legislation and wide-ranging administrative matters. Rendel comments:

> Perhaps the most striking feature of the structure of the *Conseil d'Etat* is the way it is organized as a series of committees with a considerable measure of overlapping membership. The most striking feature of the methods of work is the combination of great individual initiative and responsibility with a high degree of corporate participation through argument, discussion and voting.[60]

Apart from participating in committees with overlapping membership, members of the judicial and advisory sections have extensive informal contact. All the members of the *Conseil d'Etat* share the same physical environment—the same building, canteen, and library—and the same corporate identity. The decisions of the judicial section are therefore the decisions of the *Conseil d'Etat* and are supported as such by the advisory sections. Because of informal contact and the overlapping membership of committees, and because of the links of the *Conseil d'Etat* as a whole to the active administration, members of the judicial section have the expertise—the knowledge of administrative needs and difficulties—to command the respect of administrators required to intervene authoritatively in administrative disputes. The authority derived from the judicial section's relationship to the administration is central to Hamson's influential thesis that the double function of the *Conseil d'Etat* as both judge and confidential advisor of the administration is the reason for its success.[61]

Hamson, however, recognizes that the authority of the *Conseil d'Etat* is secured at the cost of some compromise to judicial independence.[62] Others go further and are more explicit. Shapiro, for example, because of the *Conseil d'Etat*'s links to the administration, even concludes that 'the council is not a court staffed by judges but an extremely elite segment of the high civil service designated to supervise the legal

[59] See M. Rendel, *The Administrative Functions of the French Conseil d'Etat* (London, 1970).
[60] *Ibid.* 62.
[61] Hamson, n. 44 above, especially at 46. See also Brown and Bell, n. 30 above, 271–2; J. Bell, 'Reflections on the Procedure of the Conseil d'Etat' in G. Hand and J. McBride (eds.), *Droit Sans Frontiers: Essays in Honour of L. Neville Brown* (Birmingham, 1991), 211–34 at 232–3.
[62] Hamson, n. 44 above, 70, 74.

behavior of the rest of the civil service'.[63] Whether the *Conseil d'Etat* is
described as a court or as an 'elite segment of the civil service', it does
seem to have acquired judicial independence only in the narrow sense
of absence of direct interference by the active administration in the
outcome of particular cases. Generally, it has conformed to dominant
opinion, for example, in its defence of economic liberalism and opposition to municipal socialism before the Second World War, and in its
championing of civil liberties since then.[64]

Furthermore, the links of the judicial section to the active administration are perhaps the reason for certain problems experienced with
the efficacy of its remedies. Traditionally, the *Conseil d'Etat* has been
unable to enforce its decisions against the administration because of an
incapacity either to order execution or to pronounce an injunction
against the administration.[65] It has, in the past, been less generous in
awarding damages than the civil courts.[66] Its justice, like that of the
increasingly burdened *Tribunaux Administratifs*, has usually been slow
and its interventions have chiefly been *ex post facto*.[67] In the 1960s, Weil
described the problems as follows:

One gets the impression that judicial control has been stuck onto a structure
which is profoundly foreign to it and that it constitutes a sort of excrescence
on the Administration. . . . For this reason one can understand why the man
in the street, the average Frenchman, does not feel adequately protected in his
relations with the Administration. On the contrary, he feels ill-used, the prey
of a thousand and one vexations and often obliged to bow down to ukases
which he does not understand. French Administrative Law often appears more
æsthetically satisfying to the lawyer than to the ordinary citizen. This is because
it comes into operation afterwards, and does not always make its presence felt
in the *tête-à-tête* between the Administration and the '*assujettis*'.[68]

But, although these problems are important and persistent,[69] their
scope and peculiarity to the French administrative jurisdiction with its
links to the administration must not be exaggerated. Judicial and extra-

[63] Shapiro, n. 4 above, 153.   [64] Freedeman, n. 49 above, 79, 159–63.
[65] Duguit, n. 55 above, 67, 191–6; P. Weil, 'The Strength and Weakness of French
Administrative Law' [1965] *CLJ* 242–59 at 254–5; C. Harlow, 'Remedies in French
Administrative Law' [1977] *PL* 227–48 at 230–40.
[66] Harlow, *ibid.*, 240–5; Brown and Bell, n. 30 above, 191.
[67] Weil, n. 65 above, 255–8. But see B. Ducamin, 'Recent Case Law of the French
Conseil d'Etat' (1987) 35 *AJCL* 341–57.
[68] Weil, n. 65 above, 256–7.
[69] See speech of M. Henri Nallet, 19 Feb. 1991, in (1991) 42 *EDCE* 246–247; Brown
and Bell, n. 30 above, 281–5.

judicial means of securing execution were introduced by the reforms of 1963 and 1980. Since 1963, the *Conseil d'Etat* has been able to monitor the execution of judgments through its Report Commission (now called the *Section du Rapport et des Etudes*) and, since 1980, use the civil remedy of *astreinte* to impose a cumulative penalty on an authority which has failed to execute for six months.[70] Although the *Conseil d'Etat* has seldom used the *astreinte*, its *Section du Rapport* still only receives complaints about the implementation of a tiny fraction of the total number of judicial decisions.[71] The *Conseil* has anyway only exceptionally been confronted by wilful non-execution.[72] Even were it able to pronounce judgment against the administration in the form of an injunction, its judgment could nevertheless be disregarded by an administrative authority intent on resisting judicial intervention.[73] And, while the *Conseil d'Etat* might, in the past, have awarded less in damages than the French civil courts, it has recently been more generous[74] and, unlike the English courts, at least developed a general action by which individuals injured by the administration can recover damages.

The Resilience of the *Conseil d'Etat*

Since its origin, the *Conseil* has survived numerous periods of law reform, including the post-war reforms by which the *Tribunaux Administratifs* were created as courts of first instance. As Brown and Bell point out, '[t]his robust institution has . . . survived the vicissitudes of two monarchies, two empires and five republics, not to mention a foreign occupation'.[75] Indeed, the *Conseil d'Etat* has more than survived. It has silenced much of the earlier liberal criticism of the dual jurisdiction, retained the trust of the administration, and acquired an 'unequaled prestige among French institutions'.[76] Hamson attributes its success to the maintenance of an equilibrium secured by its association with, and separation from, the administration,[77] but does not explain to his own satisfaction why the contradiction should be stable. Rather, he remains fascinated by what he regards as an 'extraordinary paradox'.[78]

---

[70] Decree of 10 July 1963; Law of 16 July 1980. See, e.g., *Menneret*, CE, 17 May 1985.
[71] See Brown and Bell, n. 30 above, 112–15, 283.
[72] Weil, n. 65 above, 255.   [73] *Ibid.* 254.
[74] Brown and Bell, n. 30 above, 191.   [75] *Ibid.* 47.
[76] Freedeman, n. 49 above, 167.   [77] Hamson, n. 44 above, 94–5.
[78] *Ibid.* 46.

Hamson's fascination must be supplemented by a sense of the contradiction's rhetorical usefulness in answering demands for independence and expertise. On the one hand, the judicialization of the judicial section of the *Conseil d'Etat* can be used, and was used,[79] to win popular confidence, or at least secure acquiescence, by answering the demand for judicial independence. David, for example, although he defends the distinction between public and private law precisely because of the state's reluctance to subject itself to legal principles and recognizes that '[p]ublicists have, and legitimately try to maintain, the outlook of the government official and the politician', nevertheless can categorically assert that the administrative courts are 'totally independent', that 'the necessary precautions have been taken to insure their full independence', and that their independence is 'universally recognized'.[80] Approving[81] and sceptical[82] foreign observers have had reason to make similar assertions. And, more recently, the *Conseil Constitutionnel* could confirm the judicial independence of the administrative jurisdiction and equate it with that of the ordinary judiciary:

[I]l résulte des dispositions de l'article 64 de la Constitution en ce qui concerne l'autorité judiciaire et des principes fondamentaux reconnus par les lois de la République en ce qui concerne, depuis la loi du 24 mai 1872, la juridiction administrative, que l'indépendance des juridictions est garantie ainsi que le caractère spécifique de leurs fontions, sur lesquelles ne peuvent empiéter ni le législateur ni le Gouvernement; . . . ainsi, il n'appartient ni au législateur ni au Gouvernement de censurer les décisions des juridictions, d'adresser à celles-ci des injonctions et de se substituer à elles dans le jugement des litiges relevant de leur compétence.[83]

On the other hand, the links of the *Conseil d'Etat* to the executive, to the extent that they compromise a broader judicial independence, can

---

[79] Hamson, n. 44 above, 74–83.
[80] David, n. 58 above, 24–30, 98–107, especially at 106, 25, 24, 30. Cf. R. David, book review (1952) 4 *Revue internationale de droit comparé* 184–5.
[81] Hamson, n. 44 above.   [82] Schwartz, n. 7 above, 312–13.
[83] *Validation of Administrative Decisions*, CC decision 80–119–DC, 22 July 1980: 'the result of the provisions of Article 64 of the Constitution on the judiciary and the fundamental principles acknowledged by the laws of the Republic, which, since the Law of 24 May 1872, deal with the administrative jurisdiction, is that the independence of jurisdictions is guaranteed as well as the specific character of their functions, on which neither the legislator nor the Government may encroach; . . . thus it is for neither the legislator nor the Government to censure the decisions of the courts, to address injunctions to them, and to substitute themselves for them in the adjudication of litigation arising out of their jurisdiction.'

be justified as a source of expertise and therefore authority.[84] Rolland, for example, could therefore conclude that:

In reality the system is for France satisfactory as a whole. It is not wise to submit to courts of justice litigations requiring knowledge of administrative law and of the necessities of administrative life. This knowledge is not possessed by judicial courts. They would be induced either to overemphasize the prerogatives of the administration or to neglect them through ignorance or partiality. The administrative judge knows administrative law. By virtue of his selection he can understand the facts and grasp them in their reality and complexity. His decision thus acquires the necessary authority to lead an administration, naturally tending to abuse its prerogative, to yield to it.[85]

As a result of the judicialization, expertise, and authority of the *Conseil d'Etat*, in one and the same breath, David can assert judicial independence and justify its absence: '[t]he administrative courts, totally independent of the executive in fact, have been able, because of their position at the very center of the executive branch, to establish a control over governmental action that would have been thought intolerable if attempted by regular judges.'[86]

The rhetorical usefulness of the contradiction between the independence of the judicial section of the *Conseil d'Etat* and its links with the administration was exemplified in the aftermath of the *Canal* case.[87] In April 1962, De Gaulle obtained through a referendum the consent of the French people to his taking all necessary measures to implement the Evian agreements putting an end to the Algerian war. In implementing the agreements, De Gaulle issued a decree establishing a military court for the trial of recalcitrant French officers. Canal, a leader of the proscribed OAS, who had been condemned to death by the military court, successfully challenged the decree before the *Conseil d'Etat*.[88] In its decision, the *Conseil d'Etat* annulled the decree mainly because it excluded *recours en cassation*. The government reacted with vigour. It first made the *Conseil d'Etat*'s judgment ineffective by ensuring that the decree was given the full force of law and, so, could not

---

[84] See Hamson, n. 44 above, especially at 70–74.

[85] Quoted by S. Riesenfeld, 'The French System of Administrative Justice: A Model for American Law?' (1938) 18 *Boston Univ. LRev* 48–82, 400–32, 715–48 at 743. See for a more recent example R. Odent, *Contentieux administratif* (Paris, 1981), 746–7.

[86] David, *French Law*, n. 58 above, 25.

[87] R. Drago, 'La réform du Conseil d'Etat' (1962/63) 18/9 *Actualité juridique: droit administratif* 524–36. See L. N. Brown and J. F. Garner, *French Administrative Law* (3rd edn., London, 1983), 38–9, 51–2.

[88] *Canal*, CE, 18 Oct. 1962.

be annulled.[89] The government then reformed the *Conseil* to halt the increasing independence of its judicial section from the rest of the administration. It issued a decree providing *inter alia* for the cross-affiliation of *Conseillers* to both the judicial and advisory sections.[90] But, despite its purpose and content, the reform was not interpreted as a compromise to the judicial independence of the *Conseil d'Etat statuant au contentieux*. Weil commented: 'in July 1963, the Government carried out a reform almost exclusively technical, satisfactory as a whole, and in no way dangerous for the *Conseil d'Etat*. The storm has died down, and the future of the *Conseil d'Etat* and Administrative Law was assured as never before.'[91] In short, the cross-affiliation of *Conseillers* to both judicial and advisory sections could be justified as a means to the greater expertise and authority of the *Conseil d'Etat*.[92]

The *Conseil d'Etat* has succeeded because of a unique political history. The *Conseil statuant au contentieux* was judicialized to meet a demand for judicial independence, and, to the extent that it has continued to lack independence, it has met a demand for expertise because of the proximity to the executive necessitated by the radical French theory of the separation of powers. Through its success in meeting contradictory demands for expertise and independence,[93] the *Conseil d'Etat* has helped entrench the underlying French separation between public- and private-law judicial institutions. It is a monument to the possible stability of contradictions.

Judicial Independence in the English Tradition

The judicial power and judicial independence were introduced to the English discussion of a separation of powers by Montesquieu,[94] but had already become central[95] to the English constitutional tradition by the end of the seventeenth-century revolutionary struggles. They had merely been neglected where separate governmental powers were discussed in the seventeenth century because of the enduring influence of the old theory of mixed government with its focus on the respective

---

[89] Law of 15 Jan. 1963.
[90] Decree 63–766 of 30 July 1963. Drago, n. 87 above, 531; *Encycl. Dalloz Répertoire de droit public et administratif* (up to date to 1973, Paris, 1973) 43–4.
[91] Weil, n. 65 above, 251.   [92] See, e.g., Brown and Bell, n. 30 above, 78.
[93] See also above, 69 ff., 119 ff., below, 176 f.
[94] Montesquieu, n. 15 above, bk. 11, ch. 6.
[95] See generally Shapiro, n. 4 above, ch. 2.

roles of King, Lords, and Commons.[96] Their importance to the English Constitution was, in fact, understated by Montesquieu. In contrast to Montesquieu and like other English writers of the seventeenth century, Locke neglected the judicial power in his analytical discussion of a separation of powers. He distinguished a *'Legislative* Power' (the power of making laws and the supreme power) only from an *'Executive* Power' (the power of executing laws) and a *'Federative* Power' (concerned with security and foreign relations).[97] But, he nevertheless repeatedly stressed the need for judicial independence or, in his words, 'indifferent judges'.[98] Locke was not the first to advocate judicial independence and some sort of separation of powers.[99] Rather, by stressing legislative supremacy and judicial independence, he described important features of the revolutionary settlement reached towards the end of the seventeenth-century struggle between King and Parliament.

Prerogative Courts and the Revolutionary Settlement

At the start of the seventeenth century, a number of prerogative courts, that is, courts which had relatively recently developed through the residuary royal prerogative of justice,[100] exercised a jurisdiction that was at least partly administrative. The Star Chamber heard complaints against officials of central and local government and especially against the Justices of the Peace[101] with their extensive powers in the countryside, ranging from the power to punish offenders to the power to administer poor relief and secure the maintenance of roads and bridges.[102] Furthermore, whereas the Court of Wards had an administrative jurisdiction relating to feudal tenures,[103] the Court of Requests

[96] Vile, n. 15 above, 33–54.

[97] J. Locke, *Two Treatises of Government: A Critical Edition with an Introduction and Apparatus Criticus* (P. Laslett (ed.)) (Cambridge, 1964), Second Treatise, chs. 12 and 13, secs. 143–9. See Vile, n. 15 above, 58–67; Friedrich, *Philosophy of Law*, n. 27 above, ch. 12.

[98] Locke, *ibid.*, Second Treatise, secs. 13, 20, 91, 125, 131.

[99] See, e.g., J. Harrington, *Oceana* (J. Toland (ed.)) (Dublin, 1737). See generally Vile, n. 15 above, 45–57.

[100] J. H. Baker, *An Introduction to English Legal History* (3rd edn., London, 1990), 135.

[101] W. S. Holdsworth, *A History of English Law*, iv (London, 1924), 60–1, 83–8; C. R. Lovell, *English Constitutional and Legal History: A Survey* (New York, 1962), 252, 274–81; J. H. Gleason, *Justices of the Peace in England 1558 to 1640* (Oxford, 1969), 65. But cf. T. G. Barnes, 'Star Chamber Litigants and their Counsel 1596–1641' in J. H. Baker (ed.), *Legal Records and the Historian* (Royal Historical Society, 1978), 7–28 at 13.

[102] E. Moir, *The Justice of the Peace* (Harmondsworth, 1969), 26–50, 59; J. P. Dawson, *A History of Lay Judges* (Cambridge, Mass., 1960), 136–45.

[103] H. E. Bell, *An Introduction to the History and Records of the Court of Wards and Liveries* (Cambridge, 1953).

had a jurisdiction not only over poor men's causes in general but also over the Royal Household in particular.[104]

Dicey and others suggested that administrative courts might have emerged from these prerogative courts to develop a system of administrative law and so to give rise to an institutional distinction between public and private law.[105] Indeed, in the early seventeenth century, Bacon justified the prerogative courts, praised the Star Chamber of his day,[106] and recognized the distinction between public and private law.[107]

But the prerogative courts and a separate realm of public law associated with them did not emerge from the seventeenth-century constitutional struggles. The distinction drawn by Bacon came to be seen as a way of setting the King above the law. The practice of the Stuart prerogative courts did not entrench their position. The Star Chamber had not been a court of tyranny[108] but in its last years was increasingly used as a tribunal for the trial of cases, if still not numerous,[109] at least of public importance, involving state security and profit.[110] Although the King's Bench was also used by the Stuart monarchs for their own purposes,[111] the prerogative courts were more clearly associated with the King and the royal prerogative. A major cause of complaint during the Interregnum was that the King abused the prerogative courts (and especially the Star Chamber), which 'did justice in a administrative way'.[112] The Court of Wards, for example, was criticized for paying too much attention to the profits of the Crown.[113] Baker concludes

[104] L. M. Hill, 'Introduction' to J. Caesar, *The Ancient State Authoritie and Proceedings of the Court of Requests* (L. M. Hill (ed.)) (Cambridge, 1975), p. xxix.

[105] A. V. Dicey, *An Introduction to the Study of the Law of the Constitution* (10th edn., London, 1959), 369–73; Holdsworth, n. 101 above, 60, 74; L. L. Jaffe and E. G. Henderson, 'Judicial Review and the Rule of law: Historical Origins' (1956) 72 *LQR* 345–64 at 353–5; J. D. B. Mitchell, 'The Causes and Effects of the Absence of a System of Public Law in the United Kingdom' [1965] *PL* 95–118 at 96–7.

[106] See B. Shapiro, 'Sir Francis Bacon and the Mid-seventeenth Century Movement for Law Reform' (1980) 24 *AJLH* 331–62 at 341–2.

[107] F. Bacon, *Works* (J. Spedding, R. L. Ellis, and D. D. Heath (eds.)), i, (London, 1857), 804–5; vii (1859), 731–2.

[108] T. G. Barnes, 'Star Chamber Mythology' (1961) 5 *AJLH* 1–11.

[109] T. G. Barnes, 'Due Process and Slow Process in the Late Elizabethan–Early Stuart Star Chamber' (1962) 6 *AJLH* 221–49, 315–46 at 330. Cf. Barnes, 'Star Chamber Litigants', n. 101 above, 9.

[110] Barnes, 'Due Process in the Star Chamber', n. 109 above, 335–6.

[111] Barnes, 'Star Chamber Mythology', n. 108 above, 11.

[112] G. N. Nourse, 'Law Reform under the Commonwealth and Protectorate' (1959) 7 *LQR* 512–29 at 516.

[113] H. E. Bell, n. 103 above, 133–4.

that '[i]t was both the strength and the ultimate downfall of conciliar jurisdiction that it depended on close association with the king's chief ministers'.[114] Because of this association, together with criticism of procedures, denunciation by common lawyers envious of the widening conciliar jurisdiction, and, in the case of the Star Chamber, involvement in ecclesiastical politics, the prerogative courts were abolished by the victorious parliamentarians early during the Interregnum.[115] Their abolition is an isolated example of a radical Interregnum reform actually implemented, surviving the Restoration, and continuing to influence English judicial institutions until the twentieth century.[116] Their abolition, together with the assumption by the common-law courts of supervisory functions over inferior administrative jurisdictions,[117] precluded the development of an English institutional distinction between public and private law.

The enduring influence of the abolition of the prerogative courts is related to the ideological significance that they acquired. They became associated with the denial of judicial independence which, alongside parliamentary supremacy, became a canon of the revolutionary settlement. Thereafter, not only was the Crown required to rule through Parliament, but judicial institutions were to be independent of the Crown. Judicial independence, although not necessarily extensive or unambiguous,[118] did become central to the English constitutional tradition in at least three respects. First, prerogative courts associated with the Crown and challenging the authority of the common-law courts were no longer tolerated. Secondly, judicial tenure *quamdiu se bene gesserint* and not merely at the pleasure of the Crown was guaranteed by the Act of Settlement of 1701. It became a symbol of judicial independence which obscured a more complex reality[119] at least in the eighteenth century.

Thirdly, judicial independence became embedded in what

---

[114] Baker, n. 100 above, 135.

[115] H. E. Bell, n. 103 above, 135–6; J. H. Baker, 'The Conciliar Courts' in *The Reports of Sir John Spelman* (J. H. Baker (ed.)) (94 Selden Society, 1978), ii, 70–4 at 74.; Hill, n. 104 above, pp. xl–xliii.

[116] Cf. B. Shapiro, 'Law Reform in Seventeenth Century England' (1975) 19 *AJLH* 280–312.

[117] S. A. de Smith, 'The Prerogative Writs: Historical Origins', App. 1, *Judicial Review of Administrative Action* (J. M. Evans (ed.)) (4th edn., London, 1980), 584–95, especially at 590.

[118] See M. Shapiro, n. 4 above, ch. 2.

[119] D. Lemmings, 'The Independence of the Judiciary in Eighteenth-century England', British Legal History Conference (Oxford, July 1991).

Henderson calls the 'doctrine of limited judicial review',[120] the juridical manifestation of the separation of powers implied by the revolutionary settlement. From about 1600 and especially after the abolition of the prerogative courts and the extension of the functions of the Justice of the Peace in 1660, the doctrine was developed through the granting of the remedies of certiorari, mandamus, and prohibition by the common-law courts to control inferior jurisdictions and local government.[121] The doctrine required a 'threefold division of labour'—the passing of general laws by the legislature to authorize and control administrators and individuals, the deciding of issues by administrators if within their jurisdiction or power, and determination of jurisdiction by judges 'independent of the day-to-day exigencies of administration'.[122]

The Eighteenth Century

As the notion of the separation of powers required by the revolutionary settlement was assimilated by the older theory of mixed government, judicial independence continued to be stressed.[123]

Montesquieu accentuated English appreciation of judicial independence in two ways. First, he linked the notion of an independent judicial power to analytical discussion of the separation of powers. Secondly, by describing judges as 'only the mouth that pronounces the words of the law', as mere mechanical appliers of the law, he emphasized an interpretation of judicial independence that was to exercise great influence in England and America in the nineteenth and early twentieth centuries.[124]

In many respects, Blackstone merely echoed Montesquieu, but in respect of judicial independence, he 'domesticated' Montesquieu by emphasizing the general importance of security of judicial tenure:

In this distinct and separate existence of the judicial power in a peculiar body of men, nominated indeed, but *not removeable at pleasure, by the crown*, consists one main preservative of the public liberty; which cannot subsist long in any state, unless the administration of common justice be in some degree separated both from the legislative and also from the executive power.[125]

---

[120] E. G. Henderson, *Foundations of English Administrative Law: Certiorari and Mandamus in the Seventeenth Century* (Cambridge, Mass., 1963), 3–7.

[121] See generally *ibid.*; De Smith, n. 117 above; A. Rubinstein, 'On the Origins of Judicial Review' (1964) 2 *UBC LRev.* 1–20.

[122] Henderson, n. 120 above, 4–5.   [123] Vile, n. 15 above, 98–118.

[124] Montesquieu, n. 15 above, 163; Vile, n. 15 above, 88–90, 101–4.

[125] W. Blackstone, *Commentaries on the Laws of England* (Facsimile of 1st edn. of 1765–9, Chicago, 1979), i, 259 (emphasis added).

Bentham attacked Blackstone and his separation of powers, but nevertheless reinforced judicial independence in another way. In his discussion of the separation of powers, Bentham distinguished between judicial and legislative powers by reference to the adversarial nature of judicial procedures:

Before a judge can issue his orders as a judge, a concurrence of circumstances is requisite, which is not requisite for legalizing the acts of the legislature:—
   1. It is necessary that an interested party should come and require the judge to issue the order in question. Here there is an individual to whom belongs the initiative, the right of putting into activity the judicial power.
   2. It is necessary that the parties to whom the orders of the judge may prove prejudicial should have the power of opposing them. Here there are other individuals who have a species of negative power—power of stopping the acts of the judicial power.
   3. It is necessary that it should have proof produced of some particular fact upon which the complaint is founded, and that the adverse party be permitted to furnish proof to the contrary.[126]

Bentham thereby emphasized a procedural implication of judicial independence—the judge as a mere umpire for a contest primarily between adversaries.

Montesquieu, Blackstone, and Bentham all contributed in different ways to reinforce the judicial independence required by the seventeenth-century revolutionary settlement: Montesquieu, by conferring upon judges a mechanical role; Blackstone, by stressing the importance of judicial tenure; and Bentham, by focusing upon adversarial judicial procedures.

Dicey's Rejection of an Institutional Distinction

Despite the domination of the theory of parliamentary government in the nineteenth century,[127] the importance of the judicial power and judicial independence was not lost from view. Alongside parliamentary control of the executive, judicial control by the ordinary courts was re-emphasized by Dicey.

Dicey was pre-eminent amongst the lawyers who came to dominate discussion of the English Constitution towards the end of the nineteenth century.[128] At times, Dicey criticized the formal separation of powers, but, implicit in his discussion of the rule of law and *droit administratif* was a separation of powers involving judicial independence. In

---

[126] J. Bentham, *Works* (London, 1843), iii, ch. 21.
[127] Vile, n. 15 above, 212 ff.   [128] *Ibid.* 228.

his Chapter 4 on the rule of law, Dicey again and again stressed the role of the 'ordinary courts' in all disputes whether they involve individuals or officials.[129] There and in his Chapter 12, Dicey rejected *droit administratif* precisely because of the association of the *tribunaux administratifs* with the administration.[130] And, to emphasize his overall argument with seventeenth-century fervour, Dicey drew an analogy between the abuse of the Stuart prerogative courts and the way in which he supposed the French administrative courts favoured or protected the administration with which they were associated. In short, Dicey rejected an institutional distinction between public and private law partly[131] because he was preoccupied with the need for that judicial independence which had become central to the English Constitution.

The theory of parliamentary government which had developed and the rule of law described by Dicey required a dual system for controlling the executive—judicial control of legality and parliamentary control of the political.[132] An administrative court, involving administrative control of the administration, was unacceptable because of the overriding importance of judicial independence. Dicey merely expressed the implications of a traditional concern with judicial independence. In so doing, he sharpened one horn of a dilemma. The other horn would be the need for expert resolution of the disputes involving an expanding and increasingly complex administration. As a result, expert administrative judges serving on the proliferating administrative tribunals would lack the necessary independence, and the judges of the ordinary courts would have independence[133] but would lack the necessary administrative expertise.

The Subordination of Administrative Tribunals

As edition after edition of Dicey's *Law of the Constitution* reiterated that the rule of law requires judicial intervention by ordinary courts, administrative tribunals were proliferating to deal with the disputes arising from the expanding social services of the developing welfare state. The administrative tribunals involved *ad hoc*, pragmatic, concessions to the

---

[129] Dicey, n. 105 above, 183–205.   [130] *Ibid.* 328–405.
[131] See also above, 78 ff., 125–8.   [132] Cf. Mitchell, n. 105 above, 98.
[133] At least in the sense of formal, institutional, assurances of judicial objectivity. See R. Cotterrell's description of the 'imperium image' dominating judicial review: 'Judicial Review and Legal Theory' in H. Genn and G. Richardson (eds.), *Government Action and Legal Control* (Oxford, forthcoming).

need for judicial expertise in an increasingly complex administration. The tribunals were conceived in confusion. They were called a variety of names, such as 'special tribunals', 'administrative tribunals', 'statutory tribunals', and 'ministerial tribunals'. They varied in personnel, procedures, and, accordingly, in their association with state departments and their degree of judicialization. Furthermore, the tribunals negated Dicey's rule of law and, so, provoked an ongoing debate.

The Debate

In 1929, Lord Chief Justice Hewart drew professional and governmental attention to the administrative tribunals by advocating their abolition in *The New Despotism*.[134] He attributed an 'administrative lawlessness' to their irregular procedures and lack of known law or justice, for which he required 'at least an independent and impartial judge who founds his judgement on evidence and reason'.[135] With Diceyan fervour Lord Hewart rejected an English administrative law associated with the administrative tribunals:

> In a country like our own, where the notion of 'droit administratif' serves only by way of comparison and contrast, for the reason that the thing itself is completely opposed to the first principles of our Constitution, the 'separation of powers' refers, and can refer only, to the principle that the Judges are independent of the Executive.[136]

At about the same time, in the first edition of *Justice and Administrative Law*, Robson, in contrast to Lord Hewart, praised the development of an English administrative law.[137] He described the tribunals as a necessary response to the inadequacies of the ordinary courts.[138] He defended the tribunals particularly because of their sympathy for the ideal of social justice inspiring the expanding administration, their understanding of the new standards necessary for resolving administrative disputes, their ability to respond flexibly, and their expertise in particular fields. He compared the tribunals to the ordinary courts to which he attributed conservatism, legalism, preoccupation with individual property rights, and neglect of social duties. He accordingly

---

[134] Lord Hewart of Bury, *The New Despotism* (London, 1929).

[135] *Ibid.* 43–58 at 44–5.   [136] *Ibid.* 37–42 at 41.

[137] W. A. Robson, *Justice and Administrative Law: A Study of the British Constitution* (London, 1928), 26–33, 249–50. See generally J. A. G. Griffith, '*Justice and Administrative Law* Revisited' in J. A. G. Griffith (ed.), *From Policy to Administration, Essays in Honour of William A. Robson* (London, 1976), 200–16. Cf. F. J. Port, *Administrative Law* (London, 1929), especially at 188–256, 358.

[138] Robson, n. 137 above, 250–75.

stressed the need for a system of administrative appeal tribunals and
advocated limited judicial supervision so as not to frustrate 'the whole
object and aim of administrative law'.[139]

The Donoughmore Committee of Inquiry prompted by *The New
Despotism* adopted neither Hewart's nor Robson's position.[140] On the
one hand, it accepted the advantages of the tribunals including their
possession 'of the requisite expert knowledge of their subject' (page 97).
It sought to allay Lord Hewart's fears, first, with the vague notion that
judicial, as opposed to quasi-judicial, decisions 'normally' (pages
115–6), 'prima facie' (page 6), or by way of 'presumption' (page 84)
should be entrusted to the ordinary courts, and, secondly, by simply
affirming their supervisory jurisdiction, albeit supplemented with an
appellate jurisdiction on points of law. On the other hand, reiterating
the importance of parliamentary sovereignty and the rule of law in a
Diceyan way, it rejected Robson's proposals for administrative appeal
tribunals and declared the 'inexpediency of establishing a system of
administrative law' (pages 110–112). The Committee therefore merely
confirmed the existing position and did not advance the developing
debate. Keeton concluded that 'few reports have assembled so much
wisdom whilst proving so completely useless'.[141] The report was useless because the Committee was indecisive, and the Committee was
indecisive because it did not begin to come to terms with the theory of
a separation of powers. Rather, its report opens with a simple recognition of a problem—the need for the separation of powers not to be
rigid, but its importance none the less to democracy (page 4).

The debate continued after the Donoughmore Report. Robson re-
asserted his position and criticized the report for 'muddling
through'.[142] Then, Jennings criticized the Committee's rejection of
specialist administrative courts (within the ordinary judicial system)
specifically because of the need for expertise. He argued as follows:

[A]dministrative questions are now so technical that legal questions relating to
them ought to be decided by a judge familiar with the problems which admin-

---

[139] Robson, n. 137 above, 304–10, 321–2, especially at 304–5.

[140] *Report of the Committee on Ministers' Powers* (1932), Cmnd. 4060. See generally
A. Suzman, 'Administrative Law in England: A Study of the Report of the Committee
on Ministers' Powers' (1933) 18 *Iowa LRev.* 160–186; D. G. T. Williams, 'The
Donoughmore Report in Retrospect' (1982) 60 *Pub. Admin.* 273–92.

[141] G. W. Keeton, 'The Twilight of the Common Law' (1949) 14 *The Nineteenth Century
and After* 230–8 at 231.

[142] W. A. Robson, 'The Report of the Committee on Ministers' Powers' [1932] *Pol.
Quat.* 346–64 at 364.

istrative law is trying to solve. . . . [T]he interpretation of administrative statutes, like the interpretation of other statutes, does involve policy. In other matters the courts generally know what that policy is. In dealing with the problems of administrative law they sometimes do not. . . . Now the reason for the Commercial Court and the Revenue Judge is that the questions with which they deal ought to be decided by someone who is, or who can become, an expert in these branches of the law. When we ask for an administrative judge— or court—we say only that these cases ought not to go to the Divisional Court but to a single judge, and that that judge ought to be familiar with the problems of modern administrative law.[143]

Elsewhere, Jennings criticized the general supervisory jurisdiction of the ordinary courts by reference to their application of the Housing Acts.[144] In contrast, Lord Denning, while appreciating the expertise of the tribunals and even the success of the French administrative courts, stressed the overriding importance of the independence of the tribunals from the policy dictates of the administration. He argued that such independence should be achieved by conferring upon the ordinary courts an appellate jurisdiction on points of law.[145]

Participants in the debate on tribunals generally adopted positions according to their assessment of the relative importance of judicial independence and expertise, but were nevertheless confused. Even the staunchest advocates and opponents of administrative tribunals seemed to be pulled in two directions. On the one side, Dicey, for example, was concerned to deny the implications of the emergent administrative tribunals in England,[146] but towards the end of his life conceded that it was 'at least conceivable' that English law would benefit from a court combining 'official experience with legal knowledge'.[147] On the other side, Robson contrasted the dangerous partiality of the experts serving on the tribunals with the laudable independence of lawyers with their 'Judicial Mind', a problem somehow to be resolved by legal and specialist personnel or training.[148] Robson rejected the 'legendary

[143] W. I. Jennings, 'The Report on Ministers' Powers' (1932) 10 *Pub. Admin.* 333–51 at 348–9.

[144] W. I. Jennings, 'Courts and Administrative Law—The Experience of English Housing Legislation' (1936) 49 *Harv. LRev.* 426–54.

[145] A. Denning, *Freedom under the Law* (London, 1949), 76–96.

[146] A. V. Dicey, '*Droit administratif* in Modern French Law' (1901) 18 *LQR* 302–18 at 304–5; *id., An Introduction to the Study of the Law of the Constitution* (8th edn., London, 1915), p. xliv.

[147] Dicey, *Law of the Constitution*, n. 146 above, p. xlviii.

[148] W. A. Robson, *Justice and Administrative Law: A Study of the British Constitution* (3rd edn., London, 1951), 383–8, 599–609.

separation of powers' but seemed to want the values associated with it.[149]

Allen simply changed sides. In *Bureaucracy Triumphant*, he preferred 'a trained judicial faculty' to 'a particular kind of specialized virtuosity', close control by 'those who are trained to look beyond the practical means of attaining an object' to Robson's Administrative Appeal Tribunal.[150] Later, however, in his foreword to Sieghart's *Government by Decree*, he claimed that English administrative law 'exists for all but the blind to see' and described his own change of position.[151] He concluded that '[t]here is no reason why an appellate administrative tribunal should not combine the purely judicial with the expert administrative elements . . . *provided always that in conception and function the tribunal remained essentially judicial and not executive*'.[152] Allen was converted but can be forgiven for wanting the best of both worlds[153] after his conversion.

In the course of the debate, however, advocacy of the traditional judicial independence became dominant. In the 1950s, it was strengthened by the work of comparative lawyers who recognized the achievements of the French administrative courts but opposed their transplantation. Hamson praised the *Conseil d'Etat* but rejected the idea of a special administrative tribunal modelled upon it because the tribunal would be contrary to the English tradition, and, in particular, would lack the necessary independence.[154] And Schwartz, after considering the work of the *Conseil d'Etat*, nevertheless emphatically asserted the importance to the Anglo-American tradition of independent judicial control over the administration.[155] He rejected the arguments for judicial expertise:

The limitations of the expert—inability to see beyond the narrow confines of his own experience, intolerance of the layman, and excessive zeal in carrying out his own policy regardless of the cost to other, broader interests of society— are subjected under our system to the trained scrutiny of the nonexpert judge,

[149] Robson, n. 148 above, 16–22. See Vile, n. 15 above, 235–8.

[150] C. K. Allen, *Bureaucracy Triumphant* (Oxford, 1931), 56–68, especially at 60, 67. Cf. *id.*, *Law and Orders* (London, 1965).

[151] C. K. Allen, 'Foreword' in M. A. Sieghart, *Government by Decree, A Comparative Study of the History of the Ordinance in English and French Law* (London, 1950), pp. xii–xiii.

[152] *Ibid.* p. xiii.

[153] Cf. Suzman, n. 140 above, 183; Jennings, 'The Report on Ministers' Powers', n. 143 above, 351; *id.*, 'Courts and Administrative Law', n. 144 above, 453–4.

[154] Hamson, n. 44 above, 21, 213–5.

[155] Schwartz, *French Administrative Law*, n. 7 above, especially at 317–20, 335–8. Cf. B. Schwartz, *Law and the Executive in Britain: A Comparative Study* (New York, 1949), especially at 143 ff. See David, book review, n. 80 above.

who, unhindered by the professional bias of the specialist, is able to take a broader view than that of merely promoting administrative policy in the case at hand without counting the ultimate cost.[156]

He concluded that the 'administrator necessarily lacks the independence that is the judge's most prized possession' and added that '[i]t is only by recourse to an independent judiciary that the citizen can be adequately protected against administrative illegality'.[157]

The Franks Report

In 1958, the Franks Committee decisively approved of the permanence of tribunals but as 'machinery for adjudication' and not 'appendages of Government Departments'.[158] It therefore recommended that the tribunals display 'openness, fairness and impartiality', that their personnel be appointed by a Council on Administrative Tribunals responsible to the Lord Chancellor, and that the tribunals be subject to appeal to the ordinary courts on points of law.[159]

Furthermore, like the Donoughmore Committee, it rejected Robson's proposal for an Administrative Appeal Tribunal particularly because it would affect the supremacy of the ordinary courts and would result in 'two systems of law . . . with all the evils attendant on this dichotomy'.[160] The Committee's recommendations, many of which were implemented by the Tribunals and Inquiries Act 1958, signified the decline of tribunals as a basis for an institutional distinction between public and private law[161] and a triumph for independent judicial control over the administration. The tribunals were to be subordinate to the ordinary courts and, in England, would not be developed into a system of administrative courts headed by Robson's Administrative Appeal Tribunal.

The Role of the Ordinary Courts

Although the battle on behalf of judicial independence was won, the peace secured by the Franks Committee was unsatisfactory. Apart from

---

[156] Schwartz, *French Administrative Law*, n. 7 above, 319.   [157] *Ibid.* 336, 337.

[158] Franks Committee, *Report of the Committee on Administrative Tribunals and Enquiries* (1957), Cmnd. 218, paras. 38–40. See generally W. A. Robson, 'Administrative Justice and Injustice: A Commentary on the Franks Report' [1958] *PL* 12–31; E. C. S. Wade, 'Administration under the Law' (1957) 73 *LQR* 470–91; H. W. R. Wade, *Towards Administrative Justice* (Ann Arbor, 1963), 44–5, 88–93.

[159] Franks Committee, n. 158 above, paras. 23–5, 41–2, 45, 49, 107, 133.

[160] *Ibid.* paras. 121–3.

[161] S. Flogaïtis, *Administrative Law et droit administratif* (Paris, 1986), 96–7.

the questionable judicialization of tribunals,[162] the role of the ordinary courts in administrative disputes was open to criticism for at least two reasons: first, because the Franks Committee had simply and vaguely asserted that judicial decisions should be made by courts 'in the absence of special considerations which make a tribunal more suitable';[163] and, secondly, because the ordinary courts still lacked that administrative expertise which was a main reason for the emergence of administrative tribunals. Robson for one criticized the Franks Report for failing to consider the appropriateness of the 'training or education of lawyers, the procedure of the courts, or the high cost of litigation'.[164] Friedmann was similarly critical: '[w]hat is needed is experience in, and understanding of, the nature of the administrative process and the basic problems of the relation between governors and governed.'[165] Then, a few years later, Mitchell explained the absence of a system of public law in the United Kingdom as a consequence of judicial failure and recommended 'the creation of a new system of courts to break the fetters upon those which now exist'.[166] Academics were not the only critics of the judicial role. Lawyers themselves from 'time to time lost confidence in their own ability to control administrative action', and administrators remained sceptical about lawyer's justice.[167]

The Crown Office List

The demand that judges dealing with administrative disputes have administrative expertise persisted after the Franks Report. In 1966, after a seminar on administrative law at All Souls College, the Law Commission recommended to the Lord Chancellor that a Royal Commission or similar body be set up to examine, amongst other questions, '[h]ow far should change be made in the organization and per-

---

[162] Council on Tribunals, *The Functions of the Council on Tribunals* (1980), Cmnd. 7805, para. 95. See C. Harlow and R. Rawlings, *Law and Administration* (London, 1984), 95–8.

[163] Franks Committee, n. 158 above, para. 38. See Robson, 'Administrative Justice and Injustice', n. 158 above, 31; E. C. S. Wade, 'Administration under the Law', n. 158 above, 485.

[164] Robson, n. 158 above, 18.

[165] W. Friedmann, *Law in a Changing Society* (2nd edn., London, 1972), 432–7, especially at 436.

[166] Mitchell, n. 105 above, especially at 118. See J. D. B. Mitchell, 'The State of Public Law in the United Kingdom' (1966) 15 *ICLQ* 133–49; M. Loughlin, 'Sitting on a Fence at Carter Bar: In Praise of J. D. B. Mitchell' (1991) 36 *Juridical Review* 135–53.

[167] Williams, n. 140 above, 290–1.

sonnel of the courts in which proceedings may be brought against the administration?'[168] Although that recommendation was in vain, it was strengthened by the establishment of an Administrative Division of the Supreme Court in New Zealand, and an Administrative Appeal Tribunal in Australia. By the 1970s, 'a groundswell of professional feeling' in favour of a specialist court or Division of the High Court had developed.[169]

While Parliament was inactive, administrators within the judiciary took action. In the process of reducing the growing backlog of cases following the procedural reforms of the late 1970s, they created the Crown Office List to ensure that judges known for their expertise in administrative law hear applications for judicial review (AJRs).[170] Lord Denning described the effect of the changes: '[t]his new procedure means that we now have an administrative court. It is a division of the High Court which might well be called the Administrative Division. It is manned by judges specially versed in administrative law'.[171]

This creation of the Crown Office List and, thus, the accompanying institutional distinction between public and private law, has been unsatisfactory for at least three reasons. First, the creation of the Crown Office List was not a principled response to the need for administrative expertise and judicial independence. Rather, it was 'achieved by administrative stealth' and without 'parliamentary or public discussion'.[172]

Secondly, the judges on the Crown Office List have only limited administrative expertise. At best, because they have the same basic training and career history as the other judges of the ordinary courts, they have administrative expertise only in the narrow sense of a knowledge of administrative-law cases. At worst, because of the recent swamping of the Crown Office, judges hear AJRs although they 'have no special background in administrative law'.[173] Either way, they have

---

[168] Law Commission, *Administrative Law* (Law Com. 20, 1969), Cmnd. 4059.

[169] L. Blom-Cooper, 'The New Face of Judicial Review: Administrative Changes in Order 53' [1982] *PL* 250–61, especially at 253–4. See, e.g., Friedmann, n. 165 above, 436; L. L. Jaffe, 'Research and Reform in English Administrative Law' [1968] *PL* 119–34; H. Street, *Justice in the Welfare State* (2nd edn., London, 1975), 125–6, 128; J. F. Garner, 'Public Law and Private Law' [1978] *PL* 230–8, especially at 236; W. A. Robson, 'Justice and Administrative Law Reconsidered' [1979] *CLP* 107–16 at 112–13.

[170] See Blom-Cooper, n. 169 above, 256–61.

[171] *O'Reilly* v. *Mackman* [1982] 3 All ER 680 at 695J.

[172] Blom-Cooper, n. 169 above, 260, 261.

[173] H. Woolf, 'Judicial Review: A Possible Programme for Reform' [1992] *PL* 221–37 at 224–5.

no special administrative training or special links with the administration. According to Blom-Cooper, 'judges have deliberately avoided any
association with public administration, because to show even the slight-
est awareness of how the executive operates might destroy the highly
prized virtue of judicial independence'.[174]

Blom-Cooper might be exaggerating, but, in his Hamlyn Lectures,
Lord Woolf recognized and discussed the problem of expertise in
detail.[175] He argued as follows:

> I regard it as being of the greatest importance that there should exist among
> the judiciary a body of judges which has the necessary insight into the progress
> of administration. . . . There is always looming the danger that the courts will
> do no more than create a minefield which will hinder any process and benefit
> no one but the lawyers who have to try and provide safe passage.[176]

He therefore recommended the 'widening of judicial experience'—that
judges on the Crown Office List sit on administrative tribunals, that
they receive administrative training from the Judicial Studies Board,
and that discussions with administrators and visits to Government
Departments be organized. Lord Woolf, however, was not prepared to
go 'so far as to suggest that English judges should for a time act as
administrators'.[177] He reiterated that, whereas the French public trust
their administrators and not their judges, the English public trust their
judges and not their administrators. He therefore rejected using the
Conseil d'Etat as a model. Despite his call for expertise, Woolf stressed
that it is 'essential that judicial review should . . . be continuously scru-
tinized by judges who are not pre-programmed by an over-exposure to
administrative law'.[178] For Woolf to have gone further than recommend a few visits, discussions, and training sessions, and advocate some
practical association with the administration that would ensure administrative expertise remotely comparable to that of the *Conseillers d'Etat*
would have negated the injunction of tradition—'[w]e must not of course
impair our independence'.[179] Even if implemented, Woolf's recommendations in his Hamlyn Lectures would make little difference.

Thirdly, because the judges on the Crown Office List lack adminis-

---

[174] L. Blom-Cooper, 'Lawyers and Public Administrators: Separate and Unequal'
[1984] *PL* 215–35 at 234.
[175] H. Woolf, *Protection of the Public—A New Challenge* (London, 1990), 18–19, 81,
115–20.
[176] *Ibid.* 117–19.   [177] *Ibid.* 116.   [178] *Ibid.* 114.
[179] *Ibid.* 117. See Lord Scarman, 'The Development of Administrative Law: Obstacles
and Opportunities' [1990] *PL* 490–5 at 493–4.

trative expertise, they have not reduced the tension between judges and administrators. Lord Woolf recognizes 'that complaints are raised by government departments that judges are insufficiently aware of the problems with which administrators are faced and that on occasions they are required to adopt unrealistic standards in order to comply with decisions of the court'.[180] The Crown Office List has not helped to bridge the gulf between administrators and lawyers.[181] On the one hand, to the extent that administrators have been aware of legal constraints, they have continued to perceive judicial intervention as an alien threat, as 'The Judge over your Shoulder'.[182] On the other hand, while most judges and practising lawyers remain ignorant of the administrative process,[183] academic lawyers have continued to use the language of confrontation, for example, by referring to *O'Reilly* as a 'retreat' from activism[184] or as a 'timely act of judicial statesmanship'.[185]

Administrative Tribunals Again

The creation of the Crown Office List has not resolved the problem of the proper relationship between independent courts and expert tribunals. A modern manifestation of that problem was illustrated in a polemic in the *Financial Times*[186] concerning judicial control over the Panel of Mergers and Takeovers with its judicially recognized public function.[187] Advocates of a legally unregulated Panel were opposed by Professor Jowell who drew attention to the Panel's lack of judicial procedures and apparent bias 'towards those with a direct financial

---

[180] Woolf, *Protection of the Public*, n. 175 above, 18.

[181] See G. Drewry, 'Public Lawyers and Public Administrators: Prospects for an Alliance?' (1986) 64 *Pub. Admin.* 173–188; Blom-Cooper, 'Lawyers and Public Administrators', n. 174 above.

[182] The name of the pamphlet prepared by the Treasury Solicitor's Department and the Cabinet Office and circulated to civil servants. See A. W. Bradley ' "The Judge over your Shoulder" ' [1987] *PL* 485–8; *id.*, 'Protecting Government Decisions from Legal Challenge' [1988] *PL* 1–4.

[183] Blom-Cooper, 'Lawyers and Public Administrators', n. 174 above, 230–5.

[184] J. Beatson, ' "Public" and "Private" in English Administrative Law' (1987) 103 *LQR* 34–65 at 41.

[185] H. W. R. Wade, 'Procedure and Prerogative in Public Law' (1985) 101 *LQR* 180–99 at 187.

[186] J. Jowell, 'Self-regulation under Threat', 9 May 1991. See letters to the editor on 15, 24, and 30 May 1991.

[187] See *R.* v. *Panel on Take-overs and Mergers, ex p. Datafin Plc* [1987] QB 815.

interest in creating more takeover activity'.[188] Seemingly this debate, along the lines of the earlier debates on judicial control of administrative tribunals, was unaffected by the emergence in the meantime of the Crown Office List.

The relationship between the ordinary courts and administrative tribunals has again been a concern of the Law Commission.[189] The debate has continued. Lord Woolf has advocated more extensive use of tribunals to unburden the High Court and to make use of specialist skills. His recent recommendations are reminiscent of Robson's:

> The way forward over a period of time should thus involve creating a unified system of tribunals for resolving administrative disputes, with the High Court and Court of Appeal required to resolve only difficult problems of law and points of principle and policy of high importance to the development of administrative law. . . . Our existing tribunals could become, with other new tribunals, specialist sections of a new tribunal system presided over by an Administrative Appeal Tribunal. Within the tribunal system, there could be deployed skills and disciplines which at present play no part in our review process.[190]

Twice before similar proposals have officially been rejected. How they are now to defy the imperative of judicial independence is unclear. The difficulties persist.

The Enduring and Intractable Problem

In this century, one attempt to introduce an institutional distinction between public and private law failed, and a second is failing. The administrative tribunals lacked the required independence; the ordinary judges on the Crown Office List lack the required expertise. Now, because of the failure of the second attempt, the first attempt is acquiring new vigour. In the absence of further theoretical development, however, it is unlikely to surmount the obstacle of judicial indepen-

---

[188] Jowell, n. 186 above. Cf. H. W. R. Wade, 'Beyond the Law: A British Innovation in Judicial Review' (1991) 43 *Admin. LRev.* 559–70; *R. v. Code of Practice Committee of the British Pharmaceutical Industry, ex p. Professional Counselling Aids Ltd* (1990) 3 Admin LR 697 at 718H-19H.

[189] Law Commission, *Fifth Programme of Law Reform* (Law Com. 200, 1991), Cmnd. 1556, item 10; Law Commission, *Administrative Law: Judicial Review and Statutory Appeals* (consultation paper 126, 1993), especially at para. 19.21; *Administrative Law: Judicial Review and Statutory Appeals* (Law Com. 226, 1994), HC 669, paras. 1.9, 3.24–6, 5.31–5. But see P. Cane, 'The Law Commission on Judicial Review' (1993) 56 *MLR* 887–96.

[190] Woolf, 'Programme for Reform', n. 173 above, 227–31, especially at 230–1. Cf. H. Woolf, 'A Hotchpotch of Appeals—The Need for a Blender' (1988) 7 *CJQ* 44–52.

dence. A separation of powers which ensures that the courts resolving administrative disputes satisfy the demands for independence and expertise has not been found. On the contrary, the separation of powers has been widely rejected or questioned since the nineteenth century.[191] Those who do now advocate some separation of powers are vague and cautious and continue to stress the centrality of judicial independence.[192]

Lord Woolf suggests that the public/private distinction accords with some separation of powers by demarcating an area of judicial restraint where the 'courts cannot usurp the duty of the public body to make the decision'.[193] But the institutional distinction rather founders[194] on the English theory of the separation of powers—its vagueness and its failure to provide for both the independence and expertise of judges resolving administrative disputes. The combination of expertise and independence resulting in an acceptable institutional distinction, achieved in France through a unique development of their separation of powers, has not been achieved in England. Because of traditional differences in approach to the separation of powers, the contradiction between expertise and independence, which was stabilized in France, is unstable in England. For want of a separation of powers which is satisfactory in the ways described in my model, an English institutional distinction, whether referring to administrative tribunals or the Crown Office List, remains questionable.

---

[191] Vile, n. 15 above, 3–7, 238; C. R. Munro, *Studies in Constitutional Law* (London, 1987), 193–5. See, e.g., M. J. Elliott, *The Role of Law in Central-Local Relations* (London, 1981), 10–11.

[192] See, e.g., E. C. S. Wade and A. W. Bradley, *Constitutional and Administrative Law* (10th edn., London, 1985), 50, 56, 59; Munro, n. 191 above, 203, 211; S. A. de Smith and R. Brazier, *Constitutional and Administrative Law* (6th edn., London, 1989), 19–22.

[193] H. Woolf, 'Public Law—Private Law: Why the Divide? A Personal View' [1986] *PL* 220–38 at 225.

[194] See also above, 87 ff.

8
A Substantive Distinction

In the last chapter, I emphasized that the English separation of powers has failed to satisfy the need for judges with both independence and administrative expertise. I concluded that the institutional distinction emerging with the Crown Office List is therefore proving inadequate. A distinction between public and private law, however, is not necessarily institutional or jurisdictional. In his book *Administrative Law et droit administratif*, Flogaïtis asserts that English commentators from Dicey to Mitchell confused administrative law with an administrative jurisdiction.[1] He argues that this confusion blinded them to the development of a native administrative law around special judicial procedures and principles of substantive law, to what I here describe as the procedural and substantive distinctions between public and private law:

[L]es avocats du système français, au lieu d'insister sur la différence de raisonnement dans les divers domains du droit public et de travailler sur la jurisprudence administrative anglaise pour bâtir une conscience administrativiste propre, ont enseigné une théorie de droit administratif importée et ont donc consacré leur efforts à demontrer plutôt les vertus du Conseil d'Etat en tant que juridiction séparée de la justice judiciaire. . . . Le prestige dont le Conseil d'Etat jouit chez les chercheurs anglais qui ont voulu étudier et contrebalancer la polémique qui lui avait été faite jusqu'il y a peu est évident. Cependant, ce prestige qui a pu restaurer complètement son autorité en Angleterre a parfois empêché ses admirateurs d'étudier à fond la réalité de leur propre système juridique déjà en évolution.[2]

Partly because Flogaïtis does not equate administrative law with an administrative jurisdiction, he identifies a convergence between *droit administratif* and administrative law. To deal with his argument and to

---

[1] S. Flogaïtis, *Administrative Law et droit administratif* (Paris, 1986). But cf. J. D. B. Mitchell, 'The State of Public Law in the United Kingdom' (1966) 15 *ICLQ* 133–49.

[2] Flogaïtis, n. 1 above, 109, 114–5: 'the advocates of the French system, instead of emphasizing the difference in reasoning in the various areas of public law and working on English administrative case law in order to build a true administrativist conscience, have taught an imported theory of administrative law and have thus devoted their efforts rather to demonstrating the virtues of the *Conseil d'Etat* as a jurisdiction separate from the justice of the ordinary judiciary. . . . The prestige enjoyed by the *Conseil d'Etat* among those English researchers who sought to study and counterbalance the polemic which had surrounded it is obvious. However, this prestige which was able completely to restore its authority in England has occasionally hindered its admirers from studying thoroughly the reality of their own already changing legal system.'

avoid presupposing an administrative jurisdiction as a requirement for administrative law, in this and the following two chapters, I will consider substantive and procedural distinctions between public and private law.

In this chapter, I will suggest that a successful substantive distinction, like an institutional distinction, depends on a satisfactory separation of powers. I will argue that the French substantive distinction is entrenched mainly[3] because the French separation of powers, as it has developed, has ensured that French administrative courts have the judicial independence and administrative expertise to develop a dynamic public law. By contrast, I will argue that the English substantive distinction is proving unsatisfactory because[4] the English theory of the separation of powers has not clarified or justified the judicial role in public law. I will conclude that the transplantation of a distinction between public and private law—whether institutional or merely substantive—to English law is unsuccessful because of enduring uncertainty about the required institutional role of the courts in the administrative process. As in the last chapter, I will presuppose a distinct state administration,[5] but with the purpose in this chapter of focusing attention on the substantive legal effect of the absence of the separation of powers described in my model.

The Extension of State Liability in France

State immunity described in pre-Revolutionary France by the maxim *le Roi ne peut mal faire* persisted after the Revolution. The maxim *les torts du soverain ne se réparent pas* remained generally valid until late in the nineteenth century. Except for liability under specific legislation, administrative authorities remained immune from liability for their *actes de la puissance publique*, that is, acts which involved their public authority, in contrast to *actes de gestion* which did not and which were justiciable before the ordinary courts.[6]

Only in 1873 did the *Tribunal des Conflits* create the means by which this general immunity would be curtailed. In the famous *Blanco* case, it established that the *Conseil d'Etat* had jurisdiction to determine the

---

[3] See also above, 69 ff.,119 ff., 149 ff., below, 212 ff.

[4] See also above, 87 ff., 130 ff., below, 221 ff.

[5] See above, 109.

[6] L. N. Brown and J. S. Bell, *French Administrative Law* (4th edn., Oxford, 1993), 124–5, 174–6; C. E. Freedeman, *The Conseil d'Etat in Modern France* (New York, 1961), 115, 143.

liability of the state for injuries arising out of the activities of a *service public*.[7] The *Tribunal* introduced the general principle of state liability but stressed that the state would be held liable according to rules different from those of private law. Waline formulates the gist of the judgment as 'l'Etat sera responsable, mais ne sera pas soumis à des règles aussi strictes de responsabilité que les particuliers'.[8] He therefore describes the principle of liability established by the *Tribunal* in *Blanco* as a cautious step away from the principle of state immunity. Indeed, the distinction between public- and private-law rules of liability, emphasized in *Blanco*, initially preserved in part the immunity of the state.

The *Conseil d'Etat*, however, acquired the independent authority gradually to eradicate state immunity. Its authority was enhanced by the Law of 1872, giving it the power to pronounce judgment in the name of the French people,[9] and by the *Cadot* decision, giving it the power to hear cases brought directly by the aggrieved.[10] The *Conseil d'Etat* used its enhanced authority greatly to extend[11] the liability of the state in the final years of the nineteenth century and early decades of the twentieth century. After initially confirming the old principle of state immunity for acts of authority,[12] the *Conseil d'Etat* abandoned the distinction between acts of authority and acts of management and began to hold the state liable for varying degrees[13] of *faute de service*.[14] Harlow rightly points out that 'the possibility of demanding from the state a modified standard of care, at first sight a privilege or immunity, in fact enabled the courts to make slow but steady inroads upon the greater administrative immunities which existed in the last century'.[15] The *Conseil d'Etat* extended state liability in various ways. In the case of *Terrier*, it established that the liability of the central state for *faute de service* was shared by a local authority.[16] Its lead was followed by the

---

[7] TC, 8 Feb. 1873.

[8] M. Waline, *Droit administratif* (9th edn., Paris, 1963), para. 13: 'the State will be liable, but will not be subject to rules of liability as strict as those governing individuals'.

[9] Law of 24 May 1872, art. 9.   [10] CE, 13 Dec. 1889.

[11] See A. de Laubadère, *Traité de droit administratif* (J.-C. Venezia and Y. Gaudemet (eds.)) (11th edn., Paris, 1990), para. 1270; L. Duguit, *Law in the Modern State* (F. and H. Laski (trs.)) (New York, 1970), 197–242.; Freedeman, n. 6 above, 143 ff.

[12] *Lepreux*, CE, 13 Jan. 1899.

[13] See C. Harlow, 'Fault Liability in French and English Public Law' (1976) 39 *MLR* 516–41 at 518–26.

[14] *Greco*, CE, 10 Feb. 1905; *Auxerre*, CE, 17 Feb. 1905.

[15] Harlow, n. 13 above, 520.   [16] CE, 6 Feb. 1903.

Tribunal des Conflits in *Feutry*[17] and *De Fonscolombe*.[18] Furthermore, the *Conseil d'Etat* extended the concept of *faute de service* to cover omissions[19] and late execution of a *service public*.[20]

Most dramatically, by beginning to develop categories of risk liability, the *Conseil d'Etat* extended the liability of the state beyond that then recognized in private law.[21] In *Blanco*, the *Tribunal des Conflits* ironically had laid the foundation for this development by distinguishing public- from private-law rules of liability. The *Conseil d'Etat* was consequently not handicapped by the principle of fault stated in articles 1382 and 1383 of the *Code Civil*. Unlike the *Cour de Cassation*, it did not need to reverse the burden of proof and manipulate provisions of the *Code Civil* in order to introduce liability without fault.[22] Already in the *Cames* case of 1895 the *Conseil* could simply find the administration responsible for *le risque professionnel*, for the risks of employment to workers in the public service.[23] Although it found that the accident in the state arsenal which injured Cames was not due to the fault of the administration, it nevertheless held the administration liable in law to compensate him. The distinction between public and private law, originally intended in *Blanco* partially to preserve state immunity, permitted an authoritative and dynamic court to create an extensive state liability.

The Conseil d'Etat*'s Extensive Judicial Role*

In this century, the *Conseil d'Etat* developed other categories of risk liability.[24] It introduced liability for dangerous state premises[25] and extended that liability to dangerous state operations.[26] In extending state liability, it dealt with the difficult problem of the kind of risk giving rise to liability. It held the state liable for a risk concentrated upon a particular area, for an exorbitant risk (e.g. where use of firearms by the police endangers bystanders), and for a calculated risk (e.g. where

---

[17] TC, 29 Feb. 1908.   [18] TC, 11 Apr. 1908.

. [19] *Département de la Dordogne*, CE, 10 May 1907.   [20] *Brunet*, CE, 18 July 1919.

[21] See Duguit, n. 11 above, 203–7; Waline, n. 8 above, para. 15; Brown and Bell, n. 6 above, 183 ff.

[22] Cf. *Guissez, Cousin et Oriolle* v. *Teffaine*, CC, 16 June 1896; *Grange* v. *Compagnie Générale Transatlantique*, CC, 30 Mar. 1897; *Jand'heur* v. *Les Galeries Belfortaises*, CC, 13 Feb. 1930. See A. von Mehren and J. Gordley, *The Civil Law System: An Introduction to the Comparative Study of Law* (2nd edn., Boston, 1977), 598 ff.; K. Zweigert and H. Kötz, *Introduction to Comparative Law* (2nd edn., Oxford, 1987), ii, 353 ff.

[23] CE, 21 June 1895. *Cames* was superseded by a Law of 9 Apr. 1898 establishing a comprehensive scheme of workmen's compensation.

[24] See De Laubadère, n. 11 above, paras. 1292–8; Brown and Bell, n. 6 above, 183 ff.

[25] *Regnault-Desroziers*, CE, 28 Mar. 1919.

[26] *Lecomte and Daramy*, CE, 24 June 1949.

an institution kept open for the rehabilitation of youngsters endangers neighbours). For instance, in the case of *Thouzellier*, institutionalized youngsters caused damage when they escaped from custody. The *Conseil d'Etat* specifically found that the institution's officers were not at fault, but nevertheless held the state liable on the basis of 'un risque spécial pour les tiers résident dans le voisinage'.[27] By holding the state liable to pay damages, it determined an important consequence of adopting a liberal policy designed to rehabilitate institutionalized youngsters. Despite far-reaching implications for government policy and expenditure, it extended state liability and determined the scope of the extended liability.

On a few occasions the *Conseil d'Etat* has even found the state liable to pay damages for losses arising out of legislation.[28] In the case of *La Fleurette*, a law which did not provide for compensation banned the making and selling of artificial cream under the name 'cream'. La Fleurette, a dairy company, claimed compensation because it could no longer market its artificial cream as cream. The *Conseil d'Etat* invoked a principle underlying no-fault state liability—*l'égalité devant les charges publiques*—to decide that La Fleurette had a right to compensation.[29] It held that the legislature did not intend to impose an unequal sacrifice on the dairy company. In introducing this right to compensation and, later, subjecting it to various limitations such as a requirement of *préjudice gravité suffisante*,[30] it has shown a willingness to determine whether a loss caused by an enacted policy should be shared by all or lie where it falls.

In other areas of *droit administratif*, the *Conseil d'Etat* has assumed a similarly extensive judicial role. I will give three further examples. First, in *le contentieux de pleine juridiction*, according to the doctrines of *imprévision* and *fait du prince*, the *Conseil d'Etat* intervenes to re-establish *l'équilibre financier du contrat* where the contract's economic basis has been upset because of unforeseen circumstances or the act of the administration.[31] For example, in a leading case, a company contracted with a commune to supply gas at a certain price. The commune refused to allow the

---

[27] *Thouzellier*, CE, 3 Feb. 1956. See the further liberalization of the requirements for liability in *Trouillet*, CE, 9 Mar. 1966. See generally R. Errera, 'The Scope and Meaning of No-fault Liability in French Administrative Law' (1986) 39 *CLP* 157–80 at 166 ff.

[28] See Duguit, n. 11 above, 207–18; De Laubadère, n. 11 above, paras. 1318–23.

[29] *La Fleurette*, CE, 14 Jan. 1938.

[30] De Laubadère, n. 11 above, para. 1323. See generally Errera, n. 27 above, 158 ff.

[31] See De Laubadère, n. 11 above, paras. 1068–76; Brown and Bell, n. 6 above, 196 ff.

company to raise that price, despite drastic increases in the price of coal as a result of German occupation of French coal-mining areas in the First World War. The *Conseil d'Etat* ordered the company to continue to supply gas, but recognized its right to indemnity in the absence of an agreement on new terms.[32]

Secondly, the *Conseil d'Etat* fulfils an extensive judicial role owing to the open-ended standards which it developed together with *violation de la loi* as a ground of review.[33] Especially since the Second World War, it has annulled administrative acts for violating *les principes généraux du droit*, which it has extended to include 'protection of the environment' and 'economic and social rights'.[34]

Thirdly, the *Conseil d'Etat* fulfils an extensive judicial role in reviewing administrative acts for *erreur manifeste d'appréciation des faits*.[35] For example, in a leading case, it evaluated the facts in the dossier and found *erreur manifeste* because the Prefect of the Var had granted planning permission for the construction of hotels that were too near the beach and that were incompatible with the surrounding buildings.[36] It therefore determined that the Prefect had granted planning permission unlawfully.

The *Conseil d'Etat* extended its judicial role further by developing the concept of proportionality, 'qui permet au juge . . . d'apprécier si une décision administrative n'est pas disproportionnée et excessive eu égard à la situation qu'elle vise'.[37] Bell describes the difference between the *Conseil*'s use of the concept of *erreur manifeste* and its use of the concept of proportionality as follows: '[t]he difference is that while both are concerned with gross administrative errors, proportionality more clearly requires a substitution of views about the merits of a case and requires a greater attention to the facts, whereas the manifest error can proceed in an apparently more objective way to consider the conception of the policy of the legislation which is to be adopted.'[38] In the leading case on proportionality, the relevant authority had declared a project for the relocation of the town of Lille *d'utilité publique*. In deciding that the

[32] *Compagnie Générale d'Eclairage de Bordeaux*, CE, 24 Mar. 1916.

[33] See generally De Laubadère, n. 11 above, paras. 864–9.

[34] Brown and Bell, n. 6 above, 214, 213.

[35] See De Laubadère, n. 11 above, para. 740; J. Bell, 'The Expansion of Judicial Review over Discretionary Powers in France' [1986] *PL* 99–121 at 108–13.

[36] *Pampelonne*, CE, 29 Mar. 1968.

[37] De Laubadère, n. 11 above, para. 900: 'which allows a judge . . . to determine whether an administrative decision is not disproportionate and excessive, having regard to the sitaution it envisages'.

[38] Bell, n. 35 above, 113.

declaration was lawful, the *Conseil d'Etat* determined whether, as a result, 'les atteintes à la propriété privée, le coût financier et éventuelle- ment les inconvénients d'ordre social' were excessive in relation to the benefit provided by the project.[39] In subsequent similar cases, it has developed the doctrine of *le bilan*, requiring the administrative court to work with a balance sheet showing the advantages and disadvantages of a proposed project.[40]

The Distinction's Entrenchment

The institutional characteristics of the *Conseil d'Etat* determined its suc- cess in extending the liability of the state and fulfilling an extensive judicial role. By the end of the last century, the *Conseil statuant au con- tentieux* had acquired the independent authority to develop a case law that gradually silenced its liberal opponents. In this century, because of its continued links with the administration, it has had the administra- tive expertise to intervene extensively in the administrative process. For example, it adapted the very concept of proportionality from the advi- sory section of the *Conseil d'Etat* dealing with public works.[41] And, because of its association with the advisory sections, it has had the administrative expertise to apply the concept of proportionality and even draw up *le bilan* stating the advantages and disadvantages of a public project.

By developing a dynamic and successful *droit administratif*, the *Conseil d'Etat* has entrenched the substantive distinction between public and private law. By extending state liability beyond that recognized in pri- vate law, it has secured an autonomous administrative law of liability:

Il en résulte que, si l'on soumettait aujourd'hui la responsabilité de l'Etat aux règles du Code civil, on risquerait, dans certains cas, une régression. Et c'est sans doute la meilleure raison qui puisse légitimer aujourd'hui le maintien d'un droit administratif autonome de la responsabilité: il tourne à l'avantage des vic- times.[42]

---

[39] *Ville Nouvelle Est*, CE, 28 May 1971: 'the encroachments on private property, the financial cost, and, where they arise, the accompanying inconveniences on the social plane'.
[40] De Laubadère, n. 11 above, para. 741; Brown and Bell, n. 6 above, 247–8.
[41] R. Errera cited by Bell, n. 35 above, 116.
[42] Waline, n. 8 above, para. 15: '[t]he result is that, if one were today to subject the liability of the State to the rules of the Civil Code, one would in certain cases run the risk of a regression. That is without doubt the best reason which is able today to legiti- mate the maintenance of an autonomous administrative law of liability: it works to the advantage of victims'.

The substantive French distinction therefore depends for its success on the institutional distinction resulting from the development of the French separation of powers which established the *Conseil d'Etat*'s independence and expertise. Brown and Bell conclude that the 'French find a justification for the distinct character of their *droit administratif* in its capacity to adapt the principles of administrative legality and administrative liability to the differing needs of the various public services, a capacity which they claim could only be found in judges who are also trained administrators'.[43] Indeed, Waline finds it difficult to conceive of a substantive distinction without a specialized administrative jurisdiction. At one point in his *Droit administratif*, he considers what might have happened had the ordinary French courts been entrusted with administrative cases. Categorically, he asserts that, then, the ordinary courts 'n'auraient sans doute pas appliqué au jugement des procès intéressant l'administration, des règles sensiblement différentes de celles qu'ils appliquent au jugement des procès civils'.[44] He concludes that the 'autonomie d'une branche du Droit suppose des tribunaux spécialisés'.[45]

The Emergence of a Substantive Distinction in England

According to the contrasting English tradition culminating in Dicey's *Law of the Constitution*, a substantive distinction between public and private law was alien to English law.[46] As described by Dicey, the rule of law required the application of the ordinary law of the land to individuals and officials alike.[47] The maxim 'the King can do no wrong' described, as in pre-Revolutionary France, immunity from legal process but well into the twentieth century continued to put the Crown beyond the law rather than into a special legal category. Whereas in France the maxim's effect was curtailed by the introduction and development of a separate realm of public-law liability determined by the *Conseil d'Etat*, in England it was ameliorated initially by governmental

[43] Brown and Bell, n. 6 above, 274.

[44] Waline, n. 8 above, para. 45: 'without doubt would not have applied to the adjudication of administrative cases rules appreciably different from those which they apply to the adjudication of civil cases'.

[45] *Ibid.*, para. 46: 'the autonomy of a branch of the law presupposes specialized tribunals'. Cf. De Laubadère, n. 11 above, para. 26.

[46] A. V. Dicey, *An Introduction to the Study of the Law of the Constitution* (10th edn., London, 1959).

[47] *Ibid.*, ch. 4.

practice in response to the petition of right[48] and eventually by the statutory extension of private-law liability. While preserving a number of Crown immunities with special statutory provisions, the Crown Proceedings Act 1947 equated the liability of the Crown in tort with that of 'a private person of full age and capacity'.[49]

Despite the traditional doctrinal rejection of a distinction between public and private law, through the course of this century, English judges and doctrinal writers used the doctrine of *ultra vires* to develop an English administrative law. By construing statutes which authorize administrative action and by implying limitations to statutory powers, the courts developed the grounds of judicial review.[50] Especially since the 1960s, after the appearance of the first editions of the systematic textbooks on judicial review by De Smith and Wade,[51] innovative judges,[52] inspired by *droit administratif*,[53] accelerated the development of an English administrative law. In landmark cases, the courts extended judicial control over the administration by beginning to apply the rules of natural justice without regard to the distinction between administrative and judicial functions and by beginning to review administrative decisions for relevancy of consideration and error of law.[54]

The transformation of English administrative law during the last few decades cannot be denied. The courts developed the grounds of judicial review, evolved legal principles specially applicable to administrative disputes, and began explicitly to use the distinction between public and private law to describe a feature of substantive law. Examples are numerous. In *Conway* v. *Rimmer*, the House of Lords entrenched the administrative authority's immunity to discovery where disclosure

[48] H. W. R. Wade and C. F. Forsyth, *Administrative Law* (7th edn., Oxford, 1994), 820 ff.

[49] S. 2(1). See generally C. Harlow, *Compensation and Government Torts* (London, 1982), 17–28.

[50] See Wade and Forsyth, n. 48 above, 41–7.

[51] S. A. de Smith, *Judicial Review of Administrative Action* (London, 1959); H. W. R. Wade, *Administrative Law* (Oxford, 1961).

[52] A. Paterson, *The Law Lords* (London, 1982), 132–89. See generally A. Denning, *Freedom under the Law* (London, 1949), 99–126; C. J. Radcliffe, *The Law and its Compass* (London, 1961); Lord Reid, 'The Judge as Law Maker' (1972/73) 12 *Jnl. of the Soc. of Pub. Teachers of L* 22–9; Lord Diplock, 'Judicial Control of the Administrative Process' [1971] *CLP* 1–17 at 17; L. L. Jaffe, 'Research and Reform in English Administrative Law' [1968] *PL* 119–34; H. W. R. Wade, 'Crossroads in Administrative Law' [1968] *CLP* 75–93 at 89. Cf. P. Devlin, 'The Common Law, Public Policy and the Executive' [1956] *CLP* 1–15.

[53] See, e.g., Denning, n. 52 above, 115–17, 122–4.

[54] *Ridge* v. *Baldwin* [1964] AC 40; *Padfield* v. *Minister of Agriculture, Fisheries and Food* [1968] AC 997; *Anisminic Ltd* v. *Foreign Compensation Commission* [1969] 2 AC 147.

would be against the public interest.[55] In *Gouriet* v. *Union of Post Office Workers*, Lord Diplock used the substantive distinction between public and private law to justify a procedural consequence—the respective roles of the court and the Attorney-General in relator actions.[56] In *Western Fish Products Ltd* v. *Penwith District Council*, the Court of Appeal virtually extinguished proprietary estoppel in public law by upholding the general rule against the raising of an estoppel 'to prevent the exercise of a statutory discretion or to prevent or excuse the performance of a statutory duty'.[57] Furthermore, in many cases this century, courts have modified ordinary contractual principles either to find a contract *ultra vires* where it unlawfully fetters a discretionary power, or to uphold a public-policy defence to an action for breach of contract.[58] Similarly, the courts have modified the ordinary law of negligence to take account of the doctrine of *ultra vires*. They have recognized a plea of public policy where the authority acted *intra vires* in furtherance of a non-justiciable public policy.[59] In *Dorset Yacht Co* v. *Home Office*, Lord Diplock went so far as to state that 'over the past century the public law concept of *ultra vires* has replaced the civil-law concept of negligence as the test of the legality, and consequently of the actionability, of acts or omissions of government departments or public authorities done in the exercise of a discretion conferred upon them by Parliament'.[60] And, in *Anns* v. *Merton London Borough Council*, Lord Wilberforce declared that the 'powers and duties [of the local authority] are definable in terms of public not private law'.[61]

The emergence of a separate English public or administrative law was given conclusive judicial recognition in the *GCHQ* case.[62] Lord Diplock noted the transformation over the preceding three decades, summarized the 'principles of public law', and suggested a new classification of the grounds of judicial review.[63]

---

[55] [1968] AC 910.
[56] [1978] AC 435 at 500C–D. See also *ibid.* 494F–G, 518D–E.
[57] [1981] 2 All ER 204 at 219C–21D.
[58] P. Cane, *An Introduction to Administrative Law* (2nd edn., Oxford, 1992), 263–9; P. P. Craig, *Administrative Law* (2nd edn., London, 1989), 502–7.
[59] *Anns* v. *Merton LBC* [1978] AC 728.   [60] [1970] AC 1004 at 1067G.
[61] N. 59 above, 754B. See also, e.g., *Hill* v. *Chief Constable of West Yorkshire* [1987] 2 WLR 1126, especially at 1140F. Cf. *Bourgoin SA* v. *Ministry of Agriculture* [1986] QB 716, especially at 788C.
[62] *Council of Civil Service Unions* v. *Minister for Civil Service* [1985] AC 374 at 407H–11H.
[63] *Ibid.*

Continuing Immunities

Because of the development described above, various commentators have concluded that English administrative law, at least in effect, has become roughly equivalent to *droit administratif*.[64] Their conclusion, however, underestimates the importance of the various legal immunities preserved by the English substantive distinction between public and private law. Many of the distinct public-law principles evolved by the courts have benefited the administration.[65] Public-interest immunity to discovery, for example, is normally raised by administrative authorities and often by those with an interest in non-disclosure. Then, as a result of the restriction of estoppel in public law, administrative authorities can seldom, if ever, be estopped from denying *ultra vires* representations upon which others have relied. Most importantly, to the extent that the distinction between public and private law has been recognized in contract and tort, the right of the individual aggrieved by administrative action to recover damages has largely been curtailed to preserve a realm of immunity. In short, the individual's action for damages in negligence or for breach of contract has often failed as a result of judicial unwillingness to interfere with public policy or the exercise of statutory powers. Harlow has reason to conclude that:

[T]he 'public/private' classification is part of another, more insular tradition. It is nothing more than an attempt by the judiciary to conceal political issues behind a formalist façade and to shield from public criticism some highly executive-minded decisions. Nevil Johnson has rightly called our legal theory 'very thin gruel indeed.' The 'public/private' distinction is not thick enough for gruel. To continue his culinary metaphor, our judges can be linked to crafty restaurateurs, seeking to pass off unpalatable common law left-overs as delicacies from the classic French cuisine. But Brown Windsor soup is not easily disguised as *Crême Vichyssoise*.[66]

The development of English administrative law is undeniable but incomparable to that of *droit administratif*.

Whereas in France the distinction between public and private law

---

[64] See, e.g., Jaffe, n. 52 above, Wade, 'Crossroads in Administrative Law', n. 52 above, 76–84; Lord Diplock, 'Administrative Law: Judicial Review Reviewed' (1974) 33 *CLJ* 233–45, especially at 244; H. Woolf, *Protection of the Public—A New Challenge* (London, 1990), 34–5, 56–62.

[65] See, e.g., above, nn. 55–61. But cf. *Derbyshire County Council* v. *Times Newspapers* [1993] AC 534.

[66] C. Harlow, ' "Public" and "Private" Law: Definition without Distinction' (1980) 43 *MLR* 241–65 at 265.

has secured an extensive state liability, in England the distinction has perpetuated numerous administrative immunities. Under the doctrines of *imprévision* and *fait du prince*, the *Conseil d'Etat* has recognized a right to indemnity where a government contract's economic basis has been upset because of supervening circumstances or the act of the administration. In contrast, English courts have continued to work with the limited doctrine of frustration. Furthermore, they have not been prepared to establish the general liability of the administration for negligence, let alone a risk liability or a liability to pay damages for losses arising out of legislation. The *Thouzellier* case, in which the *Conseil d'Etat* made the state bear the consequences of a liberal policy designed to rehabilitate institutionalized youngsters, would be unthinkable in English law.[67] Although the English courts may have the concepts with which to extend the liability of the state,[68] they have been 'unduly timorous' out of 'terror of being thought to dictate to government' even if only in regard to the calculation of risk and the payment of insurance and compensation.[69] Lord Woolf has recognized their failure as a major shortcoming: '[t]he judges have . . . failed to develop a system which would entitle a citizen to compensation if he or she has been subject to unlawful administrative activity. Here the position of a member of the public is not as satisfactory before the English courts as it is at Strasbourg or on a complaint to the parliamentary commissioner'.[70] He attributes the failure, in part, to the absence of Parliamentary support. The problem, however, is also institutional. The judges lack the institutional confidence exemplified by the *Conseil d'Etat*.

Judicial Restraint in English Public Law

Despite the expansion of judicial review, the English courts have continued to show restraint in public law. Apart from their failure to extend the liability of the state to anything approximating to the liability established by the *Conseil d'Etat*, they have failed to develop principles of public law corresponding to *les principes généraux du droit* or *le principe de proportionnalité*. English judges have mentioned or discussed the principle of proportionality but have lacked the confidence in their

---

[67] N. 27 above. Cf. *Dorset Yacht Co*, n. 60 above.
[68] See generally Harlow, *Compensation and Government Torts*, n. 49 above, 58–83.
[69] Harlow, 'Fault Liability', n. 13 above, 539–40.
[70] H. Woolf, 'Judicial Review: Have the Judges made a Mess of It?' *Law Soc. Gazette*, 17 Oct. 1991, 18.

'training or experience' needed to adopt and apply it as a standard of judicial review.[71] At most they have left it undeveloped within the vague and all-encompassing concept of reasonableness.[72]

Many of the principles that the courts have developed, they have confused. The all-encompassing concept of unreasonableness,[73] the vagueness of improper purpose,[74] and the application of the concept of legitimate expectation to both the procedure and substance of decision-making[75] illustrate the confusion. And courts must still draw the difficult distinction between jurisdictional and non-jurisdictional errors of fact, if not of law, a legacy of the doctrine of *ultra vires*.[76] In short, they have allowed the lack of a system of principles, decried in 1968 by Wade,[77] to persist,[78] and, as a result, have more easily been able to obscure their social and economic preferences.[79]

Their formal judicial restraint,[80] their reluctance to articulate and systematize clear substantive principles, which people may rely upon in their dealings with the state and by reference to which judges may be called to account, is counterbalanced only by the exceptional activism in those landmark cases used to describe the development of English administrative law. Even that activism, however, is open to question. An external commentator observed:

The four . . . major cases do not so much declare a revival [of judicial review] as announce the judges' refusal finally to be pushed entirely out of the field of judicial review of administrative decisions. *Ridge* undermines a doctrine created by the courts themselves . . . *Padfield* and *Tameside* assert that judicial review is not entirely debarred by 'subjective' clauses . . . *Anisminic* strikes at privative

---

[71] *Brind* v. *Home Secretary* [1991] 1 All ER 720 at 724H–5C, 735F–J, 738F–9H, especially at 739B; *GCHQ* case, n. 62 above, 410E. See generally S. Boyron, 'Proportionality in English Administrative Law: A Faulty Transplant?' (1992) 12 *OJLS* 237–64, especially at 245–7.

[72] *Brind*, n. 71 above, 738G. See H. W. R. Wade, *Administrative Law* (6th edn., Oxford, 1988), 428–9; Wade and Forsyth, n. 48 above, 403, 424.

[73] See, e.g., *Associated Provincial Picture Houses Ltd* v. *Wednesbury Corporation* [1948] 1 KB 223.

[74] See, e.g., *Wheeler* v. *Leicester City Council* [1985] AC 1054; J. Jowell and A. Lester, 'Beyond *Wednesbury*: Substantive Principles of Administrative Law' [1987] *PL* 368–82 at 373–4.

[75] C. Forsyth, 'The Provenance and Protection of Legitimate Expectations' [1988] *CLJ* 238–60; G. Ganz, 'Legitimate Expectation' in C. Harlow (ed.), *Public Law and Politics* (London, 1986), 145–62.

[76] Wade and Forsyth, n. 48 above, 286 ff.

[77] Wade, 'Crossroads in Administrative Law', n. 52 above, 84–92.

[78] Lord Scarman, 'The Development of Administrative Law: Obstacles and Opportunities' [1990] *PL* 490–5.

[79] Jowell and Lester, n. 74 above, 381.   [80] Cf. *ibid.* 381–2.

clauses that purport entirely to bar judicial review of some administrative decisions. Declaring on an average of once every three years that one is still in the game is not the same thing as winning it or even making a modest score. Whatever the symbolic value of these four cases, neither they nor the handful of less important decisions that have followed them constitute a major check on British administrative authority.[81]

Occasional activism has not changed an overall picture of judicial restraint. The proliferation of judicial review cases in the last few decades is not proof of successful activism but a symptom of enduring uncertainties—about the required procedure, the relevant substantive principles, and the likely judicial role.

Uncertainty about the Judicial Role

The Insecure Foundation of the Doctrine of Ultra Vires

The doctrine of *ultra vires*[82] has been the cornerstone for the development[83] of English administrative law in the twentieth century. It is the means by which the English courts have given effect to the separation of powers resulting from the revolutionary settlement and subsequent extension of parliamentary government. It justifies judicial intervention when an administrative authority acts *ultra vires*, i.e. exceeds the powers conferred upon it by statutory instruments. It accordingly supposes a threefold division of labour—the authorizing of administrative action by Parliament, the deciding of issues by administrative authorities if within their statutory powers, and determination of the scope of those powers by independent courts of review.

As stated, the doctrine justifies judicial restraint. It distinguishes judicial review of legality from an appeal on the merits. It confers upon courts of review only the control of legality and leaves policy the preserve of Parliament.[84] If Parliament has authorized administrative action, the doctrine does not justify judicial intervention.[85] Rather, it

---

[81] M. Shapiro, *Courts: A Comparative and Political Analysis* (Chicago, 1981), 118–24, especially at 121–2.

[82] See generally D. Oliver, 'Is the *Ultra Vires* Rule the Basis of Judicial Review?' [1987] *PL* 543–69; J. Bell, 'Le fondement du contrôle juridictionnel de l'administration' in P. Legrand (ed.), *Common Law d'un siécle l'autre* (Cowansville, 1992), 57–86.

[83] The origins of English administrative law are intertwined with those of the prerogative remedies. See above, 4–5, below, 227 ff.

[84] See J. D. B. Mitchell, 'The Causes and Effects of the Absence of a System of Public Law in the United Kingdom' [1965] *PL* 95–118 at 98.

[85] Cf. Shapiro, n. 81 above, 116, 123.

presupposes judicial independence and, so, discourages that association with the administration which would result in judges with the administrative expertise to intervene confidently in the administrative process.

The courts, however, have not been stifled by the doctrine of *ultra vires*. Rather, they have only been restricted, on the one hand, by the distinction between law and policy, which has been under attack since the contribution of the American realists, and, on the other hand, by statutes, which, of limited length and drafted according to a limited foresight, cannot indicate the precise scope of statutory powers. The courts have therefore been free to develop the grounds of judicial review, such as non-compliance with the rules of natural justice,[86] by implying limitations to statutory powers, that is, by assuming that Parliament intended a statutory power to be exercised according to judicial principles.[87] They have been free to blur the distinction between appeal and review.[88] Wade concludes that the courts 'can make the doctrine [of *ultra vires*] mean almost anything they wish by finding implied limitations in Acts of Parliament' and that they 'appear willing to stretch the doctrine . . . to cover virtually all situations where statutory power is exercised contrary to some legal principle'.[89] Furthermore, the courts have increasingly intervened without being preoccupied with it. In particular, they have intervened regardless of ouster clauses[90] and are prepared to review the exercise of non-statutory powers.[91]

Because of its uncertainty, the doctrine of *ultra vires* has therefore permitted judicial activism, but, for the same reason, has not justified it. The doctrine and the related theory of the separation of powers[92] have both been too vague even to begin to justify judicial intervention by answering the demand for judges with both judicial independence and administrative expertise. Rather, the doctrine has left the courts agonizing over difficulties such as the distinction between jurisdictional and non-jurisdictional error[93] or the compatibility of contract and

---

[86] See, e.g., *Cooper* v. *Wandsworth Board of Works* (1863) 14 CBNS 180.

[87] See Wade and Forsyth, n. 48 above, 41 ff.

[88] See, e.g., *Anisminic*, n. 54 above; *Page* v. *Hull University Visitor* [1993] 1 All ER 97.

[89] Wade and Forsyth, n. 48 above, 43 (author's insertion); Wade, *Administrative Law*, n. 72 above, 44.

[90] See, e.g., *Anisminic*, n. 54 above.

[91] See, e.g., *R.* v. *Panel on Take-overs and Mergers, ex p. Datafin Plc* [1987] QB 815.

[92] See above, 155–6.   [93] Wade and Forsyth, n. 48 above, 284 ff.

statutory power.[94] To the extent that the doctrine is certain, it has required judicial restraint. And to the extent that it is uncertain, it has not justified the judicial role, let alone judicial activism. The institutional foundation for English administrative law is insecure.

Unease about Justiciability

In English administrative law, the basic institutional insecurity has aggravated the issue of justiciability—the issue whether a dispute should be resolved by the courts or, alternatively stated, 'whether a court is the most appropriate organ of government to deal with the dispute'.[95] In a number of the cases introducing the distinction between public and private law, the courts have restricted their role in public law according to their sense of the non-justiciability of certain matters. The cases of *Dorset Yacht*, *Anns*, *Gouriet*, and *Western Fish Products Ltd* are illustrative. First, in *Dorset Yacht*, Lord Diplock described a range of conflicting interests and declared that the court would be extremely reluctant to find liability on the basis that the Home Office was negligent in choosing a system of control of Borstal boys.[96] His Lordship argued as follows:

[T]here is no criterion by which a court can assess where the balance lies between the weight to be given to one interest and that to be given to another. The material relevant to the assessment of the reformative effect upon trainees of release under supervision or of any relaxation of control while still under detention is not of a kind which can be satisfactorily elicited by the adversary procedure and rules of evidence adopted in English courts of law or of which judges (and juries) are suited by their training and experience to assess the probative value.[97]

Secondly, in *Anns*, Lord Wilberforce held that the court will not easily impose a duty of care in the policy as opposed to the operational area.[98] Although his Lordship did not use the concept of justiciability, he drew his policy/operational distinction because he regarded the local authority's decisions in the policy area as non-justiciable.[99]

Thirdly, in *Gouriet*, the House of Lords refused to allow Gouriet to litigate in the public interest where the Attorney-General had refused his

---

[94] See Craig, n. 58 above, 502–7.

[95] P. Cane, 'The Function of Standing Rules in Administrative Law' [1980] *PL* 303–28 at 310.

[96] *Dorset Yacht Co*, n. 60 above, 1067B–1068C.   [97] *Ibid.* 1067E–F.

[98] *Anns*, n. 59 above, 754C–5F.

[99] *Ibid.* 754C, F–H; Craig, n. 58 above, 454–5; *Rowling* v. *Takaro Properties Ltd* [1988] AC 473 at 501A–C.

consent to relator proceedings.[100] It recognized the Attorney-General's exclusive right to represent the public interest in civil litigation. By holding that the Attorney-General's decision whether or not to lend his name to relator proceedings is unreviewable, the House of Lords deferred to his decision on justiciability. In effect, it determined that the very issue of justiciability in civil proceedings is non-justiciable.[101]

Fourthly, in *Western Fish Products Ltd*, the Court of Appeal justified restricting estoppel in public law as follows:

> Parliament has given those who are aggrieved by refusals of planning permission or the serving of enforcement notices a right of appeal to the Secretary of State: see ss 36 and 88 of the 1971 Act. He can hear evidence as to the merits and take into account policy considerations. The courts can do neither. The application of the concept of estoppel because of what a planning officer had represented could result in a court adjudging that a planning authority was bound to allow a development which flouted its planning policy, with which the courts are not concerned.[102]

In this case and the other leading cases above, the courts made the substantive distinction between public and private law depend in part on some notion of justiciability and accordingly on an appreciation of institutional limitations to judicial intervention in the administrative process. The courts, however, do not argue in terms of justiciability and describe what is non-justiciable merely with vague examples such as policy issues and disputes involving many conflicting interests. Academics have similarly failed to clarify justiciability.[103] Craig, for example, advocates the concept of justiciability as an advance upon the operational/policy distinction in *Anns* but only gives the examples of decisions concerning the allocation of risk and the distribution of scarce resources. He also recognizes the uncertainty 'reflective of the broader, *unavoidable* issue of what questions are suited to judicial resolution'.[104]

Explicit use of the concept of justiciability is therefore the recognition rather the resolution of a problem.[105] By focusing on the compe-

---

[100] *Gouriet*, n. 56 above.

[101] *Ibid.* 481F–H; Cane, 'The Function of Standing Rules', n. 95 above, 309–12.

[102] *Western Fish Products Ltd*, n. 57 above, 221D–F.

[103] See G. Marshall, 'Justiciability' in A. G. Guest (ed.), *Oxford Essays in Jurisprudence: A Collaborative Work* (London, 1961), 265–87; R. S. Summers, 'Justiciability' (1963) 26 *MLR* 530–42; Mitchell, n. 84 above, 104; Cane, 'The Function of Standing Rules', n. 95 above, 311; C. Harlow and R. Rawlings, *Law and Administration* (London, 1984), 309–15.

[104] Craig, n. 58 above, 450–1.

[105] See, e.g., Craig, *ibid.*; Cane, 'The Function of Standing Rules', n. 95 above, 309–12.

tence of the court, the concept of justiciability takes us from the unknown to the more obviously unknown. It takes us from argument about the substantive principles of public law to a debate about the judicial role in public law, to a debate characterized by crudities such as the distinction between green- and red-light theory.[106] And it returns us to the institutional issue—how can English courts control or facilitate administrative action while the English separation of powers and simple ideal of judicial independence do not ensure the administrative expertise of English judges?

Attitudes to the Substantive Distinction

Underlying uncertainty about the role of the courts in public law is evident in the debate both about specific differences between public and private law[107] and about the general doctrinal distinction. Attitudes to the doctrinal distinction have varied according to varying conceptions of the judicial role. Participants in the debate adopt at least three positions—the traditional, the sceptical, and the trusting. First, certain participants defend the distinction because they accept the vague but traditional constitutional conception of a limited judicial role in public law. Lord Woolf, for example, contrasts the role of the courts in public law with their role in private law as follows:

Under public law, it is not the role of the courts to find the facts: it is not for the courts to specify what is reasonable and its views on policy questions are normally of no relevance. The explanation for the more limited role of the courts in relation to public duties is that the statute or other authority which creates the duty places the responsibility for the decision on the public body responsible for making the decision. The courts cannot usurp the duty of the public body to make the decision.[108]

Secondly, certain participants reject the distinction out of scepticism. They rely on the extension of private-law principles because they suspect that the English courts as constituted will continue to develop public law as a realm of immunity for the state. Professor Harlow, for example, identifies a fallacy in the plea for a special system of administrative liability:

---

[106] See Harlow and Rawlings, n. 103 above, 1–59. Cf. the functionalism and normativism described by M. Loughlin, *Public Law and Political Theory* (Oxford, 1992).

[107] Cf., e.g., Craig, n. 58 above, 480–6; Cane, *Introduction to Administrative Law*, n. 58 above, 225–8.

[108] H. Woolf, 'Public Law–Private Law: Why the Divide? A Personal View' [1986] *PL* 220–38 at 225.

The first fallacy is that a special system of administrative liability will *necessarily* prove more generous to the subject than the ordinary common law. Supposing this to be the case in France . . . there is no guarantee that we could reproduce the same pattern in England. It is here that the argument for special rules overlaps with the argument for special courts. After all, the English judiciary has for the most part created the special rules of which we now complain. It is unlikely, unless we rear a special new breed of administrative judges, that their outlook will suddenly and dramatically change.[109]

Thirdly, certain participants advocate the distinction out of faith. They trust in the competence of the judiciary to transform the distinction into a means to a dynamic public law which raises the responsibilities of the state. Samuel, for example, stresses the potential of the distinction:

The real issue, then, is not the distinction itself but the way it has been utilized by the judiciary. . . . The great jurisprudential advantage of the category of public law is that it describes another relationship, that between person and the state, which can *in itself* be used as a basis for conferring rights on citizens in the absence of suitable private law devices.[110]

From a different political position, but also with faith in the distinction's potential, if only as rhetoric, Collins advocates a perspective on labour relations close to that of public law because of its distributive principles. Although he accepts much of the critique of the distinction, he recognizes its rhetorical usefulness.[111]

These diverse positions are symptomatic of uncertainty about the judicial role. In the absence of a clear and justified conception of the role, or potential role, of the courts in public law, the distinction is questionable, controversial, and vulnerable to mere rhetorical use.[112] If we do not know what the courts can and should do in public law, we cannot know whether their role should be different in private law.

---

[109] Harlow, ' "Public" and "Private" Law', n. 66 above, 245.

[110] G. Samuel, 'Public and Private Law: A Private Lawyer's Response' (1983) 46 *MLR* 558–83 at 561, 564.

[111] H. Collins, 'The Public/Private Distinction in British Labour Law', Critical Legal Conference (Univ. of Kent, Sept. 1986) 13–14. See generally H. Collins, *Justice in Dismissal: The Law of Termination of Employment* (Oxford, 1992).

[112] See, e.g., K. E. Klare, 'The Public–Private Distinction in Labor Law' (1982) 130 *Univ. of Penn. LRev.* 1358–1422.

The Importance of Institutional Answers

In France, the historic development of the French separation of powers ensured that the *Conseil d'Etat* answered the need for both judicial independence and administrative expertise. The *Conseil d'Etat* could therefore develop a dynamic public law which gradually silenced liberal criticism. Its success in extending the liability of the state and fulfilling an extensive judicial role entrenched the institutional and substantive French distinctions between public and private law.

The English separation of powers has had a contrasting effect. It has not justified dynamic judicial intervention in the administrative process by ensuring independent and expert judges. Rather, it has left a legacy of judicial restraint, uncertainty engendered by the doctrine of *ultra vires*, and general unease about justiciability. For want of the required separation of powers, English administrative law has not converged with *droit administratif*[113] and has not justified the transplantation of the distinction between public and private law. The substantive English distinction has remained controversial. In short, it shares with the institutional distinction emerging with the Crown Office List the enduring and intractable problem of an appropriate separation of powers.

---

[113] *Contra* Flogaïtis, n. 1 above.

9

The Limits of Adversarial Adjudication

Apart from the institutional handicap discussed in the last two chapters, the nature of English judicial procedures has also been given as a reason for judicial restraint when the English courts deal with administrative disputes.[1] In the next two chapters[2], I will consider the procedural handicap of the English courts. In this chapter, through a critique of Lon Fuller's published and unpublished work on adjudication, I will emphasize the importance of inquisitorial judicial procedures, my model's procedural requirement[3] for a working distinction between public and private law. That requirement deserves special attention because of its controversiality and extensive implications for English public law. I will describe the need for inquisitorial procedures as the procedural implication of polycentric administrative disputes. In the following chapter, I will compare the extent to which judicial procedures in France and England respectively have answered that need. In discussing procedure, I will use the concepts 'adversarial' and 'inquisitorial' in a non-pejorative way to refer to contrasting balances between the power of the parties to prepare and the power of the court to investigate cases.[4] So as to focus attention on the judicial procedures described in my model, I will again presuppose[5] a distinct state administration giving rise to distinctly administrative disputes.

The Ramifications of Administrative Disputes

If the state administration is distinct, as is presupposed here, administrative disputes can be distinguished from private disputes by reference

---

[1] See, e.g., *Dorset Yacht Co* v. *Home Office* [1970] AC 1004 at 1067E–F; *Western Fish Products Ltd* v. *Penwith DC* [1981] 2 All ER 204 at 221H–I.

[2] These chs. include adapted sections from my following two articles: 'Fuller's Analysis of Polycentric Disputes and the Limits of Adjudication' (1994) 53 *CLJ* 367–83; 'The Procedural Reason for Judicial Restraint' [1994] *PL* 452–73.

[3] See above, 36, 39

[4] See generally R. W. Millar, 'The Formative Principles of Civil Procedure' in A. Engelmann *et al.* (eds.), *History of Continental Civil Procedure* (London, 1928), 3–81 at 11–21; J. I. H. Jacob, *The Reform of Civil Procedural Law and Other Essays in Civil Procedure* (London, 1982), 24–5; *id.*, *The Fabric of English Civil Justice* (London, 1987), 5–19; J. A. Jolowicz, 'Adversarial and Inquisitorial Approaches to Civil Litigation' in E. G. Baldwin (ed.), *The Cambridge Lectures* (Toronto, 1983), 237–44; *id.*, book review (1988) 8 *Legal Studies* 111–20 at 112–14.

[5] See above, 109.

to the involvement of the state administration. They generally have far wider ramifications than private disputes because of that involvement.[6] Administrative disputes usually have widespread ramifications, affecting limited public funds, choice of administrative action, and the public at large, who have a special interest in the collective goals that are being furthered.

Various conceptions of the state administration would explain the ramifications of administrative disputes. First, if it is characterized by its access to the public purse, a dispute involving the use of that purse affects alternative uses. Secondly, if the state administration furthers collective goals, numerous citizens may be concerned with the furtherance of those goals. Thirdly, if it has a duty to show individuals equal concern and respect, the issue of concern for one individual affects other individuals. Fourthly, if the state administration furthers a plurality of interests, rather than an univocal public interest, administrative disputes will frequently involve that plurality. And, fifthly, if it is a means by which various groups trade effectively in benefits that offset continuing hardships, then a dispute involving one benefit affects the denial of another.

Administrative disputes are not the only disputes that usually have extensive ramifications. Disputes with such ramifications have in fact become increasingly common in modern societies characterized by what Cappelletti calls 'massification'—'a mass-production, mass-distribution, and mass-consumption economy' in which '[d]amages caused by unhealthy packaging, by discharge of waste, by false publicity, or by violations of collective labour agreements may concern masses of consumers, employees, and entire communities'.[7] If this chapter's heuristic presupposition of a distinct state administration is false, administrative disputes are difficult to distinguish from private disputes,[8] but, if one of the conceptions of the state administration, listed above, is to be accepted, administrative disputes, alongside numerous other disputes, can be expected often to have widespread ramifications. How judicial procedures are affected is the difficult question that has generally been neglected by legal academics, with the notable exception of Lon Fuller.

---

[6] See Allison, 'The Procedural Reason for Judicial Restraint', n. 2 above, 457–61.

[7] M. Cappelletti, *The Judicial Process in Comparative Perspective* (Oxford, 1989), 25. See, e.g., *Texaco* v. *Mulberry Filling Station* [1972] 1 All ER 513; *Launchbury* v. *Morgans* [1973] AC 127; *Hesperides Hotels Ltd* v. *Muftizade* [1979] AC 508.

[8] On the difficulty of distinguishing the state administration, see above, chs. 4 and 5.

Fuller's Analysis of Polycentric Disputes

Fuller[9] made a leading contribution[10] to our understanding of disputes and their procedural implications. To describe disputes with wide-spread ramifications, he introduced the concept of polycentricity into discussion of adjudication. He derived it from Polanyi who used it to justify restricting central direction of the economy.[11] Fuller defines polycentric problems as 'situation[s] of interacting points of influence', which, while possibly relevant to adjudication, normally, although not invariably, 'involve many affected parties and a somewhat fluid state of affairs'.[12] He stresses the 'complex repercussions' of intervention in such situations.[13] He describes the polycentric situation with a metaphor and numerous examples:

We may visualize this kind of situation by thinking of a spider's web. A pull on one strand will distribute tensions after a complicated pattern throughout the web as a whole. Doubling the original pull will, in all likelihood, not simply double each of the resulting tensions but will rather create a different complicated pattern of tensions. This would certainly occur, for example, if the doubled pull caused one or more of the weaker strands to snap. This is a 'poly-

---

[9] L. L. Fuller and J. D. Randall, 'Professional Responsibility: Report of the Joint Conference' (1958) 44 *ABA J* 1159–62, 1216–18; L. L. Fuller, 'Adjudication and the Rule of Law' (1960) 54 *Proc. Am. Soc. of Int. L* 1–8; *id.*, 'The Adversary System' in H. J. Berman (ed.), *Talks on American Law: A Series of Broadcasts to Foreign Audiences by Members of the Harvard Law School Faculty* (New York, 1961), 30–43, *id.*, 'Collective Bargaining and the Arbitrator' [1963] *Wis. LRev.* 3–46 at 30 ff.; *id.*, 'Irrigation and Tyranny ' (1965) 17 *Stan. LRev.* 1021–42; *id.*, *The Morality of Law* (2nd edn., New Haven, 1969), 170–81; *id.*, 'Mediation—Its Forms and Functions' (1971) 44 *S Cal. LRev.* 305–39, *id.*, 'The Forms and Limits of Adjudication' (1978) 92 *Harv. LRev.* 353–409 at 393 ff. See generally L. L. Fuller, *The Principles of Social Order: Selected Essays* (K. I. Winston (ed.)) (Durham, NC, 1981); R. S. Summers, *Lon L. Fuller* (London, 1984), 90–100.

[10] For the influence of Fuller's Analysis, see J. Stone, *Social Dimensions of Law and Justice* (London, 1966), 652–6; P. Weiler, 'Two Models of Judicial Decision-making' (1968) 46 *Can. BRev.* 406–71; B. B. Boyer, 'Alternatives to Administrative Trial-type Hearings for Resolving Complex Scientific, Economic, and Social Issues' (1972) 71 *Mich LRev.* 111–70; M. D. A. Freeman, 'Standards of Adjudication, Judicial Law-making and Prospective Overruling' (1973) 26 *CLP* 166–207 at 182–9, 206–7; J. Jowell, 'The Legal Control of Administrative Discretion' [1973] *PL* 178–220 at 213–18; R. A. Macdonald, 'Judicial Review and Procedural Fairness in Administrative Law' (1980) 25 *McGill LJ* 520–64 at 540–3, 26 *McGill LJ* 1–44 at 16–21; A. Paterson, *The Law Lords* (London, 1982), 172–4; J. H. Langbein, 'The German Advantage in Civil Procedure' (1985) 52 *Chicago LRev.* 823–66 at 843–4; P. P. Craig, *Administrative Law* (2nd edn., London, 1989), 213–17; P. Cane, *An Introduction to Administrative Law* (2nd edn., Oxford, 1992), 34–6, 170, 189.

[11] M. Polanyi, *The Logic of Liberty: Reflections and Rejoinders* (London, 1951), 170 ff.

[12] Fuller, 'Forms and Limits of Adjudication', n. 9 above, 395, 397.

[13] *Ibid.* 394–5.

centric' situation because it is 'many centered'—each crossing of strands is a distinct center for distributing tensions.[14]

Fuller's examples of polycentric problems include the testamentary allocation of paintings 'in equal shares' between two galleries, 'assigning the players of a football team to their respective positions', 'allocating scarce funds for projects of scientific research', 'redrawing the boundaries of election districts to make them correspond to shifts in population', and 'allocating radio and television channels to make balanced programs as accessible to the population as possible'.[15]

Fuller focuses[16] on the problem posed for adjudication by disputes that are significantly polycentric. He characterizes adjudication principally by reference to the mode of participation of the parties—the adversarial presentation of proofs and reasoned arguments. He distinguishes that participation from the participation in other forms of social ordering, such as negotiating a contract and voting in elections.[17] Polycentricity is problematic for Fuller's adjudication because[18] participation by the presentation of proofs and reasoned arguments is affected by the complex repercussions of the judicial decision. While the range of those affected by the dispute cannot easily be foreseen and their participation organized, those who do participate—the parties to the action—lack discrete issues to address. As a result of inadequate participation, the adjudicator is inadequately informed and cannot determine the complex repercussions of a proposed solution. Fuller describes how the solution adopted by the adjudicator may consequently fail to be satisfactory: '[u]nexpected repercussions make the decision unworkable; it is ignored, withdrawn, or modified, sometimes repeatedly'.[19]

In response to the inadequacy of adjudication in a significantly polycentric dispute, Fuller did not simply depend on adjudicators in subsequent similar disputes to relax the doctrine of *stare decisis* and improve upon an initial adjudicative solution.[20] Such improvement would be at the cost of legal certainty and would only restrict unwanted repercussions as experienced in subsequent disputes which go to court.

Fuller's general approach to the inaptness of adjudicative procedures

[14] *Ibid.* 395.   [15] Fuller, 'Adjudication and the Rule of Law', n. 9 above, 3–4.
[16] See also L. L. Fuller, 'The Law's Precarious Hold on Life' (1969) 3 *Georgia LRev.* 530–45; Summers, n. 9 above, 96–8.
[17] 'Forms and Limits of Adjudication', n. 9 above, 363–5.
[18] See also Boyer, n. 10 above, 122 ff.
[19] 'Forms and Limits of Adjudication', n. 9 above, 401.
[20] *Ibid.* 398; Weiler, n. 10 above, 423.

is to use the concept of polycentricity to delimit adjudication. He opposed the general legislative use of adjudicative agencies to resolve disputes that are significantly polycentric. His analysis is also relevant to the adjudicative court or tribunal that must resolve the disputes subject to its jurisdiction. It shows that an adjudicator, informed only by the litigating parties, is ill-equipped to determine the complex repercussions of a proposed decision. Because of the adjudicator's limited competence, the legislature must avoid creating tribunals to adjudicate in significantly polycentric disputes, and the adjudicator has reason not to resolve such disputes in ways that necessitate a judicial appreciation of complex repercussions. From the perspective of the adjudicator, Fuller's analysis requires judicial restraint. To avoid exceeding the limits of its own competence, a court confronted with a significantly polycentric dispute must refrain from two kinds of activism. First, the court must not change the law where an appreciation of repercussions is required for sensible legal development. Secondly, in so far as the court has a choice under existing law, it must avoid choosing a legal solution that necessitates an appreciation of complex repercussions.[21]

Outstanding Questions

Fuller's approach begs two questions. How is the court to determine whether a dispute is significantly polycentric? And, in administrative (or other polycentric) disputes, how else, if not by adjudication, are those affected by extensive ramifications to be protected? I will deal with each question in turn.

First, to show judicial restraint, the adjudicative court must first determine whether the dispute is significantly polycentric. But, in so far as the doctrine of *stare decisis* is adhered to, almost any dispute is rendered polycentric by potential repercussions for later similar disputes.[22] The court must therefore distinguish between degrees of polycentricity. Fuller accepts that 'the polycentricity of any given problem is a matter of degree' and recalls Holmes' remark that 'a distinction may be a matter of degree and none the worse for that'.[23] Fuller's satisfac-

---

[21] See, e.g., *R. P. and T. G.* v. *Home Secretary and Criminal Injuries Compensation Board* (unreported judgment handed down on 4 May 1994), in which Neill LJ avoided an investigation of repercussions for the public purse by explicitly invoking Fuller's Analysis.

[22] See O. M. Fiss, 'The Supreme Court 1978 Term. Foreword: The Forms of Justice' (1979) 93 *Harv. LRev.* 1–58 at 42–3; F. C. Newman, letter of 19 Oct. 1959, Lon Luvois Fuller Papers, Harvard Law School Library, at no. 11.

[23] Fuller, 'Adjudication and the Rule of Law', n. 9 above, 5; *id.*, 'Forms and Limits of Adjudication', n. 9 above, 397–8.

tion with a difference of degree is possibly related to his academic appreciation of the limits to social science[24] but is of no practical help to the court. The extent of the court's difficulty is belied by the geometrical connotations of the notion of degree. Without a protractor to determine differences of degree, the court cannot be certain where to draw the line between disputes that vary in the significance of their polycentricity. The court can only estimate whether the ramifications of a dispute are sufficiently complex to require judicial restraint.

Furthermore, the court must determine the dispute's level of polycentricity only on the basis of information supplied by the parties in court. The court will struggle to determine the dispute's polycentricity for the same reason that it will struggle to resolve the polycentric dispute—the insufficiency of participation by those who are affected but are not parties to the action. Delimiting adjudication in response to polycentric disputes begs the question of their polycentricity. The court will therefore be left with nagging doubts that disputes which seem bipolar are in fact significantly polycentric.

Because of the limited participation of those affected by the dispute, the adjudicative court as described by Fuller cannot be sure of the extent of repercussions or of their legal irrelevance. For example, Fuller describes a dispute concerning an employee's contractual entitlement to a vacation as typical of 'cases that fall neatly within the competence of the adjudicative process'.[25] Such a dispute, however, would commonly involve the interpretation of vague contractual terms or an issue, such as, possibly, the timing of a vacation, on which the contracting parties have not agreed either expressly or by clear implication, If so, Fuller's adjudicative court will have reason to suspect that the dispute is perhaps significantly polycentric because of possibly relevant repercussions, not only for other employees subject to similar contracts but also for the litigating employee's colleagues whose vacations must be staggered. While relying only on the proofs and arguments of the parties, the court cannot confidently adopt a legal solution that renders such repercussions irrelevant. Similarly, it cannot be sure of the extent to which it should intervene with exclusive regard to the entitlements and interests of the contracting parties in court.

In the administrative context, the adjudicator might choose to decide on a narrow legal ground, such as a recognized case of procedural

---

[24] R. S. Summers, 'Professor Fuller's Jurisprudence and America's Dominant Philosophy of Law' (1978) 92 *Harv. LRev.* 433–49 at 442–4.

[25] Fuller, 'Collective Bargaining', n. 9 above, 31.

impropriety, which does not seem to involve a judicial determination of repercussions. It might try to avoid the issue of repercussions by showing judicial restraint. But, even when considering a narrow ground of challenge, the court cannot confidently determine the irrelevance of repercussions when it only relies on partisan argument about the scope of vague statutory formulas, general principles of review, and the judicial discretion nevertheless to deny a remedy in particular circumstances. In recognizing and resolving the issues in polycentric administrative disputes, the court is incompetent to determine the irrelevance of repercussions for the some reason that it is incompetent to determine their nature or extent—the limited participation of affected parties.

In a letter about his paper on the limits of adjudication, Fuller clarified his view of a continuum: 'calling something a continuum certainly does not mean that we can be indifferent toward the problem of clarifying what lies at the end of it. Indeed, a continuum without a definable end is not a continuum at all, but a great gray soup.'[26] But, while Fuller does define one end of his continuum—the significantly polycentric depute—with his numerous illustrations and metaphor of the spider's web, he does not successfully identify and illustrate the other end—the bipolar dispute involving discrete issues. The adjudicative court is left only with a vague sense that any dispute might have ramifications which it is incompetent to determine in reaching a decision. The adequacy of adjudication is generally threatened by the uncertainty. Application of Fuller's concept of polycentricity, used polemically by Polanyi to counter central direction of the economy, is too uncertain[27] to serve as a guide for the adjudicator. Fuller's polycentric legal dispute is like the fly somewhere in the vicinity of a spider's web.

Secondly, Fuller's analysis raises the question of alternative protection. Delimiting adjudication by reference to polycentricity exposes those affected by the repercussions of an administrative dispute. If the adjudicator is insufficiently informed to take repercussions into account, those affected by them are dependent upon other forms of social ordering to determine the relevant protective rules or principles and, so, to define, and give effect to, rights. But the other forms vari-

---

[26] 4 Apr. 1960, Lon Luvois Fuller Papers, Harvard Law School Library.
[27] See C. Harlow and R. Rawlings, *Law and Administration* (London, 1984), 63–4. Cf. Paterson, n. 10 above, 187–9, 197–8; Fuller, *Morality of Law*, n. 9 above, 170–7; *id.*, 'Irrigation and Tyranny', n. 9 above, 1034–7.

ously listed[28] by Fuller—in particular legislation, mediation, contract, and administrative or managerial direction—are not up to the task. Legislation similarly falters in the absence of discrete issues to be put to the vote.[29] If general and comprehensive, it depends heavily on adjudication for authoritative interpretation and therefore shares its limitations.[30] Mediation aims at mutual accommodation rather than the determination of existing rights.[31] Contract and managerial or administrative direction are better suited to significantly polycentric disputes[32] but have serious drawbacks. Contract is ill-suited to the inequality in bargaining power of the parties typically involved in administrative disputes and therefore 'occupies in most societies a curious twilight zone between legal entitlement and political concession'.[33] Traditionally classified as private, it is largely immune to public scrutiny.[34] Finally, administrative direction is left unelaborated by Fuller as a form of ordering—without a 'complete and explicit characterization',[35] without systematic treatment of its legitimacy,[36] dependent upon mere intuition,[37] and usually relevant by default or by the way.[38] How administrative direction can work at all satisfactorily where market checks are absent is unclear.[39]

Because Fuller perceived the insufficiency of other forms, he accepted the occasional need for the adjudication of significantly polycentric administrative disputes as a special concession to the interests at stake. In his correspondence with Frank Newman,[40] a former

[28] See K. I. Winston in Fuller, *Principles of Social Order*, n. 9 above, 27. See also, e.g., Fuller, 'Mediation', n. 9 above.

[29] Fuller, *The Morality of Law*, n. 9 above, 177–8; *id.*, 'Forms and Limits of Adjudication', n. 9 above, 399–400.

[30] See generally L. L. Fuller, *Anatomy of the Law* (London, 1968), 57 ff.; *id.*, 'Mediation', n. 9 above, 307. Cf. A. W. Blumrosen, 'The Bottom Line in Equal Employment Guidelines—Administering a Polycentric Problem' (1981) 33 *Admin. LRev.* 323–49.

[31] See generally Fuller, 'Mediation', n. 9 above.

[32] Fuller, 'Forms and Limits of Adjudication', n. 9 above, 398–400.

[33] Fuller, 'Irrigation and Tyranny', n. 9 above, 1032. See generally Boyer, n. 10 above, 164–8.

[34] Fuller, *Morality of Law*, n. 9 above, 176.

[35] Winston, Editor's Note in Fuller, *Principles of Social Order*, n. 9 above, 188; Letter of R. F. Fuchs (20 Oct. 1959), Lon Luvois Fuller Papers, Harvard Law School Library.

[36] Summers, *Lon Fuller*, n. 9 above, 87.

[37] Fuller, 'Forms and Limits of Adjudication', n. 9 above, 398–9.

[38] Summers, *Lon Fuller*, n. 9 above, 88. See, e.g., Fuller, *Morality of Law*, n. 9 above, 207–23.

[39] Boyer, n. 10 above, 150–64.

[40] Letters of L. L. Fuller (22 Oct. 1959) and F. C. Newman (19 Oct. 1959), Lon Luvois Fuller Papers, Harvard Law School Library.

Professor in Administrative Law at Berkeley, he was unwilling to condemn the American desegregation decrees of the mid-1950s but
stressed their 'serious moral drain on the integrity of adjudication'. He
also mentioned the example of employment discrimination. He concluded that '[s]ometimes in handling social problems we *may* have to
mix oil and water' and added '[w]hat I urge is that we don't pretend
when we do this that we are drinking ambrosia.'[41] But how the mixture is at all drinkable is unclear. Judicial intervention for the sake of
a litigating party might be at the expense of others seriously affected
by the polycentric administrative dispute but not heard by the court.
Fuller's analysis of adjudication and other forms of social ordering does
not provide systematically for their protection.

In short, Fuller left administrative law without appropriate procedures for resolving polycentric administrative disputes and consequently failed fully to accept[42] its development.

Administrative Law

Fuller had considerable experience in practice before administrative
agencies,[43] and perceived, to some extent, that his analysis had extensive implications for administrative law. He sent his paper, 'The Forms
and Limits of Adjudication',[44] to various administrative lawyers.[45] He
also related his analysis to the United States Senate's Sub-committee
on Administrative Practice and Procedure and initially agreed to serve
on that sub-committee.[46] In his work on adjudication, Fuller cited
numerous examples of adjudicative agencies to illustrate the improper
use of adjudication.[47] He alleged that the 'solution of polycentric problems by adjudication has most often been attempted . . . in the field of

---

[41] Letter of L. L. Fuller (22 Oct. 1959), Lon Luvois Fuller Papers, Harvard Law
School Library.
[42] Winston in Fuller, *Principles of Social Order*, n. 9 above, 188.
[43] Fuller's letter to E. V. Long (14 Jan. 1964), Lon Luvois Fuller Papers, Harvard Law
School Library.
[44] Article handed out to jurisprudence class of Harvard Law School, 1959/60, Lon
Luvois Fuller Papers, Harvard Law School Library.
[45] See, e.g., letters of F. C. Newman (19 Oct. 1959) and W. Gellhorn (19 Oct. 1959),
Lon Luvois Fuller Papers, Harvard Law School Library.
[46] See correspondence between Fuller (18 May 1959) and the Sub-committee on
Administrative Practice and Procedure (17 Sept. 1963), Lon Luvois Fuller Papers,
Harvard Law School Library.
[47] See, e.g., Fuller, 'Adjudication and the Rule of Law', n. 9 above, 7–8; *id.*,
'Irrigation and Tyranny', n. 9 above, especially at 1041–2; *id.*, *Morality of Law*, n. 9 above,
170–7; *id.*, 'Mediation', n. 9 above, 334–7.

administrative law'.[48] Elsewhere, Fuller expressed scepticism of the distinction between private and public law. As Chairman of the Harvard Law Schools' curriculum committee,[49] he wrote a report that opposed the proliferation of courses in specific branches of administrative law and advocated, in their place, courses, such as land use, unfair competition, and problems in commercial law, involving a 'synthesis of public and private-law considerations'.[50]

Fuller questioned the development of an autonomous administrative law because he was preoccupied with the limits of adjudication and because he associated administrative law initially with contract and later with managerial direction, the forms of social ordering that he considered to be better suited to the resolution of polycentric problems. In an early unpublished paper entitled 'The Philosophy of Administrative Law', he reached this conclusion: 'I see the legitimate objective of administrative law as that of fostering free contract, where practical obstacles prevent it from being free, and of imposing results similar to those which would be reached by free contract, if free contract could in fact safely be allowed to function'.[51] Later, he described administrative law as the prime example of a case 'where managerial direction and law are intertwined or merged'.[52] In his debate with legal positivists, Fuller clearly contrasted law and managerial direction.[53] Between the two, in a twilight zone, he identified administrative law. He once alleged that, in administrative law, 'if law exists at all, it exists imperfectly—it is still in process of being born'.[54]

Judicial Expertise and Investigation

Fuller's concept of adjudication affected his view of its potential. Fuller characterizes adjudication principally by reference to the participation of the parties rather than the role of the judge. He therefore distinguishes the adjudicator from decision-makers who are not informed through the parties' presentation of proofs and reasoned arguments,

[48] 'Forms and Limits of Adjudication', n. 9 above, 400. See also *ibid.* 355.

[49] See generally Summers, *Lon Fuller*, n. 9 above, 141–4.

[50] *Preliminary Statement of the Committee on Legal Education of the Harvard Law School* (1 Mar. 1947), Lon Luvois Fuller Papers, Harvard Law School Library, at 87 ff., especially at 90. See also Fuller, *Morality of Law*, n. 9 above, 176.

[51] 18 Feb. 1944, Lon Luvois Fuller Papers, Harvard Law School Library, 22. See also L. L. Fuller, 'Governmental Secrecy and the Forms of Social Order' in C. J. Friedrich (ed.), *Community: Nomos II* (New York, 1959), 256–68 at 260–1.

[52] Note, box 10, folder 12, Lon Luvois Fuller Papers, Harvard Law School Library.

[53] *Morality of Law*, n. 9 above, 204 ff.

[54] 'Adjudication and the Rule of Law', n. 9 above, 1.

such as the umpire at a baseball game and judge at an agricultural fair.[55] Fuller does not accept that such a judge or umpire is adjudicating by assessing and investigating evidence independently. He describes the office of the judge, judicial impartiality, and the responsibility to make a reasoned decision only as necessary implications of the meaningful presentation of proofs and reasoned arguments by the parties.[56]

Fuller values the expertise and investigation of the adjudicator only in so far as they facilitate the adjudicator's minimal role[57] of attending to the parties, reaching a decision which is responsive to their proofs and reasoned arguments, and explaining that decision with a reasoned reply. He commends only the competence of the expert advocate but not that of the expert tribunal 'to judge accurately in a particular case what issues will ultimately become crucial'.[58] In his discussion of adjudication in the form of industrial arbitration, he stresses that labour relations have become 'highly complicated and technical' but values the expertise and expert investigation of the arbitrator only so that the arguments of the parties do not fall on 'uncomprehending ears'.[59] And he adds a warning against the danger of an arbitrator with a 'desire to demonstrate virtuosity in his calling'.[60]

In one place, Fuller does appreciate an instance of independent expert judicial investigation but refrains from further discussion:

A slightly more sticky point is this: there are exceptional instances of decisions between disputants where no argument is ever contemplated because it is superfluous. An example is where a dispute about 'conformity to sample' arises between a seller and a buyer of textiles and the parties agree to abide by the decision of a laboratory. Whether such a process of decision should be called 'adjudication' is not a matter of real importance because its simplicity excludes the problems that are the subject of analysis in this essay.[61]

Fuller underestimated the significance of his example. In his correspondence with Fuller, Walter Gellhorn, a former Professor in Administrative Law at Columbia University, drew attention to other

---

[55] 'Forms and Limits of Adjudication', n. 9 above, 365.   [56] *Ibid.* 365–7.
[57] M. A. Eisenberg, 'Participation, Responsiveness, and the Consultative Process: An Essay for Lon Fuller' (1978) 92 *Harv. LRev.* 410–32 at 411–12.
[58] 'Forms and Limits of Adjudication', n. 9 above, 38–91, especially at 390.
[59] 'Collective Bargaining', n. 9 above, 11–12. Cf. generally Fuller, 'Irrigation and Tyranny', n. 9 above.
[60] 'Collective Bargaining', n. 9 above, 39.
[61] 'Forms and Limits of Adjudication', n. 9 above, 371–2.

similar examples which defy Fuller's analysis of adjudication.[62] He described how the Federal Trade Commission's trial examiner once took direct evidence that a lock was not 'pick proof' (as advertised) by organizing an experiment before the Commission. Then, he drew an example from the British NHS:

> I am reminded of observations I made during a field study, some eight or nine years ago, of the functioning of the National Health Service in Britain. If a patient filed charges against a dentist that, on their face, suggested departure from professional standards, the complainant and the affected dentist were summoned to a 'hearing room' in which the main furniture was a dentist's chair. The adjudicators were themselves dentists. They popped the plaintiff into the chair, poked and peered, allowed the respondent to point and argue, and then decided whether there had been an impropriety.

Although Fuller's concept of adjudication might be interpreted to cover the presentation of proofs and reasoned arguments in diverse forms, it gives little weight to the expert investigative role of the adjudicators in the examples described by Gellhorn.

Fuller's refusal to attribute much importance to the adjudicator's role is related to his belief in the adversary system as the guard against judicial bias or prejudgment. In an influential passage, he describes the danger of prejudgment and how to avert it:

> What generally occurs in practice is that at some early point a familiar pattern will seem to emerge from the evidence; an accustomed label is waiting for the case and, without awaiting further proofs, this label is promptly assigned to it. . . . But what starts as a preliminary diagnosis designed to direct the inquiry tends, quickly and imperceptibly, to become a fixed conclusion, as all that confirms the diagnosis makes a strong imprint on the mind, while all that runs counter to it is received with diverted attention. *An adversary presentation seems the only effective means for combatting this natural human tendency to judge too swiftly in terms of the familiar that which is not yet fully known.* The arguments of counsel hold the case, as it were, in suspension between two opposing interpretations of it.[63]

In this passage, however, Fuller suggests a plausible hypothesis only by exaggerating the 'natural human tendency' of adjudicators. He neglects the institutional and procedural safeguards which can protect adjudication. First, he does not take into account the ability of

---

[62] Letter of W. Gellhorn (19 Oct. 1959), Lon Luvois Fuller Papers, Harvard Law School Library. See also letter of N. L. Nathanson (29 Oct. 1959), Lon Luvois Fuller Papers, Harvard Law School Library.

[63] Fuller and Randall, n. 9 above, 1160 (emphasis added). See also Fuller, 'The Adversary System', n. 9 above, 38 ff; Summers, *Lon Fuller*, n. 9 above, 90–4.

carefully selected and well-trained adjudicators to guard against pre-judgment. Secondly, he ignores the adversarial safeguard of the principle of contradiction, the principle that the parties be given the opportunity to respond to any points raised by the judge in performing an enhanced judicial role. Thirdly, he does not mention the corrective effects of review and appeal. Fuller's powerful argument only annihilates an extreme example of untrammelled judicial investigation.[64]

Fuller does not draw on the Continental experience of adjudicative procedures involving greater judicial initiative and responsibility than is typically the case in the United Kingdom and the USA. Despite his claim to discuss 'adjudication in the very broadest sense',[65] Fuller does not give much attention in his published work to adjudicative procedures involving judicial investigation, such as the inquisitorial procedures of the French administrative jurisdiction.[66] He only occasionally mentions such procedures and, where he does, his comments are usually disparaging.[67] His empirical neglect of Continental judicial procedures generally is possibly related to the cultural relativism of his concern with the forms of social ordering. Fuller explained these forms in terms of particular purposes and regarded their number as limited in a particular society.[68] Fuller was preoccupied with adjudication in its Anglo-American adversarial form.

Partly because of his belief in the adversarial system as a guard against judicial bias and partly because of his neglect of Continental variations of adjudicative procedures, Fuller could not rely on the adjudicator's investigative abilities or expertise and initiative to help determine the complex repercussions of judicial intervention in a significantly polycentric administrative dispute. He could not depend on the adjudicator to help identify and resolve such a dispute or to help

[64] See Langbein, n. 10 above, 843–4, 857; S. R. Gross, 'The American Advantage: The Value of Inefficient Litigation' (1987) 85 *Mich. LRev.* 734–757 at 743; J. H. Langbein, 'Trashing "The German Advantage" ' (1988) 82 *Northwest. Univ. LRev.* 763–84 at 771–2. But cf. R. J. Allen, S. Köck, K. Riechenberg, and D. Toby Rosen, 'The German Advantage in Civil Procedure: A Plea for More Details and Fewer Generalities in Comparative Scholarship' (1988) 82 *Northwest. Univ. LRev.* 705–62 at 727–9.

[65] 'Forms and Limits of Adjudication', n. 9 above, 353.

[66] Summers, *Lon Fuller*, n. 9 above, 93.

[67] See, e.g., Fuller, 'The Adversary System', n. 9 above, 35–6; *id.*, *Anatomy of the Law*, n. 30 above, 19–22, 32. But cf. Fuller, *Morality of Law*, n. 9 above, 176–7.

[68] See Fuller, 'Irrigation and Tyranny', n. 9 above; K. I. Winston, review of *Lon L. Fuller* (1985) 95 *Ethics* 751–5 at 754; A. D'Amato, 'Lon Fuller and Substantive Natural Law' (1981) 26 *Amer. J of Juris.* 202–18; Boyer, n. 10 above, 137.

protect the vital interests of those whom it affects. His analysis of poly-centricity expresses an Anglo-American unease about the repercussions of adjudication, reflects the incapacity of adversarial procedures to cope with them, and suggests the implications of that incapacity for administrative law.

The Incompleteness of Fuller's Work

Although preoccupied with Anglo-American adversarial adjudication, Fuller would have resisted a straightjacket of traditional forms of social ordering. At different times spanning nearly thirty years, he attempted to distinguish and list the different forms of social ordering, but changed his list at each attempt.[69] In his correspondence, he regretted the Anglo-American bias of his paper on the limits of adjudication: 'I am acutely aware that my paper as it now stands is, as Steve Riesenfeld said, "horribly Anglo-American". This is one reason why I am not yet ready to publish it.'[70] He consequently requested a copy of the conference comments on his paper, made by Professor F. F. Stone, Director of Tulane University's Institute of Comparative Law.[71]

Another reason for the incompleteness of Fuller's work was his failure to take into account various domestic forms of adjudication. In a letter to Frank Newman,[72] Fuller said that he had 'in mind throughout' the American desegregation decrees of the mid-1950s, but he did not update his paper in the light of the further development of American public-law litigation in the civil rights era.[73] Furthermore, in his correspondence with Walter Gellhorn, he recognized that judging at an agricultural fair and umpiring at a baseball game were 'borderline' cases of adjudication and not the 'obvious cases' of something different as he had argued.[74] He also expressed the wish to include in his analysis the NHS and 'pick proof'-lock examples of adjudication mentioned by Gellhorn.[75] Fuller admitted that his own example of some different kind of adjudication—a laboratory's determination of conformity to sample in the textile industry—'is by no means as rare as I thought it was'.[76]

[69] Winston, Introduction in Fuller, *Principles of Social Order*, n. 9 above, 27. See generally Stone, n. 10 above, 654–5.

[70] 22 Jan. 1960, Lon Luvois Fuller Papers, Harvard Law School Library.

[71] *Ibid.*

[72] 22 Oct. 1959, Lon Luvois Fuller Papers, Harvard Law School Library.

[73] Fiss, n. 22 above, 39.

[74] 23 Oct. 1959, Lon Luvois Fuller Papers, Harvard Law School Library.

[75] See n. 62 above.

[76] Letter (23 Oct. 1959), Lon Luvois Fuller Papers, Harvard Law School Library.

In short, Fuller did not regard his influential paper, 'The Forms and Limits of Adjudication', as sufficiently polished for publication[77] and did not develop it in response to its critics and his own doubts. The further elaboration[78] of his concept of adjudication is necessary because of the implicit general threat posed to adjudication by polycentricity, the vulnerability of those affected by polycentric administrative disputes, Fuller's negation of judicial expertise and investigation, and his empirical neglect of Continental variations of adjudicative procedures. Incorporating the value of inquisitorial judicial procedures is required to confront the problem of polycentric administrative disputes and to provide administrative law with an appropriate procedural model.

Elaboration of Fuller's Concept of Adjudication

Fuller seems to have recognized that the objection to the adjudication of polycentric disputes was partly the result of his adversarial concept of adjudication. He was prepared to consider modifications in the light of Continental inquisitorial procedures. Although his comprehensive analysis of adjudication does not deal with such procedures, Fuller does seem to have given them some consideration. Fuller had read about the work of the French *Conseil d'Etat* and was in contact with Jean Rivero to whom he sent copies of *The Morality of Law* and 'Irrigation and Tyranny'.[79] Fuller regarded the *Conseil d'Etat* as a model possibly worth emulating:

It may be objected that without the guarantees afforded by adjudicative procedures governmental power is subject to grave abuse. This fear may underestimate the sense of trusteeship that goes with being given a job to do that makes sense and being allowed to do it the sensible way. . . . In any event, in the search for institutional safeguards against abuse we need not confine our-

---

[77] Letter (30 Nov. 1959), Lon Luvois Fuller Papers, Harvard Law School Library; Winston, Editor's Note in Fuller, *Principles of Social Order*, n. 9 above, 86.
[78] Cf. the development of adjudication in American public-law litigation: A. Chayes, 'The Role of the Judge in Public Law Litigation' (1976) 89 *Harv. LRev.* 1281–1316; *id.*, 'The Supreme Court 1981 Term. Foreword: Public Law Litigation and the Burger Court' (1982) 96 *Harv. LRev.* 4–60; Eisenberg, n. 57 above; Fiss, n. 22 above, especially at 39 ff.; Summers, *Lon Fuller*, n. 9 above, 109; Allison, 'Fuller's Analysis of Polycentric Disputes' n. 2 above, 378–83; *id.*, 'The Procedural Reason for Judicial Restraint', n. 2 above, 467–8.
[79] Letters of Fuller (14 Oct. 1964) and J. Rivero (5 Dec. 1964 and 21 Sept. 1965), Lon Luvois Fuller Papers, Harvard Law School Library.

selves to adjudicative procedures in the strict sense, but may also consider the models suggested by the French *Conseil d'Etat* [inter alia].[80]

In a note, Fuller even recognized the investigation of a French *rapporteur* as a 'special form' of adjudication which 'may by useful' and 'might accommodate a greater degree of polycentricity'.[81]

Fuller's recognition has serious implications for the validity of his analysis of the limits to adjudication. His characterization of adjudication principally by reference to the participation of the parties rather than the office of the judge becomes questionable. His opposition to the 'oil-and-water mixture of managerial and adjudicative functions' and to judicial 'reliance on considerations not advanced at the public hearing' becomes less practicable.[82] Furthermore, his concept of the polycentric dispute which he used to delimit adversarial adjudication becomes a possible justification for the enhanced judicial responsibility of an inquisitorial court.

In an important respect, however, Fuller's analysis of adjudication can be elaborated to avoid leaving him standing on his head. In his debate with legal positivists, Fuller opposed the view of law as a 'one-way projection of authority, emanating from an authorized source and imposing itself on the citizen'.[83] He emphasized the importance of 'collaboration', of 'cooperative effort—an effective and responsible interaction—between lawgiver and subject':[84]

[T]he positivist recognizes in the functioning of a legal system nothing that can truly be called a *social dimension*. The positivist sees the law at the point of its dispatch by the lawgiver and again at the point of its impact on the legal subject. He does not see the lawgiver and the citizen in interaction with one another, and by virtue of that failure he fails to see that the creation of an effective interaction between them is an essential ingredient of the law itself.[85]

To be faithful to Fuller's view, adjudication can be conceived as a kind of *organization by collaborative expert investigation* which can help complement his other basic forms of social ordering, 'organization by common aims' and 'organization by reciprocity'.[86] Then, adjudication is characterized not primarily by party-participation but by the responsible and purposive interaction between the adjudicator and the parties.

---

[80] *Morality of Law*, n. 9 above, 176–7.

[81] Note, box 10, folder 12, Lon Luvois Fuller Papers, Harvard Law School Library.

[82] Fuller in Friedrich (ed.), n. 51 above, ch. 15, especially at 267–8.

[83] *Morality of Law*, n. 9 above, 191 ff., especially at 192.   [84] *Ibid.* 220, 219.

[85] *Ibid.* 193.   [86] 'Forms and Limits of Adjudication' n. 9 above, 357–65.

The adjudicator's role is not only to respond to their proofs and reasoned arguments but also to consider the possible complex repercussions neglected by them and affecting others. In so far as the adjudicator must complement the proofs and arguments of the parties, this form of ordering contradicts Fuller's questionable advocacy of adversarial procedure as 'the only effective means for combatting' pre-judgment.[87] But it does give weight to the value Fuller accords to participation. It recognizes that persons and groups other than the moving disputants may be affected and, where practicable, provides also for their participation, for example, through consultation with an investigative judge.[88] It derives moral force or legitimacy not only from the participation of the parties but also from judicial expertise and investigation.[89]

Adjudication conceived as collaborative expert investigation has numerous advantages[90] apart from the value accorded to party-participation and judicial expertise. First, it transforms the polycentric dispute from a vague threat to adjudication to the object of judicial investigation. By considering the repercussions of judicial intervention, the adjudicator is better able to determine their relevance to a legal solution or proposed development of the law. Secondly, the troublesome examples of disputes submitted by parties for expert judicial assessment or investigation[91] can be regarded as extreme instances of adjudication involving little party-participation. Thirdly, because the possibility of a more responsible judicial role is recognized, an Anglo-American bias is absent.

Finally, adjudication conceived as collaborative expert investigation not only permits but also requires inquisitorial procedures where necessary and practicable. The court must be helped by the interested arguments of counsel and be afforded the expertise, time to deliberate, and opportunities for investigation and consultation to determine the complex repercussions of judicial intervention in polycentric administrative disputes. Adjudication so conceived requires the judicial procedures described in my model, procedures that are suited to the adjudication of polycentric administrative disputes and to the development of a satisfactory body of public law.

[87] See n. 63 above.
[88] Cf. Eisenberg, n. 57 above, 427–8; Fiss, n. 22 above, 40–1.
[89] Cf. Chayes, 'The Role of the Judge in Public Law Litigation', n. 78 above, 1307–16; Eisenberg, n. 57 above, 417, 430–2.
[90] See also Allison, 'Fuller's Analysis of Polycentric Disputes', n. 2 above, 382.
[91] See above, nn. 61 and 62.

10
The Procedural Contrast

In the last chapter, I described the need for inquisitorial judicial procedures as the procedural implication of polycentric administrative disputes. In this chapter, I will argue that, while the *Conseil d'Etat* developed procedures that broadly answered that need, the English courts have continued to be handicapped by adversarial procedures. I will suggest that the traditional prerogative writs and the recent procedural reforms resulting in the AJR involved relative technicalities and were therefore insufficient to entrench a distinction between public and private law. I will conclude that inquisitorial procedures, such as those developed by the *Conseil d'Etat*, are required for the distinction's entrenchment. I will again in this chapter use the concepts 'adversarial' and 'inquisitorial' in a non-pejorative way to refer to contrasting balances between the power of the parties to prepare and the power of the court to investigate cases.[1]

The Procedural Tradition in France

The inquisitorial judicial procedures neglected in Fuller's analysis of adjudication[2] began to prevail in France with the adoption of the canonist inquest more than 600 years ago. Their development was continuous.[3] The only radical innovation occurred in the thirteenth century. In 1258 an ordinance of Louis IX abolished the judicial duel in royal courts and adopted in its place the basic canonist inquest—investigation through the questioning of witnesses by officials of the court. Already the canonist inquest had become known through the spread of ideas from Italy and, in private arbitration, was proving preferable to the secular courts' unpredictable modes of proof such as the ordeal, judicial duel, and reliance on oath-helpers. Furthermore, while the

[1] See generally R. W. Millar, 'The Formative Principles of Civil Procedure' in A. Engelmann *et al.* (eds.), *History of Continental Civil Procedure* (London, 1928), 3–81 at 11–21; J. I. H. Jacob, *The Reform of Civil Procedural Law and Other Essays in Civil Procedure* (London, 1982), 24–5; *id.*, *The Fabric of English Civil Justice* (London, 1987), 5–19; J. A. Jolowicz, 'Adversarial and Inquisitorial Approaches to Civil Litigation' in E. G. Baldwin (ed.), *The Cambridge Lectures* (Toronto, 1983), 237–43; *id.*, book review (1988) 8 *Legal Studies* 111–20 at 112–14.
[2] See above, ch. 9.
[3] R. C. van Caenegem, 'History of European Civil Procedure' in *IECL*, xvi, ch. 2, secs. 28, 42, 47; Millar, n. 1 above, 138.

French King had limited regional authority, it could be administered in royal courts more easily than the jury inquest. The *Parlement* of Paris, which emerged from the *Curia Regis* about the middle of the thirteenth century,[4] took the lead in promoting the canonical procedure. The *Parlement* itself served as a model for courts throughout France and, in exercising its appellate function, also directly imposed its procedures upon other French courts. Through the influence of the *Parlement*, the canonist inquest was generally received by 1500. The procedural reform of Louis IX had become the cornerstone of French judicial procedure.[5]

From the fourteenth century onwards the procedure developed by the *Parlement* of Paris provided for an expert and comprehensive investigation of cases.[6] After the commencement of an appeal in the *Grand' Chambre* of the *Parlement*, *commissaires-enquêteurs* would travel to question witnesses and return with a written record of all proceedings for the *Chambre des Enquêtes*. The extensive written record required expert analysis. It necessitated that judges 'have not only an ability to read—a skill that was rare enough in itself—but an ability to dissect and scrutinize the contents of several layers of manuscript'.[7] The court would therefore appoint one of its own members—the *rapporteur*—to sift through all the material, summarize the issues, and guide the court through the evidence. The result was a thorough judicial investigation: 'a collegiate court . . . sought by refined methods to examine each case in all its aspects, with a full rehearing on facts and law together. . . . The procedural system that was being developed in the Parlement reflected a high conception of judicial responsibility.'[8]

The procedure of the *Parlement* of Paris, however, was not simply inquisitorial. The canonist procedure was adapted in France to provide for an important adversarial first stage. During the commencement of appellate proceedings in the *Grand' Chambre*, *avocats* were prominent. They would make allegations determining the scope of their dispute and engage in oral debate on points of fact and law.[9] Like the second stage of court-controlled inquest, this first stage contributed to com-

---

[4] J. P. Dawson, *The Oracles of the Law* (Ann Arbor, 1968), 274.
[5] J. P. Dawson, *A History of Lay Judges* (Cambridge, Mass., 1960), 43–70; Van Caenegem, n. 3 above, sec. 28.
[6] Van Caenegem, *ibid.*; Dawson, *Lay Judges, ibid.* 57–60; *id., Oracles*, n. 4 above, 273–8.
[7] Dawson, *Lay Judges*, n. 5 above, 60.
[8] Dawson, *Oracles*, n. 4 above, 277.
[9] Van Caenegem, n. 3 above, sec. 28, 33–4; Dawson, *Oracles*, n. 4 above, 284; Engelmann *et al.*, n. 1 above, bk. 4, pt. 2, ch. 2, sec. 20, 688–91.

prehensive investigation. The *avocats* were encouraged to cover all aspects and issues by the prospect of a second stage when the initiative would be that of the court.[10]

Through the seventeenth and eighteenth centuries, the important adversarial first stage was conserved in civil litigation.[11] Whereas in Germany the canonical procedure came to dominate civil litigation, in France 'the old idea of the law suit as a struggle fought before the judges, by the parties' was retained.[12] In 1667 oral pleading by the parties was entrenched by the *Ordonnance civile pour la réformation de la justice* of Louis XIV (the Code Louis) which unified and systematized French civil procedure.

At the time of the Revolution, inquisitorial judicial procedures were criticized but the Code Louis survived partly because of the practical difficulty of introducing completely new judicial procedures in the Revolution's immediate aftermath[13] and partly because of the extent to which party control of civil litigation had been retained. Van Caenegem explains the lasting influence of the Code Louis:

France had refrained from certain exaggerations in the previous centuries and had little need of correction: the public and oral character of debate and the role of the parties had never been lost sight of . . . It was, therefore, easy and natural to adapt the Ordinance of 1667 to serve in a period which was keen on orality and publicity, free judicial appreciation of evidence and party-control, considered as guarantees against absolutism and the abuses of the learned lawyers and as hallmarks of individual liberty and civic sense.[14]

As a result, the Code Louis provided the substance of the *Code de procédure civile* of 1806, the most conservative[15] of the Napoleonic codes.

The Development of the Procedures of the Conseil d'Etat

The *Conseil d'Etat* adopted a procedure that departed from the principle of party control. The origins of the particularly inquisitorial features of its procedure are pre-Revolutionary.[16] A *Règlement* of 28 June 1738, drafted under the direction of Chancellor d'Aguesseau, regulated

[10] Dawson, *Oracles*, n. 4 above, 285–6.
[11] Van Caenegem, n. 3 above, secs. 47, 48. See generally Engelmann *et al.*, n. 1 above, bk. 4, pt. 2, ch. 3, secs. 27–32.
[12] Van Caenegem, n. 3 above, sec. 47, 60.
[13] Engelmann *et al.*, n. 1 above, bk. 4, pt. 2, ch. 4, sec. 52, 750–1.
[14] Van Caenegem, n. 3 above, sec. 65, especially at 89.
[15] Engelmann *et al.*, n. 1 above, bk. 4, pt. 2, ch. 2, sec. 6, 664–5, ch. 4, sec. 51, 748.
[16] J.-L. Mestre, *Introduction historique au droit administratif Français* (Paris, 1985), secs. 122–130.

judicial proceedings including *procédure administrative contentieuse* before the *Conseil du Roi*.[17] It confirmed existing practice which had been affected by the *Conseil du Roi*'s general administrative role.[18] It did not provide for oral pleading and entrenched a wide-ranging expert investigation by the *rapporteur.*

L'instance introduite la procédure reste écrite et inquisitoire. Le rôle essentiel revient au rapporteur: secrétaire d'Etat, contrôleur général des finances, maître des requêtes. Il dirige l'instruction, s'adresse aux avocats pour obtenir les pièces nécessaires, les communique et pourvoit éventuellement aux incidents. Il peut demander leur avis à des personnes qualifiées: essentiellement aux officiers et aux commissaires royaux, notamment aux intendants.[19]

Despite the dissolution of the *Conseil du Roi* during the Revolution, the *Réglement* of 1738 remained influential after the creation of the *Conseil d'État*'s *Commission du Contentieux* by a Decree of 11 June 1806. Those concerned with the procedures to be followed by the *Commission* sought inspiration from the *Conseil d'État*'s pre-Revolutionary analogue—the *Conseil du Roi* of *l'Ancien Régime*. They therefore referred to the *Réglement* and modelled the decree of 22 July 1806 upon it.[20]

The role of the *Commissaire du Gouvernement* was introduced by an Ordinance of 12 March 1831, and, unlike the *Ministère Public* of the civil courts, the *Commissaire* acquired an independence from hierarchical control.[21] The *Commissaire*'s role also had pre-Revolutionary origins. Before certain *Commissions Extraordinaires* entrusted with administrative and judicial tasks by the *Conseil du Roi*, a *procureur général* was given the responsibility of protecting the interests of the King. But, like the *Commissaire du Gouvernement* in the later nineteenth century, the *procureurs* acquired a reputation for independent and general concern for individual subjects and for the *règles d'ordre public*.[22]

The particularly inquisitorial judicial procedures developed by the

---

[17] Van Caenegem, n. 3 above, sec. 48, 62.

[18] H. Lenoan, *La Procédure devant le Conseil d'Etat statuant au contentieux en première et dernière instance* (Paris, 1954), 38–40.

[19] Mestre, n. 16 above, sec. 130, 209: '[o]nce the case has begun, the procedure remains written and inquisitorial. The pivotal role belongs to the *rapporteur.* secretary of state, controller-general of finances, master of requests. He conducts the investigation, corresponds with the advocates in order to obtain the necessary documents, forwards them on and sees to the legal points that arise. He can ask qualified persons for their advice: essentially officials and royal commissioners, particularly *intendants*.'

[20] Lenoan, n. 18 above, 14–15; C. Debbasch, *Procedure administrative contentieuse et procedure civile* (Paris, 1962), 3; Van Caenegem, n. 3 above, sec. 48, 62.

[21] M. Waline, *Droit administratif* (9th edn., Paris, 1963), sec. 385.

[22] Mestre, n. 16 above, sec. 130, 210–11.

Conseil d'Etat have been justified by reference to the state's special interest in observance of the principle of legality,[23] reduction of costs for the litigant,[24] judicial restoration of the typical inequality of the parties,[25] and investigation of the complex repercussions of judicial intervention in administrative disputes.[26] These justifications, however, are not sufficient explanations for the procedure's historic development. Although as justifications they probably entrenched the *Conseil d'État*'s basic judicial procedures, they do not explain their original development. The peculiar features of the *Conseil d'État*'s judicial procedures were not deliberately created by reference to a coherent theory of procedure but were derived and elaborated from the practices of the *Conseil du Roi*.

Despite the pre-Revolutionary origins of the peculiar features of the *Conseil d'Etat*'s judicial procedures, the autonomy of *procédure administrative contentieuse* was not generally accepted until this century. Decrees and ordinances were insufficiently numerous and comprehensive to enact a systematic body of procedural law for the *Conseil d'Etat* at all comparable to the successive French codes of civil procedure.[27] Doctrine did not make up for the lack of legislation.[28] The *Conseil d'Etat* itself identified and relied upon what have come to be called *principes généraux de procédure*.[29] Because of the insufficiency of written law and doctrinal analysis, the peculiarity and therefore the autonomy of the judicial procedures of the *Conseil d'Etat* were difficult to appreciate. As late as 1903, Jacqueline argued that the *Code de procédure civile* is applicable where the law is silent, that is, in the absence of a statutory text to the contrary.[30]

Jacqueline's argument, however, was against a rising tide of doctrinal opinion. Hauriou affirmed the separate existence of a *procédure administrative contentieux* and only added the qualification that 'à la vérité, il en existe plusieurs, en ce sens qu'il y a une procédure à suivre devant le Conseil d'Etat, une autre devant les conseils de préfecture, sans

---

[23] See, e.g., B. Schwartz, *French Administrative Law and the Common-Law World* (New York, 1954), 131–2.

[24] See, e.g., Lenoan, n. 18 above, 37–8.

[25] See, e.g., J.-P. Colson, *L'Office du juge et la preuve dans le contentieux administratif* (Paris, 1970); Debbasch, n. 20 above, 442.

[26] See below, 212 ff.

[27] Waline, n. 21 above, sec. 381; Debbasch, n. 20 above, 3–4.

[28] Debbasch, *ibid.*

[29] See, e.g., A. de Laubadère, *Traité de droit administratif* (J.-C. Venezia and Y. Gaudemet (eds.)), (11th edn., Paris, 1990), i, sec. 631.

[30] R. Jacquelin, 'L'évolution de la procédure administrative' [1903] *RDP* 373–447.

parler des tribunaux spéciaux'.[31] Later, in a decisive analysis, Lenoan described how, in the second half of the nineteenth century, the *Conseil d'Etat* generally refused to apply provisions of the *Code de procédure civile* and would 'en vertu de son pouvoir prétorien' itself determine whether principles were generally applicable.[32] By 1960 Rivero could declare conclusively that 'l'autonomie du droit administratif s'affirme sur le terrain de la procédure comme sur le fond du droit'.[33]

The differences between *procédure civil* and *procédure administrative contentieuse* are nevertheless blurred by fundamental similarities and recent developments. Both procedures are inquisitorial[34] at least in comparison with the judicial procedures of English courts. The role of the expert as *auxiliaire de la justice* in civil cases[35] and the extent to which the French civil judge can introduce points of fact and law of his own motion (subject to *le principe de la contradiction*)[36] are illustrative of the inquisitorial character of *procédure civile*. In fact, relatively recent reforms of the French *Code de procédure civile* enhanced the powers of the civil judge and so reduced the contrast between *procédure civil* and *procédure administrative contentieuse*.[37] The differences are a matter of degree.

The *Conseil d'Etat*'s Inquisitorial Procedures

The inquisitorial procedures in *le contentieux de l'annulation*, partly shared by the French civil courts and partly peculiar to the *Conseil d'Etat* and the *tribunal administratif*, require the court to deliberate, investigate, con-

---

[31] M. Hauriou, *Précis élémentaire de droit administratif* (14th edn., Paris, 1938), 290–1: 'in truth, there are many, in the sense that there is one procedure to be followed before the *Conseil d'Etat*, another before the *conseils de préfecture*, not to mention the special tribunals'.

[32] Lenoan, n. 18 above, 14–32, especially at 25: 'by virtue of its praetorian power'.

[33] J. Rivero, *Droit administratif* (Paris, 1960), 179; *id.*, *Droit administratif* (13th edn., Paris, 1990), 270: 'the autonomy of administrative law proclaims itself in the field of procedure as it does in substantive law'. See Debbasch, n. 20 above, 5–7. Cf. De Laubadère, n. 29 above, sec. 632.

[34] They are 'inquisitorial' in the non-pejorative sense in which that term is used here: see above, 207.

[35] J. A. Jolowicz, 'Fact-finding: A Comparative Perspective', Colloquium of the United Kingdom Committee of Comparative Law (Aberdeen, Sept. 1991), 7–8.

[36] J. A. Jolowicz, 'The Parties and the Judge in Civil Litigation' in N. Eastham and B. Krivy (eds.), *The Cambridge Lectures* (Toronto, 1981), 160–9 at 162–4; *id.*, 'Da Mihi Factum dabo Tibi Jus: A Problem of Demarcation in English and French Law' in P. Feuerstein and C. Parry (eds.), *Multum non Multa: Festschrift für Kurt Lipstein* (Heidelberg, 1980), 79–99.

[37] See R. Chapus, 'De l'office du juge: contentieux administratif et nouvelle procédure civile' (1977/78) 29 *EDCE* 11–65; *id.*, *Droit du contentieux administratif* (2nd edn., Paris, 1990), sec. 718.

sult, and repeatedly re-examine cases. Since the reforms of 1953 and 1987, the *Conseil d'Etat statuant au contentieux* has increasingly been pre-occupied with major issues of law,[38] not of fact, but its procedures still deserve special attention because of its leading role in the formative period of French administrative law and *procédure administrative contentieuse*. In this section I will describe the various ways in which the *Conseil d'Etat* has been afforded the opportunity to determine the complex repercussions of possible decisions, whether those repercussions have been factual or legal.

First, in a *recours direct*, after the *requérant* has lodged his written complaint and a copy of the administrative decision in issue, a dossier is kept by the *Conseil*.[39] The parties may submit a range of documents to become part of the dossier. For example, where a *requérant* submitted letters from expert engineers to support his challenge to a decision ordering the demolition of his dam, the authority submitted a map and photographs to show the flooding that it caused.[40] The essentially written procedure and the prominence of a comprehensive dossier enable the court to examine various aspects of a case before decision. A French administrative lawyer observed: '[a]s for the written aspect, it is both a guarantee against surprise and a guarantee that the case will be seriously studied by the judge before decision. By obliging the parties to state all their conclusions and arguments in writing the procedure makes a clear and fair discussion certain.'[41] Furthermore, in contrast to the dramatic day in court characteristic of English judicial procedures, the written procedure encourages communication by 'permitting an intimate dialogue between court and administrator'.[42]

Secondly, the *rapporteur* directs the process of instruction according to the principle that 'les affaires dont une juridiction administrative est saisie ne peuvent pas être jugées sans avoir fait l'objet d'une instruction propre à les mettre en état d'être réglées par cette juridiction en aussi bonne connaissance de cause que possible'.[43] In a process which

[38] See Law of 31 Dec. 1987; Decree of 17 Mar. 1992; L. N. Brown and J. S. Bell, *French Administrative Law* (4th edn., Oxford, 1993), 47 ff.
[39] See generally J. Bell, 'Reflections on the Procedure of the *Conseil d'Etat*' in G. Hand and J. McBride (eds.), *Droit Sans Frontières: Essays in Honour of L. Neville Brown* (Birmingham, 1991), 211–34 at 212–14.
[40] Schwartz, n. 23 above, 137.   [41] Font-Réaulx quoted by Schwartz, *ibid.* 149.
[42] L. N. Brown and J. F. Garner, *French Administrative Law* (3rd edn., London, 1983), 180.
[43] Chapus, *Droit du contentieux administratif,* n. 37 above, 477: 'cases heard by an administrative court cannot be decided without having been the object of an inquiry suitable for reducing them to a state in which they can be adjudicated upon by such a court,

can last several months, the *rapporteur* has the responsibility of taking all the measures that appear necessary *pour établir la conviction du juge*. He can check facts, secure the availability of all relevant material, and will often consult with authorities other than the authority whose decision is in issue.

The parties can contribute to the investigation of the *rapporteur* by responding to his questions and suggesting and requesting measures of instruction. The *rapporteur* cannot act *ultra petita*, that is, introduce a head of claim not included in the *recours*, and must give the parties the opportunity to respond to legal and factual points. In short, he must abide by *le principe de la contradiction*.[44] He is not, however, similarly subject to the dispositive principle requiring that the parties have the power to dispose of all their procedural and substantive rights.[45] The *rapporteur* remains primarily responsible for the process of instruction and determines when exchanges with the parties should stop. In general, he is subject to a 'régime de liberté' which not only helps to address the inequality between the parties[46] and to reduce costs for the litigant[47] but facilitates an extensive expert investigation of the usually complex repercussions of judicial intervention in administrative disputes. A French administrative lawyer criticized the adversarial alternative as follows: '[i]n effect, if the direction of procedure is left to counsel, they, representing only their client, do not seek so much to throw light on the case as to establish the correctness of their side; and to that end they utilise as weapons every possible procedural device. This tactic leads only to pettifoggery.'[48]

Thirdly, an understanding of all the aspects of a case can be furthered through consultation. Not only can the *rapporteur* consult formally and informally with the parties, with the president of his *Sous-section*, and with various administrative agencies, but the *Conseillers d'Etat* in a case can consult with other *Conseillers* including those principally assigned to the *Conseil d'Etat*'s advisory sections. The atmosphere in the *Palais Royal* is conducive to consultation and the corporate spirit of the *Conseil d'Etat* encourages it.[49]

with as thorough a knowledge of the case as possible'. See generally *ibid.*, sec. 712 ff.; Waline, n. 21 above, sec. 388 ff.

[44] Chapus, *Droit du contentieux administratif*, n. 37 above, secs. 718–20.
[45] See J. A. Jolowicz, 'On the Nature and Purposes of Civil Procedural Law' [1990] *CJQ* 262–79 at 278.
[46] Colson, n. 25 above, especially at 9.   [47] Lenoan, n. 18 above, 37.
[48] Font-Réaulx quoted by Schwartz, n. 23 above, 149.
[49] Brown and Bell, n. 38 above, 98; Bell, n. 39 above, 216–17, 222–3.

Fourthly, the *Commissaire du Gouvernement*, in his independent examination, can stress aspects of a case neglected by the *rapporteur*.[50] He must ensure that all relevant considerations and, in particular, all relevant previous decisions are before the court. The *Commissaire* has the task 'd'exposer . . . les questions que présente à juger chaque recours contentieux et de faire connaître, en formulant en toute indépendance ses conclusions, son appréciation, qui doit être impartiale, sur les circonstances de fait de l'espèce et les règles de droit applicables ainsi que son opinion sur les solutions qu'appelle, suivant sa conscience, le litige soumis à la juridiction'.[51] In his conclusions, the *Commissaire* 'sets forth the entire case; he analyzes and criticizes all the possible grounds of decision, he does the same for all the legal rules that may be applicable; very often he indicates the direction followed by the case law, the stages already reached by it, and a foreshadowing of the stages yet to come'.[52] Because his conclusions are the only detailed decision of the *Conseil* which is made public, the aspects of a case stressed by the *Commissaire* can influence development of the law. Where the *Commissaire* disagrees fundamentally with the *rapporteur*'s report, the *Sous-section* charged with the case may be reconvened and the range of considered solutions available to the court is widened: '[s]i le rapporteur et le commissaire du gouvernement ne sont pas d'accord, alors l'organe de jugement arbitre entre eux; à moins naturellement qu'il n'adopte une troisème solution qui peut toujours être proposée, lors du délibére de l'affaire par l'un ou l'autre des conseillers'.[53]

Finally, during the *séance de jugement*, *Conseillers* not previously associated with the case contribute to a fresh examination of what might have become a range of possible solutions—solutions proposed by the parties, by the *rapporteur*, and by the *Commissaire*.[54]

The dossier, the participation of the *Commissaire*, extensive discussions

---

[50] See generally Chapus, *Droit du contentieux administratif*, n. 37 above, secs. 764–6; Waline, n. 21 above, secs. 384–7; Brown and Bell, n. 38 above, 101–3.

[51] *Gervaise*, CE, 10 July 1957: 'of setting out . . . the questions to be decided in each disputed case and, by formulating his conclusions in a completely independent manner, of making known his considered opinion, which must be impartial, on the factual circumstances of the case and the applicable rules of law, as well as his view, following his conscience, on the solutions called for in the dispute before the court'.

[52] Sauvel quoted by Schwartz, n. 23 above, 138–9.

[53] Waline, n. 21 above, sec. 386: 'if the *rapporteur* and the *Commissaire du Gouvernement* are not in agreement, the organ of judgment shall arbitrate between them; unless, of course, it adopts a third solution which may always be proposed during the deliberations on the case by one or other of the *Conseillers*'.

[54] See Brown and Bell, n. 38 above, 105–6; Bell, n. 39 above, 223–4.

with the parties and within the *Conseil d'Etat*, the direction of the process of instruction by the *rapporteur*, and repeated re-examinations often by *Conseillers* without prior knowledge of the case facilitate a collaborative and protracted expert investigation of all aspects of a case. The *Conseil statuant au contentieux* can take into account the complex repercussions of judicial intervention in polycentric administrative disputes. In *le contentieux de l'annulation*, it follows procedures that enable it to intervene confidently and to develop principles in which one has reason to be confident.

The Adversarial Tradition in England

The radically different English tradition is graphically described in this famous passage of Pollock and Maitland:

The behaviour which is expected of a judge in different ages and by different systems of law seems to fluctuate between two poles. At one of these the model is the conduct of the man of science who is making researches in his laboratory and will use all appropriate methods for the solution of problems and the discovery of truth. At the other stands the umpire of our English games, who is there, not in order that he may invent tests for the powers of the two sides, but merely to see that the rules of the game are observed. It is towards the second of these ideals that our English medieval procedure is strongly inclined. We are often reminded of the cricket-match. The judges sit in court, not in order that they may discover the truth, but in order that they may answer the question, 'How's that?'[55]

The early history of English adversarial procedures is intertwined with that of the jury. In contrast to the French royal officials who later adopted the canonist inquest, royal officials in England began to make widespread use of the neighbourhood jury in the twelfth and thirteenth centuries.[56] Henry II's reforms of 1166 made the neighbourhood jury a common feature of judicial proceedings. In 1215, the archaic mode of proof—trial by ordeal—was discouraged by the Lateran Council which forbade clerical participation. And the adoption of the neighbourhood jury was affirmed by the insistence in Magna Carta on the right to 'trial by peers'.[57] Henry II's reforms occurred before the major

[55] F. Pollock and F. W. Maitland, *The History of English Law before the Time of Edward I* (2nd edn., Cambridge, 1898), ii, 670–1.
[56] Dawson, *Lay Judges*, n. 5 above, 118–22. See generally R. C. van Caenegem, *The Birth of the English Common Law* (2nd edn., Cambridge, 1988), 62–84, especially at 79.
[57] 15 June 1215, cll. 20, 21, 22, 29, 50, 56, 57.

influence of the Roman-Canonical procedure[58] and at a time when the common-law courts lacked the expert staff to introduce the canonist inquest by examining jurors individually:

> When large-scale use of juries began in 1166 there were scarcely enough experienced men merely to direct the new court system. If, where facts were disputed, the judges were to take on the fact-finding job and interrogate individual witnesses, whether the witnesses were members of juries or not would be relatively unimportant. The judges would have been drawn irresistibly, as they were in France, into examining the testimony, determining credibility and relative weight, and making the ultimate difficult findings on contradictory evidence. It is no wonder that the English royal judges in the twelfth and early thirteenth centuries resisted the temptation to start on this long road. Crude and clumsy as it was, the early common law jury was an essential means of conserving trained manpower in a government that had taken on new tasks of immense scope and complexity.[59]

Once the required expertise was available, the alternative of the jury was established. The judge could continue to restrict his role to asking a few questions, keeping order in court, and applying the rules of the forms of action. He could leave to the parties the task of clarifying the issues.[60]

In later centuries, when the jury became a judge of the evidence, judicial investigation would defeat the purpose of the trial as a trial of fact. The alternative, investigation by a lay jury, would be inexpert and would necessitate repeated appearances of the jury, with all the accompanying expense and inconvenience. A passive judge and preparation by the parties had become a procedural necessity, at least in the common-law courts.

In the fifteenth century Chancery developed procedures resembling those of the canonist inquest.[61] The Chancery made individual testimony under oath its basic method of proof. It did not, however, create the bureaucracy to conduct elaborate investigations. Rather, it entrusted the preparation of interrogatories to the parties and their administration to lay commissioners or examiners chosen by the parties. Despite the absence of a jury, it borrowed (and reduced the rigour

[58] Van Caenegem, 'History of European Civil Procedure', n. 3 above, sec. 56, 75. See generally Van Caenegem, *Birth of the English Common Law*, n. 56 above, especially at 73, 90–2.

[59] Dawson, *Lay Judges*, n. 5 above, 123–9, especially at 128.

[60] See *ibid.* 135–6, 147.

[61] See Van Caenegem, 'History of European Civil Procedure', n. 3 above, secs. 33, 53.

of) common-law pleading techniques for the preparation of cases by the parties. In crucial respects, Chancery adopted adversarial procedures.[62]

Other royal courts of the sixteenth century were probably more strongly influenced by Roman-Canonical procedure and accordingly had adopted more inquisitorial procedures.[63] To the extent that the prerogative courts exercised an administrative jurisdiction and followed inquisitorial procedures,[64] they might have given rise to a distinction between public and private law with a procedural significance. But the prerogative courts did not survive the seventeenth-century constitutional struggles. Rather, their procedures were the subject of protest[65] and possibly[66] contributed to the abolition of prerogative courts early during the Interregnum.

During the eighteenth and nineteenth centuries, the theory of the separation of powers arising from the seventeenth-century constitutional struggles reinforced the adversarial procedures of the English courts. In his discussion of the separation of powers, Bentham distinguished between legislative and judicial powers by reference to the adversarial nature of judicial procedures.[67] Furthermore, the centrality of judicial independence to the English separation of powers reinforced the expectation of the judge as neutral umpire. The English theory of the separation of powers acquired a procedural dimension. Adversarial procedures were no longer merely a procedural necessity of the jury system but an ideological requirement that would survive the demise of the jury in civil cases.

The drastic procedural reforms of the nineteenth century called for by Bentham[68] and his followers did not affect the basic adversarial nature of English procedures. The Judicature Acts of 1873 and 1875 were mainly concerned with the system of courts and the forms of

---

[62] Dawson, *Lay Judges*, n. 5 above, 146–70.

[63] Van Caenegem, 'History of European Civil Procedure', n. 3 above, sec. 53; Dawson, *Lay Judges*, n. 5 above, 172–7; C. R. Lovell, *English Constitutional and Legal History: A Survey* (New York, 1962), 216.

[64] See, e.g., T. G. Barnes, 'Star Chamber Mythology' (1961) 5 *AJLH* 1–11 at 8–10.

[65] See, e.g., H. E. Bell, *An Introduction to the History and Records of the Court of Wards and Liveries* (Cambridge, 1953), 135–6; J. H. Baker, 'The Conciliar Courts' in *The Reports of Sir John Spelman* (J. H. Baker (ed.)) (94 Selden Society, 1978), ii, 70–4: Lovell, n. 63 above.

[66] Cf. Barnes, n. 64 above.

[67] J. Bentham, *Works* (London, 1843), iii, ch. 21 (see above, 157).

[68] See Bentham, 'The Principles of Judicial Review', *ibid.*, ii, 5–188.

action. They did not alter the principle of party-presentation.[69] Adversarial procedures were nonetheless entrenched towards the end of the nineteenth century. Analytical positivists, such as Amos, Markby, Holland, and Salmond, in their cursory treatment of civil procedure, simply accepted the adversarial system without comment.[70]

In the administrative processes of this century, despite the increasing use of other procedures by other adjudicators,[71] the adversarial tradition has retained its hold on English courts. English courts have applied and extended the rules of natural justice moulded in their own adversarial image.[72] Their exercise of an adversarial supervisory jurisdiction over tribunals and inquiries has detracted from the inquisitorial aspects of tribunal and inquiry procedure. Their supervisory jurisdiction as well as the expectation that tribunals follow adversarial rather than inquisitorial procedures were confirmed by the Franks Committee and the legislation in its wake.[73] The English courts have continued to be influenced by adversarial notions when approaching inquiries.[74] Furthermore, to their adversarial procedures, they have not developed correctives or supplements that are comparable to the class action[75] or 'managerial judging' of American 'complex litigation'.[76]

In 1945, Lord Greene expressed the traditional English rejection of inquisitorial judicial procedures with the classic warning against a judge's examining or cross-examining witnesses and so descending 'into the arena' where he is 'liable to have his vision clouded by the

[69] Van Caenegem, 'History of European Civil Procedure', n. 3 above, secs. 75–7.

[70] S. Amos, *The Science of Law* (London, 1874), 290–321; W. Markby, *Elements of Law Considered with Reference to Principles of General Jurisprudence* (6th edn., Oxford, 1905), 416–26; T. E. Holland, *The Elements of Jurisprudence* (13th edn., Oxford, 1924), 358–65, 388–90; J. W. Salmond, *Jurisprudence or The Theory of the Law* (London, 1902), 576–98.

[71] See generally G. Ganz, *Administrative Procedures* (London, 1974).

[72] *Ibid.* 1, 100–2; P. Cane, *An Introduction to Administrative Law* (2nd edn., Oxford, 1992), 163 ff.

[73] Franks Committee, *Report of the Committee on Administrative Tribunals and Inquiries* (1957), Cmnd. 218; Tribunals and Inquiries Act 1958.

[74] P. P. Craig, *Administrative Law* (2nd edn., London, 1989), 215.

[75] J. A. Jolowicz, 'Some Twentieth Century Developments in Anglo-American Civil Procedure' (1978) 7 *Anglo-American LRev.* 163–229 at 205 ff. Cf. A. Chayes, 'The Role of the Judge in Public Law Litigation' (1976) 89 *Harv. LRev.* 1281–1316 at 1289–92. See generally K. Kerameus, 'A Civilian Lawyer looks at Common Law Procedure' (1987) 47 *Louisiana LRev.* 493–509 at 503–5.

[76] See J. H. Langbein, 'The German Advantage in Civil Procedure' (1985) 52 *Chicago LRev.* 823–66 at 858 ff.; Chayes, n. 75 above; *id.*, 'The Supreme Court 1981 Term. Foreword: Public Law Litigation and the Burger Court' (1982) 96 *Harv. LRev.* 4–60; M. A. Eisenberg, 'Participation, Responsiveness, and the Consultative Process: An Essay for Lon Fuller' (1978) 92 *Harv. LRev.* 410–32; O. M. Fiss, 'The Supreme Court 1978 Term. Foreword: The Forms of Justice' (1979) 93 *Harv. LRev.* 1–58.

dust of the conflict'.[77] And, less than ten years ago, Lord Fraser re-affirmed the adversarial tradition when he refused to order the inspection of documents purely to assist the court:

In an adversarial system such as exists in the United Kingdom, a party is free to withhold information that would help his case if he wishes—perhaps for reasons of delicacy or personal privacy. He cannot be compelled to disclose it against his will. It follows in my opinion that a party who seeks to compel his opponent, or an independent person, to disclose information must show that the information is likely to help his own case.[78]

Often, however, the English belief in adversarial civil procedure is assumed and unarticulated, perhaps no more than a sense of the civil action as 'civilisation's substitute for vengeance'.[79] Its irrational justification is the continuing procedural necessity[80] created by the ghost of the civil jury which '[e]ven when physically absent . . . is morally present',[81] 'present in the spirit' if not 'in the flesh'.[82] Jolowicz describes the argument for adversarial procedures as follows:

[I]t is clearly important for the administration of justice according to law to min-imise the risk that cases may be decided by the personal preferences or preju-dices of the individual judge. This risk is at its lowest when the judge remains passive until the time comes for him to deliver his judgement . . .; as the judge's opportunities to intervene actively in the preparation of the case increase so, inevitably, does the risk that, consciously or unconsciously, he will allow his prej-udices and his political and social assumptions to influence his actions.[83]

For rational justification, the English adversarial tradition still seems to depend on the incoherent English theory of the separation of powers with its vague notion of judicial independence.[84]

---

[77] *Yuill* v. *Yuill* [1945] P. 15 at 20.

[78] *Air Canada* v. *Secretary of State for Trade* [1983] 2 AC 394 at 434D–E, 438G–9A.

[79] E. J. Couture, 'The Nature of the Judicial Process' (1950) 25 *Tulane LRev.* 1–28 at 7; J. A. Jolowicz, 'The Active Role of the Court in Civil Litigation' in J. A. Jolowicz and M. Cappelletti, *Public Interest Parties and the Active Role of the Judge in Civil Litigation* (New York, 1975), 155–277 at 167–9; *id.*, 'Comparative Law and the Reform of Civil Procedure' (1988) 8 *Legal Studies* 1–13 at 1–4.

[80] Jolowicz, 'Comparative Law and the Reform of Civil Procedure', 4–6; *id.*, 'Fact-finding', n. 35 above, 10–11. See also Langbein, n. 76 above, 841–8; Schwartz, n. 23 above, 326–7.

[81] C. J. Hamson, 'Civil Procedure in France and England' [1950] *CLJ* 411–18 at 416.

[82] M. Amos, 'A Day in Court at Home and Abroad' [1926] *CLJ* 340–9 at 347.

[83] Jolowicz, 'The Active Role of the court', n. 79 above, 275–6; N. H. Andrews, 'The Passive Court and Legal Argument' [1988] *CJQ* 125–40 at 133–4. Cf. L. L. Fuller and J. D. Randall, 'Professional Responsibility. Report of the Joint Conference' (1958) 44 *ABA J* 1159–62, 1216–18 at 1160.   [84] See above, ch. 7.

Adversarial Procedures in Administrative Disputes

The culmination of the English adversarial tradition is the passive role of the court and the active role of the parties in modern English civil proceedings. Unlike the *Conseil d'Etat*, the English court cannot determine complex repercussions of a decision by conducting its own investigations. It is dependant upon the participation of the parties to clarify the issues by formal or informal pleadings and to present the various factual and legal arguments.[85]

The court's dependence upon the parties has affected the development of English administrative law. The judicial refusal, first, to establish the general liability of administrative authorities in negligence, secondly, generally to allow an estoppel to operate against them, and, thirdly, to adopt the Continental principle of proportionality illustrates the role and effect of adversarial procedures in administrative disputes. First, in *Dorset Yacht Co* v. *Home Office*, Lord Diplock gave a procedural reason for refusing to recognize the Home Office's liability in negligence for adopting a method of supervising Borstal boys.[86] He stressed the range of interests affected by the Home Office's decision and concluded that the 'material relevant to the assessment of the reformative effect upon trainees of release under supervision or of any relaxation of control while still under detention is not of a kind which can be satisfactorily elicited by the adversary procedure and rules of evidence adopted in English courts of law'.[87] In *Dorset Yacht* (and *Anns* v. *Merton LBC*[88]), the court was informed by the administrative authority's arguments to the effect that it did not owe any duty of care. Those arguments provoked Hamson's comment:

Indeed what is striking is the degree to which our court is hamstrung. It is assailed with a mass of non-information. The alleged public interest is presented to it by a government department, that is to say with the hopeless bias of an interested party. The counter-argument is by the counsel of a private person whose dominant concern must be the immediate issue. Nobody is charged

---

[85] See generally Jacob, *Fabric of English Civil Justice*, n. 1 above, 9–15; J. A. Jolowicz, 'Civil and Administrative Procedure: National Report for England and Wales' in J. P. Gardner (ed.), *United Kingdom Law in the 1990s: Comparative and Common Law Studies for the XIIIth International Congress of Comparative Law* (London, 1990), 160–75 at 160. Order 53 makes limited provision for the participation of non-parties in judicial review proceedings: only for service on persons directly affected (R. 5(3)) and for the hearing of those who appear to the court to be proper persons, *and* desire, to be heard (R. 9(1)).

[86] [1970] AC 1004. [87] *Ibid.* 1067B–F.

[88] *Anns* v. *Merton LBC* [1978] AC 728.

here with the duty of representing to the court the considerations which may enable it to determine what the public interest really may be. . . . In the instant case it is absurd that the Home Office appeared as the protagonist of that interest and it is outrageous that in the name of the public interest a claim of total irresponsibility should have been made.[89]

Secondly, in *Western Fish Products*, the court refused to allow an estoppel to operate against the authority. It rejected the position of the court in *Lever Finance*[90] with this argument:

To permit the estoppel no doubt avoided an injustice to the plaintiffs. But it also may fairly be regarded as having caused an injustice to one or more members of the public, the owners of adjacent houses who would be adversely affected by this wrong and careless decision of the planning officer that the modifications were not material. Yet they were not, and it would seem could not be, heard. How, in their absence, could the court balance the respective injustices according as the court did or did not hold that there was an estoppel in favour of the plaintiffs? What 'equity' is there in holding, if such be the effect of the decision, that the potential injustice to a third party, as a result of the granting of the estoppel is irrelevant? At least it can be said that the less frequently this situation arises the better for justice.[91]

Thirdly, in *Brind* v. *Home Secretary*, Lord Lowry refused to recognize an English doctrine of proportionality beyond the rubric of *Wednesbury* unreasonableness, in part because 'judges are not . . . furnished with the requisite knowledge and advice' to perform the required balancing exercise.[92] Indeed, as described by Fuller, adversarial adjudicators should rely only upon the 'advice', the proofs and arguments, of the litigants, and are, therefore, ill-suited to resolve an issue of proportionality involving a determination of permissible government priorities with its extensive ramifications.[93]

The Law Lords have in the past recognized the complexity of ramifications as a reason for judicial restraint. In the early 1970s, the majority of the active Law Lords endorsed Lord Reid's guideline that the law ought not to be developed if 'it would be impracticable to foresee all the consequences of tampering with it'.[94] Paterson regards Lord

---

[89] C. J. Hamson, 'Escaping Borstal Boys and the Immunity of Office' [1969] *CLJ* 273–83 at 283.

[90] *Lever Finance Ltd* v. *Westminster LBC* [1971] 1 QB 222.

[91] *Western Fish Products Ltd* v. *Penwith DC* [1981] 2 All ER 204 at 221H–I.

[92] [1991] 1 All ER 720 at 739B–C.

[93] *Contra* J. Laws, 'Is the High Court the Guardian of Fundamental Constitutional Rights?' [1993] *PL* 59–79 at 71 ff.

[94] A. Paterson, *The Law Lords* (London, 1982), 154–89, especially at 172.

Reid's position as involving a refusal to innovate in the case of polycentric problems.[95] As a result of such a refusal, the courts could not properly innovate to resolve polycentric administrative disputes and, so, could not develop principles of public law comparable to the *Conseil d'Etat*'s principles of legality and liability.

Recently, the courts have been activist in a number of celebrated cases but their activism, however necessary in the circumstances,[96] is vulnerable to criticism. In the *Woolwich* case, the majority in the House of Lords developed the law so that 'money paid by a citizen to a public authority in the form of taxes or other levies paid pursuant to an *ultra vires* demand by the authority is *prima facie* recoverable as of right'.[97] Strong dissents, however, were voiced by Lord Keith and Lord Jauncey because of possible repercussions. Lord Keith was preoccupied with the question of the possible disruption of public finances:

It seems to me that formulation of the precise grounds upon which overpayments of tax ought to be recoverable and of any exceptions to the right of recovery, may involve nice considerations of policy which are properly the province of Parliament and are not suitable for consideration by the courts. In this connection the question of possible disruption of public finances must obviously be a very material one.[98]

Lord Jauncey was concerned with similar, wide-ranging, questions which he regarded as unsuited to judicial resolution:

To apply the Woolwich principle as initially enunciated without limitation could cause very serious practical difficulties of administration and specifying appropriate limitations presents equal difficulties. For example, what, if any, knowledge is required on the part of a payer at the time of payment to entitle him to recovery at a later date? Or how long should any right to repayment last? Is it in the public interest that a public authority's finances should be disrupted by wholly unexpected claims for repayment years after the money in question has been received? These are all matters which would arise in any reform of the law to encompass some such principle as Woolwich contend for and are matters with which the legislature is best equipped to deal.[99]

---

[95] *Ibid.*

[96] See generally J. W. F. Allison, 'The Procedural Reason for Judicial Restraint' [1994] *PL* 452–73 at 466.

[97] *Woolwich Equitable Building Society* v. *Inland Revenue Commissioners* [1993] AC 70, especially at 177F. See also, e.g., *Hazell* v. *Hammersmith and Fulham LBC* [1991] 2 WLR 372; M. Loughlin, 'Innovative Financing in Local Government: The Limits of Legal Instrumentalism—Part 2' [1991] *PL* 568–99; *Pepper* v. *Hart* [1992] 3 WLR 1032, especially at 1059B–E, 1038B–C (J. H. Baker, 'Statutory Interpretation and Parliamentary Intention' (1993) 52 *CLJ* 353–7 at 354.

[98] At 161F–G.   [99] *Ibid.* 196E–F.

The judicial restraint of Lord Keith and Lord Jauncey is at least defensible[100] because of judicial uncertainty about the repercussions of a dispute affecting public finances.

The *Factortame* litigation provides a similarly questionable example of judicial activism.[101] It raised the issue of the availability of interim relief against the Crown. The European Court of Justice affirmed that the House of Lords 'had jurisdiction, in the circumstance postulated, to grant interim relief for the protection of directly enforceable rights under Community law and that no limitation on . . . [that] jurisdiction imposed by any rule of national law could stand as the sole obstacle to preclude the grant of such relief'.[102] To give effect to the European Communities Act 1972, the House of Lords consequently disregarded the apparent rule of national law precluding interim relief against the Crown and considered the 'balance of convenience' to determine whether a proper case for the grant of relief had been made out.

The attempt of the House of Lords to determine the balance of convenience illustrates the working of adversarial adjudication in a significantly polycentric setting. Pending a ruling by the European Court of Justice on the validity of the relevant provisions of the Merchant Shipping Act 1988, the House of Lords tried to weigh the public interest in continued application of those provisions by the Crown against the damage that would continue to be suffered by Spanish-controlled fishing companies thereby prevented from fishing with vessels registered in Britain. Lord Goff in the House of Lords agreed with the conclusion reached by Neill LJ in the Divisional Court.[103] Neill LJ had tabulated the rival contentions of the applicants for interim relief and of the Secretary of State. On the one hand, by reference to supporting affidavits, counsel for the applicants had alleged that, if interim relief were not granted, 'financial consequences for them would be disastrous' because of the absence of alternative fishing grounds.[104] Counsel also argued that 'the activities of some of the applicants bring very substantial benefits to the local community'.[105] On the other hand, counsel for the Secretary of State alleged that those benefits were 'much exaggerated' and that the applicants were causing 'very consid-

---

[100] Cf. J. Beatson, 'Public Law, Restitution and the Role of the House of Lords' (1993) 109 *LQR* 1–5.

[101] *R.* v. *Transport Secretary, ex p. Factortame Ltd (No. 2)* [1991] 1 AC 603.

[102] As described by Lord Bridge in the House of Lords, *ibid.* 658D.

[103] *Ibid.* 676B–C.

[104] *R.* v. *Transport Secretary, ex p. Factortame Ltd* [1989] 2 CMLR 353, at 376, para. [49].

[105] *Ibid.*, para. [50].

erable damage to . . . the genuine British fleet'.[106] Counsel argued that
account must also be taken of the 'public interest as expressed both in
the Act and . . . in the Common Fisheries Policy, which is specifically
designed to protect national communities'.[107] Neill LJ reached the following conclusion:

I see the force of the argument that, if the Common Fisheries Policy is intended to
protect traditional fishing communities of the member-States, great importance
must be given to any measures which are designed for that purpose. In the present case, however, I am not *in the end* persuaded *on the present evidence* that there
are *identifiable* persons or communities whose activities or livelihood are at present being so seriously damaged, or will be so seriously damaged, as to out-
weigh the very *obvious and immediate damage* which would be caused by these new
provisions if no interim relief were granted to the applicants.[108]

The uncertainty of Neill LJ is suggested by the words in italics. The
adversarial procedures followed by the court did not assure a more
confident conclusion. Neill LJ had to depend on the partisan proofs
and arguments of counsel and could not draw on any independent
sources of evidence. He was nevertheless required to determine how
disapplying provisions in an Act of Parliament would affect the applicants and the public interest. Of necessity but without clear
justification, he gave overriding weight, not to the extent of damage,
but to its obviousness and immediacy, and to the identifiability of persons or communities affected.

The House of Lords was given little further evidence from the parties and was left unsure of its reliability. Their Lordships were furnished
with up-to-date evidence in the form of answers to a questionnaire sent
to owners of fishing vessels and an affidavit from the Ministry of
Agriculture, Fisheries, and Food. Lord Goff commented as follows on
the questionnaire:

None of the answers to the questionnaire was on oath; and it was not in the
circumstances possible for the Secretary of State to test the answers, or indeed
to check their accuracy. However, no objection was made to this material
being placed before your Lordships. The answers to the questionnaire were not
complete. However, from the answers received it was possible to derive the following basic information.[109]

After presenting the 'basic information' from the questionnaire
answers, Lord Goff reiterated the affidavit evidence from the Ministry

[106] *Ibid.*, para. [52].
[108] *Ibid.*, para. [55] (emphasis added).
[107] *Ibid.*, para. [53].
[109] N. 101 above, 675E–F.

of Agriculture, Fisheries, and Food to the effect that the owners of the British fishing vessels advantaged by the new register would 'suffer serious losses' if the applicants' vessels returned to the British fleet.[110] Lord Goff's conclusion is tacked on:

> However, even taking this evidence fully into account, I have, on all the material available to your Lordships, formed the same opinion as that formed by Neill L.J. in the Divisional Court on the material then before him, that there was not sufficient to outweigh the obvious and immediate damage which would continue to be caused if no interim relief were granted to the applicants.[111]

Lord Goff did not take direct evidence from the owners or managers of the British fishing vessels that had taken the place of the applicants' vessels. And he lacked an independent source of evidence upon which to rely. Like Neill LJ, Lord Goff therefore resolved a wide-ranging issue concerning access to fishing grounds, benefits to local communities, and a statute's effect on national communities by reference to the obviousness and immediacy of damage to the applicants. The obvious prevailed over what was relevant but difficult to ascertain from the adversarial presentations to the court.

In his minority judgment, Lord Bridge recognized the 'exceptional difficulty' of weighing 'irreparable damage' to the applicants against 'substantial detriment to the public interest'.[112] Unlike Lord Goff, he was 'inclined to say . . . that the public interest should prevail and interim relief be refused', but he preferred a narrow legal ground for his decision: '[i]n the circumstances I believe that the most logical course in seeking a decision least likely to occasion injustice is to make the best prediction we can of the final outcome and to give to that prediction decisive weight in resolving the interlocutory issue.'[113] His evasive tactic was necessitated by the unsuitability of adversarial procedure in a polycentric dispute involving interim relief against the Crown.

Courts have not been alone in following unsuitable adversarial procedures in administrative disputes. Because of the pervasive influence of the English adversarial tradition, other decision-makers in the administrative process have also had to depend on the interested arguments of the parties. But, to the extent that administrators,[114] admin-

---

[110] N. 101 above, 675H–6B.   [111] *Ibid.* 676B–C.

[112] *Ibid.* 659G–60A.   [113] *Ibid.* 660A–E.

[114] See, e.g., Ganz, n. 71 above, 100–2; C. Harlow and R. Rawlings, *Law and Administration* (London, 1984), 61–7; Cane, n. 72 above, 163 ff.; G. Richardson, *Law, Process and Custody: Prisoners and Patients* (London, 1993), 316–17, 324–5.

istrative tribunals,[115] and judicialized inquiries[116] have followed, or been required to follow, adversarial procedures, objections have been raised.

Implications for an English Distinction

The doctrinal effect of the unsuitability of adversarial procedures has traditionally been a certain unease about administrative or public law. Because of his traditional Anglo-American concept of adjudication, Fuller had reason not fully to recognize administrative law.[117] He realized that the adversarial adjudicative process that he identified was little suited to the resolution of administrative disputes. In the absence of an inquisitorial tradition allowing and requiring judicial investigation of their usually extensive repercussions, the courts are not competent to develop a public law distinct from private law. In the last few decades, however, while English public law in fact developed rapidly, its distinctness became associated with special procedures. An English distinction between public and private law was identified with two procedural distinctions: the old distinction between prerogative and ordinary remedies; and, the recent distinction between procedure by application for judicial review (AJR) and procedure by ordinary writ.

Prerogative and Ordinary Remedies

In his Hamlyn Lectures, Lord Woolf argued that, when the House of Lords drew the distinction between public and private law in *O'Reilly* v. *Mackman*, it 'was doing no more than recognizing that our legal system has a feature derived from the ancient prerogative writs'.[118] Certainly, the common-law courts have for centuries issued prerogative writs to supervise administrative authorities. From about 1600 they used the prerogative writs to begin to assume the jurisdiction claimed by Coke CJ, the jurisdiction to correct 'errors and misdemeanours extrajudicial, tending to the breach of the peace, or oppression of the

[115] See, e.g., Ganz, n. 71 above, 19–20, 29–35, 109–10; M. Hill, *The State, Administration and the Individual* (London, 1976), 162–7; Cane, n. 72 above, 331–2.

[116] See, e.g., P. Self, 'Planning by Judicial Inquiry' (1971) 78 *RIBAJ* 303–4; Ganz, n. 71 above, 39 ff.; Harlow and Rawlings, n. 114 above, 457–73; Craig, n. 74 above, 215–17.

[117] Above, 197 ff.

[118] H. Woolf, *Protection of the Public—A New Challenge* (London, 1990), 25–6. Cf. generally S. Flogaïtis, *Administrative Law et droit administratif* (Paris, 1986); *O'Reilly* v. *Mackman* [1982] 3 All ER 1124.

subjects . . . or any other manner of misgovernment'.[119] Particularly after the increase in the powers of the Justices of the Peace in the second half of the seventeenth century and generally through the eighteenth and nineteenth centuries, they extended their supervisory jurisdiction. By 1900 they could quash certain administrative decisions by issuing a writ of certiorari, and, by writs of prohibition and mandamus, order a wide range of authorities to refrain from illegality and to perform statutory duties.[120]

The common-law courts, however, did not develop inquisitorial procedures for issuing prerogative writs. Rather, they followed the adversarial procedures with which they were familiar and remained similarly dependant upon the pleadings of the parties. They even further curtailed their own investigations into the various aspects of a case by restricting the admissible forms of evidence. In the case of certiorari, for instance, the courts initially restricted evidence to the record and extended[121] it ordinarily to include only affidavits. In short, they adopted restrictive adversarial procedures quite unlike the inquisitorial procedures that facilitated the development of *droit administratif.*

Apart from the questionable suitability of the prerogative procedures for the development of public law, their classification as public-law remedies is open to question. The prerogative writs were available against persons or bodies who were 'in some sense "public"',[122] but only in the second half of the eighteenth century were those writs which could loosely be identified with the King's interests classified together as prerogative writs. By that time, each prerogative writ had long before developed peculiar characteristics and requirements which continued to defy systematization.[123] Unaffected by the procedural reforms culminating in the Judicature Acts, they retained their peculiarities. Their classification has remained perplexing. In this century,

---

[119] *R.* v. *Mayor of Plymouth, ex p. Bagge* (1615) 11 Co. Rep. 93 at 98 (or see Co. Inst., iv, 71).

[120] S. A. de Smith, 'The Prerogative Writs: Historical Origins', App. I, *Judicial Review of Administrative Action* (J. M. Evans (ed.)) (4th edn., London, 1980), 584–95; *id.*, 'The Prerogative Writs' [1951] *CLJ* 40–56; J. H. Baker *An Introduction to English Legal History* (3rd edn., London, 1990), 164–73. See generally E. G. Henderson, *Foundations of English Administrative Law: Certiorari and Mandamus in the Seventeenth Century* (Cambridge, Mass., 1963).

[121] See generally A. Rubinstein, 'On the Origins of Judicial Review' (1964) 2 *UBC LRev.* 1–20 at 12–13; *id.*, *Jurisdiction and Illegality: A Study in Public Law* (Oxford, 1965), 70–1, 75–6; L. L. Jaffe, 'Judicial Review: Constitutional and Jurisdictional Fact' (1956/57) 70 *Harv. LRev.* 953–85 at 957–8.

[122] Jolowicz, 'Civil and Administrative Procedure', n. 85 above, 161.

[123] De Smith, 'The Prerogative Writs', n. 120 above, 592–5.

Jenks proclaimed that there is no definition of a prerogative writ, and De Smith added that 'no lawyer has ever been able to give a satisfactory answer to the question: What is a prerogative writ?'[124]

The peculiar characteristics of each of the prerogative writs perpetuated a preoccupation with procedural technicalities similar to those produced by the forms of action until the Judicature Acts. For much of this century lawyers and courts were preoccupied generally with considering the requirements for the different prerogative writs and particularly with classifying an administrative function or a stage of an administrative process in order to apply certiorari's requirement of a judicial or quasi-judicial decision.[125] Where extensive factual disputes existed, they were preoccupied also with circumventing the deficiencies[126] of the prerogative procedures—their inadequate provision for obtaining discovery, serving interrogatories, and cross-examining deponents on their affidavits. Their preoccupation with procedural technicalities restricted substantive considerations and therefore obstructed the development of a system of public law.[127]

Furthermore, whereas the courts had formerly only occasionally made use of the ordinary remedies in administrative disputes,[128] increasingly after the Second World War, they resorted to the declaratory judgment[129] to overcome the peculiar deficiencies of the prerogative procedures. In 1949, Lord Denning concluded that: '[j]ust as the pick and shovel is no longer suitable for the winning of coal, so also the procedure of mandamus, certiorari, and actions on the case are not suitable for the winning of freedom in the new age. They must be replaced by new and up to date machinery, by declarations, injunctions, and actions for negligence'.[130] The prerogative remedies were supplemented rather than replaced by the ordinary remedies.[131] *Barnard* v. *National Dock Labour Board* was a prominent example of the

[124] E. Jenks, 'The Prerogative Writs in English Law' (1923) 32 *Yale LJ* 523–34 at 533; De Smith, n. 120 above, 595.

[125] See *Ridge* v. *Baldwin* [1964] AC 40.

[126] See H. W. R. Wade and C. F. Forsyth, *Administrative Law* (7th edn., Oxford, 1994), 668 ff.

[127] J. D. B. Mitchell, 'The Causes and Effects of the Absence of a System of Public Law in the United Kingdom' [1965] *PL* 95–118 at 106–13.

[128] See, e.g., *Dyson* v. *Attorney-General* [1911] 1 KB 410.

[129] See generally Lord Woolf and J. Woolf, *The Declaratory Judgment* (London, 1993), ch. 2; E. M. Borchard, 'The Declaratory Judgment' (1918) 28 *Yale LJ* 1–23, 105–50.

[130] A. Denning, *Freedom Under the Law* (London, 1949), 126.

[131] See Lord Denning's later recognition of the continuing importance of a prerogative remedy in *Baldwin and Francis Ltd* v. *Patents Appeal Tribunal* [1959] AC 663 at 697.

usefulness of the declaration.[132] The court made a declaratory judgment in favour of workers who had been dismissed because, by obtaining discovery, the workers were able to establish that they had been dismissed by an unauthorized authority. In the following two decades, courts concerned with administrative disputes made free use of the ordinary remedies and particularly the declaration.[133]

The various prerogative procedures were, if anything, especially unsuited to the resolution of administrative disputes. They resulted in a preoccupation with procedural technicalities which proved detrimental to the development of a substantive public law. And, because of their peculiar deficiencies, they drove the courts to rely increasingly on ordinary remedies in administrative disputes. In short, they were an insufficient basis for an acceptable procedural or substantive distinction between public and private law.

The AJR and the Principle of Exclusivity

The increasing overlap between the prerogative and ordinary remedies created further procedural difficulties. Confronted by a choice of procedures, the litigant had to weigh the advantages of a specific prerogative remedy, such as its standing requirement, with its disadvantages, such as the time-limit, requirement of leave of court, exclusion of discovery, restrictions on cross-examination, and preclusion of a claim for damages. A wrong choice could result in failure. By the late 1960s the unenviable choice of the litigant and the general confusion had attracted widespread criticism and the · attention of the Law Commission.[134]

The Order 53 reforms were intended to clear up the confusion. On the Law Commission's recommendation,[135] Order 53 of the Rules of the Supreme Court and section 31 of the Supreme Court Act 1981 were amended to create a procedural umbrella—the AJR—to cover both the prerogative and ordinary remedies and to incorporate certain procedural safeguards for administrative authorities. In *O'Reilly* v.

---

[132] [1953] 2 QB 18.

[133] See, e.g., *Ridge* v. *Baldwin*, n. 125 above; *Anisminic Ltd* v. *Foreign Compensation Commission* [1969] 2 AC 147.

[134] See H. W. R. Wade, 'Procedure and Prerogative in Public Law' (1985) 101 *LQR* 180–99 at 182–6; Lord Diplock, 'Judicial Control of the Administrative Process' [1971] *CLP* 1–17 at 16–17; Law Commission, *Administrative Law* (working paper 13, 1967); Law Commission, *Administrative Law* (Law Com. 20, 1969), Cmnd. 4059; Law Commission, *Remedies in Administrative Law* (working paper 40, 1971).

[135] Law Commission, *Remedies in Administrative Law* (Law Com. 73, 1976), Cmnd. 6407.

Mackman, Lord Diplock gave two justifications for confirming the principle that the AJR be an exclusive procedure where a claim sounded in public law.[136] First, he referred to the removal of the prerogative procedure's deficiencies that had necessitated reliance on the ordinary remedies. Secondly, he referred to the need to prevent circumvention of the AJR's procedural safeguards for administrative authorities, namely its three-month time-limit, requirement of leave of the court, and restrictions on discovery and cross-examination. Neither the procedural concerns resulting in the AJR nor the justifications in *O'Reilly* related to the general suitability of adversarial procedures for resolving administrative disputes.

The reforms introducing the AJR did not fundamentally alter the character of judicial procedures for resolving administrative disputes. They perpetuated procedural safeguards for public authorities similar to those of the prerogative procedures, and, by providing only for affidavit evidence and for discovery and cross-examination only on special application, they made judicial review procedure resemble[137] procedure by originating summons. The reforms did not enhance the investigative powers of the court to facilitate the resolution of polycentric administrative disputes.

The persisting adversarial procedures have provoked criticism and further proposals.[138] For a few years now Lord Woolf has been advocating a Director of Civil Proceedings:

I have long been concerned as to whether our adversarial procedure, which applies to judicial review in the same way as it applies to an ordinary action, sufficiently safeguards the public. It has been suggested again recently that there is a need for a Minister of Justice. If this is too dramatic a constitutional innovation, I would suggest consideration should be given to the introduction into civil procedure of an independent body who can represent the public. For the want of a better title, I should like to see established a Director of Civil Proceedings who at least in administrative law proceedings would have a status similar to that of the Director of Public Prosecutions in criminal proceedings.[139]

[136] N 118 above.

[137] Jolowicz, 'Civil and Administrative Procedure', n. 85 above, 162. See generally n. 85 above.

[138] See Allison, 'The Procedural Reason for Judicial Restraint', n. 96 above; 468 ff.; Loughlin, 'Innovative Financing in Local Government', n. 97 above; R. Baldwin and C. McCrudden, *Regulation and Public Law* (London, 1987), 63 ff.

[139] H. Woolf, 'Public Law–Private Law: Why the Divide? A Personal View' [1986] *PL* 220–38 at 235–6. See Law Commission, *Administrative Law: Judicial Review and Statutory Appeals* (consultation paper 126, 1993), paras. 9.20 and 9.28.

Lord Woolf's Director of Civil Proceedings would not only fulfil the role of the present Attorney-General in civil proceedings, but would also be 'responsible for providing arguments to assist the court . . . in those cases where in his view the issues were such that *inter partes* argument might not adequately draw attention to the broader issues'.[140] He stresses that the 'Director would have general responsibility for the development of the civil law and in particular public law' and 'could help to establish the principles of public law for which Professor Jowell and Antony Lester Q.C. have so persuasively recommended'.[141] At least implicitly, Lord Woolf recognizes the insufficiency of adversarial procedures for the development of public law.[142] Sir Konrad Schiemann recognizes a related problem: 'the effects of judicial decisions rendered in administrative law often go beyond the sphere of the parties actually present in the proceedings. Some of those persons affected by the final decision have not been heard by the court. . . . It may be that their views cannot adequately be weighed by the court.'[143] In his Harry Street Lecture, Professor Griffith proposed the establishment of a public officer comparable to Lord Woolf's Director of Civil Proceedings and recommended a general shift from adversarial to inquisitorial procedures in judicial review cases involving 'political issues and the public interest'.[144] The proposals of Lord Woolf and Professor Griffith belie Jolowicz's statement that '[t]here is not, in England, as, again, there is in France, any suggestion that litigation which concerns the public administration calls for a different and more "inquisitorial" procedure than would be appropriate in litigation between private persons'.[145] The peculiar insufficiency of adversarial procedures for the resolution of numerous administrative disputes and for the development of public law is beginning to be seen.

While the Order 53 reforms did not fundamentally alter the adversarial character of procedures for judicial review, they did confirm special procedural safeguards for public authorities. These procedural safeguards, however, were not reinforced by a clear theoretical

---

[140] Woolf, *Protection of the Public*, n. 118 above, 109–13, especially at 110.

[141] *Ibid.* 111–12.

[142] See also H. Woolf, 'Judicial Review: A Possible Programme for Reform' [1992] *PL* 221–37 at 230.

[143] 'Locus Standi' [1990] *PL* 342–53 at 349.

[144] J. A. G. Griffith, 'Judicial Decision-making in Public Law' [1985] *PL* 564–82, especially at 565. See generally M. Loughlin, *Public Law and Political Theory* (Oxford, 1992), 216–7.

[145] Jolowicz, 'Civil and Administrative Procedure', n. 85 above, 164–5.

justification in terms of the procedural demands of judicial review.[146] Rather, in *O'Reilly* v. *Mackman* they were undermined by the very decision that pretended to uphold them. By recognizing exceptions to the principle of exclusivity and leaving them unjustified and open-ended, the House of Lords has enabled the circumvention of the safeguards.[147] It protected the safeguards by adopting the principle of exclusivity and, accordingly, a procedural distinction between public and private law, but did not consider them sufficiently important to refrain from negating both the principle and the distinction with open-ended exceptions.

Academics have questioned the safeguards and criticized what has been described as the dichotomy of public- and private-law procedures produced by the principle of exclusivity.[148] McBride, for example, questions whether the three-month time-limit is invariably necessary and whether the leave requirement is necessary in addition to the courts' power under RSC Order 18, rule 19 to strike out an action when it discloses no reasonable cause of action or is scandalous, frivolous, or vexatious.[149] Without a clear sense of the invariable importance of the safeguards, academics have denied a need for a dichotomy of public- and private-law proceedings and described its result as unnecessary litigation turning on technicalities.[150]

Lord Denning, in *The Closing Chapter*, quotes his former description of the ill-suited and out-of-date prerogative remedies and comments that '[n]ow, over thirty years after, we have the new and up-to-date machinery'.[151] He seems satisfied with the recent reforms: '[b]y reforming procedure the way was laid open for the judges to reform the substantive law. In amending the law of procedure, the judges have reformed the substantive law as well.'[152] The reforms, however, have

---

[146] See Cane, n. 72 above, 100–1.　　　　　　　　　[147] See above, 133–4.

[148] See, e.g., H. W. R. Wade 'Public Law, Private Law and Judicial Review' (1983) 99 *LQR* 166–73; Wade and Forsyth, n. 126 above, 680–95; Craig, n. 74 above, 421–6; Jolowicz, 'Civil and Administrative Procedure', n. 85 above, 164–70. Cf. Law Commission, *Judicial Review and Statutory Appeals*, n. 139 above, para. 15; Law Commission, *Administrative Lasw: Judicial Review and Statutory Appeals* (Law Com. 226, 1994), HC 669, pt. 13.

[149] J. McBride, 'The Doctrine of Exclusivity and Judicial Review: *O'Reilly* v. *Mackman*' [1983] *CJQ* 268–81 at 272–7. See also A. P. Le Sueur and M. Sunkin, 'Applications for Judicial Review: The Requirement of Leave' [1992] *PL* 102–29. Cf. Woolf, 'Public Law–Private Law', n. 139 above, 229–35; *id.*, *Protection of the Public*, n. 118 above, 231–2.

[150] See, e.g., J. A. Jolowicz, 'The Forms of Action Disinterred' [1983] *CLJ* 15–18 at 18; Wade, 'Procedure and Prerogative', n. 134 above, 189.

[151] (London, 1983), 153. See *O'Reilly* v. *Mackman* [1982] 3 All ER 680 at 696C–E.

[152] Denning, *The Closing Chapter*, n. 151 above, 121. See also Woolf, *Protection of the Public*, n. 118 above, 236.

not introduced inquisitorial procedures which would have facilitated the resolution of polycentric administrative disputes and the development of public law. Rather, by merely providing a few procedural safeguards for public authorities, they provoked the courts to develop an unacceptable dichotomy. In short, they have created a 'procedural minefield'[153] nowhere near the frontline.

The Distinction's Dependence on Inquisitorial Procedures

In France, by adopting particularly inquisitorial procedures, the *Conseil d'Etat* facilitated the development of public law and so contributed to the acceptance of the distinction between public and private law. In England, the courts entrusted with the resolution of administrative disputes have remained generally handicapped by adversarial procedures. The special procedures which they have developed have become associated with unwanted or questionable procedural technicalities. By the technical deficiencies of the prerogative remedies, the courts were driven to rely increasingly on the ordinary remedies. The decision in *O'Reilly* v. *Mackman* that the amended judicial review procedure would be exclusive in public-law cases has provoked widespread criticism of the distinction between public- and private-law proceedings. Because of contrasting procedural traditions, the Order 53 reforms have not brought about a convergence of English and French law.[154] They have not entrenched the distinction between public and private law but illustrate the consequences of its ill-considered transplantation. The success of the distinction in France and its failure thus far in England confirm its dependence on inquisitorial judicial procedures suited to the resolution of polycentric administrative disputes.

[153] Cane, n. 72 above, 101.   [154] *Contra* Flogaïtis, n. 118 above.

11
Conclusions and Implications for English Law

The Distinction and its Context

The French distinction acquired significance during the nineteenth century in a context characterized by inquisitorial judicial procedures, a categorical approach to law, a conception of a distinct state administration, and a separation of powers that met the need for judges with both judicial independence and administrative expertise. By about the end of the century, it approximated to my model or ideal type of a working distinction, described in Chapter Three. By then, the distinction was entrenched within the French legal system and could survive the various legal and political changes of this century.

In contrast the English distinction has emerged and acquired significance recently, in a context lacking any of the features characterizing the French context of the late nineteenth century. The English distinction has consequently been accompanied by extensive debate and uncertainty about the proper procedure and judicial role in public-law cases and about the very idea of distinguishing public- from private-law cases. The accompanying problems are testimony to the relevance of my model and the dependence of a satisfactory distinction on the features it describes.

My model, however, does not express dogmatic conclusions. The generalizations justified by a comparative-historical analysis and Weberian method are tentative, provisional, and explicitly[1] one-sided. They are explanatory rather than conclusory. Their persuasiveness is limited by the ambit of the study upon which they are based. They therefore invite supplementary and corrective research. My generalizations regarding the context required for a working distinction are based upon a study of two legal systems, the English and the French. Their general relevance would be reduced by clear indications of a successful distinction in other contexts, possibly the Canadian, the Australian, or the German, if those contexts lack the features described in my model. No analysis can be all-inclusive. My generalizations can

---

[1] See above, 31–2.

be no more than a tentative contribution to general legal theory.[2] They explain the development of the distinction in England and France and emphasize the relationship between the distinction and its context, between a doctrinal development and prevailing theories, institutions, and procedures.

The Hazards of Legal Transplantation

My model expresses the coherence of legal and political system. It relates the distinction to features of legal and political context. Many of these features are themselves related. While adversarial procedures, for example, facilitate judicial independence by preventing the judge from identifying prematurely with a party's cause, judicial independence itself facilitates a faith in remedies and thus a remedial conception of law.[3]

Because of the coherence of legal and political system, transplantation is hazardous. The public/private distinction's transplantation to English law, like Montesquieu's adoption of the English separation of powers and Dicey's rejection of *droit administratif*, illustrates the danger of neglecting context when contemplating transplantation. It vindicates the arguments of Kahn-Freund that were challenged by Watson.[4] And it confirms the conclusion more recently reached by Atiyah and Summers in *Form and Substance in Anglo-American Law*:

[T]he ecological ramifications [of a transplant] must be fully considered. For example, English lawyers and politicians who advocate the introduction of a constitutional Bill of Rights in England, with some power of judicial review, must become more aware of the political ramifications and implications of such a move. These could, for instance, bear upon methods of judicial selection, the styles of legislative drafting, and a complete reappraisal of the relative values of certainty and justice in the individual case.[5]

Consideration of context and of the ramifications of transplantation might have prevented the transplantation of the distinction between public and private law and averted the accompanying problems.

---

[2] Cf. generally P. S. Atiyah and R. S. Summers, *Form and Substance in Anglo-American Law: A Comparative Study of Legal Reasoning, Legal Theory, and Legal Institutions* (Oxford, 1987), 415–20.

[3] See P. S. Atiyah, *Pragmatism and Theory in English Law* (London, 1987), 22. See generally Atiyah and Summers, n. 2 above, 426–30.

[4] See above, ch. 2.

[5] Atiyah and Summers, n. 2 above, 426–8, especially at 427.

Implications for Reform

Abandoning the Distinction

The English courts might further respond to their experience, and the extensive criticism, of the procedural dichotomy introduced in *O'Reilly* v. *Mackman*. They might go beyond their pragmatic disregard of Lord Diplock's principle of exclusivity.[6] As in the late 1970s and early 1980s, they might consider the recent swamping of the Crown Office—the excessive backlogs, delays, and accompanying injustices—as the occasion for dramatic procedural changes.[7] They might be influenced by the Scottish courts'[8] explicit refusal to accept a procedural distinction between public and private law. Lord Lowry has now expressed the hope that the House of Lords will reconsider *O'Reilly*.[9]

The Law Commission has had the opportunity to take the lead.[10] Again, for the last three years, it has been concerned with the procedures available by way of judicial review and particularly with 'the effect of the decision in *O'Reilly* v. *Mackman*'.[11] In its *Fifth Programme of Law Reform*, it declared that its main focus would be 'on the effectiveness of the procedural mechanisms put in place in 1977 and revised in 1980'.[12] In its consultation paper, it recognized that the 'present trend is towards limiting insistence on use of Order 53 to claims raising issues solely of public law', and it supported that trend: '[w]e provisionally support this development and the balance which it seeks to promote, but we recognise that it does not eliminate the uncertainty and the potential for continuing litigation over procedural issues.'[13] In its final report, the Law Commission confirms its support for the present position:

---

[6] But see *Roy* v. *Kensington and Chelsea and Westminster Family Practitioner Committee* [1992] 2 WLR 239 at 241F; H. Woolf, 'Judicial Review: A Possible Programme for Reform' [1992] *PL* 221–37 at 231.

[7] See Woolf, *ibid. passim*; Law Commission, *Administrative Law: Judicial Review and Statutory Appeals* (Law Com. 226), HC 669, paras. 2.12 ff.

[8] *West* v. *Secretary of State for Scotland*, 1992 SLT 636; *Naik* v. *University of Stirling, The Times*, 5 Aug. 1993. See W. J. Wolffe, 'The Scope of Judicial Review in Scots Law' [1992] *PL* 625–37.

[9] *R.* v. *Employment Secretary, ex p. Equal Opportunities Commission* [1994] 2 WLR 410 at 425E.

[10] But, see P. Cane, 'The Law Commission on Judicial Review' (1993) 56 *MLR* 887–96.

[11] Law Commission, *Fifth Programme of Law Reform* (Law Com. 200, 1991), Cmnd. 1556, item 10.

[12] *Ibid.*

[13] *Administrative Law: Judicial Review and Statutory Appeals* (consultation paper 126, 1993), para. 3. 23.

We . . . believe that the present position whereby a litigant is required to proceed by way of Order 53 only when (a) the challenge is on public law and no other grounds; i.e. where the challenge is solely to the validity or legality of a public authority's acts or omissions and (b) the litigant does not seek either to enforce or defend a completely constituted private law right is satisfactory.[14]

The Commission seeks to ameliorate, and reduce, the effect of the procedural dichotomy by recommending a procedure for the transfer of ordinary actions to Order 53 where necessary.[15] It does not, however, give much assistance with the criteria required to determine whether an AJR is to be used or a transfer is to take place. It accentuates, but does not elaborate on, 'public authority', 'completely constituted private law right', and 'issues of public law'.[16] It recognizes that '*Roy*'s case does not address the difficult question of *when* a private right is created by statute' and adds that the question 'will remain a matter of construction of individual statutes in their particular contexts'.[17] But, in the absence of clear criteria, the procedural protections re-emphasized by the Law Commission may still be circumvented by the litigants and ignored by a court without clear justification. The procedural dichotomy remains the loose pivot in the Law Commission's improved procedural system.

Apart from the procedural dichotomy, the institutional English distinction established through the creation of the Crown Office List is also in doubt. Lord Woolf proposed that the recent overload on the Crown Office be spread to judges not on the Crown Office List and to various new administrative tribunals.[18] Should this proposal be fully implemented and his further, more radical, proposal for a 'unified system' of administrative tribunals be unacceptable[19] the English institutional distinction would begin to disappear amidst a multiplicity of diverse jurisdictions.

Although the procedural dichotomy might justifiably be abandoned and the institutional distinction blurred, the substantive distinction is less criticized and more secure. In the report of the Justice–All Souls Review, for example, the procedural dichotomy is criticized while the development of administrative law is praised.[20] The procedures and

---

[14] *Administrative Law*, n. 7 above, para. 3.15.

[15] *Ibid.*, paras. 3.16 ff.   [16] *Ibid.*, paras. 3.15–16.

[17] *Ibid.*, para. 3.10. For *Roy*, see above, n. 6.

[18] Woolf, 'Programme for Reform', n. 6 above, 225–31.

[19] *Ibid.* 230. Cf. Committee of the Justice–All Souls Review of Administrative Law in the United Kingdom, *Administrative Justice: Some Necessary Reforms* (Oxford, 1988), 168–70.

[20] N. 19 above, 1–2, 148–52.

not the substantive grounds of judicial review have been the concern of the Law Commission. A waste of time and money on procedural litigation is more obviously problematic and, therefore, intolerable than the questionable application of substantive law.

Furthermore, the substantive distinction is still supported by a vague sense of various needs: first, the need to clarify and recognize the distinctness of the state administration precisely because it has been obscured by privatization;[21] secondly, the need to ensure with a distinct body of public law that the state administration remains accountable in performing what might vaguely be called a duty to show equal respect and concern to its citizens;[22] and, thirdly, the need to keep English law in line with other European jurisdictions and the case law of the European Court of Justice (ECJ).[23] This book, with its methodological emphasis on description and explanation, does not provide the comprehensive normative theory of the separation of powers or of the state in England and Europe that is required fully to evaluate these needs. It does, however, espouse a norm of systemic rationality[24] and can, therefore, spell out the difficulties and implications of meeting them.

Comprehensive Reform

If depriving the distinction of any significance be regarded as unrealistic or undesirable, other reforms are required to render it satisfactory. Because of the distinction's dependence on various features of its legal and political context, these reforms would need to be comprehensive. Lord Woolf's various proposals during the past few years illustrate the pressures created by the emergence of an English distinction between public and private law. Lord Woolf advocates a Director of Civil Proceedings as a corrective to adversarial procedures in administrative

---

[21] See M. Loughlin, *Public Law and Political Theory* (Oxford, 1992), 260–2; N. Lewis, 'Regulating Non-government Bodies: Privatization, Accountability, and the Public–Private Divide' in J. Jowell and D. Oliver (eds.), *The Changing Constitution* (2nd edn., Oxford, 1989), 219–45.

[22] See T. R. S. Allan, *Law, Liberty, and Justice: The Legal Foundations of British Constitutionalism* (Oxford, 1993), chs. 6 and 7, especially at 157–62.

[23] See the ECJ's public/private distinction between the vertical and horizontal effect of directives: *Marshall* v. *Southhampton and South West Hampshire Area Health Authority (Teaching)* (C–152/84) [1986] ECR 723, [1986] QB 401.; *Johnston* v. *Chief Constable of the Royal Ulster Constabulary* (C–222/84) [1986] ECR 1651, [1987] QB 129; *Foster* v. *British Gas plc* (C–188/89) [1990] ECR 1–3313, [1990] IRLR 353 (ECJ), [1991] IRLR 268 (HL); *Doughty* v. *Rolls-Royce plc* [1992] 1 CMLR 1045, [1992] IRLR 126.

[24] See above, 39–40.

disputes.[25] He also stresses that there 'could . . . be an advantage in
the High Court having the ability to remit issues requiring the investigation of facts to an appropriate tribunal, where they could be investigated in a more appropriate manner than is possible in adversarial
proceedings before the High Court'.[26] Furthermore, he proposes the
'widening of judicial experience' so as to equip judges on the Crown
Office List to deal with administrative disputes.[27] His proposal, however, is restricted, and will be obstructed, by the overriding demand for
judicial independence.[28] Some separation of powers that facilitates
both administrative expertise and judicial independence is required but
is yet to be established.

In the absence of an appropriate separation of powers, the English
courts will continue to lack the confidence to recognize, and the
administrative expertise to operate, the general remedy for damages
advocated by the Committee of the Justice–All Souls Review of
Administrative Law.[29] They will still struggle to articulate and systematize the principles of public law recommended[30] by Jowell and Lester.
Judicial shortcomings will be corrected only to a limited extent *ex post
facto*, through the ill-defined accountability accompanying[31] attempts to
articulate abstract principles. Without further institutional changes, the
Law Commission's preoccupation with procedure is questionable and
its faith in judicial evolution of the grounds of review is unfounded.[32]

More extensive reforms are required than those envisaged by Lord
Woolf. Apart from institutional changes and the adoption of more
inquisitorial procedures, the very approach to law in England will have
to change to accommodate the distinction between public and private

[25] See above, 231–2 ff. See also J. A. G. Griffith, 'Judicial Decision-making in Public
Law' [1985] *PL* 564–82; M. Loughlin, 'Innovative Financing in Local Government: The
Limits of Legal Instrumentalism—Part II' [1991] *PL* 568–99 at 590 ff.; J. W. F. Allison,
'The Procedural Reason for Judicial Restraint' [1994] *PL* 452–73 at 467 ff.

[26] Woolf, 'Programme for Reform', n. 6 above, 230.

[27] H. Woolf, *Protection of the Public—A New Challenge* (London, 1990), 115 ff.

[28] See above, ch. 7. Cf. Committee of the Justice–All Souls Review of Administrative
Law in the United Kingdom, n. 19 above, 168–70.

[29] *Ibid.*, 331 ff.

[30] J. Jowell and A. Lester, 'Beyond *Wednesbury*: Substantive Principles of
Administrative Law' [1987] *PL* 368–82. See also Woolf, *Protection of the Public*, n. 27
above, 112; Committee of the Justice–All Souls Review of Administrative Law in the
United Kingdom, n. 19 above, 1–2; T. R. S. Allan, 'Pragmatism and Theory in English
Administrative Law' (1988) 104 *LQR* 422–47.

[31] See Jowell and Lester, n. 30 above, 381–2.

[32] See Law Commission, *Fifth Programme*, n. 11 above, item 10; Law Commission,
Administrative Law, n. 7 above, para. 1.3; Woolf, 'Programme for Reform', n. 6 above,
222.

law. Unless the lasting rule of the forms of action be defied and a more systematic, categorical, approach to law be adopted, the distinction will continue to cause dissatisfaction and debate. The purpose of the AJR's procedural safeguards will continue to be frustrated by the open-ended exceptions recognized by Lord Diplock,[33] much used by the courts,[34] and recently confirmed by Lord Woolf.[35] And the purpose of the Crown Office List—judicial expertise in administrative-law cases—will similarly be frustrated by implementation of Lord Woolf's recommendation that its present overload be spread to other judges.[36]

   A conception of a distinct state administration suited to the application of a public/private distinction will need to accompany a categorical approach to law. Lord Woolf called upon the Law Commission to 'provide more precise markers' to define the scope of judicial review 'than exist at present'.[37] Although the Commission did not answer his call,[38] he himself suggested one such marker: 'a body should be subject to judicial review if it exercises *authority* over another person or body in such a manner as to cause material prejudice to that person or body and, if judicial review were available, that person or body could show the decision-maker had acted unlawfully'.[39] In the absence of a conception of a distinct state administration, however, Lord Woolf's concept of authority or the related and increasingly-invoked concept of power,[40] or perhaps some concept of monopoly to deal with privatized corporations and national sporting associations[41] is yet to be adopted,

---

[33] *O'Reilly* v. *Mackman* [1982] 3 All ER 1124 at 1134F.

[34] See, e.g., *Roy*, n. 6 above.

[35] Woolf, 'Programme for Reform', n. 6 above, 231–2.   [36] *Ibid.* 225–6.

[37] *Ibid.* 235.   [38] See *Administrative Law*, n. 7 above, paras. 3.10 and 3.15.

[39] Woolf, 'Programme for Reform', n. 6 above, 235 (emphasis added).

[40] See, e.g., *Breen* v. *Amalgamated Engineering Union* [1971] 2 QB 175 at 190D–H.; G. Samuel, 'Public Law and Private Law: A Private Lawyer's Response' (1983) 46 *MLR* 558–83 at 575; H. Woolf, 'Public Law–Private Law: Why the Divide? A Personal View' [1986] *PL* 220–38 at 224–5; *id.*, *Protection of the Public*, n. 27 above, 26; D. Oliver, 'Is the *Ultra Vires* Rule the Basis of Judicial Review?' [1987] *PL* 543–69 at 565–9; G. Borrie, 'The Regulation of Public and Private Power' [1989] *PL* 552–67; H. Collins, *Justice in Dismissal: The Law of Termination of Employment* (Oxford, 1992), 192, 270–4. But see Hoffmann LJ's disregard for the mere fact of power in *R.* v. *Jockey Club, ex p. Aga Khan* [1993] 1 WLR 909 at 932H.

[41] See *R.* v. *Jockey Club, ex p. Massingberd-Mundy* [1993] 2 All ER 207 at 222F; *R.* v. *Jockey Club, ex p. RAM Racecourses* [1993] 2 All ER 225 at 247E; M. J. Beloff, 'Pitch, Pool, Rink, . . . Court? Judicial Review in the Sporting World' [1989] *PL* 95–110 at 108–9; D. Pannick, 'Who is Subject to Judicial Review in Respect of What?' [1992] *PL* 1–7 at 4–5. But cf. H. W. R. Wade, 'Beyond the Law: A British Innovation in Judicial Review' (1991) 43 *Admin. LRev.* 559–70.

or reinstated[42] and elaborated, to enable the distinction between public and private to be applied satisfactorily.

Atiyah and Summers stress that 'if a given change is introduced into one system, this may call for other changes if the desired reform is to be achieved'.[43] The introduction of the distinction into English law illustrates such a change requiring further far-reaching changes.

Certain of the changes required for the accommodation of the distinction between public and private law will be easier to attain than others. Inquisitorial correctives to adversarial procedures, for example, will accord with a dawning realization of the limitations to 'trial by battle'.[44] And Lord Woolf's Director of Civil Proceedings seems a realistic although still remote prospect in administrative disputes. In civil proceedings generally, as a result of the demise of the civil jury and the improved availability of documentary evidence before trial, judges can now more fully prepare themselves and so play a more active role than in the past.[45] Jacob concludes, however, that the 'system of English civil justice has no choice but to retain its adversarial basis. It cannot replace this basis by adopting the inquisitorial system as it operates in the civil law countries of Europe, since this would require the creation of a new *corps* of lawyers, who would be career judges.'[46] Inquisitorial judicial procedures suited to the resolution of polycentric administrative disputes, like the particularly inquisitorial procedures of the *Conseil d'Etat*, cannot be introduced into England in the absence of numerous career judges available to serve on the Crown Office List. Gross gives a sober reminder of the dangers of changing to a complex and centralized procedural system:

Complex and centralized systems are not only harder to set up and more likely to break down, but they break down more thoroughly. When a central com-

---

[42] See the old common-law authorities for imposing a requirement of reasonableness on the exercise of monopolistic powers: Lord Hale, 'De Portibus Maris' in F. Hargrave (ed.), *Tracts* (Dublin, 1787), 45–113 at 77–8; *Bolt* v. *Stennett* (1800) 8 TR 606, 101 ER 1572; *Allnutt* v. *Inglis* (1810) 12 East 527, 104 ER 206. See generally P. P. Craig, 'Constitution, Property and Regulation' [1991] *PL* 538–54.

[43] Atiyah and Summers, n. 2 above, 427. See also B. Kaplan, 'Civil Procedure—Reflections on the Comparison of Systems' (1960) 9 *Buffalo LRev.* 409–32 at 421–2.

[44] B. Schwartz, *French Administrative Law and the Common-Law World* (New York, 1954), 326–7. See, e.g., J. A. Jolowicz, 'Comparative Law and the Reform of Civil Procedure' (1988) 8 *Legal Studies* 1–13.

[45] J. A. Jolowicz, 'Fact-finding: A Comparative Perspective', Colloquium of the United Kingdom Committee of Comparative Law (Aberdeen, Sept. 1991).

[46] J. I. H. Jacob, *The Fabric of English Civil Justice* (London, 1987) 17–19, 264–5, especially at 264.

ponent of a complex apparatus malfunctions, everything stops, and the failure typically requires drastic repairs. Specifically, a bad civil-law system would be worse than anything the common law can produce.[47]

Inquisitorial judicial procedures in an unfavourable environment could make matters worse. Judicious correctives to adversarial procedures will have to suffice.

In addition to inquisitorial procedures, a conception of a distinct state administration will be difficult to attain in an era of privatization, party-political disagreement, and academic uncertainty about the state.[48] Certainly, a state tradition cannot be developed overnight.[49] To provide a satisfactory substitute, a concept of monopoly would have to be freed from its etymological connotations of exclusivity and the market-place and adapted to a world of complementary and opposing authorities performing a variety of tasks. Furthermore, the increasingly-used concept of power would perplex lawyers, who long struggled with the related concept of *vires*[50] and who, before *Ridge* v. *Baldwin*, failed successfully to distinguish judicial, quasi-judicial, and purely administrative powers.[51]

To use a concept of power together with a distinction between public and private law, lawyers would need to distinguish public from private power.[52] In her article on the *ultra vires* rule, Professor Oliver mentioned a few differences:

Supervisory jurisdiction has to take account of some important differences between public and private power. Where purely private power is concerned, three factors argue against extensive judicial supervision. Respect for the individual liberty of the parties, certainty in the law, and the needs of the market, would indicate that the courts ought not, in the name of good administration, to impose too many restraints on personal liberty, or introduce a general duty to subordinate private interests to the public interest unless a statute so requires.[53]

---

[47] S. R. Gross, 'The American Advantage: The Value of Inefficient Litigation' (1987) 85 *Mich. LRev.* 734–57 at 751.

[48] See above, ch. 5.

[49] See M. Loughlin, 'Sitting on a Fence at Carter Bar: In Praise of J. D. B Mitchell' (1991) 36 *Juridical Rev.* 135–53 at 151.

[50] See E. G. Henderson, *Foundations of English Administrative Law: Certiorari and Mandamus in the Seventeenth Century* (Cambridge, Mass., 1963), especially at 6–7.

[51] [1964] AC 40. See generally E. C. S. Wade and A. W. Bradley, *Constitutional and Administrative Law* (10th edn., London, 1985), 604–7.

[52] See, e.g., *ex p. Aga Khan*, n. 40 above, 932H–3A.

[53] Oliver, n. 40 above, 566.

Oliver's references to public and private power, however, are conclusory. They do not indicate when individual liberty, legal certainty, and the needs of the market should take precedence. Later in the same article, Oliver recognizes the 'absence of workable concepts and of a framework of theory about the nature of power, whether public or private, upon which to build the supervisory jurisdictions of the courts'.[54] Oliver therefore suggests that '[p]olitical theorists and philosophers can assist lawyers in their understanding of the nature and incidence of power'.[55]

By changing a conception of the state administration for one of power, however, lawyers and legal academics would be moving from the unknown to the more unknown, from one area of complex and contested political theory to another, equally or even more complex and contested.[56] Still ill-equipped to deal with political theory,[57] they would need to elaborate a 'genealogy of powers'[58] or an 'anatomy of power' with concepts like 'condign power', 'compensatory power', and 'conditioned power'.[59] They might even be required to read the work of Foucault and his description of the ubiquity of power. Somehow Hercules would have to determine the boundaries of judicial review. He would have to determine, for example, whether someone like Mrs. Gillick should be required to proceed by way of judicial review because parental power or the power of the doctor or expert is in issue.[60] Furthermore, lawyers and legal academics would need to come to terms with the possibly wayward implications of political theories of power, for example, with Foucault's analysis of an eclipse of sovereign by disciplinary power, which undermines the importance of state law and therefore of any traditional legal distinction.[61]

The required theoretical elaboration of a concept of authority, public power, the state administration, or of some other notion like monopoly, such that a distinction between public and private law can be applied satisfactorily, will be a difficult and protracted endeavour.

---

[54] Oliver, n. 40 above, 568.   [55] *Ibid.*
[56] Cf., e.g., J. K. Galbraith, *The Anatomy of Power* (London, 1984) (see Oliver, n. 40 above, 568–9); M. Foucault, *Power/Knowledge: Selected Interviews and Other Writings 1972–1977* (C. Gordon (ed.)) (Brighton, 1980). See N. Rose, 'Beyond the Public/Private Division: Law, Power and the Family' (1987) 14 *J of Law & Soc.* 61–76.
[57] See above, ch. 5.; M. Loughlin, *Public Law and Political Theory*, n. 21 above, 23 ff.
[58] Foucault, n. 56 above.   [59] Galbraith, n. 56 above, especially at 4–6.
[60] See *Gillick* v. *West Norfolk and Wisbech AHA* [1986] AC 112.
[61] See M. Foucault, 'Governmentality' (1979) 6 *Ideology & Consciousness* 5–21; Rose, n. 56 above. Cf. M. Loughlin, 'The Underside of the Law: Judicial Review and the Prison Disciplinary System' (1993) 23 *CLP* 23–51; Collins, n. 40 above, 270–4.

Comprehensive reform has certainly been beyond the pragmatic concerns[62] of the Law Commission.

The European Movement

Progress towards European integration will facilitate a few of the changes required for a workable distinction. The ECJ's distinction between the vertical and horizontal effect of directives requires and accustoms English courts to work with criteria for distinguishing between a European public and private law.[63] European law provides leading and, in certain respects, binding examples of the application of substantive principles of public law for English courts.[64] Meanwhile, the European movement as a whole encourages some general convergence of legal[65] and political traditions, some convergence of conceptions of law and the administration, and of judicial institutions and procedures.

The European movement's influence, however, is uneven. In place of problems of transplantation, problems of harmonization will remain. As in the case of transplantation, specific instances of harmonization will continue to strain the English legal system as a whole. The English courts might, for example, be pressured into developing a general remedy for damages to secure for rights under English law the level of effective protection now given to rights under European law,[66] but, in the absence of institutional and procedural changes, they will remain hesitant and ill-equipped. They could be opening 'Pandora's box'.[67]

---

[62] See Cane, n. 10 above.

[63] See n. 23 above. This distinction has also given rise to anomalies, which have only partially been removed by the introduction of state liability for the non-implementation of directives in *Francovich* v. *Italian Republic* (C–6/90 & C–9/90) [1991] ECR I–5357, [1992] IRLR 84.

[64] See, e.g., *Woolwich Building Society* v. *IRC* [1993] AC 70 at 177C–E; *M.* v. *Home Office* [1992] 2 WLR 73 at 100B, 101C (CA), [1993] 3 WLR 433 at 448F, 463F (HL); *National and Local Government Officers Association* v. *Secretary of State for the Environment, The Times,* 2 Dec. 1992; T. Koopmans, 'European Public Law: Reality and Prospects' [1991] *PL* 53–63; N. Grief, 'The Domestic Impact of the European Convention on Human Rights as Mediated through Community Law' [1991] *PL* 555–67; Law Commission, *Administrative Law,* above n. 7, paras. 2.8 ff.

[65] See M. Cappelletti, *The Judicial Process in Comparative Perspective* (Oxford, 1989), chs. 4 and 8.

[66] See *Francovich,* n. 63 above; *Kirklees MBC* v. *Wickes Building Supplies Ltd* [1993] AC 227 at 281C–2C; R. Caranta, 'Governmental Liability after Francovich' (1993) 52 *CLJ* 272–97; C. Lewis and S. Moore, 'Duties, Directives and Damages in European Community Law' [1993] *PL* 151–70.

[67] P. P. Craig, '*Francovich,* Remedies and the Scope of Damages Liability' (1993) 109 *LQR* 595–621 at 620.

Similarly, they might be pressured into adopting the Continental principle of proportionality, but their attempts to apply it in European law illustrate an understandable discomfort. In relation to one of the Sunday-trading disputes, for example, Hoffmann J in the Chancery Division preferred to take judicial notice of the facts relevant to proportionality rather than encourage further evidence from the 'troupe of experts' touring the country and giving divergent expert advice to the courts.[68] He expressed a reluctance to investigate:

The question [of the proportionality of the Sunday-trading ban] is one on which strong and differing views may be held and which has been the subject of frequent parliamentary debate. Is the court to apply its own opinion of the importance of ensuring that shop workers do not have to work on Sundays and weigh that against its opinion of the importance of selling more Dutch bulbs or Italian furniture? . . . In my judgment it is not my function to carry out the balancing exercise or to form my own view on whether the legislative objective should be achieved by other means.[69]

The European movement is no *deus ex machina*. But accommodation of an English distinction between public and private law does depend on dramatic intervention. For English public law to develop successfully and for the Continental distinction to work in the common law, fundamental restructuring, whether through European influence or internal reform, is required.

Those who advocate the distinction's retention should countenance comprehensive reforms, reforms that are theoretical, institutional, and procedural. Because my model, described in Chapter 3, is an ideal type, which '[i]n its conceptual purity . . . cannot be found empirically anywhere in reality',[70] a rough approximation to its main features will suffice but will be, nonetheless, difficult to achieve. Despite the significant past achievements of English judges, lawyers, and academics, a satisfactory separate system of public law is still remote. A sufficient congruence between the distinction and its English context is yet to be achieved.

---

[68] *Stoke-on-Trent CC* v. *B. and Q. Plc* [1991] 4 All ER 221 at 231J-2B (Ch.), [1993] AC 900 (HL).

[69] *Ibid.* 234J–5B. See also *W. H. Smith Do-It-All Ltd* v. *Peterborough CC* [1991] 4 All ER 193 at 209J–10G; *Brind* v. *Home Secretary* [1991] 1 All ER 720, especially at 739.

[70] M. Weber, *The Methodology of the Social Sciences* (Glencoe, Illinois, 1949), 90.

Bibliography

ALLAN, T. R. S., 'Abuse of Power and Public Interest Immunity: Justice, Rights and Truth' (1985) 101 *LQR* 200.
—— 'Pragmatism and Theory in English Administrative Law' (1988) 104 *LQR* 422.
—— *Law, Liberty, and Justice: The Legal Foundations of British Constitutionalism* (Oxford, 1993).
ALLEN, C. K., *Bureaucracy Triumphant* (Oxford, 1931).
—— Foreword in M. A. Sieghart, *Government by Decree: A Comparative Study of the History of the Ordinance in English and French Law* (London, 1950).
—— *Law and Orders* (London, 1965).
ALLEN, R. J., KÖCK, S., RIECHENBERG, K., and TOBY ROSEN, D., 'The German Advantage in Civil Procedure: A Plea for more Details and fewer Generalities in Comparative Scholarship' (1988) 82 *Northwest. Univ. LRev.* 705.
ALLISON, J. W. F., 'Fuller's Analysis of Polycentric Disputes and the Limits of Adjudication' (1994) 53 *CLJ* 367.
—— 'The Procedural Reason for Judicial Restraint' [1994] *PL* 452.
AMOS, M., 'A Day in Court at Home and Abroad' (1926) *CLJ* 340.
—— 'Have we too much Law?' (1931) *Jnl. of the Soc. of Pub. Teachers of L* 1.
AMOS, S., *The Science of Law* (London, 1874).
ANCEL, M., 'Case Law in France' (1934) 16 *Jnl. of Comp. Leg. & Int. L* 1.
ANDREWS, N. H., 'The Passive Court and Legal Argument' (1988) *CJQ* 125.
ARTHURS, H. W., 'Rethinking Administrative Law: A Slightly Dicey Business' (1979) 17 *Osgoode Hall LJ* 1.
—— *'Without the Law': Administrative Justice and Legal Pluralism in Nineteenth-Century England* (Toronto, 1985).
ASARO, A., 'The Public/Private Distinction in American Liberal Thought: Unger's Critique and Synthesis' (1983) 28 *Am. J Juris* 118.
ASTON, T. (ed.), *Crisis in Europe 1560–1660* (London, 1965).
ATIYAH, P. S., *Pragmatism and Theory in English Law* (London, 1987).
—— and SUMMERS, R. S., *Form and Substance in Anglo-American Law: A Comparative Study of Legal Reasoning, Legal Theory, and Legal Institutions* (Oxford, 1987).
AUBY, J.-M., 'The Abuse of Power in French Administrative Law' (1970) 18 *AJCL* 549.
AUSTIN, J., 'Centralization' (1847) 85 *Edinburgh Rev.* 221.
—— *Lectures on Jurisprudence* or *The Philosophy of Positive Law* (5th edn., London, 1885).
—— *The Province of Jurisprudence Determined and the Uses of the Study of Jurisprudence* (H. L. A. Hart (ed.)) (London, 1954).

Azo, in F. W. Maitland (ed.), *Select Passages from the Works of Bracton and Azo* (8 Selden Society, 1895).

Bacon, F., *Works* (J. Spedding, R. L. Ellis, and D. D. Heath (eds.)), i (London, 1857), vii (1859).

Baker, J. H., 'English Law and the Renaissance', Introduction to *The Reports of Sir John Spelman, Vol. 2* (J. H. Baker (ed.)) (94 Selden Society, 1977), i, 23–51.

—— 'The Conciliar Courts' in *The Reports of Sir John Spelman* (J. H. Baker (ed.)) (94 Selden Society, 1978), ii, 70–74.

—— *An Introduction to English Legal History* (3rd edn., London, 1990).

—— 'Statutory Interpretation and Parliamentary Intention' (1993) 52 *CLJ* 353.

Baker, K. M., *Inventing the French Revolution: Essays on French Political Culture in the Eighteenth Century* (Cambridge, 1990).

Baldwin, R., and McCrudden, C. *Regulation and Public Law* (London, 1987).

Bamforth, N., 'The Scope of Judicial Review: Still Uncertain' [1993] *PL* 239.

Barker, A. (ed.), *Quangos in Britain: Government and the Networks of Public Policy-Making* (London, 1982).

Barker, E., 'The Discredited State: Thoughts on Politics before the War' (1915) *Pol. Quat.* 101.

Barker, R., *Political Ideas in Modern Britain* (London, 1978).

Barnes, T. G., 'Star Chamber Mythology' (1961) 5 *AJLH* 1.

—— 'Due Process and Slow Process in the Late Elizabethan–Early Stuart Star Chamber' (1962) 6 *AJLH* 221, 315.

—— 'Star Chamber Litigants and their Counsel 1596–1641' in J. H. Baker (ed.), *Legal Records and the Historian* (Royal Historical Society, 1978), 7–28.

Bayles, M. D., *Principles of Law: A Normative Analysis* (Dordrecht, 1987).

Beatson, J., ' "Public" and "Private" in English Administrative Law' (1987) 103 *LQR* 34.

—— 'Public Law, Restitution and the Role of the House of Lords' (1993) 109 *LQR* 1.

—— and Matthews, M. H., *Administrative Law: Cases and Materials* (2nd edn., Oxford, 1989).

Bell, H. E., *An Introduction to the History and Records of the Court of Wards and Liveries* (Cambridge, 1953).

Bell, J., 'The Expansion of Judicial Review over Discretionary Powers in France' [1986] *PL* 99.

—— 'Reflections on the Procedure of the Conseil d'Etat' in G. Hand and J. McBride (eds.), *Droit Sans Frontiers: Essays in Honour of L. Neville Brown* (Birmingham, 1991), 211–34.

—— 'Le fondement du contrôle juridictionnel de l'administration' in P. Legrand (ed.), *Common Law d'un siècle l'autre* (Cowansville, 1992), 57–86.

—— *French Constitutional Law* (Oxford, 1992).

Beloff, M. J., 'The Boundaries of Judicial Review' in J. Jowell and D. Oliver (eds.), *New Directions in Judicial Review* (London, 1988), 5–21.

—— 'Pitch, Pool, Rink, . . . Court? Judicial Review in the Sporting World' [1989] *PL* 95.

BENN, S. I., and GAUS, G. F. (eds.), *Public and Private in Social Life* (London, 1983).

BENTHAM, J., *Works* (London, 1843).

BERLIN, I., 'Two Concepts of Liberty' in A. Quinton (ed.), *Political Philosophy* (London, 1967), 141–52.

BIRKINSHAW, P., HARDEN, I., and LEWIS, N., *Government by Moonlight: The Hybrid Parts of the State* (London, 1990).

BIRNBAUM, P., *States and Collective Action: The European Experience* (Cambridge, 1988).

BLACKBURN, R. W., 'Dicey and the Teaching of Public Law' [1985] *PL* 679.

BLACKSTONE, W., *Commentaries on the Laws of England* (Facsimile of 1st edn. of 1765–9, Chicago, 1979).

BLOCH, M., *Feudal Society* (London, 1961).

BLOM-COOPER, L., 'The New Face of Judicial Review: Administrative Changes in Order 53' [1982] *PL* 250.

—— 'Lawyers and Public Administrators: Separate and Unequal' [1984] *PL* 215.

BLUMROSEN, A. W., 'The Bottom Line in Equal Employment Guidelines— Administering a Polycentric Problem' (1981) 33 *Admin. LRev.* 323.

BODIN, J., *Les Six Livres de la république* (Paris, 1583).

—— *The Six Bookes of a Commonweale* (K. D. McRae (ed.), R. Knolles (tr.)) (Cambridge, Mass., 1962).

BOHANNAN, P., 'Ethnography and Comparison in Legal Anthropology' in L. Nader (ed.), *Law in Culture and Society* (Chicago, 1969), 401–18.

BORCHARD, E. M., 'The Declaratory Judgment' (1918) 28 *Yale LJ* 1, 105.

BORRIE, G., 'The Regulation of Public and Private Power' [1989] *PL* 552.

BOYER, B. B., 'Alternatives to Administrative Trial-type Hearings for Resolving Complex Scientific, Economic, and Social Issues' (1972) 71 *Mich. LRev.* 111.

BOYRON, S., 'Proportionality in English Administrative Law: A Faulty Transplant?' (1992) 12 *OJLS* 237.

BRACTON, H., in F. W. Maitland (ed.), *Select Passages from the Works of Bracton and Azo* (8 Selden Society, 1895).

—— *Bracton on the Laws and Customs of England*, (S. E. Thorne (tr.)) (Cambridge, Mass., 1968).

BRADLEY, A. W., ' "The Judge over your Shoulder" ' [1987] *PL* 485.

—— 'Protecting Government Decisions from Legal Challenge' [1988] *PL* 1.

BREST, P., 'State Action and Liberal Theory: A Casenote on *Flagg Brothers* v. *Brooks*' (1982) 130 *Univ. of Penn. LRev.* 1296.

BRISSAUD, J., *A History of French Public Law* (London, 1915).

BROWN, L. N., and GARNER, J. F., *French Administrative Law* (3rd edn., London, 1983).

—— and BELL, J. S., *French Administrative Law* (4th edn., Oxford, 1993).

BROWN, W. J., 'The Jurisprudence of M. Duguit' (1916) 32 *LQR* 168.

BROWNE-WILKINSON, LORD, 'The Infiltration of a Bill of Rights' [1992] *PL* 397.

CANE, P., 'The Function of Standing Rules in Administrative Law' [1980] *PL* 303.

—— 'Standing, Legality and the Limits of Public Law' [1981] *PL* 322.

—— 'Public Law and Private Law: Some Thoughts Prompted by *Page Motors Ltd.* v. *Epsom & Ewell BC*' [1983] *PL* 202.

—— 'Public Law and Private Law Again: *Davy* v. *Spelthorne Borough Council* [1983] 3 WLR 742 (HL)' [1984] *PL* 16.

—— *An Introduction to Administrative Law* (Oxford, 1986).

—— 'Public Law and Private Law: A Study of the Analysis and Use of a Legal Concept' in J. Eekelaar and J. Bell (eds.), *Oxford Essays in Jurisprudence* (Oxford, 1987), 57–78.

—— 'Private Rights and Public Procedure' [1992] *PL* 193.

—— *An Introduction to Administrative Law* (2nd edn., Oxford, 1992).

—— 'The Law Commission on Judicial Review' (1993) 56 *MLR* 887.

CAPPELLETTI, M., *The Judicial Process in Comparative Perspective* (Oxford, 1989).

CARANTA, R., 'Governmental Liability after Francovich' (1993) 52 *CLJ* 272.

CHAPUS, R., 'De l'office du juge: contentieux administratif et nouvelle procédure civile' (1977/78) 29 *EDCE* 11.

—— *Droit du contentieux administratif* (2nd edn., Paris, 1990).

CHAYES, A., 'The Role of the Judge in Public Law Litigation' (1976) 89 *Harv. LRev.* 1281.

—— 'The Supreme Court 1981 Term. Foreword: Public Law Litigation and the Burger Court' (1982) 96 *Harv. LRev.* 4.

CHENOT, B., 'La notion de service public dans la jurisprudence économique du Conseil d'Etat' (1950) 4 *EDCE* 77.

—— 'L'Existentialisme et le droit ' (1953) 3 *Revue Française de science politique* 57.

CHEVRIER, G., 'Remarques sur l'introduction et les vicissitudes de la distinction du «*jus privatum*» et du «*jus publicum*» dans les œuvres des anciens juristes Français' [1952] *Archives de philosophie du droit* 5.

—— 'Les critères de la distinction du droit privé et du droit public dans la pensée savante médiévale' in *Études d'histoire du droit canonique dédiées à Gabriel Le Bras* (Paris, 1965), ii, 841–59.

COLLINS, H., 'The Public/Private Distinction in British Labour Law', Critical Legal Conference (University of Kent, Sept. 1986).

—— *Justice in Dismissal: The Law of Termination of Employment* (Oxford, 1992).

COLSON, J.-P., *L'Office du juge et la preuve dans le contentieux administratif* (Paris, 1970).

COMMITTEE OF THE JUSTICE–ALL SOULS REVIEW OF ADMINISTRATIVE LAW IN THE UNITED KINGDOM, *Administrative Justice: Some Necessary Reforms* (Oxford, 1988).

CONSERVATIVE PARTY, *The Best Future for Britain: The Conservative Manifesto 1992* (London, 1992).

CONSTANT, B., *Principes de politique applicables a tous les gouvernements répresentatifs en particulièrement a la constitution actuelle de la france* (Paris, 1815).

—— 'De la Liberté des anciens comparée a celle des modernes' in *Collection complète* (Paris, 1820), iv, pt. 7, 238–74.

—— *Political Writings* (B. Fontana (ed. and tr.)) (Cambridge, 1988).

COTTERRELL, R., *The Politics of Jurisprudence: A Critical Introduction to Legal Philosophy* (London, 1989).

—— *The Sociology of Law: An Introduction* (2nd edn., London, 1992).

—— 'Judicial Review and Legal Theory' in H. Genn and G. Richardson (eds.), *Government Action and Legal Control* (Oxford, forthcoming).

COUNCIL ON TRIBUNALS, *The Functions of the Council on Tribunals* (1980), Cmnd. 7805.

COUTURE, E. J., 'The Nature of the Judicial Process' (1950) 25 *Tulane LRev.* 1.

CRAIG, P. P., *Administrative Law* (2nd edn., London, 1989).

—— 'Dicey: Unitary, Self-correcting Democracy and Public Law' (1990) 106 *LQR* 105.

—— *Public Law and Democracy in the United Kingdom and the United States of America* (Oxford, 1990).

—— 'Constitutions, Property and Regulation' [1991] *PL* 538.

—— '*Francovich*, Remedies and the Scope of Damages Liability' (1993) 109 *LQR* 595.

CRAWFORD, M., 'Aut Sacrum Aut Poublicom' in P. Birks (ed.), *New Perspectives in the Roman Law of Property: Essays for Barry Nicholas* (Oxford, 1989), 93–8.

CRIPPS, Y., 'Dismissal, Jurisdiction and Judicial Review' (1985) 44 *CLJ* 177.

D'AMATO, A., 'Lon Fuller and Substantive Natural Law' (1981) 26 *Amer. J of Juris.* 202.

DAINTITH, T. C., 'The Mixed Enterprise in the United Kingdom' in W. Friedmann and J. F. Garner (eds.), *Government Enterprise: A Comparative Study* (London, 1970), 53–78.

—— 'The Executive Power Today: Bargaining and Economic Control' in J. Jowell and D. Oliver (eds.), *The Changing Constitution* (Oxford, 1989), 193–218.

DAVID, R., book review (1952) 4 *Revue internationale de droit comparé* 184.

—— *French Law: Its Structure, Sources, and Methodology* (M. Kindred (tr.)) (Baton Rouge, 1972).

—— 'Public and Private Law: Romanist Countries' in *IECL*, ii, ch. 2, sec. 18.

DAVIS, C. K., 'The Future of Judge-made Law in England: A Problem of Practical Jurisprudence' (1961) 61 *Columbia LRev.* 201.

DAWSON, J. P., 'The Codification of the French Customs' (1940) 38 *Michigan LRev.* 765.

—— *A History of Lay Judges* (Cambridge, Mass., 1960).

—— *The Oracles of the Law* (Ann Arbor, 1968).

252   *Bibliography*

DE LAUBADÈRE, A., *Traité de droit administratif* (J.-C. Venezia and Y. Gaudemet (eds.)) (11th edn., Paris, 1990).

DE SMITH, S. A., *Judicial Review of Administrative Action* (London, 1959).

—— 'The Prerogative Writs: Historical Origins', Appendix I *Judicial Review of Administrative Action* (J. M. Evans (ed.)) (4th edn., London, 1980), 584–95 ('The prerogative writs' [1951] *CLJ* 40–56).

—— and BRAZIER, R., *Constitutional and Administrative Law* (6th edn., London, 1989).

DE TOCQUEVILLE, A., *De la démocratie en Amérique* (Paris, 1850).

—— *L'Ancien Régime*, (G. Headlam (ed.)) (Oxford, 1904).

—— *Democracy in America*, (J. P. Mayer and M. Lerner (eds.)) (London, 1968).

—— *Democracy in America*, (P. Bradley (ed.)) (London, 1994).

DEANE, H. A., *The Political Ideas of Harold J. Laski* (New York, 1955).

DEBBASCH, C., *Procedure administrative contentieuse et procedure civile* (Paris, 1962).

DENNING, A., *Freedom under the Law* (London, 1949).

—— 'The Way of an Iconoclast' (1959/60) 5 *Jnl. of the Soc. of Pub. Teachers of L* 77.

—— *The Closing Chapter* (London, 1983).

DEVLIN, P., 'The Common Law, Public Policy and the Executive' (1956) *CLP* 1.

DEXTER, R. S., *'O'Reilly* v. *Mackman*: Further Confusion in Judicial Review' (1983) 5 *Liverpool LRev.* 187.

DICEY, A. V., *Lectures Introductory to the Study of the Law of the Constitution* (London, 1885).

—— *'Droit Administatif* in Modern French Law' (1901) 18 *LQR* 302.

—— 'The Development of Administrative Law in England' (1915) 31 *LQR* 148 (incorporated as an appendix in Dicey, *Law of the Constitution*, (10th edn.), 493–9).

—— *An Introduction to the Study of the Law of the Constitution* (10th edn., London, 1959).

—— *Lectures on the Relation between Law and Public Opinion in England during the Nineteenth Century* (2nd edn., London, 1962).

DIPLOCK, LORD, 'Judicial Control of the Administrative Process' (1971) *CLP* 1.

—— 'Administrative Law: Judicial Review Reviewed' (1974) 33 *CLJ* 233.

DONOUGHMORE COMMITTEE, *Report of the Committee on Ministers' Powers* (1932), Cmnd. 4060.

DRAGO, R., 'The Public Corporation in France' in W. Friedmann (ed.), *The Public Corporation: A Comparative Symposium* (London, 1954), 108–37.

—— 'La réform du Conseil d'Etat' (1962/3) 18/9 *Actualité juridique: droit administratif*, 524.

—— 'Public Enterprises in France' in W. Friedmann and J. F. Garner (eds.), *Government Enterprise: A Comparative Study* (London, 1970), 107–22.

—— 'La loi du 24 Mai 1872' (1972) 25 *EDCE* 13.

DREWRY, G., 'Public Lawyers and Public Administrators: Prospects for an Alliance?' (1986) 64 *Pub. Admin.* 173.

DUBY, J., *France in the Middle Ages 987–1460* (J. Vale (tr.)) (Oxford, 1991).

DUCAMIN, B., 'Recent Case Law of the French Conseil d'Etat' (1987) 35 *AJCL* 341.

DUGUIT, L., 'The Law and the State: French and German Doctrines' (1917/18) 31 *Harv. LRev.* 1.

—— 'Changes of Principle in the Field of Liberty, Contract, Liability, and Property' in *The Progress of Continental Law in the Nineteenth Century* (London, 1918), 65–146.

—— *Law in the Modern State* (F. and H. Laski (trs.)) (New York, 1970).

DURKHEIM, E., *De la division du travail social* (Paris, 1893).

—— *Le Suicide: étude de sociologie* (Paris, 1930).

—— 'L'Etat' (1958) 148 *Revue philos.* 433.

—— *The Division of Labour in Society* (G. Simpson (tr.)) (New York, 1964).

—— *Politics and the State* (A. Giddens (ed.)) (Stanford, 1986).

DWORKIN, R., *Taking Rights Seriously* (London, 1978).

—— 'Natural Law Revisited' (1982) 34 *Univ. of Florida LRev.* 165.

—— 'Law as Interpretation' (1982) 60 *Texas LRev.* 527.

—— *Law's Empire* (London, 1986).

DYSON, K. H. F., *The State Tradition in Western Europe: A Study of an Idea and Institution* (Oxford, 1980).

EISENBERG, M. A., 'Participation, Responsiveness, and the Consultative Process: An Essay for Lon Fuller' (1978) 92 *Harv. LRev.* 410.

EISENMANN, C., 'Droit public, droit privé' (1952) 68 *RDP* 903.

ELLIOTT, M. J., *The Role of Law in Central-Local Relations* (London, 1981).

ERRERA, R., 'Dicey and French Administrative Law: A Missed Encounter' [1985] *PL* 695.

—— 'The Scope and Meaning of No-fault Liability in French Administrative Law' (1986) 39 *CLP* 157.

FELDMAN, D., 'Public Law Values in the House of Lords' (1990) 106 *LQR* 246.

FINN, P. 'Public Function—Private Action: A Common Law Dilemma' in S. I. Benn and G. F. Gaus (eds.), *Public and Private in Social Life* (London, 1983), 93–111.

FINNIS, J., *Natural Law and Natural Rights* (Oxford, 1980).

FISS, O. M., 'The Supreme Court 1978 Term. Foreword: The Forms of Justice' (1979) 93 *Harv. LRev.* 1.

FLOGAÏTIS, S., *Administrative Law et droit administratif* (Paris, 1986).

FORD, F., *Robe and Sword: The Regrouping of the French Aristocracy after Louis XIV* (New York, 1965).

FORD, T. H., 'Dicey as a Political Journalist' [1970] *Political Studies* 220.

FORSYTH, C., 'The Principle of *O'Reilly* v. *Mackman*: A Shield but not a Sword?' [1985] *PL* 355.

—— 'Beyond *O'Reilly* v. *Mackman*: The Foundations and Nature of Procedural Exclusivity' [1985] *CLJ* 415.

—— 'The Scope of Judicial Review: "Public Duty" not "Source of Power" ' [1987] *PL* 356.

—— 'The Provenance and Protection of Legitimate Expectations' [1988] *CLJ* 238.

—— 'The Boundaries of Judicial Review', Public Seminar (QMW College, Dec. 1991).

FOSTER, C. D., *Privatization, Public Ownership and the Regulation of Natural Monopoly* (Oxford, 1992).

FOUCAULT, M., 'Governmentality' (1979) 6 *Ideology & Consciousness* 5.

—— *Power/Knowledge: Selected Interviews and Other Writings 1972–1977* (C. Gordon (ed.)) (Brighton, 1980).

FRANKS COMMITTEE, *Report of the Committee on Administrative Tribunals and Inquiries* (1957), Cmnd. 218.

FREDMAN, S., and MORRIS, G., 'Public or Private? State Employees and Judicial Review' (1991) 107 *LQR* 298.

—— and MORRIS, G., 'Judicial Review and Civil Servants: Contracts of Employment Declared to Exist' [1991] *PL* 485.

—— and —— 'A Snake or a Ladder? *O'Reilly* v. *Mackman* Reconsidered' (1992) 108 *LQR* 353.

FREEDEMAN, C. E., *The Conseil d'Etat in Modern France* (New York, 1961).

FREEMAN, M. D. A., 'Standards of Adjudication, Judicial Law-making and Prospective Overruling' (1973) 26 *CLP* 166.

—— (ed.), *State, Law, and the Family: Critical Perspectives* (London, 1984).

—— 'Towards a Critical Theory of Family Law' (1985) 38 *CLP* 153.

FRIEDMANN, W. (ed.), *The Public Corporation: A Comparative Symposium* (London, 1954).

—— *Legal Theory* (3rd edn., London, 1967).

—— *Law in a Changing Society* (2nd edn., London, 1972).

—— and GARNER, J. F. (eds.), *Government Enterprise: A Comparative Study* (London, 1970).

FRIEDRICH, C. J., *Constitutional Government and Politics* (New York, 1937).

—— *The Philosophy of Law in Historical Perspective* (Chicago, 1958).

FULLER, L. L., 'Government Secrecy and the Forms of Social Order' in C. J. Friedrich (ed.), *Community: Nomos II* (New York, 1959), 256–68.

—— 'Adjudication and the Rule of Law' (1960) *Proc. Amer. Soc. of Int. L* 1.

—— 'The Adversary System' in H. J. Berman (ed.), *Talks on American Law: A Series of Broadcasts to Foreign Audiences by Members of the Harvard Law School Faculty* (New York, 1961), 30–43.

—— 'Collective Bargaining and the Arbitrator' (1963) *Wis. LRev.* 3.

—— 'Irrigation and Tyranny ' (1965) 17 *Stan. LRev.* 1021.

—— *Anatomy of the Law* (London, 1968).

—— *The Morality of Law* (2nd edn., New Haven, 1969).

—— 'The Law's Precarious Hold on Life' (1969) 3 *Georgia LRev.* 530.

—— 'Mediation—Its Forms and Functions' (1971) 44 *S Cal. LRev.* 305.

—— 'The Forms and Limits of Adjudication' (1978) 92 *Harv. LRev.* 353.

—— *The Principles of Social Order* (K. I. Winston (ed.)) (Durham, NC, 1981).

—— and RANDALL, J. D., 'Professional Responsibility: Report of the Joint Conference' (1958) 44 *ABA J* 1159, 1216.

FURET, F., *Interpreting the French Revolution* (E. Forster (tr.)) (Cambridge, 1981).

—— *Revolutionary France 1770–1880* (Oxford, 1992).

GALBRAITH, J. K., *The New Industrial State* (London, 1972).

—— *The Anatomy of Power* (London, 1984).

GANZ, G., *Administrative Procedures* (London, 1974).

—— 'Legitimate Expectation' in C. Harlow (ed.), *Public Law and Politics* (London, 1986), 145–62.

GARNER, J. F., 'Public Law and Private Law' [1978] *PL* 238.

GENY, F., *Méthode d'interprétation et sources en droit privé positif: essai critique* (Paris, 1919).

GIDDENS, A., *Capitalism and Modern Social Theory: An Analysis of the Writings of Marx, Durkeim and Max Weber* (Cambridge, 1971).

—— *Durkheim* (Glascow, 1978).

—— *Profiles and Critiques in Social Theory* (London, 1982).

GILMORE, M., *Argument from Roman Law in Political Thought, 1200–1600* (Cambridge, Mass., 1941).

GLEASON, J. H., *Justices of the Peace in England 1558 to 1640* (Oxford, 1969).

GLUCKMAN, M., 'Concepts in the Comparative Study of Tribal Law' in L. Nader (ed.), *Law in Culture and Society* (Chicago, 1969), 349–73.

GOULD, M., '*M* v. *Home Office*: Government and the Judges' [1993] *PL* 568.

GOWER, L. C. B. *et al.*, *Principles of Modern Company Law* (4th edn., London, 1979).

GRAHAM, C., and PROSSER, T., *Privatizing Public Enterprises: Constitutions, the State, and Regulation in Comparative Perspective* (Oxford, 1991).

GRIEF, N., 'The Domestic Impact of the European Convention on Human Rights as Mediated through Community Law' [1991] *PL* 555.

GRIFFITH, J. A. G., '*Justice and Administrative Law* Revisited' in J. A. G. Griffith (ed.), *From Policy to Administration, Essays in Honour of William A. Robson* (London, 1976), 200–16.

—— 'Judicial Decision-making in Public Law' [1985] *PL* 564.

GROSS, S. R., 'The American Advantage: The Value of Inefficient Litigation' (1987) 85 *Mich. LRev.* 734.

GUALANDI, G., *Legislazione imperiale e giurisprudenza* (Milan, 1963).

GUIZOT, F., *Histoire générale de la civilisation en Europe* (Paris, 1828).

GUIZOT, F., *Histoire des origines du gouvernement représentatif en Europe* (Paris, 1851).
—— *Historical Essays and Lectures*, (S. Mellon (ed.)) (Chicago, 1972).
GWYN, W. B., 'The Labour Party and the Threat of Bureaucracy' (1971) 19 Political Studies 383.

HALE, M., *An Analysis of the Civil Part of the Law* (4th edn., London, 1779).
—— 'De Portibus Maris' in F. Hargrave (ed.), *Tracts* (Dublin, 1787), 45 ff.
HAMPSON, N., 'The Heavenly City of the French Revolutionaries' in C. Lucas (ed.), *Rewriting the French Revolution* (Oxford, 1991), 46–68.
HAMSON, C. J., 'Civil Procedure in France and England' [1950] *CLJ* 411.
—— *Executive Discretion and Judicial Control: An Aspect of the French Conseil d'Etat* (London, 1954).
—— 'Escaping Borstal Boys and the Immunity of Office' [1969] *CLJ* 273.
HARDEN, I., *The Contracting State* (Buckingham, 1992).
—— and LEWIS, N., *The Noble Lie: The British Constitution and the Rule of Law* (London, 1986).
HARLOW, C., 'Fault Liability in French and English Public Law' (1976) 39 *MLR* 516.
—— 'Remedies in French Administrative Law' [1977] *PL* 227.
—— ' "Public" and "Private" Law: Definition without Distinction' (1980) 43 *MLR* 241.
—— *Compensation and Government Torts* (London, 1982).
—— and RAWLINGS, R., *Law and Administration* (London, 1984).
HARRINGTON, J., *Oceana* (J. Toland (ed.)) (Dublin, 1737).
HARRIS, B. V., 'The "Third Source" of Authority for Government Action' (1992) 109 *LQR* 626.
HART, H. L. A., *The Concept of Law* (Oxford, 1961).
HAURIOU, M., *Précis élémentaire de droit administratif* (14th edn., Paris, 1938).
HAYWARD, J., *After the French Revolution: Six Critics of Democracy and Nationalism* (Hemel Hempstead, 1991).
HELD, D., 'Power and Legitimacy in Contemporary Britain' in G. McLennan, D. Held, and S. Hall (eds.), *State and Society in Contemporary Britain: A Critical Introduction* (Cambridge, 1984), 299–369.
—— *Political Theory and the Modern State: Essays on State, Power and Democracy* (Cambridge, 1989).
HENDERSON, E. G., *Foundations of English Administrative Law: Certiorari and Mandamus in the Seventeenth Century* (Cambridge, Mass., 1963).
HEWART OF BURY, LORD, *The New Despotism* (London, 1929).
HILL, C., *Reformation to Industrial Revolution: A Social and Economic History of Britain 1530–1780* (London, 1967).
HILL, J., 'Public Law and Private Law: More (French) Food for Thought' [1985] *PL* 14.
HILL, L. M., Introduction in J. Caesar, *The Ancient State Authoritie and Proceedings of the Court of Requests* (L. M. Hill (ed.)) (Cambridge, 1975).

HILL, M., *The State, Administration and the Individual* (London, 1976).

HOBBES, T., *Leviathan* (R. Tuck (ed.)) (Cambridge, 1991).

HOLDSWORTH, W. S., *A History of English Law*, iv (London, 1924), x (London, 1938).

HOLLAND, T. E., *The Elements of Jurisprudence* (13th edn., Oxford, 1924).

HOLMES, O. W., 'Codes, and the Arrangement of the Law' (1931) 44 *Harv. LRev.* 725.

HOLMES, S., *Benjamin Constant and the Making of Modern Liberalism* (London, 1984).

HOOD, C., 'Governmental Bodies and Government Growth' in A. Barker (ed.), *Quangos in Britain: Government and the Networks of Public Policy-making* (London, 1982), 44–68.

HORWITZ, M. J., 'The History of the Public/Private Distinction' (1982) 130 *Univ. Penn. LRev.* 1423.

JACKSON, B. S., *Essays in Jewish and Comparative Legal History* (Leiden, 1975).

JACOB, J. I. H., *The Reform of Civil Procedural Law and Other Essays in Civil Procedure* (London, 1982).

—— *The Fabric of English Civil Justice* (London, 1987).

JACQUELIN, R., 'L'évolution de la procédure administrative' [1903] *RDP* 373.

JAFFE, L. L., 'Judicial Review: Constitutional and Jurisdictional Fact' (1956/7) 70 *Harv. LRev.* 953.

—— 'Research and Reform in English Administrative Law' [1968] *PL* 119.

—— *English and American Judges as Lawmakers* (Oxford, 1969).

—— and HENDERSON, E. G., 'Judicial Review and the Rule of Law: Historical Origins' (1956) 72 *LQR* 345.

JENKS, E., 'The Prerogative Writs in English Law' (1923) 32 *Yale LJ* 523.

JENNINGS, W. I., 'The Report on Ministers' Powers' (1932) 10 *Pub. Admin.* 333.

—— 'In Praise of Dicey 1885–1935' (1935) 13 *Pub. Admin.* 123.

—— 'Courts and Administrative Law—The Experience of English Housing Legislation' (1936) 49 *Harv. LRev.* 426.

—— *The Law and the Constitution* (5th edn., London, 1959).

JOHNSON, D. W., *Guizot: Aspects of French History 1787–1874* (London, 1963).

JOHNSON, N., and McAUSLAN, P., 'Dicey and his Influence on Public Law' [1985] *PL* 717.

JOHNSON, W., *Chapters in the History of French Law* (Montreal, 1957), ch. 17, 228 ff., reprinted in J.-G. Castel, *The Civil Law System of the Province of Quebec: Notes, Cases, and Materials* (Toronto, 1962), 35–55.

JOLOWICZ, H. F., *Roman Foundations of Modern Law* (Oxford, 1957).

—— *Lectures on Jurisprudence*, (J. A. Jolowicz (ed.)) (London, 1963).

JOLOWICZ, J. A., 'Fact-based Classification of Law' in J. A. Jolowicz (ed.), *The Division and Classification of the Law* (London, 1970), 1–9.

JOLOWICZ, J. A., 'The Active Role of the Court in Civil Litigation' in J. A. Jolowicz and M. Cappelletti, *Public Interest Parties and the Active Role of the Judge in Civil Litigation* (New York, 1975), 155–277.

JOLOWICZ, J. A., 'Some Twentieth Century Developments in Anglo-American Civil Procedure' (1978) 7 *Anglo-American LRev.* 163.

—— 'Da Mihi Factum dabo Tibi Jus: A Problem of Demarcation in English and French Law' in P. Feuerstein and C. Parry (eds.), *Multum non Multa: Festschrift für Kurt Lipstein* (Heidelberg, 1980), 79–99.

—— 'The Parties and the Judge in Civil Litigation' in N. Eastham and B. Krivy (eds.), *The Cambridge Lectures* (Toronto, 1981), 160–9.

—— 'Civil Proceedings in the Public Interest' [1982] *Cambrian LR* 32.

—— 'The Forms of Action Disinterred' [1983] *CLJ* 15.

—— 'Adversarial and Inquisitorial Approaches to Civil Litigation' in E. G. Baldwin (ed.), *The Cambridge Lectures* (Toronto, 1983), 237–43.

—— 'Justiciable Questions are Justiciable after all' (1986) 45 *CLJ* 1.

—— 'Comparative Law and the Reform of Civil Procedure' (1988) 8 *Legal Studies* 1.

—— book review, (1988) 8 *Legal Studies* 111.

—— 'Civil and Administrative Procedure: National Report for England and Wales' in J. P. Gardner (ed.), *United Kingdom Law in the 1990s: Comparative and Common Law Studies for the XIIIth International Congress of Comparative Law* (London, 1990), 160–75.

—— 'On the Nature and Purposes of Civil Procedural Law' [1990] *CJQ* 262.

—— 'Fact-finding: A Comparative Perspective', Colloquium of the United Kingdom Committee of Comparative Law (Aberdeen, September 1991).

JONES, H. S., *The French State in Question: Public Law and Political Argument in the Third Republic* (Cambridge, 1993).

JOWELL, J., 'The Legal Control of Administrative Discretion' [1973] *PL* 178.

—— 'The Limits of Law in Urban Planning' [1977] *CLP* 63.

—— 'Courts and the Administration in Britain: Standards, Principles and Rights' (1988) 22 *Is. LR* 409.

—— and LESTER, A., 'Beyond *Wednesbury*: Substantive Principles of Administrative Law' [1987] *PL* 368.

—— and —— 'Proportionality: Neither Novel nor Dangerous' in J. Jowell and D. Oliver (eds.), *New Directions in Judicial Review* (London, 1988), 51–72.

—— and —— (eds.), *New Directions in Judicial Review* (London, 1988).

—— and —— (eds.) *The Changing Constitution* (Oxford, 1989).

KAHN-FREUND, O., 'On Uses and Misuses of Comparative Law' (1974) 37 *MLR* 1.

—— LEVY, C., and RUDDEN, B. (eds.), *A Source-book on French Law* (3rd edn., Oxford, 1991).

KANTOROWICZ, E. H., *The King's Two Bodies: A Study in Medieval Political Theology* (Princeton, 1957).

KAPLAN, B., 'Civil Procedure—Reflections on the Comparison of Systems' (1960) 9 *Buffalo LRev.* 409.

KEETON, G. W., 'The Twilight of the Common Law' (1949) 14 *The Nineteenth Century and After* 230.

KELLEY, D. R., '*Vera Philosophia*: The Philosophical Significance of Renaissance Jurisprudence' (1976) 14 *Journal of the History of Philosophy* 267.

KELLY, J. M., *A Short History of Western Legal Theory* (Oxford, 1992).

KENNEDY, D., 'The Stages of the Decline of the Public/Private Distinction' (1982) 130 *Univ. Penn. LRev.* 1349.

KERAMEUS, K., 'A Civilian Lawyer looks at Common Law Procedure' (1987) 47 *Louisiana LRev.* 493.

KLARE, K. E., 'The Public–Private Distinction in Labor Law' (1982) 130 *Univ. of Penn. LRev.* 1358.

KOOPMANS, T., 'European Public Law: Reality and Prospects' [1991] *PL* 53.

LABOUR PARTY, *Labour's Election Manifesto: It's Time to Get Britain Working Again* (London, 1992).

LANGBEIN, J. H., 'The German Advantage in Civil Procedure' (1985) 52 *Chicago LRev.* 823.

—— 'Trashing "The German Advantage" ' (1988) 82 *Northwest. Univ. LRev.* 763.

LASKI, H. J., 'A Note on M. Duguit' (1917/18) 31 *Harv. LRev.* 186.

—— 'The Responsibility of the State in England' (1919) 32 *Harv. LRev.* 447.

—— 'M. Duguit's Conception of the State' in W. I. Jennings *et al.*, *Modern Theories of Law* (London, 1933), 52–67.

—— *Parliamentary Government in England: A Commentary* (London, 1938).

LAW COMMISSION, *Administrative Law* (working paper 13, 1967) .

—— *Administrative Law* (Law Com. 20, 1969), Cmnd. 4059.

—— *Remedies in Administrative Law* (working paper 40, 1971).

—— *Remedies in Administrative Law* (Law Com. 73, 1976), Cmnd. 6407.

—— *Fifth Programme of Law Reform* (Law Com. 200, 1991), Cmnd. 1556.

—— *Administrative Law: Judicial Review and Statutory Appeals* (consultation paper 26, 1993).

—— *Administrative Law: Judicial Review and Statutory Appeals* (Law Com. 226, 1994), HC 669.

LAWS, J., 'Is the High Court the Guardian of Fundamental Constitutional Rights?' [1993] *PL* 59.

—— 'Procedural Exclusivity', Conference on the Law Commission's consultation paper 126 (Cambridge, May 1993).

LAWSON, F. H., *Negligence in the Civil Law* (London, 1950).

—— 'Dicey Revisited' [1959] *Political Studies* 109, 207.

LE ROY LADURIE, E., *The Royal French State 1460–1610* (Oxford, 1994).

LE SUEUR, A. P., and SUNKIN, M., 'Applications for Judicial Review: The Requirement of Leave' [1992] *PL* 102.

LEFORT, C., *Democracy and Political Theory* (Cambridge, 1988).

LEHMANN, W. C., *John Millar of Glasgow 1735–1801: His life and Thought and His Contributions to Sociological Analysis* (Cambridge, 1960).

LEMMINGS, D., 'The Independence of the Judiciary in Eighteenth-century England', British Legal History Conference (Oxford, July 1991).

LENOAN, H., *La Procédure devant le Conseil d'Etat statuant au contentieux en première et dernière instance* (Paris, 1954).

LESTER, A., 'English Judges as Law Makers' [1993] *PL* 269.

LETOURNEUR, M., 'The Concept of Equity in French Public Law' in R. A. Newman (ed.), *Equity in the World's Legal Systems: A Comparative Study* (Brussels, 1973), 261–75.

LEVY, E., 'Natural Law in Roman Thought' (1949) 15 *Studia et Documenta Historiae et Iuris* 1.

LEWIS, C., and MOORE, S., 'Duties, Directives and Damages in European Community Law' [1993] *PL* 151.

LEWIS, N., 'Regulating Non-government Bodies: Privatization, Accountability, and the Public–Private Divide' in J. Jowell and D. Oliver (eds.), *The Changing Constitution* (Oxford, 1989), 219–45.

LLOYD, H. A., *The State, France, and the Sixteenth Century* (London, 1983).

LOCKE, J., *Two Treatises of Government: A Critical Edition with an Introduction and Apparatus Criticus* (P. Laslett (ed.)) (Cambridge, 1964).

LOUGHLIN, M., 'John Millar', Stevenson Lecture in Citizenship (University of Glasgow, 1990) .

—— 'Sitting on a Fence at Carter Bar: In Praise of J. D. B. Mitchell' (1991) 30 *Juridical Review* 135.

—— 'Innovative Financing in Local Government: The Limits of Legal Instrumentalism—Part 2' [1991] *PL* 568.

—— *Public Law and Political Theory* (Oxford, 1992).

—— 'The Importance of Elsewhere: A Review of *Public Law and Democracy in the United Kingdom and the United States of America* by P. P. Craig' (1993) 4 *PLR* 44.

—— 'The Underside of the Law: Judicial Review and the Prison Disciplinary System' (1993) 23 *CLP* 23.

—— 'Courts and Governance' in P. Birks (ed.), *Frontiers of Liability* (Oxford, forthcoming).

LOVELL, C. R., *English Constitutional and Legal History: A Survey* (New York, 1962).

MACCORMACK, G., 'Historical Jurisprudence' (1985) 5 *Legal Studies* 251.

MACDONALD, R. A., 'Judicial Review and Procedural Fairness in Administrative Law' (1980) 25 *McGill LJ* 520, 26 *McGill LJ* 1.

MACKINNON, C. A., 'Feminism, Marxism, Method, and the State: Toward Feminist Jurisprudence' (1983) 8 *Signs* 635.

MAINE, H. S., *Dissertations on Early Law and Custom* (London, 1891).

—— *Ancient Law: Its Connection with the Early History of Society and its Relation to Modern Ideas* (London, 1930).

MAITLAND, F. W. (ed.), *Select Passages from the Works of Bracton and Azo* (8 Selden Society, 1895).

—— Introduction to O. Gierke, *Political Theories of the Middle Ages* (Cambridge, 1900).

—— 'The Corporation Sole' (1900) 16 *LQR* 335.

—— *English Law and the Renaissance with Some Notes* (Cambridge, 1901).

—— 'The Crown as Corporation' (1901) 17 *LQR* 131.

—— *The Constitutional History of England: A Course of Lectures* (Cambridge, 1908).

—— 'The Shallows and Silences of Real Life' in *Collected Papers* (H. A. L. Fisher (ed.)) (Cambridge, 1911), i, 467–79.

—— *The Forms of Action at Common Law: A Course of Lectures* (A. H. Chaytor and W. J. Whittaker (eds.)) (Cambridge, 1948).

—— *The Constitutional History of England: A Course of Lectures* (Cambridge, 1963).

MARKBY, W., *Elements of Law Considered with Reference to Principles of General Jurisprudence* (6th edn., Oxford, 1905).

MARSHALL, G., 'Justiciability' in A. G. Guest (ed.) *Oxford Essays in Jurisprudence: A Collaborative Work* (London, 1961), 265–87.

McAUSLAN, P., 'Administrative Justice—A Necessary Report?' [1988] *PL* 402.

McBRIDE, J., 'The Doctrine of Exclusivity and Judicial Review: *O'Reilly* v. *Mackman*' [1983] *CJQ* 268.

MELLON, S., *Political Uses of History: A Study of Historians in the French Restoration* (Stanford, 1958).

MERRYMAN, J. H., 'The Public Law–Private Law Distinction in European and American Law' (1968) 17 *J Publ. L* 3.

—— *The Civil Law Tradition* (2nd edn., Stanford, 1985).

MESTRE, J.-L., *Introduction historique au droit administratif Français* (Paris, 1985).

MICHELMAN, F., 'Universal Resident Suffrage: A Liberal Defense' (1982) 130 *Univ. of Penn. LRev.* 1581.

MILLAR, J., *An Historical View of English Government, from the Settlement of Saxons in Britain to the Accession of the House of Stewart* (London, 1787).

—— *Historical View of English Government* (London, 1803), iv, essay 7, 266–310, reproduced in W. C. Lehmann, *John Millar of Glasgow 1735–1801: His Life and Thought and His Contributions to Sociological Analysis* (Cambridge, 1960), 340–57.

MILLAR, R. W., 'The Formative Principles of Civil Procedure' in A. Engelmann *et al.*, *History of Continental Civil Procedure* (London, 1928), 3–81.

MILSOM, S., 'Law and Fact in Legal Development' (1967) 17 *Univ. of Toronto LJ* 1.

MITCHELL, J. D. B., *The Contracts of Public Authorities: A Comparative Survey* (London, 1954).

MITCHELL, J. D. B., 'The Causes and Effects of the Absence of a System of Public Law in the United Kingdom' [1965] *PL* 95.

—— 'The State of Public Law in the United Kingdom' (1966) 15 *ICLQ* 133.

MNOOKIN, R. H., 'The Public–Private Dichotomy: Political Disagreement and Academic Repudiation' (1982) 130 *Univ. of Penn. LRev.* 1429.

MOIR, E., *The Justice of the Peace* (Harmondsworth, 1969).

MONTESQUIEU, *The Spirit of the Laws* (A. M. Cohler, B. C. Miller and H. S. Stone (eds. and trs.)) (Cambridge, 1989).

—— *De l'esprit des loix* (J. Brèthe de la Gressaye (ed.)), i (Paris, 1950), ii (Paris, 1955).

MOUNT, F., *The British Constitution Now: Recovery or Decline* (London, 1993).

MUNRO, C. R., *Studies in Constitutional Law* (London, 1987).

NEWMAN, K. S., *Law and Economic Organization: A Comparative Study of Preindustrial Societies* (Cambridge, 1983).

NICHOLAS, B., 'Fundamental Rights and Judicial Review in France' [1978] *PL* 82, 155.

NOLTE, G., 'General Principles of German and European Administrative Law—A Comparison in Historical Perspective' (1994) 57 *MLR* 191.

NOURSE, G. N., 'Law Reform under the Commonwealth and Protectorate' (1959) 7 *LQR* 512.

ODENT, R., *Contentieux administratif* (Paris, 1981).

O'DONOVAN, K., *Sexual Divisions in Law* (London, 1985).

OLIVER, D., 'Is the *Ultra Vires* Rule the Basis of Judicial Review?' [1987] *PL* 543.

OLSEN, F. E., 'The Family and the Market: A Study of Ideology and Legal Reform' (1983) 96 *Harv. LRev.* 1497.

PANNICK, D., 'What is a Public Authority for the Purposes of Judicial Review?' in J. Jowell and D. Oliver (eds.), *New Directions in Judicial Review* (London, 1988), 23–36.

—— 'Who is Subject to Judicial Review in Respect of What?' [1992] *PL* 1.

PARKER, E. M., 'State and Official Liability' (1905/6) 19 *Harv. LRev.* 335.

PATEMAN, C., 'Feminist Critiques of the Public/Private Dichotomy' in S. I. Benn and G. F. Gaus (eds.), *Public and Private in Social Life* (London, 1983), 281–303.

PATERSON, A., *The Law Lords* (London, 1982).

PATON, G., *A Textbook of Jurisprudence* (4th edn., Oxford, 1972).

POLANYI, M., *The Logic of Liberty: Reflections and Rejoinders* (London, 1951).

POLLOCK, F., *A First Book of Jurisprudence* (6th edn., London, 1929).

—— and MAITLAND, F. W., *The History of English Law before the Time of Edward I* (2nd edn., Cambridge, 1898).

PORT, F. J., *Administrative Law* (London, 1929).

POST, G., *Studies in Medieval Legal Thought: Public Law and the State, 1100–1322* (Princeton, 1964).

POSTEMA, G. J., *Bentham and the Common Law Tradition* (Oxford, 1986).

POUND, R., 'Codification in Anglo-American Law' in B. Schwartz (ed.), *The Code Napoleon and the Common-Law World* (New York, 1956), 267–97.

RADCLIFFE, C. J., *The Law and its Compass* (London, 1961).

REICH, C. A., 'The New Property' (1964) 73 Yale LJ 733.

REID, LORD, 'The Judge as Law Maker' (1972/73) 12 *Jnl. of the Soc. of Pub. Teachers of L* 22.

RENDEL, M., *The Administrative Functions of the French Conseil d'Etat* (London, 1970).

RICHARDSON, G., *Law, Process and Custody: Prisoners and Patients* (London, 1993).

RIDLEY, F., and BLONDEL, J., *Public Administration in France* (London, 1969).

RIESENFELD, S., 'The French System of Administrative Justice: A Model for American Law?' (1938) 18 *Boston Univ. LRev.* 48, 400, 715.

RIVERO, J., 'Jurisprudence et doctrine dans l'élaboration du droit administratif' (1955) 9 *EDCE* 27.

—— 'Hauriou et l'avènement de la notion de service public' in *L'Evolution du droit public: études offertes à Achille Mestre* (Paris, 1956), 461–71.

—— *Droit administratif* (13th edn., Paris, 1990).

ROBSON, W. A., *Justice and Administrative Law: A Study of the British Constitution* (London, 1928).

—— 'The Report of the Committee on Ministers' Powers' [1932] *Pol. Quat.* 346.

—— *Justice and Administrative Law: A Study of the British Constitution* (3rd edn., London, 1951).

—— 'Administrative Justice and Injustice: A Commentary on the Franks Report' [1958] *PL* 12.

—— '*Justice and Administrative Law* Reconsidered' [1979] *CLP* 107.

ROLLAND, L., *Précis de droit administratif* (9th edn., Paris, 1947).

ROSE, N., 'Beyond the Public/Private Division: Law, Power and the Family' (1987) 14 *J of Law & Soc.* 61.

ROUSSEAU, J.-J., *The Social Contract* (M. Cranston (tr.)) (Harmondsworth, 1968).

RUBINSTEIN, A., 'On the Origins of Judicial Review' (1964) 2 *UBC LRev.* 1.

—— *Jurisdiction and Illegality: A Study of Public Law* (Oxford, 1965).

SALMOND, J. W., *Jurisprudence or The Theory of Law* (London, 1902).

SAMUEL, G., 'Public and Private Law: A Private Lawyer's Response' (1983) 46 *MLR* 558.

SCARMAN, LORD, 'The Development of Administrative Law: Obstacles and Opportunities' [1990] *PL* 490.

SCHIEMANN, K., 'Locus Standi' [1990] *PL* 342.

SCHULZ, F., *Principles of Roman Law* (Oxford, 1936).

SCHWARTZ, B., *Law and the Executive in Britain: A Comparative Study* (New York, 1949).

SCHWARTZ, B., *French Administrative Law and the Common-Law World* (New York, 1954).

—— (ed.) *The Code Napoleon and the Common-Law World* (New York, 1956).

SCHWARZE 'Developing Principles of European Administrative Law' [1993] *PL* 229.

SELF, P., 'Planning by Judicial Inquiry' (1971) 78 *RIBAJ* 303.

SERENI, A., 'The Code and Case Law' in B. Schwartz (ed.), *The Code Napoleon and the Common-Law World* (New York, 1956), 55–79.

SHACKLETON, R., *Montesquieu: A Critical Biography* (Oxford, 1961).

SHAPIRO, B., 'Law Reform in Seventeenth Century England' (1975) 19 *AJLH* 280.

—— 'Sir Francis Bacon and the Mid-seventeenth Century Movement for Law Reform' (1980) 24 *AJLH* 331.

SHAPIRO, M., *Courts: A Comparative and Political Analysis* (Chicago, 1981).

SHONFIELD, A., *Modern Capitalism: The Changing Balance of Public and Private Power* (London, 1965).

SIEDENTOP, L., 'Two Liberal Traditions' in A. Ryan (ed.), *The Idea of Freedom: Essays in Honour of Isaiah Berlin* (Oxford, 1979), 153–74.

—— *Tocqueville* (Oxford, 1994).

SIMMONDS, N. E., *The Decline of Juridical Reason: Doctrine and Theory in the Legal Order* (Manchester, 1984).

SKINNER, Q., 'Thomas Hobbes and his Disciples in France and England' (1966) 8 *Comparative Studies in Society and History* 153.

—— *The Foundations of Modern Political Thought: The Age of Reformation* (Cambridge, 1978), ii.

—— 'Introduction: The Return of Grand Theory' in Q. Skinner (ed.), *The Return of Grand Theory in the Human Sciences* (Cambridge, 1985), 1–20.

—— 'The State' in T. Ball, J. Farr, and R. L. Hanson (eds.), *Political Innovation and Conceptual Change* (Cambridge, 1989), 90–131.

SOURIOUX, J.-L., *Introduction au droit* (Paris, 1987).

STEIN, P., *Legal Evolution: The Story of an Idea* (Cambridge, 1980).

—— 'The Development of the Institutional System' in P. G. Stein and A. D. E. Lewis, *Studies in Justinian's Institutes: In Memory of Thomas* (London, 1983), 151–63.

—— 'The Tasks of Historical Jurisprudence' in P. Birks and N. McCormick (eds.), *The Legal Mind: Essays for Tony Honoré* (Oxford, 1986), 293–305.

—— 'Continental Influences on English Legal Thought, 1600–1900' in P. Stein, *The Character and Influence of the Roman Civil Law: Historical Essays* (London, 1988), 209–29.

—— 'Donellus and the Origins of the Modern Civil Law' in J. A. Ankum *et al.* (eds.), *Mélanges Felix Wubbe* (Fribourg, Switzerland, 1993), 439–52.

STONE, C. D., 'Corporate Vices and Corporate Virtues: Do Public/Private Distinctions Matter?' (1982) 130 *Univ. of Penn. LRev.* 1441.

STONE, J., *The Province and Function of Law* (London, 1947).

—— *Social Dimensions of Law and Justice* (London, 1966).

STREET, H., *Justice in the Welfare State* (2nd edn., London, 1975).

SUMMERS, R. S., 'Justiciability' (1963) 26 *MLR* 530.

—— 'Professor Fuller's Jurisprudence and America's Dominant Philosophy of Law' (1978) 92 *Harv. LRev.* 433.

—— *Lon L. Fuller* (London, 1984).

SUZMAN, A., 'Administrative Law in England: A Study of the Report of the Committee on Ministers' Powers' (1933) 18 *Iowa LRev.* 160.

SZLADITS, C., 'The Distinction between Public Law and Private Law' in *IECL*, ii, ch. 2, secs. 25–57.

TAY, A. E., and KAMENKA, E., 'Public Law—Private Law' in S. I. Benn and G. F. Gaus (eds.), *Public and Private in Social Life* (London, 1983), 67–92.

TAYLOR, A. J., *Laissez-faire and State Intervention in Nineteenth-Century Britain* (London, 1972).

THOMPSON, J. B., *Studies in the Theory of Ideology* (Cambridge, 1984).

TUNC, A., 'The Grand Outlines of the Code' in B. Schwartz (ed.), *The Code Napoleon and the Common-Law World* (New York, 1956), 19–45.

TURPIN, C., *Government Contracts* (Harmondsworth, 1972).

—— *Government Procurement and Contracts* (2nd edn., Harlow, 1989).

TWINING, W. L., ODONOVAN, K., and PALIWALA, A., 'Ernie and the Centipede: Some Theoretical Aspects of Classification for the Purposes of Law Reform' in J. A. Jolowicz (ed.), *The Division and Classification of the Law* (London, 1970), 10–29.

UNGER, R. M., *Knowledge and Politics* (New York, 1975).

—— *Law in Modern Society: Toward a Criticism of Social Theory* (New York, 1976).

—— *False Necessity: Anti-Necessitarian Social Theory in the Service of Radical Democracy*, Part 1 of *Politics, a Work in Constructive Social Theory* (Cambridge, 1987).

VAN CAENEGEM, R. C., 'History of European Civil Procedure' in *IECL*, xvi, ch. 2.

—— *Judges, Legislators and Professors: Chapters in European Legal History* (Cambridge, 1987).

—— *The Birth of the English Common Law* (2nd edn., Cambridge, 1988).

—— *Legal History: A European Perspective* (London, 1991).

VILE, M. J. C., *Constitutionalism and the Separation of Powers* (Oxford, 1967).

VINCENT, A., *Theories of the State* (Oxford, 1987).

VON MEHREN, A., and GORDLEY, J., *The Civil Law System: An Introduction to the Comparative Study of Law* (2nd edn., Boston, 1977).

WADE, E. C. S., 'Administration under the Law' (1957) 73 *LQR* 470.

—— and BRADLEY, A. W., *Constitutional and Administrative Law* (10th edn., London, 1985).

WADE, H. W. R., *Towards Administrative Justice* (Ann Arbor, 1963).

—— 'Crossroads in Administrative Law' [1968] *CLP* 75.

—— 'Public Law, Private Law and Judicial Review' (1983) 99 *LQR* 166.

—— 'Procedure and Prerogative in Public Law' (1985) 101 *LQR* 180.

—— *Administrative Law* (6th edn., Oxford, 1988).

—— 'Beyond the Law: A British Innovation in Judicial Review' (1991) 43 *Admin. LRev.* 559.

WADE, H. W. R. 'The Crown—Old Platitudes and New Heresies' (1992) 142 *NLJ* 1275, 1315.

—— and FORSYTH, C. F., *Administrative Law* (7th edn., Oxford, 1994).

WALINE, M., *Droit administratif* (9th edn., Paris, 1963).

WALSH, B. A., 'Judicial Review of Dismissal from Employment: Coherence or Confusion?' [1989] *PL* 131.

WATSON, A., *Legal Transplants: An Approach to Comparative Law* (Edinburgh, 1974).

—— 'Legal Transplants and Law Reform' (1976) 92 *LQR* 79.

—— *The Making of the Civil Law* (London, 1981).

WEBER, M., *The Methodology of the Social Sciences* (Glencoe, Illinois, 1949).

WEIL, P., *Le Droit administratif* (Paris, 1964).

—— 'The Strength and Weakness of French Administrative Law' [1965] *CLJ* 242.

WEILER, P., 'Two Models of Judicial Decision-making' (1968) 46 *Can. BRev.* 406.

WEIR, T., 'Public and Private Law', *IECL*, ii, ch. 2, secs. 115–34.

WILLIAMS, D. G. T., 'The Donoughmore Report in Retrospect' (1982) 60 *Pub. Admin.* 273.

WINSTON, K. I., review of *Lon L. Fuller* (1985) 95 *Ethics* 751.

WOLFFE, W. J., 'The Scope of Judicial Review in Scots Law' [1992] *PL* 625.

WOOLF, H., 'Public Law–Private Law: Why the Divide? A Personal View' [1986] *PL* 220.

—— 'A Hotchpotch of Appeals—The Need for a Blender' (1988) 7 *CJQ* 44.

—— *Protection of the Public—A New Challenge* (London, 1990).

—— 'Judicial Review: Have the Judges made a Mess of It?' *Law Soc. Gazette*, 17 October 1991, 18.

—— 'Judicial Review: A Possible Programme for Reform' [1992] *PL* 221.

—— and WOOLF, J., *The Declaratory Judgment* (London, 1993).

WRIGHT, V., 'La réorganisation du Conseil d'Etat en 1872' (1972) 25 *EDCE* 21.

—— *The Government and Politics of France* (2nd edn., London, 1983).

ZWEIGERT, K., and KÖTZ, H., *Introduction to Comparative Law* (2nd edn., Oxford, 1987).

Index